Life
Should Be

AF149478

Life
Should Be
Transparent

Conversations about
Lithuania and Europe
in the Twentieth Century
and Today

Aurimas Švedas · Irena Veisaitė

TRANSLATED FROM THE LITHUANIAN BY Karla Gruodis

Central European University Press
Budapest–New York

© 2020 Aurimas Švedas, Irena Veisaitė
English translation © Karla Gruodis, 2019

Originally published in Lithuanian as *Irena Veisaitė. Gyvenimas turėtų būti skaidrus* by Aurimas Švedas (Aukso Žuvys, Vilnius, 2016).

Published in 2020 by
Central European University Press
Nádor utca 9, H-1051 Budapest, Hungary
Tel: +36-1-327-3138 or 327-3000
E-mail: ceupress@press.ceu.edu
Website: www.ceupress.com

224 West 57th Street, New York NY 10019, USA

All rights reserved. No part of this publication may be reproduced, stored in a retrieval system, or transmitted, in any form or by any means, without the permission of the Publisher.

ISBN 978-963-386-359-6

Library of Congress Cataloging-in-Publication Data

Names: Švedas, Aurimas, interviewer. | Veisaitė, Irena, interviewee. | Gruodis, Karla, translator.
Title: Life should be transparent : conversations about Lithuania and Europe in the twentieth century and today / Aurima Švedas, Irena Veisaitė ; translated from the Lithuanian by Karla Gruodis.
Other titles: Irena Veisaitė. English
Description: Budapest ; New York : Central European University Press, 2020. | Includes index.
Identifiers: LCCN 2019047409 | ISBN 9789633863596 (paperback)
Subjects: LCSH: Veisaite, Irena | Theater critics--Lithuania--Biography. | Theater critics--Lithuania--Interviews. | College teachers--Lithuania--Biography. | Jews--Lithuania--Biography. | Holocaust survivors--Lithuania--Biography.
Classification: LCC PN1708.V45 S8413 2020 | DDC 891/.928303--dc23
LC record available at https://lccn.loc.gov/2019047409

CONTENTS

Engaging Memory and History

*Irena Veisaitė and Aurimas Švedas at Veisaitė's home in May 2015,
during the last meeting in their marathon of conversations.
Photo by Algimantas Aleksandravičius.*

When we contemplate a person's fate we inevitably engage memory and history, and begin telling a story. To paraphrase the English writer Graham Swift, this action helps us to fill the existential void and dispel the fear of darkness.[1]

I am an explorer of the past—a servant of Clio, the muse of history—and this book was born of my wish to talk to Irena Veisaitė, who, in this context, is in the care of Mnemosyne, the goddess of memory. A German literature scholar and theatre critic, Veisaitė has been one of the main driving forces behind the Open Society Fund–Lithuania and has played a crucial role in her country's development after the fall of the Soviet Union. In the course of thirteen conversations between 2013 and 2015, I sought to ask Irena Veisaitė questions that would help me to reflect on the meaning of a person's existence in history.

Why did I, a historian, feel the need to hear Veisaitė's story? Initially, I will mention only a few aspects in the hope that they will serve as benchmarks for the reader.

First of all, Veisaitė's personal history enables us to take a look at four periods of the twentieth century from the perspective of an inhabitant of Lithuania and Central Europe. These are: the inter-war period (1918–1940), during which Lithuania reestablished itself as an independent state; the Second World War, which, for the people of the Baltic countries, began with the first Soviet occupation (1940–1941), followed by four years of Nazi occupation and the horrors of the Third Reich (1941–1944); the third period includes the second So-

---

1   I am referring to Graham Swift's novel *Waterland* (1983, Lithuanian edition 2009). The principal character is Tom Crick, a history teacher living in London in the 1980s, who tells his pupils many stories that have little to do with the school curriculum, yet encourage them to keep asking questions: "Why? What is the meaning of this?"

viet occupation (1944–1990), when life and spiritual freedom were smothered, and the later collapse of that totalitarian regime; the fourth saw the revival of Lithuanian independence, in 1990, and the country's consolidation as a democratic European country by the end of the millennium. In the collective memory of Lithuania, the Baltic States, and Central Europe, these periods are often subject to a lack of shared understanding. Our protagonist's life story helps us to interpret this history and build bridges across its chasms.

During our conversations I did not simply ask Veisaitė to describe her experiences, but rather looked for ways to contemplate how and why we remember what we do and to explore the significance of such historical experiences and memories in the twenty-first century.

Veisaitė's continuous involvement in cultural life during the Soviet era and in independent Lithuania enabled my interlocutor to accumulate unique knowledge about people, phenomena, and events that today are accessible to us only through the reading of texts, looking at photographs, watching film footage, or... listening to tales of living history.

Both Veisaitė's fate and the ethical stance that she, as a Holocaust survivor, has taken qualify her to talk about the common traumatic experiences of Lithuanian and Central European people. It is my deep conviction that the experience of someone like Irena Veisaitė, who was able to understand, forgive and live on and then went on to work for the common good of Central Europe, is relevant not only for twenty-first-century Lithuanian society, but for the people of other countries touched and traumatized by history in some way. Learning how to coexist with a complex and painful past is therefore another very important leitmotiv in the book.

Finally, there is one more reason why Irena Veisaitė's life story is so important to us. It is the story of a woman and her efforts to survive in extreme times, and to live a dignified, creative and purposeful life. Until our current epoch it was rare for people to speak openly about their experiences and suffering; until the second half of the twentieth century, women's voices were even more rarely heard, and even less frequently in Central Europe and the Baltic countries.

These aforementioned aspects of Veisaitė's remarkable life determined the themes of our conversations and the structure of this book.

In the first and second chapters, Veisaitė talks about her childhood, family, Kaunas between the wars, the first Soviet occupation, and the outbreak of the Second World War.

Chapters three and four reveal the most dramatic episodes of Irena Veisaitė's life, including her mother's arrest by the Nazis, her life in the Kaunas Ghetto and her escape from that death zone, her attempts to find refuge in Vilnius, and how she met her savior and second mother Stefanija Ladigienė.

Chapters five and six are devoted to the early post-war years, in particular Veisaitė's high school studies at Salomeja Nèris Gymnasium and her university studies in Vilnius, Moscow and Leningrad (now Saint Petersburg).

In chapter seven Veisaitė shares insights into her work at Vilnius Pedagogical Institute, the challenges of teaching under the Soviet regime, the Theatre Club she created and the club's annual "Theatre Mosaic" event.

In chapter eight Veisaitė talks about Lithuanian theatre, her friendships with its most prominent figures, and the most important productions of the era.

In chapter nine we discuss different strategies for surviving under an oppressive regime, and the intellectual life that, in the Soviet era, was confined to so-called "islands"—private gatherings of like-minded people in Vilnius, Moscow and Leningrad.

The tenth and eleventh chapters are devoted to literature—both Lithuanian and foreign authors—and the works whose ideas were of existential significance to Veisaitė.

Chapter twelve offers an outline of Irena Veisaitė's personal history.

Chapter thirteen tells the story of the Open Society Fund (OSF) in Lithuania. During the first decade of Lithuanian independence the OSF developed and implemented numerous programs that had a fundamental impact on post-Soviet Lithuanian society and stimulated many positive developments in the humanities and culture, as well as education, law, and other spheres.

In the Epilogue, Veisaitė and I share our thoughts after having completed the marathon of these thirteen conversations.

The appendices section, titled "Voices of the Past" presents additional textual material that extends, deepens, and contextualizes the book's main questions and themes, offering the reader one more opportunity to look at familiar historical narratives from new perspectives.

The book we present to readers has been written as an oral history: Irena Veisaitė's narration was edited lightly in order to preserve her unique voice, intonation, and her emphasis on certain meanings. Some statements and views have been clarified and explained in the contextual commentaries.

I hope that my dialogue with Irena Veisaitė and the supplementary texts will be interesting and meaningful not only for researchers of the past but will complement the portrait of this extraordinary individual that was presented in Yves Plasseraud's 2015 book about Veisaitė.[2] A French lawyer and long-time friend of Veisaitė's, Plasseraud took a more documentary approach: he addressed readers who might be unaware of the history of the Lithuanian and Jewish communities in the twentieth centuries, and unfamiliar with Veisaitė's story. The goal of my conversations with Veisaitė has been to reflect, together with her, on her remarkable life journey, focusing, as mentioned above, not so much on "what was it like?" but rather on more complex issues related to the meaning of human existence. I hope that the questions Irena and I explore here will be interesting to our readers.

Writing is a solitary occupation. However, when writing a book of oral history, this rule no longer applies. Comprehending the past through conversations—relating it and commenting upon it—becomes a joint effort. I would like to sincerely thank those without whose help this book would not have come to be: first and foremost, of course, Irena Veisaitė, for her collaboration and sharing her life story, and for enabling us to forge a mutual spiritual understanding.

※

---

2   Yves Plasseraud, *Irena Veisaitė: Tolerance and Involvement*, Amsterdam: Brill, 2015.

ACKNOWLEDGEMENTS

We would like to sincerely thank all those without whose help this book would not have come to be: our heartfelt thanks therefore go to: Karla Gruodis, for her skilled translation of the text into English; historian Stanislovas Stasiulis and theatre critic Laura Blynaitė, for their help with writing the contextual commentaries; Professors Tomas Venclova, Saulius Sužiedėlis, Šarūnas Liekis and Dr. Lara Lempert, as well as theatre director Gintaras Varnas, all of whom read, commented on and reviewed the text; our special thanks go to Katalin Koncz, who supported the translation and publishing of the book from the very beginning; Alina and Michael Slavinsky, for their careful proof-reading of the translation; Marius Mikalajūnas, for assistance in selecting and scanning the additional photographs that appear in the English version of the book; the Open Society Institute, for its financial support, and Julija Motiejūnienė, the Open Lithuania Fund's financial director, for managing the project's finances.

Aurimas Švedas and Irena Veisaitė

Life Should Be Transparent

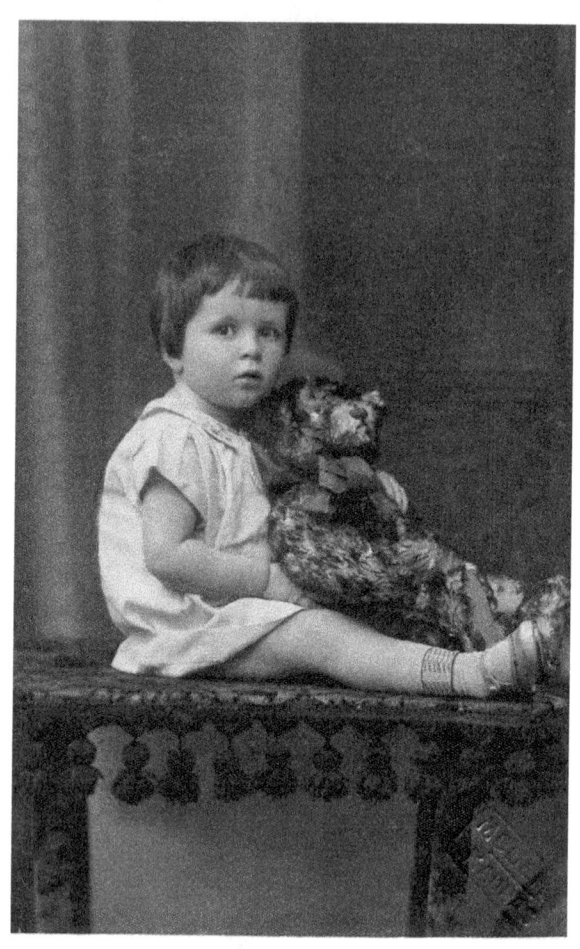

Irena Veisaitė holding a teddy bear. Kaunas, 1930.

Your life has been especially rich in dramatic events and intense experiences. Have you never thought of writing about some of them?

Of course I have, and I have often been encouraged by others to do so. But, for a variety of reasons, I simply could not, or did not want to delve into my memories. To return to the past one has to re-experience it, and that, for me, is simply unbearable. You see, I live behind a suit of armor. To help you better understand this metaphor, I will tell you about one incident. One day, I went to see Andrzej Wajda's film *Holy Week* (Pol. *Wielki tydzień*) with two of my former students, now my very close friends, Audra Žukaitytė and Reda Pabarčienė.[1] My friends left the cinema in tears, but I accepted the disturbing story we had witnessed on the screen—about the fate of a Jewish woman living in Warsaw during the Second World War—with perfect calm. Naturally, I, too, was baffled by my reaction, and had to ask myself, "What is going on?" That was when I realized very clearly that I live behind a suit of armor.

Another reason why I never wrote a memoir, and never wanted to, has to do with how I live, and probably also my personality. I have always, in psychological or spiritual terms, lived actively in the present, and therefore simply never had any time left for the past. I always had so many things to think about, write, work on, and participate in. Also, I put a lot of time and love into my teaching, which I saw as a type of mission.

---

1   Audra Žukaitytė—founder and former artistic director of the "Sirenos" international theatre festival; international tour manager for Oskaras Koršunovas Theatre.
Reda Noreikaitė-Pabarčienė—professor of Lithuanian and Comparative Literature at the Lithuanian University of Educational Sciences.

And there is a third reason that prevented me from writing about my experiences. It seems to me that, when a person undertakes such writing, they must reveal themselves completely. And if that self-revelation does not take place, the resulting text cannot be interesting. During the Soviet period, that kind of openness was utterly impossible! I am speaking about deeply personal revelations. I don't know how to, and cannot speak about certain very private, personal experiences. Knowing this, I therefore asked myself: "If I cannot write completely openly, why bother writing at all?" On the other hand, I have expressed my views on numerous questions that I care about in articles as well as papers presented at various conferences in Lithuania and abroad.

And there is one more thing I should say. After the war, when, by some miracle, I was still alive, one of my main motivations going forward was the desire to tell the world what had actually happened. But no one wanted to hear about my own, or others', horrific experiences. So talking about them was utterly pointless.[2] It was more important to simply survive, and I quickly realized that reliving painful memories was draining. The only family member of my parents' generation to have survived the war was my aunt Ona Štromaitė, my mother's cousin.[3] She survived the Kaunas ghetto, and then later even the Stutthof concentration camp. For Aunt Anuška, as everyone called her, life became a perpetual period of mourning. She withdrew completely from public life (after the war she never once went out to the theatre or the cinema) and simply mourned all that had been destroyed and lost. Perhaps that is why my aunt died so young. But I wanted to live, and life captivated me! I therefore had to somehow find my place in it, to establish myself, to find my own purpose and meaning.

---

2   This post-war silence was the result of Soviet policies regarding the shaping of how the Second World War was remembered. The main leitmotif of that remembrance was "the war against fascism," and losses experienced by different nationalities were concealed under the idea of the victims being "peaceful Soviet citizens." This policy is accurately summarized in the following passage by Lithuanian historian Alfonsas Eidintas: "The Soviets upheld their well-known position that Jews exist but there is no Jewish problem. In terms of the Holocaust this simplified matters greatly: many Jews were killed by the fascists but there was no specific Holocaust; mass extermination of Soviet citizens took place during the course of the war, so individuals of all nationalities fell within the general group of people who were killed." C.f.: *Žydai, lietuviai ir holokaustas* [Jews, Lithuanians and the Holocaust], Vilnius: Vaga, 2002, 326.

3   Ona (Anuška) Štromaitė (1901–1967)—owner of a shop in Kaunas, Irena Veisaitė's aunt.

For a conversation to take place, and for it to be successful, it is very important for the interviewer to gradually get to know their collocutor. Some people are able to recall events that took place decades ago in the minutest detail; others brilliantly reconstruct images from the past in very broad strokes, but do not focus on detail; still others need photographs or fragments of diary text to revive their memories. How does the past come alive in your own mind?

The most vivid images in my memory are connected to emotions. I might not be able to recall the contents of an event or work of art, or some of the conditions surrounding it, but I can always remember what that event or work made me feel.

In thinking about how your life might be described, I suddenly remembered the thought that both you and I are inclined to see living life as an art form. Could you elaborate on how you developed that attitude?

Every work of art must have some kind of structure and narrative rhythm. Only then can art be effective. I feel that we can apply this analogy of the work of art to our lives, because our lives, too, must have structure and rhythm, not to mention clear governing ideas and values. I felt that very distinctly when I was married the second time, to my beloved husband Grigori.[4] Being with him helped me understand that every day is special, that it opens up new possibilities for creating one's life. It is very important to sense the rhythm of time and not let events or processes drag on (as often happens in films or performances). In other words—one must live creatively. I can give you an example. We were not wealthy, but you could say that we wanted to give each other the whole world. If we saw a new building, an interesting painting or landscape or flower, or read a meaningful book, we would say to each other: "This is a present for you!" Obviously, such gifts did not have any material value, but they let us get closer to beauty and to fill our existences with meaning.

---

4   Grigori Kromanov (1926–1984)—Estonian theatre and film director and Irena Veisaitė's second husband. For more about Kromanov and his work c.f.: *Lavastaja Grigori Kromanov: mälestused, artiklid, kirjad, päevikud* [Director Grigori Kromanov: Memories, articles, letters, diaries], ed. Irena Veisaitė-Kromanova, Tallinn: Eesti Raamat, 1995.

This may sound somewhat didactic, but I believe that life should be transparent. It should not be polluted by either alcohol or compromises. We can take this even further. The experiences that I have just told you about allowed me to understand that one's life, too, is a work of art—that it needs meaning, a theme, and a rhythm. I can, perhaps a little immodestly, share something that the great sociologist Zygmunt Bauman inscribed for me when giving me his book *The Art of Life*: "To Irena, a great master of life."[5] That dedication is very dear to me.

You are a theatre critic, so our conversations inevitably veer toward the theatre, but theatre will likely also be important here as a metaphor. I would hazard to say that your life during the twentieth century was played out in a theatre of horror, absurdity, and metaphor.

That last comparison is perhaps a stretch, though, as Shakespeare wrote in *Macbeth*:

> *Life's but a walking shadow, a poor player,*
> *That struts and frets his hour upon the stage,*
> *And then is heard no more.* (Act 5, Scene 5)

Theatre has been present in my life in various ways. While still a tiny girl, I dreamt of becoming a singer. There were many records in our home, including recordings by Fyodor Shalyapin, Amelita Galli-Curci, Enrico Caruso, Joseph Schmidt, and Kipras Petrauskas.[6] When famous musicians such as David Oistrakh or Emil Gilels were performing in Kaunas, my parents would take me to the concerts. I even attended a concert by Shalyapin, which I believe took place in Kaunas in 1934.[7]

---

5   Zygmunt Bauman, *The Art of Life*. Cambridge: Polity, 2008.
6   Fiodor Shalyapin (Rus. Фёдор Иванович Шаляпин, 1873–1938)—opera singer, bass.
    Amelita Galli-Curci (1882–1963)—opera singer, soprano.
    Enrico Caruso (1873–1921)—opera singer, tenor.
    Joseph Schmidt (1904–1942)—opera singer, tenor.
    Kipras Petrauskas (1885–1968)—opera singer, tenor.
7   Davyd Oistrakh (Rus. Давид Ойстрах, 1908–1974)—violinist.
    Emil Gilels (Rus. Эмиль Гилельс, 1916–1985)—pianist.
    Fyodor Shalyapin was a friend of the Lithuanian opera singer Kipras Petrauskas. Petrauskas arranged Shalyapin's 1934 tour to Kaunas, where the famous opera singer performed the role of Mephistopheles in Charles Gounod's opera *Faust*.

So the world of the arts was not foreign to me and, as I mentioned, I wanted to be a singer. But sadly, God did not give me a good ear. I have to thank my parents for hiring a music teacher; my musical abilities improved, but, at the age of ten, I had to make a difficult "decision": "Alright—I won't become a singer … but I'll definitely become an actress!" I have to admit that I was very ambitious at the time. Every year, our school put on a play, and I always tried to get the lead role! And if it was not assigned to me, I would be very upset. Another example of my stubbornness and youthful maximalism was when I blurted out to my parents, "If I can't become either a singer or an actress—I'll kill myself!"

Naturally, I loved going to the theatre and the cinema. The first play I saw was Kazys Binkis's *Atžalynas* (The undergrowth), and I remember just loving it.[8] Of course, with time, the details of the plot have faded from my memory, leaving only a general feeling of the mood, and perhaps also the actress Vanda Lietuvaitytė's lead performance.[9] When I saw a recent production of the play by director Jonas Vaitkus, it was wonderful to feel those memories come alive in me again.[10]

I would also attend the opera with my parents, and was enthralled by Kipras Petrauskas. I remember when Valerija Barsova and Marija Maksakova came to Kaunas on tour.[11] Soviet Russia would send performers of great stature abroad to represent its culture. Even though I was still very young, these encounters with artists of the highest calibre made a deep impression on me.

After the war, when I was studying in Moscow, I also intensely followed what was happening on that city's theatre stages, and especially liked to attend classical music concerts. I tried not to miss a single concert by Oistrakh, Gilels, Safronicki, Heinrich Neuhaus, and especially Sviatoslav Richter.[12] They gave me a great deal.

---

8   Kazys Binkis's play *Atžalynas* [The undergrowth], directed by Borisas Dauguvietis, premiered in Kaunas in 1938. This play was very popular in 1940s Lithuania and was staged in Panevežys, Kaunas and Šiauliai.

9   Vanda Lietuvaitytė-Kauneckienė, Staneikienė (1910–1977)—theatre and film actress.

10 *Atžalynas* [The undergrowth]—dir. Jonas Vaitkus, Lithuanian National Drama Theatre, premiere 2013.

11 Valerija Barsova (Rus. Валерия Барсова, 1892–1967)—opera singer, soprano.
    Marija Maksakova (Rus. Мария Максакова, 1902–1974)—opera singer, mezzo-soprano.

12 Vladimir Sofronicki (Rus. Владимир Софроницкий, 1901–1961)—pianist.
    Heinrich Neuhaus (Rus. Генрих Нейгауз, 1888–1964)—pianist and pedagogue.
    Sviatoslav Richter (Rus. Святослав Рихтер, 1915–1997)—pianist.

Indeed, in Moscow I learnt how to get into expensive concerts for free, and even to sneak some of my friends in. For example, four of us would purchase one ticket; at the entrance I would show it to the usher and then, as I chatted him up, my friends would sneak into the concert hall. I never felt guilty about this deception—on the contrary, I was proud of it. In doing so, we didn't harm anyone—we never even sat down in empty seats, always remaining on the steps after the lights went down.

Sometimes I tried the same technique to get into the theatre, but it did not always work, so I had to buy cheaper tickets. Watching performances at the MHAT, I could not have imagined how closely tied to theatre my life would end up being.[13] After all, I was studying German language and literature at the time.

When I returned to Lithuania and began to work at Vilnius Pedagogical Institute [now the Lithuanian University of Educational Sciences], my journey into the world of the theatre began with work on a book about Bertolt Brecht, titled *Motušė Kuraž*.[14] I was very interested in Brecht's views on theatre and acting, which differed significantly from Konstantin Stanislavsky's.[15] Brecht was not concerned with reflecting reality, but rather with changing it. He created what he called "epic theatre," which he wanted to be a "school of life" for viewers—to force them to think, rather than merely experience. All of this was new and it utterly fascinated me.

At the Pedagogical Institute, I had the experience of working with the theatre scholar and excellent Shakespeare scholar Dovydas Judelevičius.[16] We were close friends. He encouraged my interest in theatre in every way and helped me to find my way in the theatre world, something for which I am deeply grateful to him.

In speaking about my relationship with the theatre, it is not my intention to become involved in an intellectual debate. I only want to say that I still expe-

---

13 The Moscow Artistic Academic Theatre (MAAT, or MHAT) was founded in 1898 by Konstantin Stanislavsky and Vladimir Nemirovitch-Danchenko.

14 Irena Veisaitė's article "Bertoltas Brechtas—Minties teatro kūrėjas" [Bertolt Brecht—Creator of epic theatre], c.f.: *Bertoltas Brechtas, Motušė Kuraž: pjesės* [Mother courage: plays], Vilnius: Vaga, 1964, 5–16.

15 Konstantin Stanislavsky (Rus. Константин Станиславский, 1863–1938)—theatre director who developed the Stanislavsky method for training actors.

16 Dovydas Judelevičius—literary scholar, critic, translator. Taught at Vilnius Pedagogical Institute, 1951–1994.

rience the same feeling that I did in childhood—the excitement of sitting and waiting for the curtain to go up, for a miracle to take place on the stage. Even though curtains have long since ceased to be used, or are used rarely, I still wait for that miracle.

Sadly, it does not always occur.

The theatre remains the place where I can think about life, humanity, and creativity.

Let us start from your maternal grandfather, Chielis Štromas. You have described him as a dairy farmer from Babtai and have said that your grandmother, Chaja Katz-Štromienė, (and again I am quoting you) held the four corners of the house upon her shoulders.[17] They were Jewish farmers—not a very typical situation?

In this case it is very important to remember that my normal contact with my grandparents broke off when I was thirteen years old, so most of my memories about them were formed in childhood. But Waldemar Ginsburg gave me the opportunity to become reacquainted with them through his book *...And Kovno Wept,* where they are described.[18]

We will talk more about his book later. But all I can say is that remembering my grandfather fills me with a wave of the goodness that emanated from him. My grandfather seemed to glow from within. He had blue eyes and was fair-haired, though of course I remember him after he had gone grey. I so admired that he was not fanatical. My grandmother, on the other hand, strictly adhered to kosher rules. When my grandfather came to visit our home (which was not a kosher one), he was not supposed to eat anything. But despite that, he would take the occasional bite and right there ask me not to tell my grandmother. I liked that so much. We had our secrets.

My grandfather visited us frequently. During my childhood, it was my grandparents, and especially my grandfather, who provided me with a feeling

---

17 Chielis Štromas (approx. 1860/70–1944)—dairy farmer, Irena Veisaitė's maternal grandfather.
Chaja Katz-Štromienė (approx. 1870–1942)—homemaker, Irena Veisaitė's maternal grandmother.

18 Waldemar (Val) Ginsburg—Irena Veisaitė's counsin and the only member of a large family of fourteen to have survived the Holocaust. He emigrated to England and wrote the memoir *...And Kovno Wept* (The Holocaust Centre, 1998; Lithuanian translation 2010).

of warmth and cosiness. Although we did not celebrate religious holidays in our own home, my parents encouraged me to respect other people's beliefs and faith. That is why I have such strong memories of Easter and Hanukkah, when, together with my cousins Aliukas (Alexander) and Liovenka Štromas, I visited my grandparents.[19] While the adults sat at the table, we played underneath it, thinking up all sorts of pranks. These incredibly beautiful holidays are, more or less, my only memories of Jewish religious traditions, and I experienced them thanks only to my grandparents. But I never doubted that I am a Jew.

I remember a trip my father and I took to Berlin in 1938. We had Lithuanian passports, so we were not treated like Jews. We stayed in a hotel on Kurfürstendamm, one of the city's most famous streets. I can still remember the delicious apricot jam pastries that were served at breakfast ... But I remember other things too, that I want to tell you about, now that I have touched on what being Jewish meant to me. One day, my father took me to Unter der Linden, the main boulevard of Berlin, where there were regular benches as well as other ones that were painted yellow. Jews, as you have probably already understood, were only allowed to sit on the yellow ones. I remember clearly how my father sat down with me on one of those benches and said: "I want you to understand that Jews are singled out in Germany. We, too, are Jews. Of course, we are not obliged to sit here, because we are Lithuanian citizens. But I want you to understand what it feels like to be singled out." I have taken us on this excursion to the past because I wanted to illustrate how my parents understood perfectly well who they were, and how they never tried to renounce or deny that. But they did not observe Jewish customs or traditions, which, as I have mentioned, I only learnt about from my grandparents.

Remembering my grandparents, I should mention that, while my grandmother's health was quite poor, you could say that she ran the show. My grandfather was under her thumb. He was a man who liked to philosophize, to dream, while my grandmother made all the practical decisions in the family. My grand-

---

19 Aleksandras (Aliukas) Štromas, later Alexander Shtromas (1931–1999)—Irena Veisaitė's cousin and very close, lifelong friend; Lithuanian lawyer, political scientist, dissident, professor, and author. Emigrated to the UK in 1973; taught at Bradford University and Salford University in the UK, Hillsdale College in the US. A detailed portrait of Shtromas is available in Leonidas Donskis's *Identity and Freedom: Mapping Nationalism and Social Criticism in Twentieth-Century Lithuania*, London and New York: Routledge, 2002.
Liova (Liovinka) Štromas (d. 1941.10.28)—Irena Veisaitė's cousin.

parents had ten children, and by the time I was born, five of them were still alive. During the interwar period, after my birth, two more of my mother's brothers died. In 1941, during the first week of the war, my uncle Jurgis Štromas was killed and then, at the end of July, so was my mother. In the end, only one member of this large family remained—my aunt Polia, the mother of my cousin Waldemar, whom I mentioned earlier.[20] But she, too, died during the war, while trying to help someone else. In 1945 she was being transported by boat from Stuttfhof concentration camp to the depths of Germany. Another woman settled down next to her on the deck and picked up a cigarette that had been tossed by a soldier who was guarding the Jews. An SS officer noticed this and wanted to throw this poor woman overboard. Because she spoke German, my aunt tried to defend the unfortunate woman, but did not succeed in softening the SS officer's heart. Instead of the woman, it was my aunt who was thrown over the edge of the boat. She drowned.

And now about my grandparents' fate . . . My grandmother died in the ghetto, probably from a stroke. We found her, dead, early one morning in 1942, and buried her in the ghetto. My grandfather was later sent to Šančiai concentration camp, near Kaunas, where, during the so-called "old people's and children's action" of March 26–27, 1944, he was taken to the Ninth Fort and shot.[21]

You have mentioned that you did not know your paternal grandparents.[22] But did your father, Izidorius Veisas, tell you anything about them?

I can show you a photograph of my grandfather on my father's side. You can see that he was a very intelligent-looking man. It is true that I did not know him, because he died in 1926, before I was born. Nor did I know my father's mother, my grandmother. After my grandfather's death, she moved to Moscow, where two of her sons and two of her daughters lived. She died in 1931. So I only knew these grandparents from other people's stories. I learnt that, during tsarist times,

---

20   Paulina (Polia) Ginsburg-Garzon (1900–1944)—bookkeeper, Irena Veisaitė's aunt.

21   In the fall of 1943 a portion (approx. 4,000) of Kaunas Ghetto prisoners were distributed to work camps in the Lithuanian towns of Aleksotas and Šančiai.

22   Lazaris Veisas (d. 1926)—businessman, Irena Veisaitė's paternal grandfather.
      Aniuta Štein-Veis (d. 1931)—homemaker, Irena Veisaitė's paternal grandmother.

Irena Veisaitė's grandfather,
Lazaris Veisas, prior to the
First World War.

my grandfather was a successful merchant and a member of the Second Guild.[23] Indeed, until the First World War, he lived in Grodno, after which he moved to Kaunas, where he was the owner of the Red Cross Lottery. My father later inherited this business, because his brothers and sisters were all living in Moscow. My grandfather's business was the determining factor in my father's success as a businessman in interwar Lithuania; together with my mother's brother, he eventually became director of the Senior Agency of the State Lottery.[24]

What else can I tell you about my paternal grandfather? As far as I know, he was intelligent, organized, and knew how to make the most out of life. He

---

23 A tradesman of the Second Guild [Rus. *купец второй гильдии*], according to 1775 rules regulating the possibilities for Jews to enter one of the three tradesmen's guilds that existed in Imperial Russia. According to further regulations passed in 1824, Third Guild members had to have capital over 8000 rubles; Second Guild members—over 20,000 rubles; First Guild members—over 50,000 rubles. First Guild members were permitted to conduct wholesale and retail trade of any goods without financial limits. Second Guild members were permitted to conduct retail trade not exceeding 15,000 rubles.

24 After the Lithuanian government took over the profitable lottery business from the Red Cross Society in 1932, State Lottery tickets were sold through the Senior Agency and several other institutions.

took care of his children and made sure that each one of them received a university education. Nevertheless, before the First World World, all of Lazaris Veisas's sons were involved with the revolutionaries. My grandfather was repeatedly forced to deal with the tsarist police—his sons would be arrested and imprisoned, and he would have to pay bribes to rescue them. In an effort to protect his youngest son from revolutionary ideas, my grandfather sent him to study in Germany. That is how that boy found himself in a high school in Hamburg. But the First World War interrupted my father's studies and he was forced to return to Lithuania. He did so with great difficulty, travelling many days on foot. Some Russian soldiers thought he was a German spy and wanted to shoot him, and it was only by a miracle that he survived. I do not know the details of this incident; my father was arrested, but, thank God, was later released.

In trying to remember my father, I am forced to state a banal truth, which I am sure many people have to face: we begin to take interest in family history only when there is no one left to ask about it.

And how did your parents meet?

I know that my mother, Sofija, or Sonia, as everyone called her, worked at the Senior Agency of the State Lottery, which my father owned. I used to have a photograph of my mother sitting in the agency's offices with some of the other workers, but, sadly, it got lost. My father fell in love with her. But my mother was already engaged to an engineer named Tedi Bliumentalis, who lived in Paris. Mr. Bliumentalis's dream of marrying my mother was thwarted by very practical problems—he was having trouble finding a job.

And at the time, as you very well know, it was thought that a man can start a family only after he has established himself and can support it financially.

Moreover, my father was very determined to win my mother's heart. If she went out for a walk, for example, she would be met by a driver in a horse-drawn carriage called a *droškė*, who was ready to take her anywhere she wanted. My father was constantly sending her all sorts of expensive bouquets. If she went to buy groceries, she would find out that her admirer had already paid for her purchases. My mother told my father that this kind of squandering of money was offensive to her. So, one day, my father tried to prove his indifference to material wealth by throwing a large sum of money into the fireplace. This was an ec-

Ona Štromaitė, Eugenija Štromienė, and Sofia Štromaitė-Veisienė. Kaunas, around 1926.

centric gesture, as my father was, fundamentally, an intelligent, rational, and re-served person. He was also a handsome, elegant, and, of course, a wealthy man. According to the standards of the day, he was the ideal suitor, and my grand-mother urged my mother to marry him. She was supported by other members of the family, who reminded my mother to "play her cards right."

Finally, after three years, my mother made up her mind and said, "Yes." I re-member seeing a photograph in her album; Mr. Bliumentalis had sent it to her after learning that she was engaged. His eyes are so sad in that photograph, and there was an inscription on the back of it . . .

Remembering my mother, it must be said that she always had many ad-mirers.

In speaking about your parents, you have said, "They were Europeans."

As I have already mentioned, my parents respected traditions, but did not ad-here to them. Their relationship to European culture can be described in sever-al ways. For example, they did not dress like Jews, but like Europeans; they had secular educations; and they spoke many languages. My father did not attend university—he was what the English call a "self-made man."

My mother, on the other hand, had graduated from the Handelshoch-schule, or Trade School, in Berlin, where she had studied economics, and, in around 1930, she began further studies in the Faculty of Law at Vytautas Magnus University, in Kaunas. But she dropped her studies after three years and never received her diploma. After the war, I spoke to some of her classmates, who remembered my mother as a talented student.

How would you describe the atmosphere in your home?

We were not a typical Jewish family; we did not adhere to religious traditions and were open to the world. For example, at Christmas and New Year's I always had a Christmas tree. I remember my mother saying that it is always meaningful to adopt other cultures' beautiful customs. Although each of my parents cared about me a great deal and gave me much attention, the atmosphere in our home was never very good. And I felt that very acutely. I received emotional warmth from my grandparents and my aunt Anuška. Aunt Anuška lived in Kaunas, on Donelaičio Street, I believe at number 16, where she had a small grocery store, and I loved to visit her there. Aunt Anuška loved me a great deal and always spoiled me. She was a very warm and intelligent person.

At home, however, the discord between my parents was palpable. One of my warmest childhood memories—I was five or six at the time—is of going for a walk on Laisvės Alėja.[25] I was so happy that both of my parents were walking with me! Such emotions clearly reveal that this was not a typical event for our family. And then, my parents spent quite a lot of time abroad, while I remained at home with governesses.

I remember being very small—perhaps about five years old—and entering my parents' bedroom, sitting down in the middle of their double bed, and saying: "I don't want you to fight or split up. I'm so frightened of that!" So I clearly felt that their separation was a possibility.

My father played a very big role in raising me. I can give you several examples, though I know that, from today's perspective, they will sound rather harsh, perhaps even shocking . . . Once, he and I were taking a walk and he said to me: "Irutė, you mustn't keep staring up at the sky while you're walking—you'll

---

25   Laisvės Alėja [Freedom avenue]—pedestrian boulevard running through the centre of Kaunas.

bump into something!" I was quite a stubborn child and did not always heed my parents' advice. That time, I did not react to my father's warning—and nor did he warn me that I was about to crash into a pole! And that is exactly what happened. I was injured by staring at the clouds. My father did not scold me; he simply took me to Bielski's Pharmacy, next to the Opera and Ballet Theatre.[26] There, he applied some ointment to my forehand and attached a sticking plaster. I had learned a painful lesson.

Here is another example. I was obsessed with chocolate. Naturally, my parents tried to rein in my appetite, but I was always trying to get around their restrictions. One day, to my mother's horror, my father came home with a kilogram of chocolate and said, "Eat as much as you want!" I ate it all and became ill. After I recovered, there was a conversation with my father.

And here is another example. I hated marrow soup and did everything I could to avoid it. Once, at dinner, my father said, "Since you are not eating your soup, you are clearly not hungry, so you can go to your room." My dinner ended before it had even begun. The same soup awaited me in the evening, and was served it again in the morning, until, by then famished, I finally ate it.

I was never scolded or beaten. For one of my birthdays, I received a doll that could blink its eyes. One of my friends wanted to play with the doll, but I would not let her. My father said, "This girl is your guest—you must give her your doll. After that you can play with it yourself." But I did not follow suit, so my father took the doll from me and gave it to the girl. When I started to shout and cry, I was taken to another room. When I calmed down, my father came and once more explained: "You must show your guest respect. That is why I asked you to give the girl your doll." When the emotions that had overtaken me finally abated, I was allowed to re-join the guests.

As you can see, my parents always calmly explained to me why I should behave in one way or another. And, as I have already mentioned, I was never either hit or shouted at.

In raising me, my father made a great effort to ensure that I would not abuse the fact that I was from a wealthy family, so that I would not stand out among other children. I was not, therefore, driven to school by car, and, if I went to the cinema, I was not allowed to buy the most expensive tickets. The same rule ap-

---

26 Now the Kaunas State Musical Theatre.

Izidorius Veisas. Brussels, 1949.

plied when I went to the theatre. If I went without my parents, I always sat in the gallery. I am still thankful to my parents for these lessons.

I remember other kinds of incidents, too. During a holiday by the sea, my father put me on his shoulders and swam far, far out. He was a very good swimmer. You can imagine how happy I felt! So although my father gave me some painful lessons, I loved and even worshipped him!

But sadly, my parents divorced. It happened in 1938, and it was the great tragedy of my childhood. I had heard all of the night-time discussions. Prior to the divorce, my father had slept in his office, which was next to my bedroom. Hearing those nighttime discussions pained me deeply. I can even remember some moments when I was prepared to kill him! At the time, it seemed to me that my father was offending my mother.

Following their divorce, my father left Lithuania. He returned once, in 1939, but only briefly. I had scarlet fever at the time. I remember him coming to my bedside . . . I would see him again only thirty years later.

After leaving Lithuania, my father married a German woman named Mary. In separating, my parents had decided that I would spend summers with my father and the rest of the year with my mother, in Lithuania. In the summer of 1938, my father took me on a trip to Western Europe. We travelled a great deal. The story I told about sitting on a yellow bench is one of my memories from that summer. We visited Germany, Switzerland, Belgium, and France.

Upon arriving in Switzerland, I was put up in a guesthouse in the resort town of Arosa, while my father and his future wife checked into a hotel in Engadin. But I didn't want to stay in the guesthouse—I wanted to spend time with my father! So I wrapped my belongings up in a scarf, went to the station and took the train to Engadin, where I announced: "I am not staying in Arosa!" My father gave in immediately. He got me a room in the same hotel and hired me a nanny, and I was finally introduced to his future wife. To be sure, I knew about my father's plan to remarry, as he had told me about it some time before that. Then I asked him if he planned to have children. He said no, so I calmed down. But not entirely. I was ten years old at the time, and looking at Mary made me wonder. My father's fiancé was a very refined lady who devoted a lot of attention to her appearance.

One morning, hoping to dispel my doubts and anxieties, I marched into Mary's room and said: "I have several questions for you. Do you love my father?" She replied, "Yes." Then I asked a second question: "Would you still love him if he was no longer wealthy?" She again replied, "Yes." When I heard that, I answered, "Then everything is fine. I don't have to worry." And I went back to my room.

I remember how, during that stay in Switzerland, my father bought me a very pretty dress and, for the first time, at a party we attended, I was asked to dance. Why is this memory so vivid? My father was very strict about my not standing out in relation to my peers, so I did not have fancy clothes. It is for that reason that I can remember my father's gift—an especially beautiful dress with a bright blue lining—to this day. I was also very excited by the fact that the gentleman who invited this ten-year-old girl to dance even kissed my hand. At the time, I was sure it was because of my beautiful dress.

At the beginning of the war, my father and his second wife were living in Brussels, Belgium. He possessed a foreign travel Lithuanian passport, which did not specify his nationality or religion.[27] No one betrayed him and he avoided attracting attention to himself, and he therefore survived the German occupation.

In 1951, my father decided to emigrate to the United States. I do not know anything about his financial situation after the war, except that he had lost most

---

27 Lithuanian foreign travel passports were issued by the Citizens' Protection Department to any Lithuanian citizen travelling abroad. Indeed, this kind of passport did not specify nationality or religion.

of his wealth, as it had remained in Lithuania. After arriving in the United States, my father and his wife, Mary, went to California and settled in Los Angeles, where, in the San Fernando Valley, he established a chicken farm; he even spent two years diligently studying the specificities of that business at a local university.[28]

Mary did not want to be a farmer's wife, so she left my father. After the divorce, he had to pay a sizable settlement. My father later told me that the years working on the farm were the happiest in his life, because he had never liked the business world.

By the time I visited my father, he was recovering from a serious heart attack. He had already sold the farm, so he had to take me to visit a farmer he knew so that I could form some idea of how he had lived. My father told me that he had learned more about human beings from the behaviour of chickens than one would imagine. I was especially struck by his story about how a chicken transferred to a different cage will be pecked to death . . .

My father died in 1973, in the United States.

During the Soviet period, a close relative living abroad was a source of potential problems. How did you avoid such problems?

I was not able to avoid them. For this and other "sins" there were plans to expel me from Vilnius University. Some friends warned me this was a danger. That is when, and why, I left for Moscow. I was also running from persecution by the KGB.

I was a good student. During my final year at Moscow University, I was a candidate for the Stalin Prize. But to receive it I had to fill out a form requiring various biographical details. After I filled out the form, I had no chance of winning the prize. I also stopped receiving the Lermontov Bursary, which, if I remember correctly, I had received from my third year.

My father stopped writing to me in 1949. We lost contact and I did not know anything about him. This was his decision, as he believed that correspondence between us would put me at risk. Indeed, after the war he had sent me a package with twelve pairs of silk stockings. I gave most of them away to

---

28   This refers to University of California at Los Angeles.

my girlfriends—we were a group of seven—and one pair to my guardian. And then I experienced the truth in the Russian expression *Ни одно доброе дело не остается безнаказанным.*[29] In other words, rumours began to fly around Vilnius that I was incredibly wealthy, and that came to haunt me.

What do you mean? What happened?

During the post-war period, women's silk stockings were extremely scarce and coveted items. The fact that I handed them out and only kept two pairs for myself intensified the rumours that I was from a bourgeois family. And that placed me within the ranks of potential enemies of the people . . .

How, then, did you succeed in visiting your father in the United States?

My father had been what was called a "drawing-room communist." At least that's what people called him. Although, in Soviet terms, he lived as a bourgeois, he supported communist ideas about social equality. He clearly had a sense of justice and wanted to help people who were harassed, victimized, and imprisoned in Smetona's Lithuania.[30] I know that he regularly made donations to the MOPR.[31] Antanas Sniečkus even briefly lived in our home.[32] At the time, I was told that he was a cousin of Petras Cvirka.[33]

---

29 No good deed remains unpunished. (Rus.)

30 Antanas Smetona (1874–1944)—one of the most influential politicians of the interwar period, the first Lithuanian president (1919–1920) and one of the leaders of the military coup of December 17, 1926. Elected President of the Republic of Lithuania on the day of the coup, he remained in this position until June 15, 1940.

31 MOPR (Rus. МОПР)—also known as the International Red Aid, an international organisation that provided support to revolutionaries; established in 1922 by a decree of the Fourth World Congress of the Comintern.

32 Antanas Sniečkus (1903–1974)—Soviet Lithuanian Communist Party figure and political leader, from 1940 to 1974 First Secretary of the Central Committee of the Lithuanian Communist Party and de facto leader of the republic. For more about Sniečkus in Lithuanian historiography c.f.: Vytautas Tintinis, *Sniečkus: 33 metai valdžioje. Antano Sniečkaus biografinė apybraiža* [Sniečkus: 33 Years in Power. A biographical study of Antanas Sniečkus], Vilnius: Lietuvos karo akademija [Military Academy of Lithuania], 1995; Marius Ėmužis, *Sovietų Lietuvos partinis elitas 1944–1974 metais* [The Soviet Lithuanian party elite 1944–1974], PhD Diss, Vilnius University, 2016. The most conceptual analysis of the "Sniečkus factor" by a Western historian to date is Walter A. Kemp's *Nationalism and Communism in Eastern Europe and Soviet Union: A Basic Contradiction?*, London: MacMillan Press, 1999.

33 Petras Cvirka (1909–1947)—left-leaning Lithuanian writer whom the Soviet authorities turned into an icon of Soviet Lithuanian literature following his death.

After the war I met Sniečkus again myself. As it turned out, at the end of the war his family took in my cousin Alexander Shtromas, who had been rescued by the Macenavičius family in Vilijampolė.[34] When the Soviet army entered Kaunas, Aliukas ran to the ghetto to see if anyone had survived. But he was met with a horrific scene: burning buildings, ruins, scattered corpses, and not a single living soul . . . That is where Aliukas met Sniečkus, who had also gone to inspect the ghetto territory. Sniečkus initiated a conversation, and when it emerged that Aliukas was the son of Jurgis Štromas, who had also been a longtime supporter of the leftists and contributor to MOPR, Sniečkus said to him, "Come with me, you'll live with us." That is how Aliukas ended up living in Sniečkus's home.

So it was thanks to Aliukas that I came to know Sniečkus and his family quite closely.

Nor did Sniečkus forget my father. When my father's health began to decline, Sniečkus helped me to travel to the US to visit him in 1968 and 1971. He convinced the KGB that I would not run away, so they did not harass me: before I left, there were no requests that I cooperate, or observe anyone, and, upon returning from America, I was not forced to write any reports.

Tell me about your trip.

Travelling to America was, as the English say, the experience of a lifetime. I spent five months in the US and another month in Great Britain, where my cousin Margarita and my eldest cousin Waldemar were living.[35] I returned to Vilnius through Paris, which was full of policemen and rioting students at the time.

The trip to see my father shook me to my roots, opened my eyes, and led me to rethink many things. And most valuable of all was that I had a taste of FREEDOM.[36] I was enchanted with how people dressed, walked, danced, openly expressed their thoughts, discussed. I remember my conversation with American university students about the difference between "fun" and "joy." I often heard people say "have fun," "take it easy," and so on. I tried to explain to them that

---

34 The family of Marija and Antanas Macenavičius sheltered Alexander Shtromas in 1943–1944.
35 Reference to Margarita (Mara) Štromaitė-Kagan (Lady Mary Kagan) (1924–2011)—Slavic Studies scholar, businesswoman, social activist.
36 Here and hereafter some words were capitalised by Irena Veisaitė during the review of the text.

fun is a short-term pleasure, while even a difficult task can, in the end, provide long-term joy. You could speak about anything openly. Though I have to admit that I was still afraid of snitches, and often avoided discussing political questions among strangers. So I was not entirely able to avoid the shadow of the KGB.

I'm trying to imagine how you felt...

I saw America as the land of freedom. And I felt that everywhere. On the other hand, during my trip I also noticed that Americans were especially proud of and valued material wealth. Most of them would show me their homes, which were often grand and luxuriously decorated. I was forced to tour kitchens, living rooms, and bedrooms—and even bathrooms! As you know, luxury homes have a bathroom connected to every bedroom ... Eventually these "excursions" began to grate on me. I would remember our *chruščiovkės*.[37] During one such tour, I politely thanked my host and said that it was not necessary to show me every single bathroom, because, if I needed to use one, I would simply do so. I wonder what those Americans thought about me ...

By the way, traveling around the United States there are three places where I cried.

The first time that I broke down in tears during my trip was when I went to a bookstore. When I saw such vast numbers of books, each one of which offered exciting new information that was inaccessible at home, I felt as though I would explode. How much had the Soviet government taken from me—simply stolen from me! All of those books and the ideas collected in them belonged to me too!

The second place where I broke down was in a shoe store. I have flat feet and had therefore always suffered from bad shoes. And so did all of my girlfriends. My father gave me $6000 to spend anyway I wanted. That was an enormous sum at the time. I remember buying shoes not only for myself, but for my friends.

The third place that I cried was a dentist's office. That is where I learned that it is possible to receive dental care without the terrible pain we all experienced going to Soviet clinics. The word "drill" alone terrified us.

---

37 *Chruščiovkės*—Lithuanian slang term for Khruschchev-era high-density, residential apartment buildings. These kinds of buildings appeared during Nikita Khrushchev's rule (1953–1964) with the claim that "it may be small, but it offers each family privacy."

There was another significant aspect related to my trip. While still in the United States, I began to think about how I would describe my impressions upon returning to Lithuania. Naturally, I knew that I would be able to be open only with my closest friends. But what would I do in public or with strangers, not to mention with representatives of the "authorities"? That was a real headache for me. How to describe what I had experienced in America in such a way that those "ears" would not have the opportunity to find fault with me? Then I thought of the solution. I would talk about calories and diets! So I became an "expert" in weight-loss and counting calories. While very popular in the United States at the time, such things were practically unknown in Lithuania.

Upon returning, I held a party, perhaps it was even my birthday. I served my friends screwdrivers, which no one here had heard about, though today anyone could tell you that they are made with vodka and orange juice. At the time, I liked to joke that a screwdriver was the straightest path to happiness: if you're miserable, just drink one on an empty stomach and it will be sure to help you unwind. Next to each dish I placed a card noting how many calories it contained. I even gave my guests a short presentation about how many calories one should consume every day if one wants to eat healthily and, if necessary, lose weight. Of course, we surpassed all of those limits, but we had a lot of fun.

It may also be hard for you to imagine that I returned from the United States with my suitcases full—not only of books and shoes, but also various household and other products which were unavailable in Lithuania. I even brought back two litres of orange juice, which were of course intended for the above-mentioned screwdrivers. At the party, I didn't tell any of my guests that the orange juice had been cut with vodka. To be sure, I had chosen a fairly reasonable ratio of vodka to juice, so no one lost control of their legs or their tongues, but everyone relaxed very quickly. So, we all drank screwdrivers, knew how many calories we were consuming, and talked about diets. That was how I presented my trip to the United States. It was probably the liveliest birthday party I ever gave.

Of course, I did not only talk about food and calories when describing my trip to the United States. But if even one person we weren't sure about joined a gathering, everyone automatically knew: "Today we won't be speaking openly."

There is another detail, which today might seem tragicomical: when we were talking about things that could not be shared openly, we always placed a pillow on the telephone so that no one could listen in to our conversations, or—in the worst case—it would be impossible to identify those speaking.

Better than anything else, such seemingly insignificant details help us to understand the Soviet era and how people felt during it. Listening to you speak I keep thinking to myself, "Thank goodness that is all over!"

I could not agree more. I'm so very happy that we now live in a free society, in a free Lithuania.

My trip to the United States was important to me in one additional way: it allowed me to learn English. Before visiting my father I spoke Russian, German, and French, and also Yiddish, but not English. Before leaving for America, I had sixteen English lessons, clearly not a very substantial foundation.

On the first day that I was staying with my father, he moved the television into my room and said: "This is the best way to learn the language. I myself learned English by watching television and constantly listening to radio programs." For my part, I asked him to speak with me only in English. I urgently needed to learn English, but the price I paid by making that request was enormous. Every night I wanted to cry—I was so tired from all of that English and so missed speaking Lithuanian and Russian!

The turning point occurred two months later, when, one day, I was finally able to express myself in English. As you know, my knowledge of that language later came in very handy. With the restoration of Lithuania's independence, I was immediately able to enter into dialogue with people from the West and to undertake various international projects. Very few members of my generation knew any English at all.

How did you feel upon returning to Lithuania? Did you have any hope of ever returning to the United States, or did you think that this was the first and last time that you would visit your father?

I certainly did not think that I would never see my father again. As I have mentioned, I returned to the United States in 1971, this time bringing his granddaughter—my daughter Alina—to meet him.

Already, then, I could see that he was weakening. I can still see him standing by his house and waving goodbye to us. It was hard to leave him. Less than two months later he died. His ashes were scattered in the Pacific Ocean. That was what he wanted . . .

Let us now return to interwar Kaunas. Where did your family live before moving into the house that your father built?

We lived at the very beginning of Laisvės Alėja. Our neighbour was Colonel Jurgis Bobelis.[38] He often came over to play cards with my parents. I suspect that he was also my mother's secret admirer. And I was friends with the Bobelis's daughter Laimutė, who was the same age as me. As I have already told you, in 1936 my father built a house on Trakų Street in Kaunas. After that we saw the Bobelis family less often.

For some reason I have trouble remembering our time on Laisvės Alėja, but my memories of the home on Trakų Street are very vivid.[39] In 1936 the house received an award for being the best residential building in Kaunas. Later, the Soviets nationalized it. During the first Soviet occupation, Antanas Sniečkus lived in it; under the Germans, it housed Gestapo leaders.

It was not a very big house but it was a very pleasant one. The first floor contained an apartment for a guard, but my father's cousin lived there instead. The second floor contained two rental apartments. We lived on the third floor, where I had my own room with a separate washroom. Next to my room was my father's office, which was painted blue, and where I loved to read books from our library. Indeed, I believe that a library is an essential part of any home. My parents' library, which contained many great works of Western and Russian literature, played a crucial role in my development. Although I was primarily looking for books such as *Uncle Tom's Cabin*, at the same time I would see volumes by Molière, Shakespeare, Balzac, Schiller, Byron, Flaubert, Zola, Dostoevsky, Goethe, Pushkin, and Thomas Mann. Perhaps that is why, after the war, I always felt a great hunger for books.

My parents' bedroom, which had its own very modern washroom and toilet, was opposite mine. Our apartment, of course, also contained a dining room,

---

38   Jurgis Bobelis (1895–1954)—Lithuanian military officer, War Commandant of the city of Kaunas and Kaunas Region in 1937–1940. City of Kaunas and Kaunas Region commander during the uprising of June 23, 1941.

39   18 Trakų Street, now 20 Trakų Street.

and kitchen with an adjoining pantry. The dining room opened onto a large balcony or terrace, where, during the summer months, we could eat, read books, and sunbathe.

As I tell you about our house, I can clearly see all of the rooms and their contents. I could draw it in detail if I had any artistic talent.

My father had also bought two lots adjoining our house and yard, but he later sold them. One was bought by the US government, which erected a consular building on it. The other lot was bought by Dr. Milvidas, who built himself a house.

After my parents' divorce, my mother and I moved into a three-bedroom flat on Vytautas Prospect.[40] That building was also of interwar construction and was very comfortable to live in. I can remember it, and our third-floor flat, but not as distinctly as the house my father built.

With the first Soviet occupation of 1940–41, my mother and I were forced to move out of that flat and into a three-bedroom communal apartment on Krėvos Street.[41] I recall that the artist Vytautas Jonynas lived in the same building.[42] We shared our apartment with Jewish refugees from Poland. A Mr. Rabinovich and his wife occupied one room, while, as I'm sure you have gathered, the kitchen, bathroom and toilet were common. It was what people called a *komunalka*.

From that apartment I would later be forced to move into the ghetto.

Tell me about your school, about your teachers. You have mentioned that you were taught there in the "Šapoka spirit." What was distinctive about that kind of education?

We were taught from Adolfas Šapoka's *Lietuvos istorija* (History of Lithuania, 1936).[43] Indeed, I was the only child within the large Štromas clan to go to a Yiddish school—I attended Sholom Aleichem High School, on Gardino Street.[44]

---

40   85 Vytautas Prospect.

41   11 Krėvos Street.

42   Vytautas Kazimieras Jonynas (1907–1997)—Lithuanian artist.

43   Adolfas Šapoka (ed.), *Lietuvos istorija* [History of Lithuania], Kaunas: *Šv. ministerijos K.L.K. leidinys*, 1936. *Lietuvos istorija* and its editor, Adolfas Šapoka, remained very popular in Lithuanian society during the twentieth century.

44   Sholom Aleichem High School (originally called the Commercial High School) was a Jewish, Yiddish-language high school that existed in Kaunas between 1926 and 1940 at 16 Gardino (now Puodžių) Street.

My father was convinced that it had the best teachers in Kaunas, and that I would receive the best education there. On the other hand, all of my cousins went to Lithuanian schools.

With the exception of the religious societies, during the interwar period the Jewish community was divided into at least two groups: the "Zionists" and the "Yiddishists." The Zionists had their sights set on Palestine; they dreamed about the creation of a Jewish state and studied Hebrew. The Yiddishists, on the other hand, were oriented toward Lithuania, as they held the view that one must build a life in the place where one was born. The conflict between them was overt.

At our school, we were constantly mocking the Zionists, whose views and behaviour we found unacceptable. The Zionists did the same with us and were ever thinking of ways to make fun of us. I can remember that we had nasty, sometimes even obscene names for the students of the Hebrew schools, as they did for us.

Our teachers at Shalom Aleichem High School were truly excellent. I have fond and grateful memories of my Lithuanian language teacher, Mrs. Majerovičiūtė-Brikienė. She was from the town of Rokiškis and had completed her studies in Lithuanian language and literature at Vytautas Magnus University. She taught me Lithuanian grammar and helped me to see the beauty of the language. At the end of my first year at Vilnius University, when taking an exam with Professor Juozas Balčikonis, I did not make a single error on the accentuation dictation.[45] Still, I did not receive a "perfect five" score, but I will have to tell you about that incident later.

So, in high school we were taught from Šapoka's textbook. I was therefore steeped, you might say, in a Lithuanian perspective on the Grand Duchy of Lithuania and Lithuanian patriotism. For that reason, no one was surprised that we Yiddishist school students sang songs like "We will not rest without Vilnius!" in class.[46]

---

45 Juozas Balčikonis (1885–1969)—Lithuanian linguist. According to the grading system of the time, five was the highest grade.

46 Petras Vaičiūnas's poem "Mes be Vilniaus nenurimsim!" [We will not rest without Vilnius!] was very popular during the interwar period; the composer Antanas Vanagaitis set it to music. The poem and, later, the song, expressed Lithuanians' hopes of regaining Vilnius and Vilnius region, which were occupied by the Polish general Lucjan Żeligowski in 1922 and incorporated into the Republic of Poland.

Indeed, my favorite of the Lithuanian grand dukes was Kęstutis. I can't quite remember why he became my hero, but I was simply in love with him. Perhaps it was because of the romantic love story of Kęstutis's relationship with Birutė.

Looking back at my youth, I can now assess the "Šapokian" understanding of history that was instilled in us. But that critical perspective does not spur me to undertake any act of deconstruction. After all, the Lithuanian perspective on history and the state that I gained in school shaped my relationship to my native Lithuania—a relationship that was not altered by even the most tragic events. Of course, a lot of this has to do with my parents, who instilled and reinforced within me a feeling of tolerance for people of other nations, religions, and cultures. I have carried this feeling with me throughout my life and it has protected me from the greatest dangers, even from hatred and the thirst for revenge. After all, if one becomes infected with hatred, one harms oneself most of all.

※

We Could All See That Lithuania Was Trapped

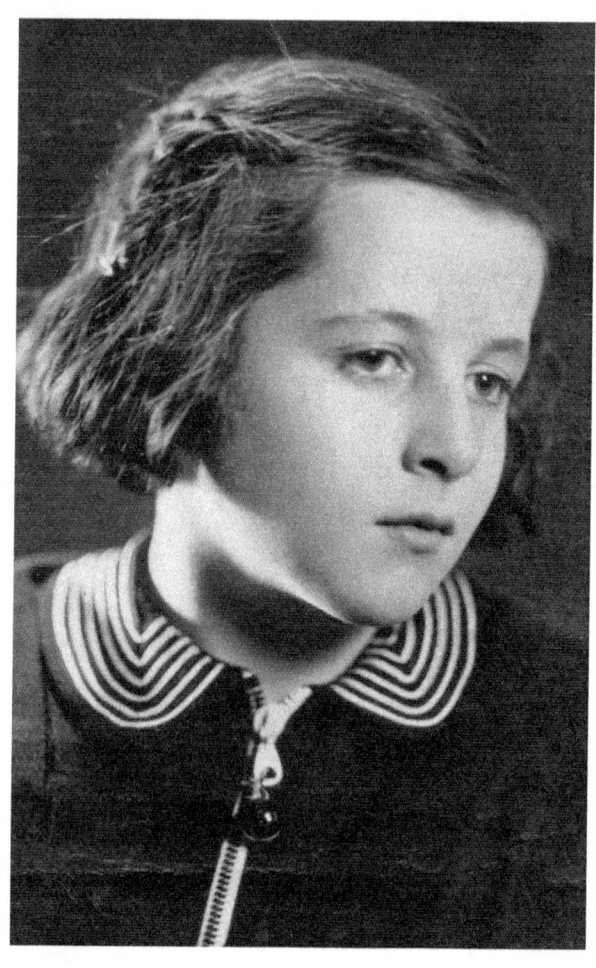

Irena Veisaitė. Kaunas, 1938. On 2 September 1943 this photograph was given to Jaša Braunsas, who, wanting to save it, buried it in the territory of the Kaunas ghetto. It was found after the war.

In an interview with the magazine **Moteris** *(Woman), you said that your mother was "oppressed by her status as a divorced woman."*[1]

In many ways, interwar Lithuanian society still functioned according to nineteenth-century values and ideas, and a patriarchal concept of the family still dominated. The man was the force that created and organized both family life and the social macrocosm. During the interwar period, divorce was a rare and almost unimaginable thing. In any case, among my relatives, friends, and acquaintances there was not a single other divorced family.

I have already described how, when my father fell in love with my mother, she was already engaged to another man. You have also heard about how persistently my father sought my mother's hand. In the end, my mother not only gave into his and her own family's pressure and agreed to break off her engagement with Mr. Bliumentalis and marry my father, she also came to love him. The divorce was therefore extremely painful for my mother, in terms of both its social and emotional consequences.

She cried frequently. I witnessed it myself, and that was the most painful thing for me.

After the divorce, it seemed to her that some men started to think that she would be more "available," and she found this humiliating. All of these things depressed her, and I am still not sure whether I want to, or am even capable of talking about them.

---

1   Virginija Majorovienė, "Stebuklas, kad išlikau" [It is a miracle that I survived], *Moteris*, 2013, nr. 11, 184–190.

I understand your hesitation and your desire to keep some things to your-self. But there is one question I have to ask, as it will help me to better understand your mother's fate. As far as I know, she had the opportunity to enter into a fictitious marriage with a man living in Sweden, and in that way could have emigrated to the United States. Why did your mother not take advantage of this opportunity?

It was a question of destiny . . . By 1939, it was clear that Lithuania was trapped. My father wanted to leave the country, and so did my mother. She asked him to pay her alimony in a foreign currency so that she could leave Lithuania and live somewhere else. For some reason unknown to me, my father refused to do this.

At the time, my mother travelled frequently to Western Europe and had many friends there. In Sweden she met a German Jew who had a visa for the United States. Peter—I can remember only his name—liked my mother and was perhaps even in love with her, but she did not feel ready for a new relationship. Then Peter offered that they form a fictitious marriage so that she and I could leave for America. My mother agreed, because she did not want to stay in Kaunas any longer.

Sofija Štromienė, Irena Veisaitė, and Alexander Shtromas (Štromas),
crossing the Nemunas River by ferry, near Birštonas, 1939.

When she made this decision, she was not in Lithuania, but in Stockholm. I was supposed to get onto a plane that was flying from Warsaw to Helsinki, with a stop in Kaunas. In Helsinki, I was to be met by the former French consul to Lithuania, Mr. Georges-Henri Duménil, who would then accompany me to the Swedish capital. My uncle Jurgis Štromas had made all of the travel arrangements.

On the scheduled date, my uncle drove me to Kaunas Airport. It was September 1, 1939. I made it through the customs inspection, which at this time was especially thorough. The customs officers likely thought that I was trying to take some family heirlooms out of the country—they inspected every single object I had with me, even a container of talcum powder, which they poked at with an enormous knife. Following this inspection, the other passengers and I waited for the plane for what seemed an eternity, but of course it never arrived. That day, Nazi Germany attacked Poland. World War II had begun, and my mother soon returned to Lithuania.

I will shortly have to ask you many painful questions about this fateful decision, but for now, I would like you to go back to before September 1, 1939—to the time when Lithuania and Kaunas had not yet become trapped. I want to hear more about that interwar city that no longer exists—the temporary capital of Lithuania. What was your Kaunas like? How do you remember it?

I have a very special relationship with the city of my birth. Kaunas is in my blood. Despite the circumstances that have led me to live in Vilnius since 1943, I still consider myself first and foremost a kaunietė—the feminine term for someone from Kaunas. Perhaps my relationship to Kaunas is something like that of the great twentieth century Lithuanian poet Marcelijus Martinaitis's relationship to the village of his birth, which he describes in his brilliant autobiography *Mes gyvenome* (We lived).[2]

It is at once quite easy and very challenging to describe these sentiments. To this day, I feel Kaunas in my pores. I need only to see a three-paned window—

---

2   Marcelijus Martinaitis (1936–2013)—Lithuanian poet. Reference to his book *Mes gyvenome: biografiniai užrašai* [We lived: Biographical notes], Vilnius: Lietuvos rašytojų sąjungos leidykla, 2009.

many Kaunas buildings had windows with three vertical panes—and a wave of
memories flows through me, as I associate such windows with 1930s Kaunas
and my father's house. The city's streets and buildings have preserved, for me,
many beautiful memories—this is where I romped, played pranks, visited my
closest relatives and friends. But after the war, after the Holocaust, Kaunas became a city of shadows for me. Even today, when I walk that city's streets, I remember which houses different people lived in, but these are usually painful
memories . . . Despite my very special relationship to Kaunas, I would not want
to live there again.

When Lithuania regained independence and the process of restoring private property began, I went to Kaunas to see my father's house, the house I had
inherited. I went up to take a look at our apartment and walked through all of
the rooms—rooms that had been my parents' bedroom, my father's office, our
living room, and my bedroom. Although everything had been changed and re-
arranged, it still reminded me of my lost world . . . It took me about one month
to recover from this excursion to Kaunas . . . I could not have imagined how
deeply I would be affected by the memories revived by this visit to my family's house.

As it was, the building had already been partially, if illegally, privatized.
I could have gone to court to contest the deals that had been made and defended
my rights, but I decided not to do so. This was a conscious decision. I accepted
the small monetary compensation that was due to me by law, and raised only
one condition—that this money be paid to me in full, not in parts over several
years, as was customary at the time.

Why did I make that decision? One of the main reasons is that I did not
want to live with the anger that I would have inevitably felt once the trials and
battles over the house began. And, as my good friend, the lawyer Vytautas
Merkšaitis pointed out, I would have lost anyway, as I don't know how to give
bribes.

In short, I did not want to live in a world full of bad emotions. Many people had trouble understanding this decision. Some of my relatives condemned
me for letting my father's house fall into the hands of strangers. But I do not regret it.

To answer your questions about what my Kaunas was like, I can only reply
by saying that it was a rapidly growing and increasingly beautiful city.

Many important buildings were erected during the 1930s, including the Lithuanian Bank headquarters, the War Museum, the Central Post Office, modern residential buildings, and the Church of the Resurrection was under construction. Today, all of these buildings are internationally recognized as having historical value and for being excellent examples of interwar modern architecture.[3]

And today, whenever I visit Kaunas, I am so happy to see that its beauty is being steadily revived.

The city's development was interrupted by the first Soviet occupation (June 15, 1940). How do you remember that time? What images and emotions surface when you think about that period when your world began to crumble?

As I have already mentioned, even before the war everyone in my family clearly sensed that Lithuania was trapped. We lived with this presentiment for more than a single month or year.

When the Soviet army marched into Kaunas, none of us met its soldiers joyfully—we all knew that no good would come of their arrival. But we had to continue to live. My father had already left Lithuania, and I can remember my mother sitting at the kitchen table with her head in her hands . . . She was not among those who went out into the streets of Kaunas to greet the Red Army with flowers. I can understand my mother's emotional reaction . . .

The mood was completely different at Sholem Aleichem High School. With the arrival of the Soviets, "Yiddishist" Sholem Aleichem high school was merged with "Zionist" Švabės high school, a Hebrew school, which had a much better building on the banks of the Nemunas.[4] Under the Soviets, all of the

---

3   In recent years, Lithuanian cultural and architecture historians are increasingly using the terms "Kaunas Modernism" and "architecture of optimism," which describe the architecture of Lithuania's interwar capital and its society's creative aspirations during that era. C.f.: Marija Drėmaitė, *Progreso meteoras: modernizacija ir pramonės architektūra Lietuvoje 1920–1940 m.* [Meteoric progress: Modernisation and industrial architecture in Lithuania 1920–1940], Vilnius: Lapas, 2016; *Optimizmo architektūra: Kauno fenomenas*, 1918–1940 [Architecture of optimism: The Kaunas phenomenon, 1918–1940], ed. Marija Drėmaitė, Vilnius: Lapas, 2018.

4   Kaunas Švabės Hebrew High School was a Jewish, Hebrew-language high school founded by Mošė Švabė and which existed in Kaunas from 1927–1940, on Prieplaukos Kranto Street (now 11 Karaliaus Mindaugo Prospect).

Hebrew schools were closed and the Hebrew language was banned, so the lessons at the new combined school were all in Yiddish. I have already mentioned that we had been educated according to values and ideas that fed Lithuanian society as a whole. On the other hand, Sholom Aleichem High School had been quite left-oriented, with many of the students coming from disadvantaged Jewish workers' families, and pro-Soviet teachers who had considerable illusions about the "paradise" the communists were creating.

I was twelve years old at the time, so could not yet see these things with adult eyes, and I was primarily interested in what was happening here and now. Before we knew it, Communist Youth and Pioneer organisations had formed in the school, and I joined the Pioneers myself.

I remember our wonderful music teacher, with whom we put on an opera. It contained a song that went something like this: "Somewhere on this Earth there is a land where the rye and wheat are not owned by the masters . . ." There were other incidents too, that are difficult to talk about today, because they illustrate that I, too, was affected by the pro-Soviet attitudes that permeated the school. For example, I was not even very upset when we were moved from our separate flat on Vytautas Prospect to a communal one on Krėvos Street.

But I experienced other struggles during that time which had nothing to do with the arrival of the Soviets. A real "war" broke out in the school, and I was quite involved in it. While I had been the top student at Sholom Aleichem, the leading student at Švabės high school was a certain Buby Blumbergas, a very handsome, blond-haired, blue-eyed and ambitious boy. He was very upset that I had toppled him from his position as the best student in our grade, and he turned his friends against me. One of them, a talented artist who later become an architect, named Osia— Josifas Judelevičius—drew and distributed caricatures of me. And I gave back in kind.

Buby Blumbergas survived the war and later left for the United States, but he was deeply traumatized by the Holocaust and hid his Jewish identity for the rest of his life. I never had any more contact with him. In speaking about the first Soviet occupation, it is important to understand that Lithuanian Jews and ethnic Lithuanians were in very different existential situations. To the Lithuanians, the beginning of the war and the German occupation looked like they would bring liberation from the "red plague"—from the horrors of the deportations.[5] Although Lithuanian Jews were also transported to Siberia in cattle cars together with ethnic Lithuanians, to the Jews the Nazi regime meant death, while the Soviets, and even deportation, offered some chance of survival. We must understand this and stop blaming each other.

How did members of your family resolve the question of what to do if the war came to Lithuania?

No one in our family had the slightest doubt that the war would eventually reach Lithuania. I felt that anxiety constantly, and heard much talk about it. Once, I even dreamed that I found myself in Adolf Hitler's camp; I was told that I must go to his tent, sit down on his lap and call him papi, the German word for "daddy." Overwhelmed by fear and tension, I could not say the word, and then I woke up.

In the meantime, everyone was trying to find the answer to the question of "what to do?" We were all deeply shaken by the arrests and deportations. My father's cousin Maksikas Šteinas and his family, my parents' friends the Perelšteins, and many others were taken away.[6] I was heartbroken for Hermanas Perelšteinas.[7] I can remember being so impressed by Haris, who had tremendous musical talent and sang a beautiful coloratura soprano. I would listen, enchanted, to a recording that we had of his singing. Haris was older than me, and I thought he looked like a young god. His father was executed in Siberia, his mother died in a camp, but he, thank God, survived, returned to Lithuania, and later became the founder and director of the famous "Ąžuoliukas" boys' choir.

---

5   Once established in Lithuania, the occupying Bolshevik government began an active campaign of identifying, isolating, and exterminating potential threats to the regime. The list of potential threats to the regime included many members of Lithuania's political, economic, and cultural elite. In 1940–1941, approximately 6,600 Lithuanian residents were arrested. The second wave of Bolshevik terror descended on Lithuania on June 14, 1941, when the mass deportation of Lithuanian citizens began. The deportation of families to remote northern regions of Russia and Siberia played a key role in the Bolsheviks' system of terror. On June 14, 1941, approximately 17,600 Lithuanian residents were deported to the Komi Autonomous Republic, Altai, and Krasnoyark regions. By 1952, at least 130,000 people, 70 per cent of them women and children, had been forcibly removed from Lithuania to remote regions in the Soviet Union. Approximately 150,000 more, including partisan resistants and political prisoners, were imprisoned in the Soviet gulag system.

6   Maksas Šteinas—businessman, Irena Veisaitė's father's cousin.

7   Hermanas Perelšteinas (1923–1998) and his parents were deported to Siberia in 1941; they returned to Lithuania in 1956; in 1959, Perelšteinas established the boys' choir "Ąžuoliukas," which was a major cultural phenomenon in Lithuanian during the Soviet period.

During the first Soviet occupation, no one knew who was fated to be arrested or deported, and this had a terrifying and paralysing effect on people.
Hitler spoke about his goals openly and everyone knew that he posed mortal danger to Jews, gypsies, homosexuals, and the mentally disabled, but Stalin
was more inclined to shroud his horrors in silence or lies. This is extremely relevant in speaking about how the Jews of that era felt. It is essential, in thinking
about those times, that we put ourselves in people's shoes and to try to imagine how they thought, what kinds of emotional states they were in. only then
can we assess the behaviour of Lithuanian interwar left-leaning intellectuals
such as the socialist avant-gardist writers and critics who called themselves the
trečiafrontininkai (Third Frontists).[8]

So, let us not evaluate other epochs drawing only on the knowledge, values,
and ideas of our own times. It took me a long time to understand this. The famous
Russian historian Aron Gurevich's *Categories of Medieval Culture*, which was
published in Lithuanian in 1989, helped me to fully grasp this principle.[9] Gurevich argues that we are very mistaken in speaking about "dark medieval times" because we cannot sufficiently grasp the ideas and values that people held during
that era. Medieval people were not worse or more brutal than us; they simply had
a different understanding of the importance and meaning of God's word. When
they were drowning or burning "witches," they were convinced that God would
never touch a hair on the head of an innocent person. According to this logic, if
a woman who had been accused of being a witch were innocent, she would not
be burned by fire or drowned by the stone tied to her legs. We can draw paral-
lels between this and our relationship to things that occurred in Lithuania during the 1930s. Totalitarian ideologies are just as dangerous as religious fanaticism.

*One the one hand, what you have been saying is very familiar to me as a
historian. But on the other hand, even when one understands that such
distance between a researcher and the past is essential, it is so easy to make*

---

8   Trečias frontas [The third front] (1930–1931)—avant-garde, leftist grouping of Lithuanian writ-
     ers (Kazys Boruta, Antanas Venclova, Kostas Korsakas, Jonas Šimkus, Petras Cvirka, Bronys Raila,
     and others) who criticised the official ideology of the day, as well as clericalism in society at large
     and literary forms and tendencies of the times.

9   Aron Gurevich—historian who promoted the ideas of the French Annales School in the Soviet Union
     and Russia; his book *Категории средневековой культуры* [Categories of medieval culture] (Москва:
     Искусство, 1972) was a major intellectual event.

mistakes and allow contemporary "viruses" to "infect" one's view of a historical period. Both society as a whole and certain researchers have the tendency to view the Soviet period either as a "dark age" or, in the case of a few eccentrics, a period of "enlightenment."

In examining various historical events and phenomena, our society has a tendency toward extremes—as though everything can be painted either black or white. I remember a conversation I had with Professor Vanda Zaborskaitė about the writers Maironis and Vincas Mykolaitis-Putinas.[10] She published a very important monograph about the great Lithuanian romantic writer Maironis in 1968 and devoted a great deal of her research to the interwar and Soviet-era writer Putinas. Zaborskaitė believed that there was no sense in probing such literary personages' biographies for details, as these might topple the myths around them. I thoroughly disagreed with her position. I argued that we are all fallible, that even geniuses are human and have their weaknesses, and that, if one wishes to know and understand a person, especially someone who creates, one should not idolize them. Such people only become more accessible, understandable, and powerful when they are fully revealed to us.

I am inclined to take your side in this debate. Tomas Venclova[11] put it very well when he said that the truth is more important than, say, a single person's, or even nation's, honour.

---

10 Vanda Zaborskaitė (1922–2010)—literary scholar, pedagogue, essayist. One of the most prominent figures in the Lithuanian humanities community during the Soviet period. Published a monograph about the Lithuanian poet Maironis in 1968 and was the authority on the poet and on the personality and work of Vincas Mykolaitis-Putinas.
   Maironis (Jonas Mačiulis, 1862–1932)—priest, poet. Maironis's poetry and his writings about the history of the Lithuanian nation had an enormous impact on Lithuanian national consciousness at the end of the nineteenth century and the first half of the twentieth century. In this case, Maironis's most important work is *Lietuvos istorija arba apsakymai apie Lietuvos praeigą* [History of Lithuania or stories about Lithuania's journey], published in 1891 under the name of Stanislovas Zanavykas.
   Vincas Mykolaitis-Putinas (1893–1967)—Lithuanian poet, prose writer, playwright and key interwar figure. During the early Soviet period, Mykolaitis-Putinas was a very important symbolic figure for students and members of the Vilnius University community who were trying to find ways of surviving in the new and aggressive Soviet reality.
11 Tomas Venclova—poet, translator, cultural historian, literary scholar and critic, essayist; notable Lithuanian and Central European cultural figure of the second half of the twentieth century and early twenty-first century; Professor Emeritus of Slavic Languages and Literatures, Yale University.

I agree completely, but sadly only a minority of people in this country understands this.

Many would probably theoretically agree that this principle is important, but the decision to hold to the truth is often a painful one.

Yes, but that kind of decision does not humiliate a person or cause them to enter into potentially shameful compromises. To the contrary—it allows one to remain oneself. That is not easy and it is often painful. I have to admit that I have not always managed to behave in a principled way. For example, when I was studying German language and literature at Moscow University, I was in the same year as Simon Markish, the son of the famous Jewish poet Perets Markish. Stalin ordered Simon's father to be executed for being a member of an anti-fascist committee, and their entire family was deported to Siberia in 1953. Sima was a very talented young scholar. Professor Radsig, with whom he studied classics, once said, "In classical languages, a talent such as Simon is born only once every hundred years."[12]

I believe that it was in 1950 that we celebrated New Year's Eve in the apartment of our classmate Tamara Smaradinskaya, the daughter of a Soviet Army general, who was studying French. Incidentally, following the events of January 13, 1990, Tamara came from Moscow to see me; she bought one hundred tulips and laid them by the victims' graves in Antakalnis Cemetery and apologized for the massacres her countrymen conducted on January 13 in Vilnius and at the Medininkai border crossing.[13]

But let's return to 1950. Because we were all living in various student residences, Tamara's invitation to celebrate the New Year in her flat was met with

---

12   Perets Markish (Rus. Перец Маркиш, 1895–1952)—poet and writer who lived in the Soviet Union and wrote in Yiddish. Arrested in 1949 and executed in 1952; rehabilitated after his death in 1955. Simon Markish (Rus. Симон Маркиш, 1931–2003)—Perets Markish's son, translator, literary scholar, pedagogue. Simon was forced to abandon his studies in 1953 because he and other members of his family were deported to Kazakhstan.
     Sergej Radsig (Rus. Сергей Радциг, 1882–1968)—classical languages expert, translator, literary scholar, pedagogue.
13   In January 1991, Soviet armed forces, including Soviet Internal Ministry and Soviet State Security forces, attempted to topple the newly independent Lithuanian state. The January 13, 1991 storming of the Vilnius Television Tower as well as the Radio and Television building by Soviet forces resulted in the deaths of fourteen Lithuanian citizens who had been using peaceful means of blocking the Soviet Army's actions.

universal enthusiasm. The party was attended by German, English, and French philology students. The "classicist" Sima was also there; at the time, he was dating an English Studies student, Inna Bernstein, whom he later married.[14] When I was at university, it was very popular among students to sing revolutionary songs in various languages, but especially Spanish. That night, as we were waiting to ring in the New Year, we were therefore singing. We were all in a good mood, but then suddenly Sima got up, stood in a doorway, and began to sing a very sad Yiddish song. I can't remember which one, but of course I knew it and understood the words. To this day, it is terribly painful for me to remember this episode, because Sima sang in complete silence, all alone, and I could not muster the courage to join him . . . I am still very ashamed of that.

I can understand perfectly, because I have often admitted to myself, in thinking about those times, that "I probably would not have been one of the brave ones."

Nobody can fault you for that, but I am obliged to admit to myself that my behaviour that night was shameful, and morally wrong. No one would have persecuted or punished us for singing a song, but I still did not have the courage—anti-Semitic sentiments were especially strong in the Soviet Union of that time!

As it turned out, fate would twice bring Sima and me together in Lithuania. Thank God that he survived deportation. He returned to Moscow and later, when the opportunity arose, emigrated to Switzerland, where he decided to stay. Once, when about fifteen years had passed since our studies, we met in Vilnius and Sima asked me, "How can you live in Lithuania? It is a land stained with blood!" I answered him very simply: "It is my native land. I love it despite everything." After all, parents love their children, and children—their parents, come what may . . . Besides, I saw and continue to see not only evil in Lithuania, but also much that is light and good, and many wonderful, outstanding people. But that is a whole other topic.

---

14 Inna Bernstein (Rus. Инна Бернштейн, 1929–2012)—translator, Simon Markish's wife. Inna Bernstein and Simon Markish later divorced; both remarried in the 1970s.

You have mentioned that your father supported the leftists. Was this not an important factor for you when the Soviets came? Despite your family's former wealth, you were not touched by the repressions, and those kinds of people were the new regime's first targets.

My father had already left Lithuania. It goes without saying that my mother could not expect any further financial support or alimony from him. So she had to work and she found a job at the Lithuanian SSR People's Commissariat for Trade and Industry, where she became head of the Trade Council.[15]

At the time, a man named Marijonas Gregorauskas was the People's Commissar for Trade.[16] He was already divorced from his wife, Kazimiera Kymantaitė, and fell in love with my mother.[17] Things between them were serious, as my mother even asked me whether I would not object to them marrying. I replied that I did not have any objections. Agnė Gregorauskaitė once told me that her father was a womanizer and that I should not make much of that story, but I'm not so sure that she was right.[18]

One way or another, I do know that, once the war began, Gregorauskas had to flee to the Soviet Union together with the Red Army. On either Sunday evening or Monday morning he went to the Red Cross Hospital to get my mother. But she was too weak to travel. On June 16 Professor Kanauka had operated on her to remove a benign but very large tumour that had formed on one of her kidneys.[19] The operation was successful and my mother was expected to make a full recovery. But even though the prognosis was good, Dr. Kanauka would not let my mother travel. "She would lose too much blood during the journey," he said. Gregorauskas had to leave without my mother, but he left a small doll as a

---

15   Trade and Industry Council—the People's Trade Commissariat of the Lithuanian SSR, which fulfilled the function of a trade ministry.

16   Marijonas Gregorauskas (1908–1995)—economist. With the beginning, in 1940, of intense Sovietisation of occupied Lithuania, Gregorauskas, as someone loyal to the new regime, was appointed Lithuanian SSR People's Commissar for Trade (held this position 1940–1944); from October 1944 to September 1946—LSSR Deputy Director of the Council of Ministers. Gregorauskas later shifted his focus to research and teaching.

17   Kazimiera Kymantaitė-Gregorauskienė, Banaitienė (1909–1999)—actress, first professional female theatre director in Lithuania.

18   Agnė Gregorauskaitė—actress, daughter of Marijonas Gregorauskas and Kazimiera Kymantaitė.

19   Vincas Kanauka (1893–1968)—physician, surgeon, Director of Surgery of the Kaunas Red Cross Hospital 1940–1944.

Irena Veisaitė with her mother. Kaunas, 1938. Studio Zinaida Bliumental.

talisman . . . I believe that her connection to Gregorauskas was also one of the reasons why she was later arrested. But no one from our family was deported in June 1941, and I have no idea why.

You have more than once described how, after a Lithuanian baltaraištis, or "white armband," came to the hospital to arrest your mother . . .[20]

Yes, a man with a white armband, holding a rifle . . .

. . . you and she had a conversation that would later have a significant impact on your life. What did you talk about?

I have spoken about this in numerous interviews, and also written about it.[21] On Friday, before my mother was taken to prison, we discussed what I would have to do: which people I must go see, what to tell them, how to manage things at home.

---

20   *baltaraištis*—a "white armband." Members of the June 1941 anti-Soviet uprising wore white armbands on their sleeves.

21   C.f.: Elvyra Kučinskaitė, "Renkuosi meilę, (...)" [I Choose Love (...)], *Tapati*, 2011, Nr. 2, 6–12; Virginija Majorovienė, "Stebuklas, kad išlikau" [It is a miracle that I survived], *Moteris*, 2013, Nr. 11, 184–190.

My mother hoped that everything would be all right. But then she also said things to me that I would only fully understand much later, and which had a great impact on the course of my life. She instructed me to be independent and to live within my means; to always be on the side of truth, because, as the German saying goes, "lies have short legs"; and to never seek revenge, especially for personal reasons.

That was the last time we were together; I never saw her again. On Sunday a "white armband" took her away to the prison on Mickevičiaus Street in Kaunas. Someone told me that they had still seen her on the hospital's balcony on Sunday morning.

By the way, it was Dr. Kanauka who prevented my mother from being taken away on the first day of the arrests. "While this woman is ill, she belongs to me," he told the "white armband." I will always be grateful to the professor for his bravery.

What happened to you from June until August, when you had to move to the ghetto?

After my parents' divorce, I had done everything I could to take care of my mother, and she often said that I had become the man in the house. The independence that my father taught me helped me on more than one occasion.

After saying goodbye to my mother, I returned to Krėvos Street. I wanted to stay at our flat, because it was near the Red Cross Hospital and I still hoped to see my mother again. But I often went to see my grandparents, and I visited my aunt Edia, who also lived near the hospital.[22]

My mother had suggested that I seek help from Vladas Skorupskis and Jurgis Bobelis.[23] Skorupskis refused to help me, so I went to see Bobelis, who was Commandant of the City of Kaunas and the Kaunas Region at the time. He agreed to try to get my mother out of prison but explained that funds would be needed for various bribes. I took him my mother's valuables: a diamond ring, a diamond broach, and a set of silverware. Sadly, Bobelis was not able to rescue my mother; apparently he was not able to, but after that incident I never again visited his home.

---

22   Eugenija (Edia) Štromienė—wife of Irena Veisaitė's maternal uncle Ovsiejus Štromas (d. 1938).
23   Vladas Skorupskis (1895–1959)—military officer, state figure.

At the same time, I want to mention another event. When my aunt Ženia— Jurgis Štromas's wife and Alexander's mother—was arrested in the street and incarcerated at Security Headquarters, following an order from Bobelis she was immediately released. So, as you can see, nothing was simple or straightforward.

※

What Had Happened to the World?

Margarita Štromienė. Kaunas ghetto, 1942.

Now we must turn to the most difficult, horrific period of your life—the Holocaust.

As far I remember, the order to move to the ghetto was announced on July 15.[1] My biggest concern at the time was where and how to obtain food. I also wanted to help my aunt Edia and her little boy Liovenka, who was my youngest cousin. They felt completely lost—the stores for Jews had almost nothing, only empty shelves! I would remove the mandatory Star of David from my clothes and go into the Lithuanians' stores.[2] I was saved by the fact that I spoke Lithuanian perfectly. If I bought a loaf of bread, I would take it to either my grandparents or my aunt. Usually it went well, but a few times I did hear someone shout, "You, Jewish girl—get out of here!" Remembering that, I now realize, without any irony, that I was lucky: I could have been shot or handed over to the "white armbands."

At the time, we still did not fully grasp how dangerous a situation we were in. My uncle Jurgis Štromas did not flee to Russia because his son Aliukas was in the seaside resort of Palanga, attending a Pioneers' camp. Nor did he want to leave his elderly parents or my mother, who was in hospital after her operation. So he stayed.

---

1   On July 10, 1941, Kaunas City Commandant Jurgis Bobelis and Kaunas Mayor Kazys Palčiauskas issued an order for the transfer of Jews to a ghetto that was being established in the Kaunas neighborhood of Vilijampolė. The order specified that all Jews had to move to the ghetto within one month—from July 15 to August 15.

2   According to Kaunas City Commandant Jurgis Bobelis and the Kaunas mayor's July 10, 1941 order, all Jews living in Kaunas were required, starting July 12, to wear an 8–10 cm yellow Star of David on their left breast.

Jurgis Štromas, Eugenija Štromienė, and Margarita Štromaitė. Berlin, c. 1936.

Uncle Jurgis was the director of the "Parama" cooperative.[3] Even though, by Monday, anti-Semitic sentiment was running rampant in Kaunas, he went to the cooperative to hand in his keys. "People will still want to eat, they will need bread," he said. As soon as Uncle Jurgis appeared at work, he was arrested. On Wednesday or Thursday, either June 25 or 26, by pure chance I came across my uncle near the Soviet Embassy at the beginning of Laisvės Alėja. He was part of a group of arrested Jews being sent off to do some kind of farm work. I went up to my uncle and said, "Uncle, let's escape!" Indeed, that day it was still easy to escape, but he replied, "I can't. We have all been counted, and if I escape, the guard will have problems. In any case, I'll be let go. I haven't done anything wrong."

As I have already said, no one—including my beloved, intelligent uncle— imagined what danger hung over our heads. By Friday he had been slaughtered in the Lietūkis Garage massacre.[4] I learned about that only after the war.

---

3   The "Parama" cooperative, whose director was Jurgis Štromas, controlled a bread bakery in Kaunas and a network of stores that operated under the "Parama" banner throughout Lithuania.

4   The Lietūkis Garage massacre took place on June 27, 1941. The exact number of victims is not known, but it is estimated that at least 60 people were killed. As Christoph Dieckmann and Saulius Sužiedėlis put it, "The particular resonance created by the Lietūkis killings reflects the especially gruesome method of killing conducted in public view, rather than the scale of the atrocity." C.f.: Christoph Dieckmann and Saulius Sužiedėlis, *The Persecution and Mass Murder of Lithuanian Jews During Summer*

A man who had worked as a security guard at my parents' home saw it with his own eyes.

Aliukas, thank God, was able to return safely from Palanga to Kaunas; he didn't give himself away, as he did not at all look like a Jew and had attended Ateitininkų High School. But most of the Jewish children at that Pioneers' camp would never return home . . .

The story of the Kaunas ghetto is horrific: on August 18, 1941, the "intelligentsia action" took place; on September 26, the "action of 1000" happened; and on October 4, the Small Ghetto was liquidated.[5] Within barely three months, half of the ghetto population had been annihilated. And that is only a few episodes and far from a full history of the Kaunas ghetto. But these preliminary facts are enough to raise the question: how do survivors manage to keep their sanity and not be broken by such extreme existential experiences as the Holocaust?

Far from all of the survivors managed to keep their sanity. All I can say, in reflecting upon my experience, is that it had much to do with the basic instinct to survive: I never wanted to live as much as during that time spent in the ghetto. And when you want to survive, you simply try to focus all of your attention on the moment you are in. For example, "I need to find something to eat so that I will have enough strength to go to work." One of the things that most motivated me to stay alive was the desire to tell the world what had happened, what my loved ones and I were forced to experience—because that unrestrained killing was simply incomprehensible.

That desire to survive also had much to do with my love for my relatives.

To be honest, even now, as I sit here speaking with you, I am still searching for the answers to many questions, some of which remain mysteries to me. I have often asked myself, "How could a crowd of tens of thousands of Auschwitz

---

and Fall of 1941. In series *The Crimes of the Totalitarian Regimes. The Soviet Occupation*, Vol. II, 121. Vilnius: Margi raštai, 2006.

5   The massacres of Kaunas ghetto residents at the Fourth and Ninth Forts were called "actions": during the August 18, 1941 "Intelligentsia Action," 534 Jews were killed; on September 26, the ghetto hospital was burned down and 1608 patients were shot; on October 4, 1845 Jews were killed during the liquidation of the Small Ghetto.

prisoners stand and watch children being hanged?" I am referring to a situation described in Elie Wiesel's book *Night*.[6] After all, such a crowd could have defeated a few dozen SS officers. Nevertheless, this huge crowd just stood there speechless and did nothing as three starving children were hanged . . . At one point someone asked, "Where is God now?"

Most likely each person in that crowd clung to the hope that they themselves might be able to survive and knew perfectly well that any kind of revolt would instantly shatter that hope.

But all that is nothing more than conjecture. I never stood by a pit and I don't know what people in those situations felt. To blame them for not resisting is, in my view, foolish, and even cruel.

I also believe that pure chance determined our fates. We lived in constant fear and could never know what repercussions one or another decision might have. Life turned into some kind of lottery. For example, my cousin Valdemaras wanted to join a group of 500 Jews being selected by the SS to work in the Kaunas archives . . . who were shot dead instead. They did not take my cousin because he was number 513, I believe, on the list. So he survived only by pure chance.

Such chance events are as difficult to explain as the helplessness of that enormous crowd in the face of the horrors being committed by a few dozen, albeit armed, villains.

By the way, if I have started to speak about twists of fate, there is another story that I should tell you. At the beginning there were two ghettos in Kaunas—the Big Ghetto and the Small Ghetto.[7] The Small Ghetto contained an infectious disease hospital. My friend Yasha's father, Dr. Moisiejus Braunsas (Moses Brauns), was an infectious disease specialist. When he went to work, he often took his teenaged son with him. One morning, it was October 4, 1941, they were a few minutes late; the gates of the Small Ghetto were closed and they never reached the hospital. That chance event saved both of their lives, be-

---

6   Elie Wiesel's book *La nuit* [Night] (1958, Engl. trans. 1960) draws on memories of experiences at Auschwitz and Buchenwald concentration camps.

7   The Large and Small Ghettos were connected by a bridge over Panerių Street. The Small Ghetto was liquidated on October 4, 1941. In the fall of 1943, the ghetto was reorganised as a concentration camp. As the front approached, the ghetto was liquidated; on July 8–13, 1944, its buildings were burned and approximately 1,000 residents were killed; the remaining inhabitants of the ghetto (approx. 6–7,000 people) were transferred to concentration camps in Germany.

Irena Veisaitė's cousin Liova Štromas' birthday. Kaunas, 1934. Veisaitė is seated first from the left; behind her stands her grandmother Chaja; her mother Sofija is standing second from the left.

cause on that wretched day the Nazis burned down the entire hospital with all the patients and staff in it . . . [8] It is clear that something like fate exists, but it is tremendously difficult to understand how it works, let alone to speak about it.

There were many such chance events in my own life. I could have been shot at least ten times—I would fall into the hands of the kinds of "white armbands" who would take a watch, or harass or humiliate me, but did not shoot me . . .

Another terrible blow to the ghetto was the "Great Action" that was conducted on October 28, 1941. Tell me how you managed to survive this inhumane "death lottery."[9]

8   Jokūbas/Yasha (Jack) Brauns wrote a memoir about the Kaunas Ghetto, c.f.: Jack Brauns, *Recollections and Reflections: How I Turned Despair into an Appreciation of Life*, Portland: Vallentine Mitchell, 2007.

9   The "Great Action"—the largest massacre of Jews during the Nazi occupation, on October 29, 1941, when 9,200 Jews were executed at the Ninth Fort.

Before this "action," all able and working ghetto inhabitants were issued so-called "Jordan Certificates."[10] Everyone thought that these certificates were some kind of guarantee of survival—everyone wanted to obtain one and people literally fought over them.

When the "Great Action" was announced, all residents of the ghetto—young and old, able and decrepit—were ordered to go out into Democrats' Square. Wanting to look older (I was thirteen at the time)—in other words, able-bodied—I dressed up in my mother's clothes, put on her brassiere and stuffed some socks into it so that my chest would look like a grown woman's.

I remember how we stood in columns, generally according to our workplaces, as Gestapo officer Helmut Rauca walked the columns and indicated which Jews were to go to the left, which to the right.[11] In other words, some were being sent to their deaths while others were being given the chance to live a little longer. It was very cold. We stood there from early morning, waiting for Rauca to reach our column. Our "sorting" began as it was beginning to get dark, at around 4 p.m. I saw how Valdemaras, Aunt Polia and Uncle Samuilas, her husband, were sent to the "good side" because they looked healthy and able-bodied.[12]

My grandparents were already over 70 years old. They looked quite frail, but I still had hope that I could save them. When Rauca approached us, I looked him straight in the eyes, perhaps with some kind of hypnotic power, so that he did not even notice my grandparents. I heard him say, "The girl has pretty eyes. Go to the right!" I remember how I dragged my grandparents, how we ran to the right and how my grandmother cried, "Don't rush so, my dear child. I can't run any more!" But I continued to drag them with almost superhuman strength...
That time we were still destined to return to our ghetto quarters...

According to Waldemar Ginsburg's highly moving memoir ...And Kovno Wept, which you have already mentioned, the period of November 1941 to October 1943 was one of "relative peace" in the ghetto. But during some

---

10   "Jordan Certificates"—certificates issued to Jewish craftsmen by the Kaunas Ghetto Commandant, SS Hauptsturmfuhrer Fritz Jordan.

11   Helmut Rauca—SS officer and war criminal who contributed to the murders of 11,584 Jewish men, women and children in Kaunas during the Second World War. When the war ended, Rauca succeeded in hiding and avoided taking responsibility for his crimes. He was located in Toronto in 1982 and arrested. He died in prison while awaiting trial.

12   Reference to Samuilas Garzonas—died in the Dachau concentration camp in 1945.

Irena Veisaitė. Vingis Park, Vilnius, 1947.

of our un-recorded conversations, you yourself have touched on "high moments of ghetto life." Did you experience any such moments during that period of "relative peace," during which an organized ghetto cultural life began to flourish?

We were young …

In 1942, the ghetto orchestra was formed. I had a friend, Buby Rozenbaum, who loved music. He and I would go to hear the orchestra and sometimes listened to records at his home, and during those moments I would once again feel human. You must understand that the experiences that I have described to you today not only terrified and depressed me, but also forced me to ask: "What has happened to the world? Why have Jews, myself among them, come to be so cruelly persecuted?" When you find yourself in such an extreme situation, it is difficult not to ask yourself, "What if there really is something about us Jews, something in me myself, that really is repugnant or evil, that has led us to find ourselves in this situation?"

As I have already mentioned, music had the power to disperse such thoughts, assumptions, and doubts. And so did literature. An underground school was established in the ghetto. I can remember reading Schiller's ballads, which spoke about friendship, goodness, love, morality, truth, and loyalty. Reading the German poet's sublime verse, I would feel my faith in humanity, in life, being once again restored.

※

To Forgive
and Build the Future
—These are the Duties
of the Living

Irena Veisaitė's rescuers, Juozas Strimaitis and Ona Bagdonavičiūtė-Strimaitienė.
Brussels, 1938.

I would now like to hear about how you managed to escape from the Kaunas ghetto.

For a long time, a false hope prevailed—that we would be allowed to survive as long as we were useful to the Reich. But, as time went on, it became very clear that all of the Jews of the ghetto were condemned to death—that our own demise was only a matter of time. So everybody started to look for a way out. Some of the young people joined the partisans. But, to be honest, no one there was waiting for them with open arms; one of the conditions for being accepted into the Soviet partisans was that one had to have a weapon, and where to find one? Some people tried to find refuge for themselves or their children with Lithuanian families. But that too was no easy task. After all, the Nazis threw Jews and their rescuers into the same pits . . . Moreover, Nazi and LAF propaganda had deeply affected society's views—the Jews were seen as responsible for all of Lithuania's woes.[1]

I myself did not want to leave the ghetto. My grandfather, aunt, and other relatives and friends were still alive. But then, in 1943, I received a letter from Onutė Bagdonavičiūtė-Strimaitienė . . .[2]

---

1   LAF (Lietuvių aktivistų frontas) [Lithuanian activists' front]—anti-Soviet resistance organisation (1940–1941) that organised and implemented the June Uprising of 1941. The LAF united a wide range of anti-Soviet forces: the core LAF group in Kaunas was formed from a secret student coalition; in Vilnius, LAF was headed by former military officers; and the Berlin branch was established by former ambassador to Germany Kazys Škirpa. For political reasons, the Berlin LAF leadership collaborated with German military intelligence and Senior Armed Forces leadership. LAF's ideology contained distinctly anti-Semitic elements.

2   Ona Bagdonavičiūtė-Strimaitienė (Strimatis) (1913–2007)—recognised by Yad Vashem World Holocaust Remembrance Center as one of the Righteous Among the Nations (non-Jews who took great risks to save Jews during the Holocaust) for her role in rescuing Irena Veisaitė.

*Irena Veisaitė and her lifelong
friend Lilė Bokšickytė. Moscow,
around 1950.*

Onutė had worked for my father at the head office of the Lithuanian State Lottery. I loved her dearly and knew her family well. Onutė's father was the organist at the church in the town of Kudirkos Naumiestis and I sometimes visited them there in the summer. I was friends with Onutė's brothers and sisters and was close to her entire family. Onutė was married in 1938. My mother and I were invited to her wedding and I still have a few photographs from that celebration. Onutė's husband, Juozas Strimaitis, was a Lithuanian army officer.[3] He was sent to study in Belgium and went there with his wife before the first Soviet occupation, so they were spared deportation. They were in Belgium when the war started, and returned to Kaunas in 1942.

I am making the assumption that they saw my father in Belgium; as I mentioned previously, he was by then living there with a Lithuanian passport.[4] I suspect that he spoke to Juozas and Onutė about me.

---

3   Juozas Strimaitis (1908–1979)—civil engineer and military officer. Recognised by Yad Vashem World Holocaust Remembrance Center as one of the Righteous Among the Nations (non-Jews who took great risks to save Jews during the Holocaust) for his role in rescuing Irena Veisaitė.

4   Izidorius Veisas (1900–1973)—businessman, Irena Veisaitė's father.

In any case, let us get back to Onutė's letter. It was passed on to me by some-one from the ghetto work brigade who worked in the city. Onutė informed me that documents were being prepared for me and that I must escape from the ghetto—that I was sure to die if I remained. After reading the letter I debat-ed for a long time—what should I do? I did not want to leave my loved ones. Aliukas and Mara were also getting ready to flee.[5] In the end, all the people close to me convinced me to try to escape from the ghetto; they pointed out that we could not all get out together, so we would have to save ourselves one by one.

It was finally decided that I would leave the ghetto on November 7, 1943, with the evening work brigade. Arrangements were made with the Jewish po-liceman in charge of the ghetto that day that he would not count me. I was to remove the Stars of David from my clothes—I would only pin them on light-ly, so that I could quickly remove them after passing through the gates. I would then slip away from the column of workers.

I can remember how long we seemed to wait by the policemen's booth near the ghetto gates; the brigade was late that day. Usually, the evening brigade would leave for work in the city at four in the afternoon, but this time it only left after six. The column was escorted by a "white armband" with a gun, or it may have been a Lithuanian policeman.[6] Everything seemed to be going smoothly.

The most frightening moment was when I had to leave the column. Had the guard noticed me, he would certainly have shot me on the spot. I can remember taking a step away from the column and toward the sidewalk. It felt as though the guard's weapon was aimed at my back. I walked slowly toward the sidewalk while repeating a single thought in my mind: "Don't panic! Don't rush! Stay calm! Don't give yourself away!" Thank God that the guard did not notice me slip away. From Krikščiukaičio Street, I turned toward Jurbarko Street, which leads to the bridge where Onutė was supposed to be waiting for me. But I did not find her at the arranged spot because, as I explained earlier, I was more than two hours late for our meeting.

---

5   Alexander (Aliukas) Shtromas survived the Holocaust and, during his teenage years, lived with the family of Antanas Sniečkus, First Secretary of the Communist Party of the Lithuanian SSR.
Margarita (Mara) Štromaitė-Kagan (Lady Mary Kagan) escaped the Holocaust with her husband, Joseph Kagan, and settled in the UK.

6   It is known that, at the time of Irena Veisaitė's escape from Kaunas ghetto, the so-called *baltaraiščiai* ["white armbands"] had been disbanded (in the summer of 1941). The brigade that was walking to do work in the city was therefore most likely led by a policeman.

I knew Kaunas very well, so I went to Onutė and Juozas's building at the beginning of Donelaičio Street, only to realize that I did not know their apartment number.

I had no choice but to knock on the first door I found and, as I learned later, met the building guard. This could have been a fateful encounter—at the time, many building guards were collaborating with the Gestapo. Once again, it was likely my flawless Lithuanian that saved me. The guard did not suspect anything, but when Onutė and Juozas learned that before knocking on their door I had met the guard, they became terrified. After what must have been a sleepless night for them, Juozas and I rushed out early in the morning to catch the "Kaunas-Vilnius" diesel train. That is how I ended up in Vilnius, and the Vilnius period of my life began. From November 8, 1943 I became a *vilnietė*—a Vilnius resident.

When we arrived in the city, Juozas took me to his sister's home in the residential neighbourhood of Žvėrynas. She was a very sweet woman, but, with good reason, was very frightened that she might get into trouble by sheltering me. For three nights—the whole time I was there—she did not sleep a wink. It was clear that I would have to find refuge elsewhere. That was how I ended up in the home of Pranas Bagdonavičius, Onutė's brother.[7] I had known and dearly loved Pranas from childhood. He was a wonderful person with an incredibly good heart and an excellent sense of humour. While Pranas was a surgeon by training, he was also a talented writer and was very interested in the other arts too, in particular theatre. All sorts of fascinating people—such as Antanas Škėma, Jeronimas Kačinskas, Romualdas Juknevičius, and Balys Lukošius—gathered at his home.[8] We lived at 4 Didžioji Street, in Chodkevičiai Palace, which is now the National Painting Gallery; my old room is now the office of the assistant director of the National Art Museum, Vytautas Balčiūnas, a former student of mine. Anyone

---

7   Pranas Bagdonavičius (1900–1992)—medical doctor. Recognised by Yad Vashem World Holocaust Remembrance Center as one of the Righteous Among the Nations (non-Jews who took great risks to save Jews during the Holocaust).
8   Antanas Škėma (1910–1961)—writer and playwright, one of the most important Lithuanian literary innovators in the twentieth century.
    Jeronimas Kačinskas (1907–2005)—composer, the most notable representative of modernism in interwar Lithuanian musical culture.
    Romualdas Juknevičius (1906–1963)—theatre director and actor.
    Balys Lukošius (1908–1987)—actor.

who dropped by to see Pranelis—as his friends and family called him—was told that I was a relative of his from the country. I was very interested in what they talked about and always tried to nestle into some corner and listen to their conversations. It's a pity that I did not write any of it down.

I felt very good staying with Pranelis. Once he gave me some money to get a permanent for my hair, so that, in his words, I would look "like all the other young girls." But it was a mistake, because with curly hair I looked even more Jewish.

While living with Pranas, I used the documents of Feliksas Treigys's daughter, Irena Treigytė; Juozas and Ona Strimaitis had procured them for me. Treigys was a mathematician, a teacher, and director of the Marijampolė high school, and his daughter spent the war years in that town. I never knew Treigys, but my friends must have simply asked him to help me. Thanks to him, my life in Vilnius could appear legitimate. A wonderful woman named Marcelė Kubiliūtė helped me to find a job as a cleaner in the nursery of Dr. Izidorius Rudaitis's clinic at 16 Subačiaus Street.[9] Marcelė was a great Lithuanian patriot and, as I later learned, a Lithuanian intelligence agent.

In the nursery I fed the children, washed floors and cleaned the wards, changed bedding, and did laundry. A week after I started there, the head nurse Gabriūnienė rushed into the ward in which I was working and began to ask me questions: "Who are you? Where are you from? What is your last name?" I had the impression that she was asking all of these things quite angrily and that she suspected I was a Jew. Of course, I answered all of her questions and immediately told Pranas and Marcelė about the encounter. We learned that some of the personnel had begun to suspect that I was Jewish. But Dr. Rudaitis categorically denied the rumors and it seemed that, for now, I was safe. Indeed, Dr. Rudaitis did not know the whole truth—Marcelė had told him that I was "half-Jewish."

Everything seemed to settle down. But then, exactly a week later, a nurse ran into the ward and announced that the Gestapo had surrounded the building. I was sure that they had come for me. I frantically asked myself, "What do I do now?" I tried to gain control of my emotions . . . I went into the washroom, flushed the toilet, and began to think it through logically. If I tried to run, they

---

9   Marcelė Kubiliūtė (1898–1963)—social activist, intelligence agent (worked with Lithuanian military intelligence), public servant.

would surely catch me. Then, since I was registered as living at Pranas's home, he, too, would suffer consequences. If I stayed in my workplace, I wouldn't give myself away. But if I were arrested, I might have the chance to explain to the Gestapo that Pranas had known nothing about my background when he rented me the room. After weighing all of the pros and cons, I returned to the ward, and, because it was mealtime, picked up a bowl of porridge and began feeding one of the infants. Just then we heard soldiers marching down the corridor. Dr. Rudaitis entered the ward with several Gestapo officers. I cannot remember their faces, but the image of their perfectly polished boots is fixed in my memory. I'm not sure, but I think that Dr. Rudaitis may have winked at me when he came in. The Gestapo officers looked around the ward and then left. Some time later I learned that they had come to the clinic after receiving a complaint that there were some Jewish children in the nursery. There was a shortage of blood for injured German soldiers and Jewish children were in demand as blood donors.[10] Dr. Rudaitis did not let the Gestapo have a single one of the children in the nursery. Even though several circumcised boys were discovered during the inspection, Dr. Rudaitis said that they were not Jewish, but Karaite children.

The Gestapo's visit to the nursery "legalized" me. I became "reliable" in the eyes of both the staff and people visiting the nursery, and I was able to work there until the end of the German occupation.

Every day I would walk to work along Subačiaus Street. At the time, 2 Subačiaus Street housed a bordello that "serviced" German soldiers. Every Tuesday was a day off for the women; they were mostly Polish, and would sit in the windows chatting up passersby. Walking past that house I received a thorough "education" in matters of sexual relations.

After the Gestapo inspection of the nursery there was a period of "relative" calm. I continued to live at Pranas's home, but it eventually became clear that I would have to move out. Pranas had a fiancé named Janė, who lived in the town of Šiauliai, and she was not terribly happy that some young woman was living in her future husband's home. There was no "subtext" in my relations with Pranas, but rumours began to circulate in Šiauliai. After all, I was already fifteen at the time...

But the main factor that made it necessary to move out was a seemingly meaningless event. One evening, the usual bohemian crowd had gathered at

---

10   This statement is of questionable historical accuracy.

Pranas Bagdonavičius. New York, 1970s.

Pranas's home. Someone had brought a rather poor-quality album of Van Gogh reproductions, and everyone was eager to take a look. I liked Van Gogh very much and had seen some of his paintings in Paris, so I forgot myself and said, in front of everyone, "Van Gogh is my favorite artist!" Naturally, this caused great surprise: how could a girl from the country be familiar with Van Gogh?

I am sure that none of Pranas's friends would have betrayed me. But they all enjoyed a drink, and a person under the influence often blurts out things that they would not normally say. It therefore became unsafe for me to continue living in that welcoming home. I had to leave.

My protectors—Onutė and Juozas—arranged for me to go live with Mrs. Marija Meškauskienė, who lived at 32 Gediminas Prospect.[11] Mrs. Meškauskienė's husband was a Lithuanian army colonel who had been arrested during the first Soviet occupation and was imprisoned somewhere in Russia. She had a ten-year-old daughter named Saulė and a maid named Jadvyga. Marcelė Kubiliūtė also lived there. She was a great source of comfort to me—I could speak to her, as they say, from the heart.

I lived with Mrs. Meškauskienė for two months. I am eternally grateful to her for the shelter she provided me and for the great risks she took in doing so,

11 Reference to Česlovas Meškauskas (1904–1942)—military officer. Following the Soviet occupation of Lithuania in 1941, Meškauskas was convicted and spent eight years in a Soviet gulag near Pechora (currently in the Komi Republic).

but, for various reasons, I did not feel comfortable in that home. I would hazard to guess that Mrs. Meškauskienė had decided to help me because she was a devout Catholic, and Father Norbertas Skurskis, who had christened me at Saint Ignatius Church, was an advocate of mine. So that I would not stand out and raise suspicions, I had to attend mass every Sunday. But that was not just for "show." I truly felt very good during the services . . . After all, Christ loves those who suffer perhaps even more than the fortunate, and they will be rewarded in Heaven. In church I could feel like a full human being, loved and protected by God—not some outcast, someone beneath others. Eventually, I asked to be christened. My christening name is Marija, and my confirmation name is Kotryna. I received the sacrament of confirmation from Bishop Mečislovas Reinys.[12] For a long time, even during the Soviet period, I was a strong believer and attended mass regularly.

As you have probably noticed, we are sitting in a room where a menorah stands on a table and a cross hangs on the wall. My bedroom also contains both a menorah and a statue of the Blessed Virgin Mary. Eventually, I began to find the stereotypical thinking often expressed in priests' sermons distasteful, and I turned away from the Church. From around 1949, I stopped going to mass. But to this day I painfully seek answers about our existence, and, if I can put it that way, am always searching for God . . .

But let us return to the event that forced me to find somewhere else to live. As I have explained, Onutė and Juozas had found shelter for me with Mrs. Meškauskienė. I was given a place to sleep in a room full of all sorts of odd objects, clothes, and boxes—in effect, a storage room. A stranger, upon opening the door, would never suspect that a bed stood somewhere in the depths of the room. In fact, this detail saved me. One day, the Gestapo knocked on Mrs. Meškauskienė's door. I don't know what they were looking for, but when they poked their noses into the room where I was slept, they didn't notice me.

As soon as the Gestapo left, Mrs. Meškauskienė told me that I would have to leave her home immediately. I can't even remember where I spent the next few days, probably with Juozas's sister in Žvėrynas, but, after that, Juozas and Onutė took me to the home of Mrs. Stefanija Ladigienė, who lived on Trakų

---

12 Mečislovas Reinys (1884–1953)—Catholic cleric, archbishop, pedagogue, activist.

Stefanija Paliulytė-Ladigienė, 1920.
She welcomed Irena Veisaitė into her
family in 1944.

Street.[13] It was evening, and the whole family was seated at the dinner table. Mrs. Ladigienė had six children, but three of them no longer lived there. Her eldest son, Algis, was guarding the Ladiga family estate in Gulbinai; another son, Linas, was working in Germany; and her daughter Irena was, I believe, working as a teacher in Varėna.[14]

When I arrived, Mrs. Ladigienė sat me down at the dinner table and said to her children: "This is Irena—she is now your sister and I want you to love her." Later, Mrs. Ladigienė liked to joke that she had two daughters named Irena— a white one and a black one, because of the color of our hair.

---

13 Stefanija Paliulytė-Ladigienė (1901–1967)—pedagogue, social activist, journalist, married military Kazys Ladiga in 1921. She welcomed Irena Veisaitė into her family in the spring of 1944. Recognised by Yad Vashem World Holocaust Remembrance Center as one of the Righteous Among the Nations (non-Jews who took great risks to save Jews during the Holocaust) for her role in rescuing Irena Veisaitė. For more about Stefanija Ladigienė c.f.: *Esame: Stefanija Ladigienė (dienoraštis, atsiminimai, laiškai, publikacijos)* [We are: Stefanija Ladigienė (diary, recollections, letters and articles), ed. Ema Mikulėnaitė, Vilnius: Lietuvos gyventojų genocido ir rezistencijos tyrimo centras, 2003.

14 References to Stefanija Paliulytė-Ladigienė's children: Algis Marijonas Ladiga; Linas Pranas Ladiga; Irena Ladigaitė-Eiva; not mentioned—Benediktas Ladiga; Marija Ladigaitė-Vildžiūnienė; Joana Irena Ladigaitė.

Mrs. Ladigienė had an older maid named Agnietė working for her, who had cooked dumplings with bacon for dinner. When I sat down at the table, I noticed that Mrs. Ladigienė served me a slightly bigger portion of dumplings than she did her own children. She must have understood how hungry I was. I can't begin to tell you what a sharp feeling of hunger I had felt throughout the years of the Nazi occupation! I was deeply moved by Mrs. Ladigienė's generosity. After dinner we sat for a long time at the table and talked—Mrs. Ladigienė's children Marytė, Jonė, Benediktas, and I.

In that home, there was a longstanding tradition that the mother, after putting all of the children to bed, would visit each one: she would kiss them on cheek and make the sign of the cross on their forehead.

I was given Linas's bed, the bed of the son who was in Germany. When she came to my bedside, Mrs. Ladigienė also kissed me and made the sign of the cross on my forehead. I didn't even realize it when the tears began to flow

Marija Ladigaitė (Stefanija Ladigienė's daughter) and Irena Veisaitė. Moscow, 1947.

from my eyes. Mrs. Ladigienė was startled and began to ask what had so hurt or saddened me. I asked her, "Did it not disgust you to kiss a Jew?" Then Mrs. Ladigienė wept as well.

Neither she nor I slept that night—we talked right through to the morning. That was how she became my second mother, and I—her daughter. I stayed with Mrs. Ladigienė's family even when the Soviets occupied Lithuania and right up to her deportation to Siberia.

You are probably wondering what made me cry and what led to that dramatic conversation between Mrs. Ladigienė and myself. Here it is important to say one key thing: when a person is constantly surrounded by humiliation and hatred, when they are constantly hounded and persecuted—this kind of situation has a profound psychological effect. Living within that steady stream of hatred, I could feel the worm of doubt beginning to gnaw at my heart: "Maybe there really is something wrong with me?"

I felt very comfortable in Mrs. Ladigienė's home and was showered with love and attention. Although she was a woman of profound faith, she never displayed it, and she always demanded more of herself than of others. Her whole being was permeated by love for her neighbour. But Mrs. Ladigienė was also a secular and an artistic woman. How beautifully she recited poetry! I can remember how we—the whole family—would sit in the living room after dinner and she would recite poems by the Lithuanian writers Salomėja Nėris, Bernardas Brazdžionis or Maironis, and sometimes also poems in Russian, by Pushkin, Apuchtin, and others.[15]

Once, Mrs. Ladigienė surprised me by giving me a small box of rouge, so that I could paint my cheeks and would not look so pale. This kind of behaviour was unheard of in a Catholic Lithuanian family! According to the attitudes of the day, a girl who bought and used rouge was at the very least seen as unseri-

---

15 Salomeja Nėris (1904–1945)—poet, one of the most distinct Lithuanian women poets of the interwar period, a person of a complex and tragic fate, who contributed to the establishment of the Soviet regime in Lithuania.
  Bernardas Brazdžionis (1907–2002)—Lithuanian poet, one of the most respected writers of the interwar independence period. During the occupation period Brazdžionis acquired the status of national poet; like Maironis before him, Brazdžionis had a profound impact on Lithuanian national consciousness.
  Alexander Pushkin (Rus. Александр Пушкин, 1799–1837)—Russian poet.
  Aleksei Apuchtin (Rus. Алексей Апухтин, 1840–1893)—Russian poet.

ous. But Mrs. Ladigienė knew how to separate true faith from public displays of devotion. As I have already mentioned, the main thing that motivated all of her actions was love for her fellow human beings. No one ever left Mrs. Ladigienė's home hungry, and anyone appealing to her for help could be sure that they would receive sympathy and understanding. I remember a discussion that frequently took place between her and Agnietė. "Madam, maybe we should not be feeding guests? We may not have anything to feed the children tomorrow," Agnietė would say. "Don't worry—God will provide," was Mrs. Ladigienė's reply. As strange as it may seem, Mrs. Ladigienė was right. The next day, someone would arrive from the countryside with bacon, eggs, flour or potatoes, and the family, despite Agnietė's fears, would not go hungry.

Another person who lived with us on Trakų Street was the teacher Adelė Dirsytė, who is currently being beatified by the Catholic Church.[16] She was teaching German at Vilnius Girls' High School. And there was also a Mr. Česlovas Mečys, a man with a wonderful sense of humour. He was short and plump, and he liked to joke that he only needed to wave his little finger and "all the girls would come running to him." I have no doubt that both Adelė and Mr. Česlovas knew that I was Jewish, but they were on our side. On the other hand, Mrs. Ladigienė's children knew nothing. I remember one funny incident. Marija Ladigaitė (later Vildžiūnienė) was in the same class as Irena Žemaitytė (later Geniušienė). They had to participate in some kind of thematic evening wearing folk costumes, and were talking amongst themselves: "What sorts of Lithuanian girls do we make? But look at Irena—she really looks Lithuanian!" Of course, hearing such talk, all I could do was smile silently. To this day, it makes me happy to remember that conversation.

I was happy and felt loved in Mrs. Ladigienė's home. What was my everyday existence like during that period? I continued to work in the nursery at Dr. Rudaitis's clinic. I was dying to go the theatre or the cinema. I did not dare go to the theatre, even though Ibsen's *Nora* was being performed at the time, with Monika Mironaitė playing the title role.[17] But I did go the cinema once. I saw

16   The process of Adelė Dirsytė's beatification began in 2000. For more about Adelė Dirsytė c.f.: *Adelė Dirsytė: Gyvenimas ir darbai* [Adelė Dirsytė: Life and work], ed. Mindaugas Bloznelis, Vilnius: Katalikų akademija, 2003.

17   *Nora*—theatre director Romualdas Juknevičius's production of Henrik Ibsen's play, Vilnius City Theatre, premiere 1942.

a film that was very popular at the time, Veit Harlan's *Die goldene Stadt* (The golden city), which was based on a work by Richard Billinger.[18] After the screening, the doors of the cinema were blocked and Gestapo officers were checking documents at the exit. You can imagine how I felt. But luckily—thank God—everything went well.

By then it was 1944, and the situation was changing dramatically. Everyone could see that the Germans would lose the war, and it seemed that the Germans understood that themselves. In July, the battles over Vilnius began. In reaction to the rapidly shifting situation, Mrs. Ladigienė's family began to debate: what should they do—remain in Lithuania and experience a second Soviet occupation, or flee to the West? They decided to stay.

As the front approached Vilnius and the city was being bombed daily, Mrs. Ladigienė decided to take her children to stay with a Mr. Stabinis, who lived in what is currently the neighbourhood of Žirmūnai, but which Vilnius residents then called "Losiuvka." At the time it was a suburb of Vilnius. She hoped that this area would not be bombed, and Mr. Stabinis had a basement in which they could hide if needed.

I announced that I would not leave Mrs. Ladigienė's home, because someone had to guard it. I was afraid that her Polish neighbours would loot the empty apartment as soon as the opportunity arose. As you know well, I have nothing against Poles, but try to imagine what an atmosphere of intolerance had developed, and we were the only Lithuanians in that large building. Mrs. Ladigienė tried to talk me out of this plan, but it was impossible to reason with me. I loved her greatly and wanted to repay the kindness she had shown me, at least in this way. No matter what she said, my response was: "At night I will guard the apartment, and during the daytime I will join you."

For some time, that is what I did. I would sleep in our apartment and spend the days with Mrs. Ladigienė's family. But when battles erupted on the streets of Vilnius, I could no longer keep my promise. Finally, fierce fighting reached Trakų Street and I found myself imprisoned in the apartment. Trakų Street changed hands at least three times. I have to admit that it was quite terrifying.

---

18   *Die goldene Stadt* [The golden city, 1942]—film directed by Veit Harlan, based on Richard Billinger's *Der Gigant* (The giant, 1937).

During the shooting and bombing, the residents of the building would hide in the basement. A few times the building superintendent asked me to give him the keys, saying that he had to regularly check the third-floor apartments to see if fires had caught in them. I did not give him the keys, but a few times I took him and some of the other neighbours to check the apartment. Not realizing that I could understand some Polish (since I spoke Russian perfectly), the neighbours were constantly gossiping about Mrs. Ladigienė's family and me. *Czy ona żydówka?* —I heard them ask each other a few times.[19] Of course, I did not give myself away; I knew that if the Germans should win Trakų Street from the Russians yet another time, the neighbours could report me.

I remember how, five days into my "imprisonment," it was a Thursday, and my nerves were at a breaking point. The days were very hot. It seemed as though the air itself was quivering from the heat. Moreover, the constant tension and the brutal killing taking place before our eyes were very hard to handle. The final drop of horror, after which I lost my self-control, was the following episode . . . I believe it was on Wednesday that a gang of Russian soldiers—they were sixteen-year-old boys—turned into Trakų Street from Pylimo Street. There were about thirty of them. A German tank stood hidden behind a chapel on Pranciškonų Street, which runs into Trakų Street. As the Russian soldiers approached the chapel, the tank drove into Trakų Street and opened fire. All of the Russian soldiers were killed. It happened right under our windows . . .

The next day the Germans drove us out of our buildings and made us bury the soldiers' bodies. The stench was terrible. When we would move one of the boys' bodies, a brown liquid would pour from it. It was ghastly. Suddenly I saw that, among the pile of corpses, one of the soldiers was still alive. A neighbour and I dragged the wounded soldier into the stairwell of our building. Of course, we had neither medicine nor any other means to help him properly, so we just gave him some water and a slice of bread. But the young man's state was quickly deteriorating. He was in terrible pain and was feverish. When he briefly revived, he kept asking us to let his family and his girlfriend know what had happened to him. He had a photograph of her in his pocket. Thank God that, when the Russians appeared on the street, we were able to give them the wounded boy. I would like to think that he survived.

---

19 "Is she a Jewess?" [Pol.]

You cannot imagine what a horrific thing war is! It is nothing more than legitimated murder! Most of the people who had been sucked into the gears of this killing machine deserved pity more than condemnation. What was some Russian or German, who had been forced by his government to take up a weapon and go and kill innocent people, guilty of? In situations of mandatory military service, we can hardly blame conscripts who are fighting on one side of the front or the other. I finally grasped this after reading the play *Der Stellvertreter*, by the then famous German writer Rolf Hochhuth, which blames the Vatican for its concordat with Nazi Germany.[20]

As I have already mentioned, by Thursday of that week I had realized that I could not bear it any longer. I packed my most valuable possessions into two suitcases and prepared to hike to Žirmūnai. It seemed that the fighting had died down somewhat, but as soon as I got to the gates of the yard I once again heard an exchange of gunfire. So I had no other choice but to pick up my suitcases and go back up to our apartment.

As the Nazis retreated from Vilnius, German soldiers were running along the rooftops, setting buildings on fire. The entire Old Town was in flames. It was so hot in our apartment that the wallpaper was peeling away from the walls. Next to the window stood a buffet, and on it was a painting of the Holy Virgin Mary of the Gates of Dawn. I can remember praying to that painting and asking that the spreading fire bypass our building.

That time misfortune spared us . . .

On July 13, 1944, the Soviets took Vilnius and the shooting stopped. At around lunch time there was a knock on the door. It was the composer and choirmaster Mr. Konradas Kaveckas, a close friend of Mrs. Ladigienė's. He was living on Klaipėdos Street at the time and, taking advantage of the restored calm, had come to see how we were doing. I told him that the rest of the family had gone to stay with Mr. Stabinis, and so the two of us decided to walk to Žirmūnai together. I can remember the terrible sights that we saw as we walked through the Old Town and then along the Neris River: collapsed buildings; streets scattered with the corpses of Russian and German soldiers, intestines and brain matter spilling from them; streams of blood, already dry, on the roads. . . . Fires were still raging in some places. The city looked so awful! But, strange as it may sound, life did not

---

20　Rolf Hochhuth, *Der Stellvertreter* [The deputy], 1963.

stop for a second. As we approached the Neris, at the spot where King Mindaugas Bridge now stands, a boatman was already waiting to take people to the other side of the river. All you needed was a little bit of money. So, with that boatman's help, we found ourselves on the other side of the river, in Žirmūnai.

It is difficult to convey the emotions that overwhelmed us when we were reunited in Mr. Stabinis's home. Everyone was exhausted from the long week of uncertainty. Mrs. Ladigienė could not forgive herself for leaving me to guard the apartment. And I, having spent a week on Trakų Street, realized how heavily the solitude, fear, and constant tension had weighed on me.

When I saw them all alive and well, still sitting in the cellar, I began to shout quite hysterically. There are moments in life when one cannot control oneself... when one is simply carried by emotion. And Mrs. Ladigienė—as she told me later—was terribly frightened and even thought that my intense experiences had caused me to lose my emotional balance, or perhaps even my mind. In the end, we all simply embraced, crying and laughing from the joy of being reunited. For my part, I was happy that the apartment had been preserved, and a few days later we all moved back to Trakų Street.

But soon new worries emerged. Mrs. Ladigienė was very concerned about her son, Algis, and her sisters. Algis was in Gulbinėnai, while her sisters were in the village of Vabalninkas.[21] We had not had any news of them for a long time, so all sorts of thoughts came into our heads. I offered to go to find out if they were all right. It was a hazardous journey, but once again I was happy to help my second mother. The train to Biržai, through Panevėžys, took three days. It barely crept along, stopping constantly. I remember sitting on the station platform, freezing; a man hugged me to warm up, but I quickly got away from him. Then I walked from Biržai to Vabalninkas, a distance of 26 or 27 kilometres. I found both Algis and the sisters alive and well, so I was able to return to Vilnius with good news.

And then the Soviet period began...

Before we enter this period, I would like to ask you one more question. There were many times in your life when your life was in danger. How did you handle the extreme tension of those situations? After all, there

---

21 Stefanija Paliulytė-Ladigienė's younger sister—Irena Marija Cecilija Paliulytė, and three older sisters—Natalija Ona Paliulytė, Severina Pranciška Paliulytė, and Kotryna Paliulytė.

were many cases when your fate clearly depended on whether you would know how to control yourself and calmly analyse the situation in which you found yourself.

I certainly did not always succeed in controlling myself. On the other had, as I have said already, there is some kind of survival instinct that comes into force in extreme circumstances and helps a person make quick decisions. I have already told you about my escape from the Kaunas ghetto and the time when the Gestapo unexpectedly visited the clinic nursery. I am eternally grateful to my father, who raised me to be independent and taught me to think logically. Besides, much also comes down to chance events, and we have already spoken about some of those.

How would you explain the causes of horrific things such as the Holocaust? There are generally two approaches: those who adhere to the first argue that, under certain circumstances, and especially during periods of want and misfortune, a small, average person is an easy target for various chauvinistic ideologies; those who support the second view argue that evil can only be explained using metaphysical categories.

Personally, I often find that the sources of evil first of all lie within us. People are imperfect and are easily manipulated. They are easily infected by feelings of hatred and revenge. It is normal people who spread evil. The philosopher Hannah Arendt, who observed the Eichmann trial, spoke about the banality of evil.[22] She came to the conclusion that Eichmann, who directed the mass killing of Jews during the Holocaust, saw himself as a good German citizen; he felt no guilt and was a good son, husband, and father. Eichmann simply believed in Hitler's ideas and obediently executed them. The sociologist and philosopher Zygmunt Bauman has warned us that a potential Eichmann exists within each of us. It is therefore very important to preserve our critical thinking in every situation, and not to succumb to indoctrination.

---

22 Adolf Eichmann—one of the main masterminds and organisers of the Holocaust, Obersturmbannführer. Eichmann's trial took place in Jerusalem and began on May 31, 1961. The trial sentenced him to death on December 15, 1961; Eichmann was executed on June 1, 1962.
Reference to Hannah Arendt's book *Eichmann in Jerusalem: A Report on the Banality of Evil* (1963).

I can only hope that I was protected from "banal evil" by two things: critical thinking and the desire to remain myself; and the tendency, in any situation, to see not only evil, but also the goodness and beauty of life and human beings. That is probably why I cannot remember the faces of any of those who persecuted me, whether Gestapo or NKVD officers. All that remains in my memory is the image of their shiny boots.

I have probably told you about a dream that I have had several times. I'm sitting in a room full of Persian rugs with my daughter, who is around ten years old. We are happy and are experiencing a state of perfect harmony. It's cosy. But then the door, which is also covered in a Persian rug, opens suddenly and a man approaches us. I cannot see his face—only his shiny boots. He holds a pistol in one hand and there is a very pretty, blond, blue-eyed boy of around six standing next to him. Thrusting the pistol into my hand, the man screams in an unearthly voice: "Shoot this boy or I will shoot your daughter!" I am holding the pistol in my hand and pressing my daughter even closer to me when . . . I wake up. My first thought upon awakening is: "Thank God that I did not shoot the boy, even in my dream!"

Those who want to sow the seeds of evil are highly skilled, so their efforts are often successful, even when we believe that we are immune to lies and manipulation.

I can remember an incident which I hope will better illustrate my thoughts about the dangers we all face. It was 1951 and I was studying in Moscow. I was chosen to participate in an athletes' parade that was due to take place on May 1 in celebration of International Workers' Day. I can remember how thoroughly we were drilled. May 1 finally came and we were marching through Red Square. As we approached the Mausoleum, Stalin suddenly appeared. You cannot imagine the scene in the square! People thought that they were seeing God himself, descended from Heaven . . . Our rows fell apart as everybody turned toward Stalin, screaming like madmen, reaching their hands out toward him!

As we left Red Square and approached Saint Basil's Cathedral, I suddenly realized that I was shouting with the rest of the crowd . . . Can you imagine that? I knew perfectly well who Stalin was and what he had done, and I did not worship him! But I had unwittingly succumbed to the mass psychosis. It's lucky that I only shouted and did not, unwittingly, become part of a lynching mob and killed a person! It's entirely possible . . .

That rally in the Red Square was one of the most horrific experiences of my entire life. Elias Canetti has written very insightfully about crowd psychology, but it is one thing to read books and quite another to experience that in reality, and to realize that one, too, is susceptible to manipulation.[23]

Perhaps I am going on a tangent, but I have often thought that, during the Second World War, a portion of ethnic Lithuanians also succumbed to manipulation, especially with regards to the Jewish question. The anti-Semitic baggage was substantial ... For a long time I was surprised that post-war Lithuanian literature spoke so little about the tragedy of the Jews. After all, Lithuanians had seen how their Jewish neighbours were arrested, tortured, and murdered *en masse*, and how the entire Jewish world that had existed in Lithuania was destroyed! Yes, I know that the Lithuanian poet Sigitas Geda put together an anthology of poetry about the Holocaust, titled *Mirtis, rečitatyvas ir mėlynas drugelis* (Death, a recitative, and a blue butterfly); that the journal *Pergalė* (Victory) published Antanas Jonynas's story "Šuliny" (In the well); that Jonas Avyžius wrote about the Jewish tragedy in his novel *Sodybų tuštėjimo metas* (When the homesteads died); and that Algimantas Mackus wrote the wonderful poem "Jurekas."[24] There are many examples, but in general the theme of the Holocaust has only been treated marginally in Lithuanian literature.[25] I understand that

---

23   Reference to Elias Canetti's *Masse und Macht* (Crowds and power), 1960.

24   *Mirtis, rečitatyvas ir mėlynas drugelis. Lietuvių poetai apie holokaustą* [Death, a recitative and a blue butterfly: Lithuanian poets on the Holocaust], ed. Sigitas Geda, Vilnius: Vaga, 1999.
Fragments of Antanas Jonynas' unfinished novel *Šuliny* [In the well] were first published in the literary journal *Pergalė*, later published in a collection of Jonynas's works; c.f.: *Šuliny: proza, kino dramaturgija* [In the well: Prose, film scripts] ed. Antanas A. Jonynas, Vilnius: Vaga, 1982. *Šuliny* was translated into English by Juval Lirov and published in the United States: *The Hill*, Marlboro, NJ: Affinity Billing, 2007.
Jonas Avyžius, *Sodybų tuštėjimo metas* [When the homesteads died], Vilnius: Vaga, 1973.
Algimantas Mackus, *Augintinių žemė* [Land of the adopted], Chicago: A. Mackaus knygų leidimo fondas, 1984.

25   The tendencies that Veisaitė outlines have to some degree been corrected by the appearance of Sigitas Parulskis's novel *Tamsa ir partneriai* [Darkness and partners] (Vilnius: Alma Littera, 2012; Eng. *Darkness and Company*, trans. Karla Gruodis, London: Peter Owen, 2018). This work inspired intense public discussion, debate, and self-reflection about the Holocaust in Lithuanian society. The discussion further intensified with the publication of Rūta Vanagaitė's book *Mūsiškiai* [Our people] (Vilnius: Alma Littera, 2016); c.f. further discussion of *Mūsiškiai* in section "Voices from the Past," p. 340. Irena Veisaitė's steady raising of the question of Lithuania's relationship to the Holocaust has been explored in depth by Hektoras Vitkus in his dissertation "Holokausto atminties raida Lietuvoje" [The development of Holocaust memory in Lithuania] (PhD diss., Klaipėda University, Lithuanian Institute of History, 2008).

this was partly the result of the Communist Party's anti-Semitic policies, but still . . . In speaking about such things, writers, not just historians, could help us to feel empathy, to oppose evil. But how little has this theme appeared even in the diaries of our most prominent writers and literary critics. As the historian Egidijus Aleksandravičius has correctly noted, "The Holocaust did not survive in Lithuanians' collective memory."[26]

The Jewish Lithuanian writers Grigory Kanovich and Icchokas Meras wrote about the Holocaust, but I believe it is very important that ethnic Lithuanians also remember that tragic page in the country's history—that they attempt to understand what happened.[27]

I too am a Lithuanian, but one of Jewish ethnicity. For that reason it is always easy to accuse me of being biased. That is why I generally avoid speaking about the Holocaust, and do not bring up this topic unless I am asked about it directly.

I was very struck by your thought that it is not only the work of historians, but also of artists, that is important when we are speaking about the common tragedy that befell the Jews and the Lithuanians.

And I greatly value that you just said the "common" tragedy of the Jews and the Lithuanians. In making that point I wish to recall the writer and dissident Vasilij Aksionov's mother's, Yevgenia Ginzburg's 1967 book *Journey into the Whirlwind*, which made a profound impression on me.

Ginzburg and her husband were intellectual communists, but, in 1937, her husband Pavel Aksyonov was arrested.[28] Certain that he was innocent, Ginz-

---

26 Egidijus Aleksandravičius—Lithuanian historian and commentator, long-time colleague of Irena Veisaitė's at the Open Lithuania Foundation.

27 Grigory Kanovich—Lithuanian and Israeli writer, author of numerous books and stories in Russian about Litvak culture and history, and about how the tragedy of the Holocaust destroyed the world of Lithuania's Jews.
Icchokas Meras (1934–2014)—Lithuanian writer. His novel *Lygiosios trunka akimirką* (Vaga, 1968; Eng. trans. Jonas Zdanys: *Stalemate: A novel*, New York: Other Press, 2005) is recognised as one of the great works of Holocaust literature.

28 Vasily Aksyonov (Rus. Василий Аксёнов, 1899–1991)—writer, one of the most famous representatives of the "Sixties Generation," son of Pavel Aksyonov and Yevgenia Ginzburg.
Yevgenia Ginzburg's (Rus. Евгения Гинзбург, 1904–1977) 1967 memoir *Крутой маршрут* (Journey into the whirlwind) written in 1967 (second volume 1975–1977)—one of the first literary texts to descibe the Stalinist repressions. The book was first published in Milan from audio recordings prepared by Ginzburg; it was distributed in the Soviet Union in *samizdat* [self-published, Rus.] format.

burg—just like Joseph K. in Kafka's *The Trial*—went from one bureaucratic office to another explaining that there had been an error, that her husband was not an enemy of the people. Eventually she too was arrested and she spent many years in the Gulag. In speaking about her own and others' suffering, she comes to the following conclusion (I am citing from memory): "How fortunate that I became a victim rather than an executioner."

The fact that the Holocaust was our common tragedy, and one for which I feel a degree of responsibility, is illustrated by the contradictory emotions I experienced during our last conversation. And I have to admit that, when I think about this horrific chapter in our history, I cannot give an unequivocal answer to the question, "What would I have done?" I might have stood quietly under a tree.

No one can answer that question unequivocally. But most importantly—you certainly would not have joined the murderers.[29]

But is silent observation of evil's triumph not, in some way, equivalent to supporting the killers?

I am deeply convinced that you have formulated your question much too categorically. As I have already said, what is most important is to not spread evil or become a murderer oneself. I know that, as long as I am of sound mind, I will never deliberately kill another person—that I will try not to add to the evil that exists in the world. Do you remember my story about how I stood in line for bread? Nobody forced that woman to say angrily, "Get out, you Jew!"

Pavel Aksyonov (Rus. Павел Аксёнов, 1899–1991)—Soviet Communist Party figure. Arrested in 1937 based on falsified claims and condemned to death. His sentence was commuted to imprisonment in a gulag in 1939; spent 18 years in Inta gulag and in exile in the Krasnoyarsk region. Rehabilitated in 1956.

29　While reviewing the text, under the sentence "But most importantly— you certainly would not have joined the murderers" Veisaitė wrote the following comment: "While reading Rūta Vanagaitė's *Mūsiškiai*, I was very happy to discover that 117 Lithuanian volunteer recruits, having understood that they would not be defending their homeland but would be used to kill Jews, ran away from their battalion. That did not save the lives of the condemned Jews, but those escapees saved their own human dignity and did not contribute to the implementation of a horrific crime."

And I have already explained that I understand perfectly what kind of a situation Lithuania had found itself in. The first Soviet occupation, in 1941, and the deportations that ensued were a shock to everyone. But, as I have already said, the existential situations of the ethnic Lithuanians and the Jews were very different, and that has to be taken into account when discussing 1941. The Lithuanians thought the Germans would liberate them, but to the Jews, the Nazis meant death. That is why they saw the situation differently. Add to that the deep traditions of anti-Semitism, and the powerful propaganda of Joseph Goebbels and the LAF... I don't want to condemn anyone, but there are boundaries that should not be crossed—otherwise you will destroy yourself as well. Perhaps you know of a Jew-killer with a happy fate, but I'm not aware of any.

Thank God that life did not present you with such dilemmas.

You are correct—whenever I think of the bloody nature of the twentieth century, I am grateful that I did not have to experience what my grandparents did, that I did not have to face the decisions that tormented them. That is why, when most of my intellectual friends reacted with irony and doubt to the Nobel committee's decision to award the 2012 Peace Prize to the European Union, I saw it quite differently.

Yes, the European Union is not a perfect political community, but, thanks to its existence, we have had seventy years of peace on this continent. And Lithuania, as a member of the EU, is protected from military aggression and the threat of occupation, although the situation has recently changed somewhat... I do not understand people who only berate the EU instead of trying to contribute to its improvement. After all, we have to recognize that our geographic situation and cultural traditions make us part of Europe.

With that in mind, what are the moral imperatives that govern your own life? More than once you have stressed how important it is to resist giving in to the thirst for revenge—that is especially important when speaking of experiences such as the Holocaust and learning how to live afterwards...

Revenge is a horrible thing; it only leads to a dead end—to greater and interminable bloodshed. I was protected from taking the wrong path by the principles my mother instilled in me. I never felt the need to take revenge on anyone for the wrongs that were done to me. But I have had conversations with people who cannot understand my position, who say: "How can you forgive the Holocaust? What right have you to do so? My mother or my uncle, who were murdered, could forgive. But you certainly cannot!" I don't think that the person who spoke in that way was right, but I can understand him. To forgive, especially after some time has gone by, and to create the future, are the duties of the living.

I believe that, if my mother's torturer or murderer were standing in front of me and truly repenting for what he had done, I would definitely forgive him. It is probably impossible to forgive someone who has no regrets about their crimes. But to seek revenge on such a person is pointless...

Remember how Pope John Paul II behaved with Mehmet Ali Ağca, who attempted to kill him.[30] The Pope forgave him, but the man had to serve his sentence.

※

---

30 In 1981 Mehmet Ali Ağca attempted to kill Pope John Paul II in St. Peter's Square.

I Was Surrounded by Very Good People

Irena Veisaitė preparing for a music lesson. Vilnius, 1946.

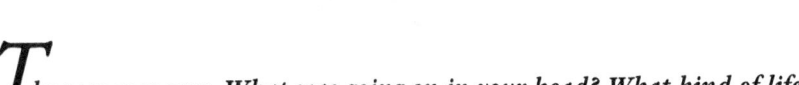

The war was over. What was going on in your head? What kind of life did you want? What did you want to study? Where did you want to live?

I felt liberated and lucky to once again be like everybody else. I was finally free of the constant fear of death. I lived among very good people and felt their love.

The first thing I did was to search for survivors. I checked all of the lists that were being posted and waited for my dear mother and uncle to return. But these hopes were not destined to be fulfilled, as they were long dead. I kept finding the same news: "Deceased," "Killed," "Perished," "Executed." But despite loss, life always moves forward. Especially when sad news was sometimes replaced by happy discoveries: my aunt Anuška, my eldest cousin Valdemaras, and my cousin Margarita with her husband Juozapas all turned out to be alive.[1] As was Aliukas, who had been taken in by Sniečkus. But when I thought about the future, a single thought occupied my mind: "I must study!" As soon as it was possible, that is, in August 1944, I went to sign up at Salomėja Nėris High School.[2] After the war, it moved to a former monastery next to the Church of Saint Catherine. It was often freezing cold in the classrooms.

Salomėja Nėris High School was run by a very intelligent, refined and noble-minded woman named Aldona Rapoportienė-Končiuvienė. Meeting her made a great impression on me. To know someone who was so pure, who glowed from within, was a great fortune after the darkness of the German occupation.

---

1   Reference to Juozas (Joseph) Kagan.
2   Vilnius High School Nr. 2, which Irena Veisaitė began to attend after the war ended, was named after the Lithuanian poet Salomėja Nėris in 1946. It was a girls' school until 1954, when it was reorganized into a co-educational high school.

Classmates and award winners. From left: Sigita Paleckytė, Irena Veisaitė, Birutė Baužaitė, Lilė Bokšickytė. Vilnius, 1947.

When I started going to school, I met a girl of my age named Lilė Bokšickytė, who wore a shabby brown coat and wooden clogs. She became a lifelong friend. Lilė was from Alytus, but had come to Vilnius before the war to attend a Lithuanian high school. She was imprisoned in the Vilnius ghetto, but, during its liquidation, had managed to jump over the barbed wire fence and escape. At first she was given shelter by Kazys Janavičius and later by his mother, who lived in Alytus. Her former teacher, Vanda Daugirdaitė-Sruogienė provided Lilė and other Jewish girls with her deceased students' identification cards.[3] As soon as the war ended, Lilė returned to Vilnius and began to look for opportunities to continue her studies. We both entered the same fifth-year high school class. She lived in great poverty, was always short of clothes, food, and money, and lived in a student residence. She was a strong student with a great deal of talent, and her goodness knew no bounds. We graduated from high school in three years, as we both "skipped" the sixth year.

I had the opportunity to know some excellent teachers at that school, first and foremost Vanda Zaborskaitė, who was our homeroom teacher in the seventh and eighth years, but there were others as well.[4] My first Lithuanian lan-

---

3   Vanda Daugirdaitė-Sruogienė (1899–1997)—historian, pedagogue, social activist. Wife of writer Balys Sruoga.
4   Vanda Zaborskaitė—c.f. note 10, p. 47.

guage teacher there was Mrs. Mackevičienė, who taught us in the fifth year. She was an excellent specialist in that field and a very interesting, sensitive person. Mrs. Mackevičienė gave me an edition of the writer Vaižgantas's Lithuanian epic *Pragiedruliai* (Cloud clearings), with the inscription "So that even in the darkest night you may see the brightening sky!" I cherish this book to this day. Our music teacher was Pranas Sližys, who later directed the Vilnius University Choir. We were very fond of him.

In her autobiography, Vanda Zaborskaitė recalls that there was a core group of seven girls in our class: Sigita Paleckytė, Birutė Baužaitė, Lionė Nekrošaitė, Lilė Bokšickytė, Sulamita Gordonaitė (Sulamita and I had attended Shalom Aleichem High School in Kaunas together; she was rescued from the Kaunas ghetto by Dr. Kutorgienė), Genovaitė Šukytė and myself.[5] We got along very well and were all very active in school life. Four girls from our class were even awarded gold medals with their diplomas: Sigita Paleckytė, Birutė Baužaitė, Lilė Bokšickytė, and myself. I have kept a photograph of the four of us in Lithuanian national costumes, from after the graduation ceremony. This photograph was published in the daily newspaper *Komjaunimo tiesa* (Komsomol truth) together with a short article.[6] Following the ceremony, in the early morning and following a sleepless night, we hiked to the top of Gediminas Castle Hill and signed the following oath: "In the early morning, the white witches granted me happiness and prophesied that I would remain eternally young. We, the girls of class 8b, who graduated from Salomėja Nėris High School in 1947, will meet in Vilnius again in exactly ten years, in the spring of 1957. Signed on June 29, 1947." It was signed by every girl in class 8b, and also by Vanda Zaborskaitė.

Salomėja Nėris High School was a very happy and interesting place for me to study.

Did you fulfil this promise?

In part—our group of seven did, as we remained very close. It is interesting that very different kinds of students made up classes 7 and 8b. I later learned that

---

5   Vanda Zaborskaitė, *Autobiografijos bandymas* [Autobiographical sketch], ed. Virgilija Stonytė, Vilnius: Lietuvos rašytojų sąjungos leidykla, 2012.

6   "Nepaprasta diena Salomėjos Nėries gimnazijoje" [A special day at Salomėja Nėris high school], *Komjaunimo tiesa* [Komsomol truth], July 2, 1947, 3.

there were children of deportees among us who, understandably, did not speak about what had happened to their parents. After all, we attended Salomėja Nėris High School during an era of fear. People were very guarded and were reluctant to share private information. But within our group of seven girls, we were very open with each other, even in those times.

And now let us return to your teachers.

The biggest star at Salomėja Nėris during that time was unquestionably our homeroom teacher, Vanda Zaborskaitė, who, as we learned only later, was still completing her own university studies. Indeed, while reading her autobiography, I found out that we were not that interesting to Vanda. She was teaching high school because she needed to earn a living, and her thoughts were primarily occupied with her studies at Vilnius University. But I must stress that none of us sensed this. She knew how to create a very special atmosphere in the class-

Vanda Zaborskaitė, Irena Veisaitė's high school home-room teacher. Vilnius, 1947.

room. We all felt very close to her and trusted her completely. Zaborskaitė's lessons were always rich and interesting. She taught us Lithuanian language and literature, and also German. Her lessons about Tolstoy and Goethe, and the Lithuanian writers Maironis, Vaižgantas, and Putinas made a great impression on us. I believe that she had a fundamental impact on the shaping of all of our worldviews and values.

Who were some of your other teachers?

I have already mentioned Rapoportienė and Sližys . . . We also had a very good chemistry teacher, Miss Staniulytė. She knew her material very well and inspired trust. I would also like to mention our Latin teacher, Miss Melaikytė, as she introduced me to the texts of Ovid, Horace, and Cicero. We were taught history by Mr. Biziulevičius, physics by Mr. Janonis, and Russian by Mrs. Archipovienė. Although I recall all of these teachers with a great deal of gratitude, as I have mentioned it was Vanda Zaborskaitė who had the greatest impact on me personally.

In your short reminiscences about Zaborskaitė, I read a lively account of how, when a rumour was circulating that she was going to be let go, some of her students expressed their opinion by going to the Ministry of Education. Obviously, no one would have so defended a "regular" teacher.

That was exactly the case . . . As far as I can remember our delegation consisted of Paleckytė, Šukytė, Bokšickytė, and myself. We very emphatically stated that, if Zaborskaitė was taken away from us, we were prepared to leave the school ourselves. This was early 1947, a period when it was generally dangerous to express one's views freely . . . But what is most interesting is that our efforts bore fruit!

What are some of the texts that you read during high school?

I read a great variety of books from the selection that was available to me at that time. I cannot say whether I understood, or, to be more precise, grasped, all of the texts that I read. Some things were only revealed to me much later. I could mention Antanas Baranauskas and his famous long poem *Anykščių šilelis.*[7] While in high school, I learned the poem by heart, as we were required to do. Twenty or so years later, my husband Grigori and I were walking in a forest. We both loved picking mushrooms. It was early morning and the natural world was awakening. And, then, suddenly, I remembered Baranauskas's poetry, and I sensed its beauty and meaning. I grew up in the city, so my relationship with nature is different from that of someone who was raised in the country. That morning, I finally, truly, saw Baranauskas's world. Surrounded by the profound beauty of the forest, I thought to myself, "How lucky that we had to memorize so much poetry in school!"

Of course, we did not only study Lithuanian classics, but great works of world literature as well. Teacher Zaborskaitė recommended so many books to us that I doubt I would have had time to look for anything else.

While reading your answers to the questionnaire that Zaborskaitė gave to students, I noticed one sentence in particular: "I am drawn to study a field that has no future and which it would not be interesting to study under our present circumstances."[8] *What did you have in mind when you wrote that?*

I wanted to study psychology—to better understand human nature and thinking, how people's values and characters are shaped. This probably came from my family, because my mother was very interested in psychoanalysis. She read a great deal on the topic. I remember seeing books by Sigmund Freud, Carl Jung, and Alfred Adler on her table. She often travelled to Vienna, where she attended various psychoanalytic seminars, which were fashionable at the time. Her interest in psychology undoubtedly influenced me. But after the Holocaust, I was also trying to understand the motivations behind human behaviour, the roots of brutality.

As I have already mentioned, I had relatives in Moscow. My uncle—my father's brother, Aleksandr Veis—belonged to the academic community. He worked at the Moscow State Alpine Institute and was responsible for the de-

---

7   *Anykščių šilelis* [The forest of Anykščiai, publ. 1861]—poem by Seinai (Sejny) bishop and poet Antanas Baranauskas (1835–1902), considered one of the most important classics of Lithuanian literature. In the poem, forest and tree imagery is a powerful romantic symbol of freedom, used by the poet in discussing the need for a Lithuanian national revival during the period of csarist Russian imperial rule.

8   C.f. full questionnaire text in "Voices from the Past" section, p. 303

partment of colored metals. When he learned that I was interested in psychology, he offered to introduce me to a famous psychologist of that time, Sergei Rubinstein, who was in charge of the Psychology Department within the Academy of Science's Philosophy Institute.[9] "What interests you?" Professor Rubenstein asked me. I answered that I was especially interested in psychoanalysis. Because he knew my uncle, the conversation was relatively open. "You know, my dear girl," replied the professor, "in the Soviet Union psychology is not a science. There would certainly not be any opportunities to study or write about the authors who interest you. I do not recommend that you study psychology!" So ended our conversation. When I realized that I would not have studied true psychology but Marxism-Leninism thinly veiled behind a few academic concepts, I gave up that plan, and am still grateful to Professor Rubinstein for helping me to grasp the situation.

I made the most important decisions about my life path while living with Dr. Moses Brauns's family.[10] By that point, Mrs. Ladigienė had already been deported to Siberia, and her children were scattered and living in different places.[11] Although we continued to stay in touch, our home had been ripped apart.

Dr. Brauns was a man of rare kindness. If he visited a patient and learned that he or she was having difficulty making ends meet, he would not only refuse to accept payment but would leave them some money to purchase medication. But most importantly, he was someone who was always capable of looking at a situation from an optimistic perspective. "If you broke your arm—be happy that at least you did not break your neck!" he would say in reaction to most accidents. By some miracle, the doctor himself had survived Dachau concentration camp. He told me about how, while at Dachau, he fell ill with typhus

---

9   Sergei Rubinstein (Rus. Сергей Рубинштейн, 1889–1960) established a Department of Psychology at Moscow State Lomonosov University and initiated the creation of the first psychologists' association in the country (connected to the USSR Academy of Sciences). During the anti-Semitic campaign in the second half of the 1940s he was removed from his positions but remained one of the most influential researchers in the field of psychology in the USSR.

10 The family of Moses and Betty Brauns supported Irena Veisaitė from 1946 to 1960. After the Braunses emigrated to the US, Veisaitė continued to maintain close ties with the family.

11 Stefanija Ladigienė was accused of membership in the interwar Catholic organisation "Ateitininkai" and the Catholic Women's Association, which the Soviet regime viewed as "anti-Soviet." She was arrested in March 1946 and sentenced to ten years in a gulag and four years of exile. In July 1947 she was transported to Stroika [Construction] 501 gulag in Tyumen Oblast, and later to the Angarlag [Angar construction] gulag in Irkutsk. From 1955 she lived in exile in the Golumet region of Irkutsk.

and was at death's door when the following thought flashed through his mind: "Why on earth should I die? Let Hitler kick the bucket—I will live!" That was the turning point that led to his recovery.

The doctor's wife, Betty Brauns, was a very dear and intelligent woman who, during the interwar period, had written one of the first English-language textbooks for Lithuanians.[12] She was incarcerated in Stutthof concentration camp, but also survived.

And so, after Mrs. Ladigienė's family was ripped apart, destiny was once again kind to me—I was taken in by exceptionally good-hearted people who gave me much help and support in choosing my path in life, applying for doctoral studies, and even raising my daughter Alina, who was born in 1955.

By the way, the Braunses encouraged me to become a doctor. But, as often happens, when a person is pressured, they tend to resist. I felt more drawn to the humanities. I decided to study Lithuanian language and literature, and have never regretted it.

What were your first impressions of Vilnius University?

My first contact with Vilnius University was, shall we say, ambiguous. While still at Salomėja Nėris High School, I had gone to the university several times to take the German language entrance exam—I knew the language quite well and sat it for some of my older schoolmates. At the time, entrance applications did not include a photograph, which opened the door to various "creative strategies."

The university impressed me in many ways, beginning with the ancient architecture and ending with the notable personalities who worked there, including Vincas Mykolaitis-Putinas, Vasily Sezeman, Juozas Baldžius-Baldauskas, Kostas Korsakas, Jonas Dumčius, Jonas Balčikonis, and others.[13] I was happy

---

12 Reference to the textbook *English grammar* = *Anglų kalbos gramatika*, Kaunas: Leidimo B-vė literatūra, 1924.

13 Irena Veisaitė lists the most noteworthy figures of the Lithuanian humanities community—individuals who chose not to flee at the end of the war and worked at Vilnius University.
Vincas Mykolaitis-Putinas taught courses on various subjects related to Lithuanian literature.
Vasily Sezeman (Vosylius Sezemanas) (1884–1963)—Lithuanian philosopher of Swedish descent.
Juozas Baldžius-Baldauskas (from 1939) (1902–1962)—ethnologist, folklore scholar.
Kostas Korsakas (1909–1986)—Lithuanian literature scholar, critic.
Jonas Dumčius (1905–1986)—classical languages scholar.
Juozas Balčikonis (1885–1969)—linguist, translator.

at Vilnius University and felt that I belonged there. But, unfortunately, I never finished my Lithuanian literature studies.

What happened? Why did you have to break off your studies?

Because I had completed high school with a gold medal, I was accepted into the program without an entrance exam.

During the first year, I had to take a course with Juozas Balčikonis. I have already mentioned how, in a dictation on accentuation, I received a perfect score of five from this professor. But, during the oral part of the exam, the professor asked me the usual question: "Where are you from, young lady?" "From Kaunas," I replied. "Ah, from Šančiai," responded the professor and wrote a score of four points in my grade booklet, even though I felt I had answered all of the exam questions correctly. "A girl from Kaunas who speaks without the dialect cannot know the Lithuanian language perfectly!" This was how Balčikonis explained his decision. Nevertheless, I was very happy with the grade!

What other professors did I encounter at Vilnius University? We were taught German by Eugenija Vengrienė, Latin language and literature by Jadvyga Tijunelytė, psychology by Alfonsas Gučas, and aesthetics by Professor Sezemanas. The spirit of the Lithuanian ancient literature scholar Jurgis Lebedys was still alive in the university.

As you already know, the NKVD arrested Mrs. Ladigienė on March 14, 1946. For three days, an armed security service officer sat in her apartment and detained everyone who came through the door. Very quickly there was a room full of people whom the NKVD officer did not permit to leave. We lived like that for three days and, in that way, all found ourselves within the "authorities'" field of vision.

Later that May, a very close friend of mine, a young physicist names Tadas Masiulis , was arrested. I went to the NKVD prison regularly to visit him and Mrs. Ladigienė and to bring them packages of food. At the time I was also very religious, so I was going to mass often. It was obvious that I appeared unreliable in the eyes of the security service. And if we add to that the fact that my father was living abroad . . .

One fine day—it was late spring, 1948—I learned that the Vilnius University Communist Youth Committee had "deliberated" about me and had de-

Tadas Masiulis and Irena Veisaitė meeting on the shore of the Neris, after Masiulis
returned from eleven years of imprisonment and deportation. Vilnius, late 1970s.

cided that I must be expelled. By that point the NKVD had attempted to recruit me.

Some time in April, I believe, I was walking with my closest friend, Genė
Šukytė (we recently celebrated the seventieth anniversary of our friendship!)
along Didžioji Street, which at the time was called Maxim Gorky Street. As
we passed Chodkevičiai Palace, I was suddenly detained by two men in civil-
ian clothes who took my passport, led me to Saint Casimir's Church, and then
let me go. As I would later learn, Genė was also detained that day; the security service men took her to the NKVD building on what is now called Gediminas Prospect, near Lūkiškių (then Lenin) Square, where they tried to recruit
her. Several days later, late in the evening, they came to Trakų Street and led me
to their headquarters as well, where I was interrogated through the night. I was
"handled" intensively by two different security service brigades. One of them
played the role of "good NKVD men," the others—"bad NKVD men." The
"good" ones said to me: "We rescued you, an orphan, we can help you finish your
studies, obtain an apartment; we'll take care of you." All the while, they were
urging me to "help them in the struggle against the fascists." To this I replied,
"I will always help you to fight the fascists. What would you like me to do?" "It's

all very simple," they would reply. "For example, you are friends with a certain Alė Naginskaitė.[14] Find out what she writes in her diary, listen to her conversations with others, and then report back to us." I answered as follows: "I cannot do that. My parents raised me differently. My mother never once opened a letter that was addressed to me. She respected my privacy." Of course, my answers did not satisfy the "good" NKVD men, so they continued to pressure me, while I continued to reply that I would not be able to break with my moral principles, even citing excerpts from Maxim Gorky and Alexander Fadeyev's *The Young Guard* to support my argument.[15]

When the "good guys" did not succeed, they were replaced by the "bad guys." A powerful spotlight was aimed at my face and a pistol lay on the table, while the NKVD men shouted and cursed: "You ungrateful girl! We rescued you, and how do you thank us? You associate with fascists! We'll make sure that you rot in Siberia!" These and similar words were interspersed with a flood of swearwords which I cannot repeat. This continued through the night.

They did not succeed in talking me into collaborating with the NKVD. It went on until seven in the morning. Finally, two pieces of paper were brought in. "Sign!" I heard them order. "I will certainly not sign anything," I replied. "Then you will not leave here!" they informed me. The situation was at a deadlock. "Before arguing anymore, read what is written here," they suggested. One of the documents stated that I swore not to tell anything about that meeting. That one I agreed to sign. The other document contained my pledge to cooperate with the "authorities." That one, it goes without saying, I did not sign. I am happy, even quite proud of that. Yes, I was ready to be sent to Siberia, but... I don't have any idea if I would have been able to resist physical torture... Maybe I would have agreed to everything after the first needle was dug under my nail?

That time, they let me go, despite all the threats that I would rot in prison. But they did not leave me in peace. I was continuously watched and persecuted, and was regularly led to secret NKVD apartments to "have a talk." During

---

14 While studying at Vilnius University, Alė Naginskaitė-Vajegienė belonged to a young writers' group supervised by Vincas Mykolaitis-Putinas. She was expelled for her "formalist experiments" and was forced to return to her native town of Rokiškis.

15 Up to the 1980s, Aleksander Fadeyev's novel *Молодая гвардия* [The young guard; first edition 1946, second edition 1951] was an ideologically sanctioned literary version of the history of the Communist Party.

these meetings they continued to attempt to convince me to collaborate and provide information about various people. It was clear that this process would not lead to a good outcome—I would be expelled from the university for having been involved in "anti-Soviet" activities, which would sabotage any attempts to continue my studies. Seeing this situation, my closest friends and advisors recommended that I leave Vilnius.

As I have already recounted, my father's brother and two sisters lived in Moscow, and they urged me to move there. Eventually, I made up my mind, packed my bags, and left Vilnius.

Was your decision to flee justified? Did the authorities leave you alone after that?

Yes. This is most likely because the security service, like most other Soviet institutions, were very inefficient. It seemed that I disappeared from their field of vision. To be sure, many years later, my Moldovan friend Liuda Chebotarenko, who was in the same year at university, told me that the Moscow security service had once called her in to "have a talk" about me. By they never again bothered me personally.

※

I Needed a Change

Alexander Shtromas (Štromas). Moscow, 1958.

*During the Soviet period, Moscow State Lomonosov University, where
you studied German, was quite a legendary place, as though it had a particular aura . . .*

I haven't heard any legends about it. I only knew that it had a high rating and
was considered a prestigious university.

Although I had completed one year at Vilnius University, Lomonosov University refused to accept me straight into the second year, so I once again became
a first-year student. I had to spend the first semester in the part-time studies department, but after completing that semester with high grades and, apparently, making a good impression on some of my professors, they decided to transfer me into the full-time studies program.

As I have already mentioned, I was studying German language and literature, which was part of the Western section of the Faculty of History and Philology. People studying the different languages interacted quite a lot and even
had some common lectures. I felt comfortable with the people surrounding
me and the atmosphere in Moscow seemed freer to me than Vilnius at that
time, though this impression was likely shaped by the frightening encounters
I had had with the "authorities" in Vilnius. In Moscow no one dragged me
to secret apartments, and I gradually shed the tension that had so long oppressed me.

And now onto my studies . . . During the first half-year, I took notes on the
lectures, which were all in Russian, in Lithuanian, but then there was a turning point and I began to write all of my notes in Russian, which I had known
since childhood. My exam grades were always very high, and, from the third

year, I believe, I began to receive a Lermontov bursary, which was bigger than a standard one.[1]

Unfortunately, while studying in Moscow, I also had to join the Communist Youth League, or Komsomol.[2] I was not an especially active member, but I did work for the university's wall newspaper. Thankfully, I managed to avoid participating in various "actions." I have already described to you how, during one New Year's Eve party, I did not have the courage to join in when my classmate Simon Markish sang a song in Yiddish. I can't remember in which year it was that they began to attack him during Komsomol meetings. I was asked to write a negative, discrediting article about Sima. I refused to do this, and am very happy that I did. If I had agreed, my conscience would have tortured me for a long time.

When I think about the level of instruction at Lomonosov University, I have to say that I was not terribly impressed. I graduated from it with the feeling that they mostly taught us all sorts of things related to Marxism-Leninism, which were meaningless to me. My assessment probably does not surprise you. At the time, Lomonosov University had "lost a lot of blood." For example, just as I began my studies, the university fired the famous Shakespeare and Western literature scholar, the erudite and enlightened professor Leonid Pinsky.[3] Perhaps you have heard of his seminal study of Shakespeare? They also dismissed docent Jevgenija Lvovna Galperin, an expert in Western literature, as well as the irreplaceable scholar of nineteenth century Russian literature, docent Bielkin.[4] If I am not mistaken, all three were Jewish, so in addition to their other "sins" they were also labelled as "cosmopolitans."

Another scholar forced out of Lomonosov University, whose lectures in Medieval and Renaissance literature I was fortunate to attend in my first year,

---

1   Refers to a bursary named after Michail Lermontov (Rus. Михаил Лермонтов, 1814 – 1841)—Russian poet.

2   Communist Youth League, or Komsomol (Rus. Всесоюзный ленинский коммунистический союз молодёжи)—established in 1918. The goal of the All-Union Leninist Youth Communist League was to shape generations of young "Homo sovieticus" loyal to the Communist Party.

3   Leonid Pinsky (Rus. Леонид Пинский, 1906–1981)—philologist, scholar of 17–18th century Western literature. Irena Veisaitė mentions the following monograph by Pinsky Шекспир. Основы драматургии, Москва: Художественная литература, 1971.

4   Jevgenija Galperin (Rus. Евгения Гальперина, 1905–1982)—literary scholar, critic, editor. Abraham Belkin (Rus. Абрам Белкин, 1907–1970)—philologist and pedagogue whose research focused on the works of Fyodor Dostoevsky and Anton Chekhov.

was Professor Boris Ivanovich Purishev, who later taught at Moscow Pedagogical University.[5]

Indeed, these individuals' erudition and inner intelligence did not impress me alone. My classmate Elena Markovich wrote a poem, on her own and my behalf, dedicated to Professor Galperin.

The person who took over the Department of Western Literature, Professor Roman Samarin, was very well-read, but was a *konjunktursikas*—as we called political operators who played the system—par excellence.[6] To this day, I remember how, for example, when speaking to us about the supposedly reactionary German writer Novalis, he blurted out, "At least he died young!"[7] I have no doubt that Samarin had a hand in driving out the best professors in the faculty.

My thesis advisor was Professor Vladimir Neustrojev.[8] Elena Markovich wrote a poem about him as well. We would grin while reciting it:

> *And every time he was asked*
> *He answered so:*
> *On the one hand "Yes,"*
> *On the other hand "No."*[9]

He was probably a decent man, but it seemed that he lacked the courage to oppose the system. And when one is surrounded by professors like that, the Lomonosov University "atmosphere" that you mentioned tended to evaporate . . .

I was very disturbed by several things that happened during my third year. The "Campaign against Cosmopolitanism" and the "Doctors' Plot" clearly showed that Jews were considered unreliable and undesirable by the Soviet regime.[10] At the time, I was writing my undergraduate thesis about Georg

---

5   Boris Purishev (Rus. Борис Пуришев, 1903–1989)—Russian literary scholar, pedagogue.

6   Roman Samarin (Rus. Роман Самарин, 1911–1974)—literary scholar.

7   Novalis (a.k.a. Georg Philipp Friedrich Freiherr von Hardenberg (1722–1801)—poet and philosopher.

8   Vladimir Neustrojev (Rus. Владимир Неустроев, 1911–1986)—literary scholar.

9   И он на любой вопрос / Такой предлагал ответ: / С одной стороны, это "да," / С другой стороны, это "нет." (Rus)

10   The "Campaign Against Cosmopolitanism" was a Soviet 1948–1953 policy which had a clear anti-Semitic subtext, as it was generally individuals of Jewish ethnicity who were the focus of criticism. The "Doctors' Plot" was a 1952–1953 criminal case against a group of prominent Soviet doctors, many of whom were Jewish. They were accused of organising a conspiracy to murder several Soviet leaders. The

Weerth, the nineteenth-century German poet and bard of the revolution of 1848.[11] It was not a bad paper for those times. After reading it, Neustrojev did not have any major criticisms. But lecturer Oleg Melichov's review was such that I could have received a three or a five.[12] С одной стороны, это „да," а с другой, это „нет."[13] I understood clearly that Neustrojev always left himself the possibility to detach himself, so I was not sure what to expect. If my memory does not fail me, the thesis defence took place on April 7, 1953, while the "doctors'" trial that was due to take place on April 4th was cancelled. My fiends, who had gathered to hear my defence, saw Samarin enter the auditorium and hand the committee a note that read, "Veisaitė and Markovich are to receive five." And that is the grade that I received. But it did not make me very happy, as that incident made the whole process appear suspicious to me . . .

The various manipulations around my thesis defence and grade did not end there. Based on my grades, I should have received a "red diploma," as my grade book contained only perfect scores of five. But during the state exam on foreign literature, Professor Samarin began to ask me provocative questions. Out of nervousness, I gave the wrong date for Molière's death—I said 1683 instead of 1673. This was not a fundamental error, as nothing occurred during that decade that would have changed the course of Molière's writing. On the other hand, my fumble became an excuse for more questions of that nature, until Samarin was eventually able to give me a score of four. So, in the end, I did not receive a "red diploma." But I was not very upset about that. I was much more disturbed by the ugliness of the whole incident.

As you can see, I do not feel very sentimental about Lomonosov University, though of course I have many fond memories: our German instructor Liubov Moisejvna Volf, all the time that I spent in the library, my friends.[14] Besides, Moscow itself was fascinating: the people, the classical music concerts, the exhibitions and museums. At the beginning of my studies, I stayed with my relatives, but after two years I moved to a student residence flat on Stromynka Street, at

"guilty" doctors were also accused of having established ties with the bourgeois international Jewish nationalist organisation "Joint," established by US intelligence.

11   Georg Weerth (1822–1856)—German journalist, writer and poet; one of the first German Marxists.
12   Oleg Melichov (Rus. Олег Мелихов)—literary scholar.
13   On the one hand "Yes," on the other hand "No." (Rus.)
14   Liubov Volf (Rus. Любовь Вольф)—German language professor.

Lithuanian students attending Lomonosov University in Moscow.
Irena Veisaitė is in the front row, second from the left. Moscow, 1951.

number 32, I believe. I lived there for three years. There were eight of us sharing the room—a true "international."

My cousin Aliukas lived in the same residence. I remember going to wake him every morning, because my cousin, who made fun of me for going to bed at midnight, would sit with his books until four or five, so he struggled to wake up in the morning. You can't imagine how hard it was to rouse Aliukas! Eventually, he would rise from his bed, white as a sheet, and we would go off to our lectures.

Quite a lot of other Lithuanians were studying in Moscow at the time, and we all stuck together. I was friends with Elena Gaškaitė (Červinskienė), Vera Lisauskaitė, Jonas Bulota, Dovydas Judelevičius, Zacharijus Grigoraitis, and others.[15] Fate later brought some of us together again in Vilnius.

Let's talk about Moscow's libraries...

Oh, Moscow's libraries! At one time, Vilnius University Library, and especially Pranciškus Smuglevičius Hall, where the rare manuscripts are held, had made a

---

15 Elena Gaškaitė-Červinskienė (1920–2003)—literary scholar, pedagogue.
   Vera Lisauskaitė—philologist, Russian language specialist.
   Jonas Bulota (1923–2004)—journalist, pedagogue.
   Zacharijus Grigoraitis (1928–1988)—editor at the Lithuania Film Studio.

great impression on me.[16] I can also remember, with pleasure, how I was sometimes allowed to work in the Professors' Reading Room, even though I was only
a first year student. The libraries of Moscow were on a completely different scale.
Their collections were enormous, but it was quite difficult to get into the actual
reading rooms. For example, on weekends we would go to either the Lenin Library or the Foreign Literature Library.[17] On Sundays, we would take turns—
one of the girls in our room would wake up very early and catch the first Metro
train to get to the library, where she would save us all places in the line of people waiting to enter. The rest of us would arrive just before the opening time. If
someone had to leave during the day, it was practically impossible to get back
in, so we often brought some food with us or had lunch at the library cafeteria.
Lomonosov University also had an excellent library, on Mochovaja Street, but
it was similarly difficult to gain access.

Those three places were very important to me and I spent a great deal of
time in them. I so admired the elderly Russian women—book-loving members
of the intelligentsia—who worked there.

The daughter of my uncle Veis (he was shot in 1937), whose name was Leah,
was married to the professor, violinist, and pedagogue Piotr Abramovich Bondarenko, so she had many contacts in the world of the arts.[18] Piotr Abramovich
knew and worked with David Oistrakh at the Moscow State Conservatory.[19]
Their family lived in an apartment on Mansurovsky Lane, then another one on
Nezhdanov Street. Sviatoslav Richter and other famous musicians would visit
the latter apartment. Piotr Abramovich often obtained complementary tickets
for me, so I went to practically all of the best concerts. And while living on Stromynka I learned how to sneak into the great Conservatory hall without a ticket.

Richter's concerts probably made the greatest impression on me. They left
me feeling exalted, as though I had been close to something very real, valuable,

---

16   The oldest and most impressive library at Vilnius University, built in the second half of the seventeenth
      century and decorated by artist Franciszek Smuglewicz; currently contains a permanent display of old
      manuscripts and books.
17   Reference to USSR State V.I. Lenin Library, currently the Russian State Library; the Foreign Litera-
      ture Library—currently the Rudomino Russian All-State Library for Foreign Literature.
18   Davyd Veis was arrested in 1937 and in 1938 the USSR Supreme Court's Military College proclaimed
      a verdict that had no basis in reality, accusing Veis of involvement in an anti-Soviet terrorist organisa-
      tion. He was sentenced to death and executed, and rehabilitated in 1956.
      Davyd Veis's daughter—Leah Bondarenko.
19   Piotr Bondarenko (Rus. Петр Бондаренко, 1903–1985)—violinist and pedagogue.

and perfect. I also greatly admired his teacher, Professor Heinrich Neuhaus's, person and playing.

During my student years, in addition to music there was, of course, also theatre, but it is my experiences of classical music concerts that remain most vivid in my memory.

When you returned from the intensity of Moscow's culture to Vilnius, did you not experience something of a culture shock?

No, definitely not! Indeed, I was simply dying to return to Vilnius! To some people at the time (and probably still today), this ardour of mine must have seemed strange. After all, Lithuania was the land where my dearest family members had perished. But during all of those student years, I still felt a strong urge to return to my native land. A few weeks after I first left to study in Moscow, I returned to Vilnius for no reason at all—simply because of a great feeling of longing. I also felt this strong need to return after I completed my studies. Very simply, I always felt that this was where I belonged. That it was only here that I could do meaningful work...

When the "distribution" process took place, I was supposed to be sent to the Soviet republic of Belarus, to work as a teacher in some small town with just a train station.[20] I can't even remember its name. I was in complete despair. But I was spared my "deportation" to Belarus. In early spring 1953, on March 5th, Stalin died. All of Moscow was in a state of complete emotional paralysis. It seemed as though the city had gone mad—everyone was crying and no one could imagine how it would be possible to go on without "the nation's great leader." After all, we were all forced to wake up and go to sleep "together with Stalin." And suddenly, this deified *generalissimus* had died and left the people of the Soviet Union to their fate. What a chasm must have opened up to those who sincerely believed the propaganda about the "great leader and teacher." Personally, I did not have any illusions about Stalin, but of course I could not show my true feelings openly... I did not participate in the *generalissimus'* funeral, not even out of curiosity. Indeed, it took quite a few lives, as the crowds of peo-

---

20 According to the "distribution plans" that existed during the Soviet period, university graduates were sent to work in locations across Lithuania or even other Soviet republics, often without regard for individual desires, needs, or possibilities.

ple desperate to say goodbye to Stalin were unimaginable. To be honest, at that time I was much more concerned with our "allocations" to our future workplaces than with Stalin's funeral.

It is likely that I would have been forced to go to Belarus if it had not been for my classmate Lena Markovich and her father, the famous power engineer Isaac Moiseyevich Markovich.[21] When I visited their home and told them about my anxieties, Lena's father said: "Go and speak with Sniečkus—he is definitely in Moscow right now!"

Indeed, we learned that Sniečkus had come to attend Stalin's funeral and was staying at the Moscow Hotel. I was nervous about approaching him, but Lena's father simply insisted that I go to the hotel and I am grateful to him for that to this day.

When Sniečkus learned that I wanted to see him, he gave me an appointment immediately. I was very surprised to see that he was not at all sad about Stalin's death. On the contrary, he seemed to be in quite a good mood. He offered to help me right away—he called the Lithuanian mission, and 45 minutes later I had permission to return to my homeland.

At the time, the vice rector of the Lithuanian Pedagogical Institute was my former physics teacher, Antanas Janonis.[22] I must have once made a good impression on him, as he offered me a position at the Institute. It was only part-time at first, but within a year I had a full-time job. That was how my 43-year long career at the Pedagogical Institute began.

This is not the first time that Antanas Sniečkus's name has flitted through our conversation. You had the opportunity to see this person in a range of situations and in varied time periods. How do you remember him? I am not asking you to assess his interwar and Soviet-era activities. Rather, I am interested in seeing him better as a person.

I realize that Sniečkus was a very complex and contradictory figure. He was a convinced communist and had been involved in the pre-war communist underground. Under Antanas Smetona's rule, he spent a fair amount of time in prison.

---

21 Isaac Markovich (Rus. Исаак Маркович, 1901–1974)—engineer and pedagogue.
22 Antanas Janonis was Assistant Director of Vilnius State Pedagogical Institute (further: VSPI) in 1948–1951 and 1953–1955.

With the first Soviet occupation, Sniečkus became secretary of the Communist Party of Lithuania. As far as I remember, people used to call him "the boss." There is no question that Sniečkus was largely responsible for the suffering that befell the Lithuanian nation as well as Lithuanian citizens of other ethnicities: deportations, imprisonments and persecution, and the incredibly painful process of the collectivization of Lithuanian agriculture.

But I also knew Sniečkus as a man. He was very intelligent and principled, and was a man of his word. He was also very charismatic. I was impressed that he never divorced his wife, Mira Bordonaitė, even when, from 1938, anti-Semitism was rising and many communist men were divorcing their Jewish wives.[23] Sniečkus never forgot anyone who had helped him. Perhaps that is why, when he found Aliukas amid the burning ruins of the Kaunas ghetto, he took my cousin into his home.

Sniečkus was good to me as well because my parents had helped him during the interwar period, when the Communist Party was banned in Lithuania and he was being persecuted.

This will sound paradoxical, but I am certain that Sniečkus cared about Lithuania. He wanted Lithuania—rather, Soviet Lithuania—to flourish. I believe that, at the time, he firmly believed in the ideals of communism, but at the same time he cared about Lithuania's survival. Under his rule, industry was developed only in moderation—Lithuania needed to increase its workforce, but he was concerned that our country not be overrun by foreigners. He carefully oversaw agricultural development and took considerable risk in defying Khrushchev's order that corn be planted everywhere.[24]

I know that, during the Khrushchev era, every time Sniečkus travelled to Moscow he was not sure whether he would return as First Secretary or would instead be arrested.

---

23 Mira Bordonaitė-Sniečkuvienė (1910–1992)—member of the communist underground in Lithuania between the wars, later was a Party activist, teacher, and Antanas Sniečkus's second wife.

24 Antanas Sniečkus's view of Khrushchev's agricultural "innovations" has not been studied by Lithuanian historians. This question is, to some degree, discussed in Aaron T. Hale-Dorrell's dissertation "Khrushchev's Corn Crusade: The Industrial Ideal and Agricultural Practice in the Era of Post-Stalin Reform, 1953–1964," (PhD diss., University of North Carolina at Chapel Hill, 2014). To date, the most thorough assessment of the "Sniečkus factor" by a Western historian is Walter A. Kemp's *Nationalism and Communism in Eastern Europe and the Soviet Union. A Basic Contradiction?* London: MacMillan Press, 1999.

Your and Sniečkus's biographies are connected by your cousin Alexander Shtromas's story. Did Alexander tell you about how Sniečkus reacted when he realized that his ward was developing very different—anti-Soviet and generally right wing—views, and later took a different path in life? Why do you think Sniečkus initially tolerated Alexander's views and behaviour?

I think that everything was quite a bit more complicated. When Aliukas found himself in Sniečkus's home, he sometimes behaved . . . I'm not quite sure what word to use . . . he loved and respected Sniečkus, but he allowed himself too many liberties. For example, he used Sniečkus's library without permission; he even made annotations in his guardian's books, and took the liberty of calling for a chauffeur. Sniečkus did not like this because, in his own home, he was quite modest. Then the ideological conflicts began. In Vilnius, Aliukas organized a revolutionary educational institute to prepare workers for higher studies. Aliukas simply did not fit into any standard moulds! Finally, Sniečkus sent him to live in Kaunas. More serious ideological differences emerged when Aliukas was studying in Moscow—their paths separated for good and Sniečkus stopped having anything to do with Aliukas.[25] But Sniečkus maintained contact with me. I sometimes visited his home, he always sent me a New Year's greeting, and we spoke occasionally. I did not pretend to be a communist and was not afraid to occasionally express my views to him. I remember how, one time, he asked me what I thought about Solzhenitsyn's expulsion from the Soviet Union.[26] I replied that I could not have an opinion as no one had let me read his works, and that I did not believe the official dribble printed in *Pravda*.

As I have already said, it always seemed to me that Sniečkus was a Lithuanian—but, I have to once more stress, a Soviet Lithuanian—patriot. So one can

---

25   For more on Shtromas' public opinion of Sniečkus c.f.: "Su Antano Sniečkaus mirtimi pasibaigusi Lietuvos gyvenimo epocha" [With Antanas Sniečkaus's death, a chapter of Lithuania's life comes to an end], and "Man Sniečkus buvo Lietuvos Stalinas" [In my view, Sniečkus was Lithuania's Stalin] in *Laisvės horizontai* [Horizons of freedom] ed. Liūtas Mockūnas, Vilnius: Baltos Lankos, 2001.

26   Aleksandr Solzhenitsyn (Rus. Александр Солженицын, 1918–2008)—writer and dissident, social activist, Nobel Literature Prize Laureate (1970). With the January 1974 appearance of the first publications of Solzhenitsyn's work *The Gulag Archipelago* in the West, the Central Committee of the Soviet Union decided to expel the writer from the country. In 1974 Solzhenitsyn was convicted of betraying his country, stripped of his citizenship, and sent to the German Democratic Republic.

say that he cared about the country. For example, when, under Stalin, Lithuania was offered the opportunity to annex the Kaliningrad region, Sniečkus refused; he knew that Lithuania did not have enough people to inhabit that territory and that it would have been necessary to bring more foreigners into the republic.

I have heard that you also knew Sniečkus's wife, Mira Bordonaitė. What was she like—in public as well as in private? You have spoken to me about a conversation you had with her during the independence movement, when she was already in hospital. Would you mind returning to this episode and telling the story again?

Mira Bordonaitė was a very intelligent, well-educated, and well-read woman from a wealthy Vilijampolė Jewish family. She left home quite young and became a revolutionary. She was persecuted and had spent time in prison under Smetona, and that is where, as far as I know, she met Sniečkus. She was definitely a convinced Communist.

One could disagree with her, but she commanded respect. I remember how, when Sąjūdis independence movement started, she criticized the First Secretary of the Lithuanian Communist Party at that time, Ringaudas Songaila, for trying to block its activities.[27] She once told me that before Sąjūdis she had never doubted her life path, but that once the independence movement began, she could no longer say that categorically.

An already very ill Mira Bordonaitė found herself in the Antakalnis *nomenklatura* hospital, sharing a room with a former deportee. They got along perfectly well. It seemed to me that Mira understood a great many things. I respected her and visited her up to her death.

---

27 Ringaudas Bronislovas Songaila—Soviet party and state figure. During the "rebirth" period in Lithuania, Songaila was First Secretary of the Lithuanian Communist Party and de facto leader of the Lithuanian SSR (December 1987–October 1988). When the Communist Party of the Soviet Union elected Michail Gorbachev as General Secretary, democratisation of the state, political system and society began to take place.
Reacting to these changes, a group of prominent members of the Lithuanian academic and arts communities formed the Sąjūdis Initiative Group, which quickly grew into a Lithuanian-wide movement whose members sought wide-ranging changes at the state and societal levels, and restoration of Lithuania's independence.

And now I would like to ask you about something that is very hard to mea-
sure rationally, so I am most concerned with feelings and impressions. You
have lived in Vilnius, Moscow, and Saint Petersburg (called Leningrad at
the time). In which of these cities could a Soviet-era person breathe most
easily? Which one had the strongest feeling of freedom?

Moscow is a great academic and cultural centre. As you know, I had relatives in
that city. Thanks to them, I quickly became acquainted with some of the great
academic and art figures of that time. I was enchanted by the Russian intelligentsia—their broad view of the world, their capacity for critical thinking. I
was especially impressed by the dissidents and their courage, determination,
and self-sacrifice in opposing Soviet ideology. I continue to hold the true Russian intelligentsia in high esteem. It is a role model for me.

I had the good fortune to know the writer and activist Viktor Shklovsky,
the families of the academics Abrikosov and Otten, the poet Nikolai Panchenko and the bard Alexander Galich, and I also visited Tarusa, which was something of a dissident centre.[28] There, I became acquainted with dissidents like
Anatoly Marchenko, Lyudmila Alekseyeva, Yuli Daniel, and others.[29] These
were people of true courage and broad thinking. In that sense it was easier to
breathe in Moscow.

Comparing Moscow's Lomonosov University and Leningrad's Zhdanov
State University, where I also studied, I have to say that the former, while headed by Samarin, was a place of real stagnation. In contrast, the Leningrad aca-

---

28 Viktor Shklovsky (Rus. Виктор Шкловский, 1893–1984)—writer, literary critic, screen writer. Dur-
ing the period Irena Veisaitė is referring to, Shklovsky was married to Vasilisa Shklovskaya-Kordi (Rus.
Василиса Шкловская-Корди, 1890–1977).
Alexei Abrikosov (Rus. Алексей Абрикосов, 1928–2017)—theoretical physicist, awarded Nobel
Prize in Physics.
Nikolai Otten, pseudonym Potashinski (Rus. Николай Оттен-Поташинский, 1907–1983)—writ-
er, translator, screen writer, film critic. Otten was married to translator Elena Golisheva (Rus. Елена
Голышева, 1906–1984). The Otten family lived in Tarusa. For more about Irena Veisaitė's friendship
with Otten see Conversations X and XI.
Nikolai Panchenko (Rus. Николай Панченко, 1925–2005)—poet.
Alexander Galich (real name—Ginzburg, Rus. Александр Галич-Гинзбург, 1918–1977)—poet,
singer, cinematographer, dissident.
29 Anatoly Marchenko (Rus. Анатолий Марченко, 1938–1986)—writer, dissident, and political prisoner.
Lyudmila Alekseyeva (Rus. Людмила Алексеева, 1927–2018)—social activist, dissident; one of the
founders, in 1976, of the Moscow Helsinki Group.
Yuli Daniel (Rus. Юлий Даниэль, 1925–1988)—poet, translator, dissident.

Professor Maria Tronskaya,
Irena Veisaitė's philology thesis
supervisor. Leningrad, 1960.

demic community was still living in the spirit of the academic Viktor Maksimovich Zhirmunsky and the critic Grigory Gukovsky.[30]

My thesis advisor, Mariya Lazarevna Tronskaya and her husband, Josef Moiseyevich Tronsky, a professor of classical languages and literature, were truly enlightened people.[31] The head of the Department of Foreign Literatures was Boris Reizov, a specialist of eighteenth and nineteenth century literature who had written numerous important studies.[32] Thanks to them, I gained much more professional and methodological knowledge than I had in Moscow; they helped me develop a great respect for academic work.

Tell me more about the phenomenon of Tarusa. After all, it is in Tarusa that Joseph Brodsky hid from the threat of arrest, and Galich and Solzhenitsyn were frequent visitors. Did you get to know any of these people?

Tarusa was a very special place. When I went there, I would stay with the Ottens, who, together with the writer Konstantin Paustovsky, edited and published the *Tarusa Pages*, which simply exuded freedom and independent

---

30 Viktor Maksimovich Zhirmunsky (Rus. Виктор Жирмунский, 1891–1971)—linguist, literary scholar, pedagogue.
   Grigory Gukovsky (Rus. Григорий Гуковский, 1902–1950)—philologist, literary scholar, critic. Considered the leading specialist in eighteenth-century Russian literature.

31 Mariya Tronskaya (Rus. Мария Тронская, 1896–1987)—literary historian and scholar, pedagogue. Josef Tronsky (Rus. Иосиф Тронский, 1938–1970)—classical languages scholar. Considered the leading classical literatures scholar of his time.

32 Boris Reizov (Rus. Борис Реизов, 1902–1970)—literary scholar, translator.

thinking.[33] While staying there, I met Anatoly Marchenko, Natalia Stoliarova, and, I believe, Natalia Gorbanevskaya.[34] While I did not have the opportunity to meet either Brodsky or Solzhenitsyn, I had access to and read books by Solzhenitsyn and other dissident writers. I did meet Brodsky once, many years later, in London, during an event marking the hundredth anniversary of Mandelstam's birth. When I met him, I passed on the best wishes of his friend, the Lithuanian physicist Ramūnas Katilius and his wife Elė. Brodsky gave an excellent presentation about Mandelstam's poetry; I can still remember the unique, song-like manner in which he read, and how he smoked one cigarette after another, without a pause. But that meeting did not give me any better sense of the man.

How did you find yourself in the company of dissidents such as the people you have just mentioned? Were you not afraid that the "authorities" would once again start taking interest in you?

I met members of the dissident community through my cousin Alexander Shtromas, the Otten and Shklovsky families, and other friends of mine. It would have been terribly shameful to give into my own fears before these people. Although there was definitely fear, Alexander was much more daring than I. If a fearful thought passed through my mind, I would immediately suppress it.

How did you decide to study in what was then called Leningrad?

My daughter Alina was born in 1955. After half a year, I suddenly realized that I was suffocating from the domestic routine of diapers and bottles. My first hus-

---

33　Following an idea suggested by Nikolai Panchenko, the writer Konstantin Paustovsky edited the first and final edition of the *Tarusa Pages* almanac. The main idea was to provide an opportunity for poets and writers whose texts were not accepted by the country's main journals and publishing houses to see their work published. Appearing in 1961, the *Tarusa Pages* drew not only broad public attention but also harsh criticism, and even the attention of the Central Committee of the USSR. Publication of the almanac was halted and remaining copies of its only edition were pulled from circulation. C.f.: http://imwerden.de/pdf/tarusskie_stranitsy_1961_text.pdf.

34　Natalia Stoliarova (Rus. Наталия Столярова, 1912–1984)—translator and a woman who lived a brilliant and dramatic life among the highest level of the Soviet-era Russian intellectual elite. Natalia Gorbanevskaya (Rus. Наталья Горбаневская, 1936–2013)—poet, translator, dissident and human rights advocate.

band and my former protectors, the Braunses, became very concerned and saw that I needed a new challenge—that I needed to return to my books and studies. I can't remember any more who first proposed the idea that I go to Leningrad and look for a thesis supervisor. I had heard about some of the professors working there, about their books and lectures. I was very impressed by the scholar Viktor Zhirmunsky, but missed my chance to study with him, as he had just retired. However, his wife, Nina Alexandra Sigal, still worked at the university and kept her husband's academic traditions alive.[35]

While I was still in Vilnius, someone had given me the address of the German literature professor Gelman, who worked at Herzen Pedagogical Institute. When he learned that I wanted to write my dissertation on Heinrich Heine, he immediately referred me to Mariya Lazarevna Tronskaya, a Heine scholar and professor at Leningrad University.[36] That was how I found myself in this unique, exceptional woman's hands!

I presented myself to her, we spoke for about twenty minutes, and she made her decision right there: "You may go ahead and apply to the doctoral programme." Apparently, during the course of our conversation I managed to convince her. I remember my advisor and our work together with much gratitude. Every visit to her and her husband, professor Josif Tronsky's, apartment at the beginning of Nevsky Prospect was very special to me. Josif Moiseyevich was an important Classics scholar. His enormous study—it was 80 or 100 square meters!—was simply filled with bookshelves. It felt like one had entered a labyrinth made of books, where a little space had been cleared by a window for his desk, chair, and a sofa. Mariya Lazarevna, on the other hand, worked in the dining room at an impressive antique table that also stood by a window. So, she only had a corner to herself. The dining room was also filled with books.

Interacting with the Tronsky professors gave me a great deal in both professional and personal terms. Josef Tronsky was a very dignified, extremely subtle person—a walking encyclopaedia of tremendous erudition. It could seem that the professor existed in another world, but, in fact, he noticed everything. I loved my advisor very much and did everything that my means and abilities

---

35 Nina Sigal (Rus. Нина Сигал, 1919–1991)—literary scholar, translator, pedagogue.
36 Heinrich Heine (1797–1856)—poet, one of the most important European literary figures of the first half of the nineteenth century.

allowed me to help her. At that time, Mariya Lazarevna was already of a very respectable age. Indeed, she defended her habilitation thesis at the age of 72! My desire to occasionally help her seemed perfectly natural to me, but Mariya Lazarevna did not want any help. One day, when she was not at home herself, Professor Tronsky invited me into his study and said, *"Иреночка, Вы должны понять—Марусенька не хочет стариться!"*[37] That was a very gracious way of telling me that I should behave more carefully.

I sometimes think that Mariya Lazarevna gave me much that she had not been able to give her own daughter. She had not had any children herself, but had raised the daughter of her brother, who was killed during Stalin's purges. She loved Lena very much, but her niece tragically died at a young age. I came into Mariya Lazarevna's home when Lena was already terminally ill.

But let us return to my studies. I was accepted into the doctoral program in 1958, when my daughter was three years old. Both my husband and the Braunses did everything they could to support my desire to continue my studies. I received a graduate student stipend and was able to support myself in Leningrad, but my family in Vilnius needed financial help. Mr. and Mrs. Brauns had not only agreed to take care of my daughter; they also agreed to help us financially. When I tried, several times, to pay back at least a portion of my debt, they categorically refused to take any money. In 1960, their son, who lived in Los Angeles, sponsored their immigration, and they lived in that city until they died. As a result, my debt became a gift.

That is a brief account of how I found myself in Leningrad.

After completing my comprehensive exams, I began to work on my thesis, which was on the topic "Heinrich Heine's Late Poetry: *Romanzero*." I had always been interested in Heine's late poetry, when he was already lying in his *Matrazengruft*, or "mattress grave," and was trying to assess his revolutionary past.

When I remember my studies in Moscow, there is not one professor who I can say was a true teacher for me, but Leningrad University was full of enlightened people who, as I have said, had a great influence on me both academically and personally . . . Foremost among them was my thesis supervisor, Mariya Tronskaya.

---

37 Irenochka, you must understand—Marusienka does not want to grow old! (Rus.)

And why Heinrich Heine?

To this day I cannot say why, during my studies in Moscow, I chose to write my bachelor thesis about Georg Weerth. Somebody simply suggested it to me. But Heine, as you have probably gathered by now, was a very conscious decision on my part. I have always loved his poetry and been fascinated by him as a person. I had studied German Romanticism quite deeply—its connections to folk art, its exalted and spiritual sense of nature, its glorification of love and Woman. From what I understood, Heine was both a Romantic and a critic of Romanticism. His Romantic irony was unique—it at once created and undermined. Through it Heine expressed his bitterness, his love, and his pain.

I was also very interested in Heine's relationship with his German homeland. In his satirical poem "Germany: A Winter's Tale," he mocks Germany mercilessly for its backwardness, narrow thinking, and provincialism, but it is also clear that he loves it.[38] I believe that a true satirist is always in pain . . . That, by the way, is evident in the work of the famous nineteenth-century Russian satirist Saltykov-Shchedrin.[39] If you do not suffer over the object of your satire, then what you are writing is not satire, but more likely an expression of disdain or derision.

There was another aspect, too. I was interested in Heine because he was a Jewish writer with a unique fate—he became part of the German literary canon and was as beloved as he was loathed. Although his poetry was banned by the Nazis, his poem "Lorelei," which became a popular folk song, was identified as a "work by an unknown author." To this day, it is debated whether Heine was a German poet, or a Jew who wrote in German.

Another significant reason why I chose Heine was that Soviet-era scholarship did not focus very much on his late poetry, which expressed disillusionment with the idea of revolution.

I never regretted that I chose to write about Heine. His portrait still hangs in my room amid those of other people who are dear to me.

When I wrote the first chapter of my dissertation, I took it to Mariya Lazarevna. When I returned to meet with her some time later, I saw that every page

---

38 Ger. *Deutschland: Ein Wintermärchen*, 1844.
39 Michail Saltykov-Shchedrin (Rus. Михаил Салтыков-Щедрин, 1826–1889)—writer, journalist, editor of the journal *Otechestvennye Zapiski* [Notes of the fatherland].

of my text was crossed out—every single one! My advisor explained that I cannot write that way—that a thesis cannot be a simple recounting of events, that it is not like stringing beads. It must contain a central idea and a strong argument. "You already have enough material," Mariya Lazarevna explained to me. "Now you must analyse it, and present it completely differently."

It was an utter disaster for me. I remember walking home, in tears, along Nevsky Prospect. "I can't write. I'm not good enough for the doctoral programme. I should just pack up my bags and go home!" I think that my violent reaction was the result of my experience up to that point—the "top student" syndrome. I was used to constant praise and always receiving the highest grades for my work.

Of course, some time passed and I succeeded in taking charge of my emotions. There was a technique that I always used when I found myself in a practical or creative dead end. Before going to sleep, I would clearly formulate a question in my head; sometimes I even wrote it down on a piece of paper and put it under my pillow. Then, as soon as I awoke in the morning, while still not completely conscious, I would try to catch the answer and quickly write it down. And usually it was the correct and decisive answer. That time I understood that I must not give up.

Over the following week or two, I rewrote the first chapter of my thesis, and this time my advisor did not have any major criticisms. From that point on everything went very smoothly. In remembering that episode I can only say that I am eternally grateful to Mariya Lazarevna for that painful but important lesson.

※

I Saw My Work as
a Kind of Mission

*Irena Veisaitė at a "Theatre Mosaic" event at Vilnius Pedagogical Institute. Late 1970s.
Photo by Ona Pajedaitė.*

In talking about your studies in Leningrad, we almost skipped over a very important biographical moment. Upon returning from Moscow in 1953, you began to work at what was then called Vilnius State Pedagogical Institute. How did you fit in with the staff community? What courses did you teach?

When I came to the Pedagogical Institute, I was assigned to teach a course in the literature of Western Europe. I decided to focus on the Middle Ages, the Renaissance, and the seventeenth and eighteenth centuries. By nature, I am a very contemporary person—I'm more interested in today, in our life here and now. But I chose those periods consciously in the hope of avoiding direct connections to Soviet ideology. I understood perfectly well that if I had taught nineteenth and twentieth century literatures, I would not be able to say what I think and feel. Some time later I was also given a course on German literature. I did not always limit myself to the chronological and thematic boundaries of the courses, especially when I wanted to tell the students something important, to stimulate their critical thinking.

When I began to work at the Institute, I quickly realized that a heavy Soviet atmosphere hung over it. It was headed by Professor Marcelinas Ročka, a scholar of early Lithuanian literature from the older generation of the intelligentsia and a very decent man. But it seemed to me that, in reality, all the decisions were made by the vice rector, Ivan Ariskin.[1] Ročka was succeeded by

---

1   Marcelinas Ročka (1912–1983)—scholar of early Lithuanian literature and books. Rector of VSPI (1951–1955).
    Ivan Ariskin (Rus. Иван Арискин)—Communist Party figure, VSPI Vice Rector, academic and pedagogical affairs (1949–1953).

Juozas Mickevičius, who was a very Soviet person.[2] A relatively liberal man, Vytautas Uogintas, became vice rector; though he did not succeed in fundamentally changing the atmosphere, it improved markedly.[3]

When I began my teaching career, the Institute was located in the Vilnius Basilian Monastery ensemble. Later, we moved to a new building that was erected on the other side of the Neris River.[4] As the result of another move, the Faculty of Philology found itself in a building on Taraso Ševčenkos Street, which had formerly housed the Higher Party School.

At the beginning of my career at the Institute my courses were attended by students of Russian and Polish languages and literatures, while analogous courses were taught to Lithuanian literature students by Ipolitas Cieška, a lovely man who was very popular with the students.[5] Following his death, I was invited to teach in the Lithuanian Language and Literature Department, where I felt that I had finally found my place. Perhaps that was because it had many interesting students, but it could also have been because I was finally able to lecture in Lithuanian.

I became a full-time staff member after one year. I found teaching very interesting and hope that I had a knack for it. Besides, I loved literature, which allowed me to say the occasional important thing to the young people sitting before me. Naturally, it was a long process and one during which I, too, grew in maturity—I figured out my own values and developed an understanding of how I should talk about all of it. I can only hope that the fruit of these searches came across in my lectures. At the beginning, for the first three or four years, it took me a great deal of time to prepare my lectures—I would prepare very detailed notes. This exhausting work paid off in the end: once I had gathered and systematized the material for a course, I only needed to review my notes before each new semester and sometimes make minor additions or revisions. In the end, I did not use them for much more than to check a date or the spelling of a name. I am happy and grateful that life gave me the opportunity to know and work with so many lovely young people; I like to think that we had some meaningful conversations.

---

2   Juozas Mickevičius (1907–1974)—Communist Party figure, VSPI rector (1955–1960).
3   Vytautas Uogintas (1918–1994)—historian, VSPI rector (1960–1979).
4   VSPI was located within the Vilnius Basilian Monastery ensemble at 9 Aušros Vartų Street in 1939–1943 and 1946–1960. It moved to a new campus on Studentų Street in 1960.
5   Ipolitas Cieška (1908–1960)—philologist.

In sharing these memories of my work as a teacher during the Soviet period, I must add that, although anti-Semitism existed, I did not personally experience it directly. But nor did I ever forget that I am a Jew.

Could you explain what it was that reminded you of that?

It is difficult to answer this question in a clear and succinct way . . . Perhaps it was the pervasive atmosphere of anti-Semitism in the Soviet Union. But I should note that it was less strong in Lithuania than in the other republics. Sometimes I was reminded of it by something a colleague said in passing. For example, once a fellow teacher was telling a story about how she had sold her automobile to a Jew. She was simply sharing a piece of information. But when she noticed that I was there she apologized and said that had not wanted to insult me, as though the word "Jew" was something offensive.

Then there was the famous Petrulis case, which shook all of Vilnius in the mid-1960s, in 1965, I believe. A five-year-old girl was found dead in the basement of 13 Jakšto (then called Communard) Street. I can even remember her last name—Bartusevičiūtė. This horrific crime was committed just before Passover, so a rumour instantly spread through Vilnius and people were saying that the Jews were responsible because they needed Christian blood to make matzos. This rumour was quickly embellished with all sorts of stereotypical interpretations. Some "witnesses" even materialized, who claimed to have seen how the bowl of blood had been passed on to the pilots of a mysterious plane, or something like that. The atmosphere became electrified. My daughter was even frightened to go out into the street. Just imagine—some of my colleagues even believed these things!

Or perhaps this extreme sensitivity to anti-Semitism was simply a vestige of my past? I cannot say precisely . . .

On the other hand, the main reason probably lay in my personality. I always just wanted to be myself. I remember how, when I was eighteen, someone suggested that I try a face cream called "Metamorphosis," which eliminated freckles. I refused, saying that if someone were going to fall in love with me, they would come to love me just as I am. I would say that I would remain a Jew until there was not a single anti-Semite left in the world. When the war ended, I immediately changed my last name—from Treigytė I once again became Veisaitė.

Did this stance inform your general attitude and bearing, or your work, lectures, and texts?

In a certain sense, yes. For example, when I began to work in the area of theatre studies, I decided that I would never write about productions based on Lithuanian literature or about Lithuanian playwrights, as I did not want to give anyone the opportunity to say, "What can you know about these things? This is not your business!" I therefore wrote primarily about productions based on world literature. After Lithuania's independence was restored, there was no longer any need for me to limit my interests in this way, but by that time I had little to do with the theatre any more.

Who were your closest colleagues at the Pedagogical Institute?

My closest colleague there was always the well-known Lithuanian Shakespeare scholar Dovydas Judelevičius, to whom I am grateful for many reasons. The general atmosphere in our department improved considerably when Vanda Zaborskaitė and the semiotician Kęstutis Nastopka joined us.[6] I was very close to them as well. I had a great deal of respect for the literature scholars Albertas Zalatorius and Vytautas Martinkus, who also taught there.[7] Indeed, I had good relations with most of my colleagues.

You have described how you prepared your lectures. Everyone knows, of course, that, during the Soviet period, scholars and educators had to make great efforts to "hunt down" the books they needed, which were often hidden away in "special collections" or were simply unavailable in Lithuania. How did you handle this issue?[8]

---

6   Vanda Zaborskaitė worked at VSPI 1971–1992.
    Kęstutis Nastopka—literary scholar and critic, translator; worked at VSPI 1972–2012.
7   Albertas Zalatorius (1932–1999)—literary scholar and critic.
    Vytautas Martinkus—literary scholar, critic, and writer.
8   During the Soviet period, a strict and consistent policy regarding the hierarchical ordering, control, and limitation of different kinds of information existed in Lithuania. This policy was first of all reflected in the nature of the interaction between libraries, as mediators between information (various kinds of texts), and readers. From the first years of the Soviet occupation a campaign of destroying all "ideologically dangerous"—from the viewpoint of Soviet authorities—publications and books related to the independent Lithuanian state, as well as a large portion of the humanities and social science works

There were many texts that, despite my best efforts, I simply could not obtain. I taught a course on German literature that included contemporary writers. It was impossible to find any of their books. For example, I only read Kafka when I travelled to America...

On the other hand, I was in a somewhat better position than some of my colleagues because I knew several foreign languages. So, despite all of the prohibitions and obstacles, I was sometimes able to collect more information on questions that interested me.

There is no question that my perspective and opportunities broadened after I visited my father in the United States in 1968. I have already told you about that, and about how I learned English there and was able to purchase a lot of books and successfully send them back to Lithuania. These packages also included the works of Franz Kafka. I also visited the University of California at Los Angeles, where I met with professors and students and even gave a lecture, though I can't quite remember the topic. After all, the Stalinist era had passed...

During the Soviet period, you knew a great variety of people through whom you had access to all sorts of books. Tell me about some of these people and titles, and where the books came from.

Samizdat literature mostly reached me through my cousin Aliukas and my very close friend Kazys Saja, a playwright who was friends with Aliukas and who was responsible for a considerable amount of dissident literature reaching Lithuania.[9] In fact, there was one incident in which a young man named Vidmantas Putelis wanted to give me some books from Aliukas. He later became a good friend and a well-known journalist, but we did not yet know each other. Imagine this situation: a stranger wearing a beret rings my doorbell. There was some-

---

published during that period. Newspapers, magazines and books that escaped destruction were, as a rule, housed in special collections that were only accessible to a small percentage of readers. Most of the books, newspapers, and magazines that reached Soviet Lithuania from Western Europe and the United States also ended up in such special collections.

9   *Samizdat* [Rus. самиздат]—"self-published" literature that was copied and circulated clandestinely. Self-publishing was a phenomenon unique to Soviet society and a key form of dissident activity. It emerged spontaneously as society's response to Soviet state censorship and other limitations on public life. Kazys Saja—writer, playwright, social activist.

thing about his appearance that made me suspect he might be a KGB agent . . .
I became very frightened and wouldn't let him in. Aliukas later explained to
me that he was very trustworthy and was supposed to bring me greetings and
some *samizdat* books.

I would also gain access to all sorts of books whenever I travelled to Moscow. You asked earlier whether Vilnius then seemed provincial in comparison
to Moscow. To some degree it did, and for that reason I liked to make several trips a year to both Moscow and Leningrad. I especially felt Vilnius's provincialism when I returned from visiting my father in the US. In Lithuania we
were too insular and too inward looking, though, given our situation, that was
probably inevitable.

But let us return to the dissidents. Personally, I felt that the Russian intelligentsia was very sympathetic toward us. Many of them admired Lithuania and,
later, actively supported our quest for independence.

I was able to read Alexander Solzhenitsyn, Varlam Shalamov, and other authors who were banned because they were considered to be "unreliable,"
"not recommended," or seen as "overt enemies of the Soviet government."[10]
This list also included contemporary classics such as Akhmatova, Tsvetaeva,
Mandelstam, Pasternak, and others.[11] Usually you had one, or at best two nights
to read these books that circulated in typewritten copies.

Sadly, I did not see an edition of *Lietuvos Katalikų Bažnyčios kronika*
(Chronicle of the Catholic Church in Lithuania) during the Soviet period, as I
did not cross paths with the people who circulated that publication.[12]

---

10 Varlam Shalamov (Rus. Варлам Шаламов, 1907–1982)—writer, political prisoner and author of a lit-
     erary cycle describing life in the Soviet gulags during the 1930s to the 1950s (*Kolymskiye raskazy* [The
     Kolyma tales], first published in whole in London, 1978).
11 Veisaitė is referring to authors who were out of favor with the Soviet authorities and who therefore suf-
     fered persecution and lived on the outskirts of official public life.
     Anna Akhmatova (Rus. Анна Ахматова, 1889–1966)—poet.
     Marina Tsvetaeva (Rus. Марина Цветаева, 1892–1941)—poet.
     Osip Mandelstam (Rus. Осип Мандельштам, 1891–1938)—poet.
     Boris Pasternak (Rus. Борис Пастернак, 1890–1960)—poet and prose writer, winner of the Nobel
     Prize for Literature in 1958.
12 Lietuvos Katalikų Bažnyčios kronika [Chronicle of the Catholic Church in Lithuania, further—
     CCCL]—the first serious underground publication in Lithuania during the Soviet occupation. It was
     the longest running and most broadly read undergound publicaiton in 1972–1989. A total of 81 issues
     of the CCCL were published.

I have had the opportunity to know some of your former students. They, of course, have warm memories of your lectures and have spoken to me about what helped them to understand your pedagogical approach. They said that a single lecture could contain thirty or more references or excerpts. This detail has made me wonder whether you believed that students of that era could manage such an intellectual load? Your former students have also told me that they were given a very wide range of literary texts to read outside of class.

I think that my former students are exaggerating a little. It would have been very difficult to cite and comment upon thirty or more sources during one ninety-minute lecture. But I certainly did everything I could to broader their perspectives, open their eyes, and dislodge some deeply rooted stereotypes.

My relationship with my students and my teaching methods were probably mostly driven by the fact—and I know this could sound rather pathetic—that I saw my work as a kind of mission. I would describe that mission as an argument, or even a battle, with Soviet ideology.

It was vitally important to me that my students understand that the world is much more varied and complex than was claimed by the Soviet Marxists, who seemed to have simplistic answers to all the existential questions. And, of course, it was impossible that they should. It was a lie, because there are no such answers. I tried to support my view by drawing on literary texts of the highest quality.

Yes, I certainly gave my students a broad range of readings that related to my courses. There were lists of both required and recommended readings.

Sadly, students at the Pedagogical Institute, who were mostly from the provinces, were not very enthusiastic readers. I suppose they needed more time to feel the need for, and importance of, great literature. But I am convinced that most of them began to sense that importance during the course of their studies.

I would say that I was not so much concerned with the number of texts or pages on my reading lists as with crystallizing and communicating certain values. I was horrified by the "Pavlik Morozov" morality that permeated our world and filled every moment with a blend of hypocrisy and lies.[13] In his book

---

13   Pavel (Pavlik) Morozov—a young man whose violent (and never thoroughly investigated) death was used by the Soviet propaganda machine to generate a myth about a pioneer hero, and to promote the

Terror und Traum: Moskau 1937, Karl Schlögel says a very obvious, but important thing: neither Nazism nor Communism would have survived if there had not been an aspect of their ideology that was appealing to the masses.[14] It was important to fight against that!

Some of my former students are surprised, to this day, that I referred to and quoted from the Bible in my introductory lecture. But that was essential. Any analysis of the sources of European culture must speak about Antiquity, the Bible, and folk culture. How can one understand European literary history without understanding such fundamental things? That is why, during that lecture, I always recommended that my students find their grandparents' or parents' old Bible and study it carefully.

As I have already mentioned, the literature that I taught helped me to refine certain concepts for myself. For example, one book that was very important to me was Aron Gurevich's *Categories of Medieval Culture*.[15] It was only published in Lithuania in 1989, so I would encourage my students to read it in Russian. Gurevich's book helped me to explain to my students that each era can only be evaluated within its own context. We have spoken about that before, but I must return again to Gurevich because what he said is relevant today, when we are trying to assess our own cultural heritage.

I was also strongly influenced by works of literary scholars that were accessible at different points during the Soviet period, in particular those of Bakhtin, Alexander Veselovsky, Yury Tynyanov, the sociologist Yuri Levada, and the semiotician Yuri Lotman, as well as Lithuanian literary scholars such as Vanda Zaborskaitė, Vytautas Kubilius, and Albertas Zalatorius.[16]

---

idea that it was necessary to sacrifice oneself "in the name of higher goals" (in other words, in the interests of the Communist Party). This could involve sacrificing morality, harming one's loved ones and even denouncing them to the police, the security forces or the Party (like Pavlik Morosov, who informed on his father to the NKVD).

14 In English: Karl Schlögel, *Moscow 1937*. Cambridge: Polity Press, 2012.

15 See note 9, p. 46.

16 Mikhail Bakhtin (Rus. Михаил Бахтин, 1895–1975)—philosopher, cultural historian, semiotician. One of the most prominent figures in Soviet-era humanities.
Alexander Veselovsky (rus. Александр Веселовский, 1838–1906)—literary historian.
Yury Tynyanov (Rus. Юрий Тынянов, 1894–1943)—writer, playwright, literary scholar.
Yuri Levada (Rus. Юрий Левада, 1930–2006)—sociologist.
Yuri Lotman (Rus. Юрий Лотман, 1922–1993)—semiotician, literary and cultural studies scholar.
Vytautas Kubilius (1926–2004)—literary scholar and critic.

It goes without saying that literary analysis always formed the basis of my courses. Here are a few examples of how we used literary texts to explore the complexities of life and human existence. For example, Boccaccio's *Decameron*, in particular the third story from the first day (which raises the question of which kind of faith is best), helped us to explore the question of tolerance. Dante's *Divine Comedy* provided the opportunity to discuss how life and human behaviour can be assessed, and the importance of always searching for the truth. Erasmus's *In Praise of Folly* was excellent material for both lectures and discussions, especially when wanting to show how any kind of dogmatism, even of the religious kind, can lead to inhumanity.

I myself was probably most interested in analysing Cervantes's *Don Quixote*, Shakespeare's tragedies and Goethe's *Faust*.

We examined Don Quixote's "insanity," which was essentially his protest against the injustices and humiliations of life. As we delved deeper into Cervantes's work, we inevitably came up against the question of who was actually insane: Don Quixote, with his knightly ideals, or the "wise men" of the world, who considered him insane. Who is right—the duke and duchess who mock Don Quixote and Sancho Panza and finally drive them out of their castle, or Don Quixote, who, after leaving the comfortable life of the palace, says to Sancho something to the effect of: I say to you, Sancho—the duties that come with good deeds and favors are like tethers tangling the wings of the soul.

And another important question: in the end, Don Quixote abandons knightly ideals, so it seems that reason triumphs. By why is everyone—including Sancho Panza and the reader—left so sad?

Goethe's *Faust* was excellent for exploring existential questions. Can man change the world? Can he avoid sin? What is the dialectical relationship between good and bad? How can we understand Mephistopheles's words—that he is "... part of that power which eternally wills evil and eternally works good?"

Why was Faust saved, even after he had joined forces with Mephistopheles?

And then there is Shakespeare! *Romeo and Juliet* allowed us to dive into debates about the nature of love. *The Merchant of Venice* helped us raise the question of the fate of the despised Other. I would tell my students about seeing a production of that play in London, starring the great British actor Laurence Olivier. At the end of the play, when Portia has triumphed and Shylock is condemned, an old Jewish prayer could be heard as a counterpoint ... It was a way for the director to show sympathy for this horrible and vengeful, but continuously debased, man.

Sometimes, with my students, we discussed performances as well as books. I would tell them about productions I had seen in Moscow, Leningrad, Riga, Tallinn, London, and the US. We also often discussed films we had seen.

As you can see, literature helped me to shape my students' values and cultural tastes. I was very happy when I succeeded in achieving this goal. I often felt that I could have paid more attention to these and other works' aesthetics, styles, and genres, but I felt that my approach was justified because, during Soviet times, it was most important to help students develop an alternative, non-Soviet value system. For that reason I was most concerned with the works' metaphorical meanings.

Were there any situations in which someone would "take issue" with your lectures?

Naturally, my lectures were often inspected by the administration of the Pedagogical Institute (for example, Vice Rector Ariskin, whom I mentioned earlier, once visited my class) and by my colleagues. But, as I have already said, the subjects that I taught were not considered "ideologically dangerous," and naturally, when such inspections were taking place, I made sure not to complicate things and avoided controversial themes. In other words, I applied some "self-censorship."

Fortunately, such inspections were quite rare.

I can honestly say that I was open with my students and never lied to them. For example, during one lesson I was unexpectedly asked what I thought about Solzhenitsyn's writing and his forced emigration to West Germany in 1974. That time, I sincerely replied that I was not familiar with his writing—I had not yet read Solzhenitsyn's books—so I could not have an opinion about it. But I said that I believed that forcing someone from their homeland for their views was an extreme and unjustified approach.

Things like that occurred regularly, especially when I was in charge of one of the grades. For example, if a "red holiday" were coming up, we would have to herd the students to demonstrations. In such situations, I would address the students in the solemn tone of radio announcer Yuri Levitan and would say: "The

Rector has requested that I tell you that you should . . ."[17] This would be followed by a list of duties and responsibilities. I would read the Pedagogical Institute administration's official document without adding a single word of my own. The students understood everything perfectly well . . .

Such behaviour did not require any special courage. If I had been truly brave, I would have been in a prison cell—not in a classroom with my students.

Of course, there were also some more difficult situations that did require a bit more courage. The first of these occurred when the office of Dean of Lithuanian Language and Literature was taken over by Ričardas Mironas, who held that post in 1953–1954.[18] I respected him as a serious scholar but at the same time I was somewhat frightened of the man. Even his appearance terrified me. I can still remember his stern expression and frequent, angry outbursts. At the time, there was an extremely bright young man studying French language and literature, named Dangis Čebelis. He was, as they say, someone with a history; he had spent five years in Siberia for having distributed copies of Mykolaitis-Putinas's poem "*Vivos plango, mortuos voco*" (I lament the living, I call the dead).[19] Indeed, he never revealed the author to the KGB. After returning from exile, Dangis was accepted into the Pedagogical Institute and wrote an essay about Balzac for my course. Our institute, like other schools of higher learning, had a Student Scholarship Association, which organized an annual academic conference. Because Dangis's essay was very strong, I included it in the conference program.

Suddenly I was called to Dean Mironas's office. As I entered the room, I immediately realized that he was thoroughly irate—he was even quite red in the face. "How could you dare to recommend that such an enemy of the people participate in the conference?" he shouted at me. To which all I managed

---

17 Reference to well-know Soviet radio and television announcer Yuri Levitan (Rus. Юрий Левитан, 1914–1983), who had an unusually expressive tone of voice. His career received a boost when Stalin noticed the young announcer's talent. During the Second World War Levitan read "Sovinformbiuro" announcements. He was given the responsibility of conveying news of the occupation of Berlin and Nazi Germany's surrender, as well as the flight of the first human being to outer space, Yuri Gagarin.

18 Ričardas Mironas (1908–1979)—linguist, translator, Dean of the VSPI's Faculty of Lithuanian Language and Literature (1953–1954).

19 In the poem "Vivos plango, mortuos voco" [I lament the living, I call the dead, 1945], Vincas Mykolaitis-Putinas expressed criticism of the totalitarian regime, condemned its "infection of moral degeneracy" and begged God for help. Although the poem's poetic expression is abstract, its readers—who circulated copies of it—understood perfectly well that it referred to Soviet reality. The KGB attempted to identify the author and began to suspect Mykolaitis-Putinas, but Čebelis, then a Vilnius University student, accepted responsibility and was convicted for the alleged crime.

to reply was, "How could I have possibly known that my student is an enemy of the people?"

You would not believe the horrible names that Mironas called me! But I did not give in, and Čebelis read his paper at the student conference. As you can imagine, following that incident Dean Mironas's opinion of me was not very good.

I had another conflict with the administration, this one with the rector of the Institute, Jonas Aničas, regarding my student Audra Žukaitytė, who has long been my closest friend.[20] Audra had announced to the committee responsible for student "workplace allocations" that she did not want to work as a teacher. When Aničas heard this, he called me to his office and told me that I had not educated her correctly, because she did not have the right values. Naturally, I had a completely different opinion about Audra than the rector, and I defended her to the end. I told him that, instead of being criticized, Audra should be respected for her openness and courage.

Another incident occurred in the spring of 1987, right before the state exam period. At the time, I was in charge of the Theatre Club, which was very popular among the students. The Theatre Club was headed by a talented Lithuanian Studies student. I would rather not mention his name. Suddenly, there was a decision that an open Party meeting be called. I was not a member of the Party, but all teachers, even non-Party members, were expected to attend such events.

I was very surprised when, at one point during the meeting, the Theatre Club head asked to speak. He stated that he believed that the club was being led in the "wrong direction." In other words, an ideological critique was being directed at me. This attack had been planned for the end of the party meeting. As I listened to the criticisms being levelled against me, I kept looking at my watch; I could see that it was getting close to two o'clock, when a meeting of students from our faculty was scheduled with the writer Romualdas Granauskas.[21] Everyone was looking forward to it very much.

It would not be hard to imagine my reaction—I had not expected the attack, so I was stunned and speechless, all the more so because the head of the Theatre Club was speaking in all of its members' names.

---

20 Jonas Aničas—historian, Soviet party figure, VSPI rector (1979–1989).
21 Romualdas Granauskas (1939–2014)—writer, playwright, essayist.

I was sitting next to Dovydas Judelevičius and another colleague, and they both recommended that I not engage in the conflict, that I not react to the lies being thrown about. I did just that, but, when I returned to our department, I heard our chair say that my silence suggested that I agreed with the criticisms.[22]

I was very shaken by that student's betrayal.[23] I had not experienced anything like it during my entire teaching career. I always showed my students a great deal of respect and expected the same from them.

Three or four days went by . . . I experienced them in a fog and could barely eat or sleep. I only woke up from this paralysis when, as I was walking home after my lectures, three students from the Theatre Club came up to me and asked: "What happened at the Party meeting?" All I could say in reply was "You should know as well as I—the head of the theatre club said he was speaking for all of you." When they heard this, the students rushed to defend themselves: "We knew nothing about it. He had not discussed his statement with us, so he did not have any right to speak on the group's behalf. What should we do now?" I replied to them that, because this matter involved me, I could not suggest anything to them.

A week later a meeting of the Theatre Club was called. Rector Aničas was invited (he did not come), as was the department chair, who did attend.

The entire auditorium, probably Room 301, was filled with current and past Theatre Club members. The meeting was chaired by a student named Violeta Pašaitytė, who later married the teacher Vytautas Toleikis.[24] Addressing the student who had spoken during the Party meeting, she asked, "Tell us what you said during the meeting and why."

To which the student replied: "I cannot remember anything about it and do not want to discuss the matter further. Besides, I hereby resign as head of the Theatre Club."

---

22 At the time, i.e., 1985–1989, the head of the Department of Lithuanian and Foreign Literature was the linguist and folklorist Stasys Skrodenis.

23 This attack upon Veisaitė was not an isolated event in the VSPI Department of Lithuanian and Foreign Literature. According to witnesses of the events mentioned here, various department members' "ideological purity" was repeatedly questioned in 1987, and Vanda Zaborskaitė also received heavy criticism.

24 Violeta Pašaitytė–Toleikienė—former student of Irena Veisaitė, worked with her former teacher at the Open Lithuania Fund (in the Social Welfare Program), civil servant.
Vytautas Toleikis—pedagogue, essayist, social and community activist.

You should have seen Violeta Pašaitytė's reaction! That tiny girl was incensed and shouted out loud: "It is not you who are resigning—we are removing you!" I had never imagined that she had such inner strength.

The meeting turned into a triumph for truth and I could sense my students' affection, confidence, and respect. I heard so many kind words and received so many flowers that it felt as though we were celebrating an important anniversary of mine. It was one of the moments of true happiness in my life.

That meeting clearly illustrates that your method of looking for "diamonds in the rough" was effective . . .

I respected all of my students, but then I would occasionally encounter young people of rare talent, whom it was a gift of fate to know. As a lecturer at the Lithuanian Conservatory, I had the good fortune to work with the future theatre director Gintaras Varnas, who was one of strongest students I ever had—well-read, interested in everything, witty, an individual of very refined taste.[25] Another one of my most talented students was Oskaras Koršunovas, now a world-renowned theatre director. I sensed his talent intuitively and gave him a passing grade in an exam, even though he had read none of the required readings. He must have been focused on other things during that period. At the time, I felt that I was compromising myself and felt quite guilty about it, but now I am happy that I behaved that way, as my intuition was correct. I realized that one must never "stick to the letter," even for principles.

At the Institute I also had the good fortune to work with Dangis Čebelis, whom I mentioned earlier; the future priest Robertas Grigas (sadly, I was not able to defend him when the Party organization attacked him for his views and ultimately expelled him); with Vytautas Balčiūnas, Vytautas Toleikis, Reda Noreikaitė (Pabarčienė), Audra Žukaitytė, Dainora Rakauskaitė (Eigminienė), Marius Mikalajūnas, Nijolė Banaitytė (Kezienė) and many others.[26]

I can remember the circumstances under which I discovered Audra

---

25 Lithuanian Conservatory—currently the Lithuanian Music and Theatre Academy.
26 Robertas Grigas—priest, member of the anti-Soviet resistance movement and persecuted for activities related to that.
   Marius Mikalajūnas—Lithuanian language teacher at Vilnius St. Christopher's High School, co-author and editor of various literary textbooks and teaching materials.

Žukaitytė. We first became acquainted during the Faculty of Lithuanian Language and Literature entrance examinations. She drew a ticket to answer a question about the poet Vytautas Montvila.[27] She answered the question perfectly and knew all of the poet's works by heart, as the examination required, but she frankly admitted that she did not like his writing. I was elated to hear her say that, as I understood that I would have the opportunity to converse with a person who has an interesting way of thinking and is not afraid to express her views. Naturally, Audra received a score of five for her answer and was accepted to the Faculty of Lithuanian Language and Literature. Indeed, I can still remember the excellent review of Jonas Vaitkus's 1983 production of Albert Camus' *Caligula* that Audra wrote while in her second year. It is a pity that she does not write much any more.

Remembering some of those "little diamonds," as you called them, I must mention Vytautas and Violeta Toleikis—two excellent students and wonderful people, close friends of mine to this date and like-minded people—they are simply a part of my life. Many people in Lithuania know Vytautas Toleikis as an excellent ethics teacher and essayist; he received a diploma from the Sugihara Foundation for promoting tolerance and for his life achievements.[28] Violeta holds an important position at the Ministry of Social Security and Labour.

There was also Dainora Rakauskaitė (Eigminienė), a very serious, well-read Lithuanian literature student; she is now a master teacher at St. Christopher's High School in Vilnius. While still a student, Dainora was eager to become friends with me, but I tried to maintain a certain distance, because I did not know her well and was unsure of her intentions. That was simply a defence mechanism on my part—during the Soviet period you never knew if you could trust someone who wanted to enter your life. But one day, I met Dainora with her mother, Mrs. Renata Rakauskienė, and all the barriers dissolved. I understood that I could trust these people implicitly.

27　Vytautas Montvila (1902–1941)—poet, known for combining avant-garde style with social and revolutionary motifs.

28　The Sugihara Foundation–Diplomats for Life was founded in December 1999 following the efforts of Lithuanian and Belgian intellectuals and business people who sought to honour the memory of the Japanese diplomat Chiune Sugihara (1900–1986). During the Second World War Sugihara was one of a small number of diplomats worldwide who helped European Jews facing death at the hands of the Nazis. Sugihara issued approximately 6,000 transit visas to Lithuanian, Polish, and German Jews, thus giving them the opportunity to escape from Europe.

It also makes me happy to remember Nijolė Banaitytė, an interesting, constantly searching and very expressive student. She became a teacher but remained devoted to the theatre; she infects all those around her with her enthusiasm.

One of my best students was Vytautas Balčiūnas—a well-read, insightful, and creative young man. It is not surprising that he would later become an excellent Deputy Minister of Culture. Vytautas contributed a great deal to the founding of the Thomas Mann Centre and organisation of the festival. He has devoted his entire life to the world of culture and is currently Deputy Director of the Lithuanian Art Museum.

I must also mention Deimantė Kažukauskaitė (Kukulienė), who now works at the Writers' Union. I remember her listening to lectures with bright, almost burning eyes. I often looked at her while lecturing—one always looks for a sympathetic gaze.

And Edita Šicaitė, who became a Benedictine nun and now lives at Pažaislis Monastery; she is a teacher in Kaunas and remains a great theatre fan.

Although I can still see all of my students' faces, unfortunately my memory has not preserved the names of all those that I could mention.

Because our conversation veered to the Pedagogical Institute's Theatre Club, I would like you to tell me more about this aspect of your work. How did the idea for the Theatre Club emerge?

From about 1964, I was both intensely attending theatre performances and writing theatre reviews. I quickly began to make contacts with people in the theatre world, and I always sought to pass on any positive experiences that I had to my students.

The Theatre Club was not my idea—I borrowed it from the Lithuanian writer Balys Sruoga, who was very active in interwar cultural life and is famous for his powerful literary memoir based on the two years he spent in the Stutthof Nazi concentration camp.[29] This is a tangent . . . I can remember Sruoga

---

29 Balys Sruoga (1896–1947)—poet, playwright, literary scholar and critic. During the Second World War, Sruoga was one of a group of 47 Lithuanian intellectuals incarcerated in Stuthoff Nazi concentration camp; these arrests were a form of punishment on the part of Nazi authorities for resistance to the formation of Lithuanian SS units. This experience was the basis of Sruogas's semi-autobiographical novel *Dievų miškas* [Forest of the gods, written 1945, published 1957], which presents a highly ironic

from Kaunas before the war—a tall, well-built man who walked around Kaunas wearing rather strange golfer-style pants. I was, of course, too young to really understand who he was and only grasped his cultural importance and the beauty of his personality quite a bit later, well after the war.

Sadly, after he returned from Stuthoff and moved back into his Vilnius apartment on Tauro Street, Sruoga sometimes drank himself into a black stupor. I imagine this was from the despair and depression he felt at having been separated from his wife and daughter, who had fled to the West not knowing that he would return to now Soviet Lithuania. And then all of the problems he had with his masterpiece, *Dievų miškas* (Forest of the gods), which was not acceptable to the Soviet authorities and was only published in 1957, well after the writer's death. Mrs. Ladigienė, who was a lifelong friend of Sruoga's, would go to see how he was doing. I would often accompany her, but would wait outside of the apartment.

Later, having taken an interest in Sruoga's writing, I learned that he had taught foreign literature at Vilnius University, during the Nazi occupation, before his imprisonment. Searching in the university archives, I found his course notes, which were written on small pieces of paper, and studied them carefully. They contained quite a lot of jibes against the Nazis. I also knew that Sruoga had created a theatre discussion group in which he met with students, often in his own home, to discuss performances they had seen and theatre in general. I thought this was an excellent idea, and this is how the theatre club idea came to be. Imitating Sruoga, I invited students to come to my home, but after several such meetings, I was called in to see Rector Aničas, who said that work with students can only take place at the Institute and that my project would not be tolerated. We therefore began to meet at the Institute. First we would see a performance and meet with the actors and director, and later would have a discussion about it all.

The Theatre Club was intensely active during the late 1970s and through the 1990s, when Lithuanian theatre was at a high point of creativity and innovation, with the directors Juozas Miltinis, Jonas Jurašas, Eimuntas Nekrošius, Jonas Vaitkus, Rimas Tuminas, Saulius Varnas, and Romanas Viktiukas developing a powerful and often metaphorical theatrical language to counter the Soviet regime's attempt to ideologically control culture.

---

portrait of camp life. The work was not acceptable to the Soviet party elite and the cultural controllers of the day, and was only published in 1957 with extensive cuts by censors. Sruogas's course notes are preserved in the manuscript library of the Institute of Lithuanian Literature and Folklore.

The Vilnius Pedagogical Institute's Theatre Club meeting with actress Nijolė Gelžinytė. Vilnius, 1986.

This surge in theatrical activity could be felt beyond Lithuania's borders. The director Anatoly Efros was working in Moscow, Leningrad had Georgy Tovstonogov and Lev Dodin, there was Adolf Shapiro in Riga, and Tallinn had Jaan Tooming, Evald Hermaküla, and others.[30]

The Theatre Club was not constrained by any bureaucratic regulations, so it was a very creative atmosphere. Most of the students involved in it were first or second-year students taking my courses, but there was also the odd stray from one of the other departments.

---

30   Yuri Liubimov (Rus. Юрий Любимов, 1917–2014)—theatre director and pedagogue, one of the founders of the Taganka Theatre in Moscow (1964) and its long-time director.

Anatoly Efros (Rus. Анатолий Эфрос, 1925–1987)—theatre and film director who had an important influence on numerous Moscow theatres.

Georgy Tovstonogov (Rus. Георгий Товстоногов, 1915–1989)—theatre director and pedagogue, director of the Gorky Bolshoi Drama Theatre in Leningrad (1956–1989), currently Tovstonogov Great Drama Theatre.

Lev Dodin (Rus. Лев Додин)—theatre director, from 1975 worked with the Small Theatre in Leningrad and was its director from 1983.

Adolf Shapiro (Rus. Адольф Шапиро)—director, head of Riga Youth Theatre (1964–1992).

Jaan Tooming—actor and theatre director.

Evald Hermaküla (1941–2000)—theatre director.

In this context Irena Veisaitė's article about Estonian theatre "Ieškojimų kelyje" [On the path of discovery] is relevant (c.f.: *Literatūra ir menas* 23 April 1977, Nr. 17, p. 11).

Our annual "Theatre Mosaic" event was very popular. We would invite theatre critics to join a discussion about the year's most important productions. Our guests included the critics and theatre experts Antanas Vengris, Irena Aleksaitė, Audronė Girdzijauskaitė, Egmontas Jansonas, literary scholar and critic Algis Samulionis, theatre professor Laima Tupikienė, and others. The event was attended by students from the entire Institute, many of whom had not participated in the club during the year. The auditorium was always full to the rafters! Recently, my dear friend Vytautas Toleikis, who had been a very active member of the group, told me that, at the time, the Theatre Club seemed like a real "oasis of freedom" to him. It was wonderful to hear that from Vytautas's lips.

Indeed, "Theatre Mosaic" activities were documented by the photographer Ona Pajedaitė—thanks to her we have many excellent photographs of that time.[31]

⁂

31   Ona Pajėdaitė (1925–2016)—Lithuanian literature scholar, photographer, cultural chronicler.

The Theatre Suits My Interests and Temperament Perfectly

From left: Irena Veisaitė, Jonas Jurašas, Kalju Haan.
Below: Aušra Marija Sluckaitė-Jurašienė. 1960s.

Today, I would like to continue our conversation about theatre. But I have to admit that I hope that our exchange will not devolve into an academic account of the history of Lithuanian theatre and an attempt to name and discuss everything. Would you agree with my approach?

I agree completely. Indeed, as I was waiting for you to arrive, it occurred to me that, until now, I have never had time for the past, for reminiscing—I have always lived very intensely in the present. I never had enough time, so I experienced almost constant stress. I touched on this during our first conversation. Now these thoughts have come back to me, because our conversations force me to look back upon the past. It is like a completely new stage in my life. It is only a pity that my memory has not preserved everything.

I wish I could remember even more, but I never kept a diary. When I arrived in Moscow in 1948, my uncle Sasha tore up my letters and many of the photographs that I had, explaining that, in the Soviet Union, keeping a diary is like reporting on oneself, like writing a denunciation—a *донос*, in Russian.[1] Later, I was neither very good at, nor had time, to keep my papers in order, so my archives are quite a chaotic mess . . . I am especially sorry that I did not preserve the notes, letters, and other texts that contained my impressions of different theatre experiences, especially since theatre has played such an important role in my life. A lot of it I simply burned . . .

As I was gradually transformed from a student of German literature into a theatre critic, I realized the obvious—that the theatre corresponds to my inter-

---

1   Reference to Irena Veisaitė's uncle Aleksandr Veis.

ests and temperament! At the same time, under Soviet rule, the theatre was a very special place in which, using Aesopic language, it was possible to say things about existential matters, ethics, morality, and human values, all of which were very important to me.

During the Soviet period, Lithuanian theatre went through several stages. It received a big push, albeit in terms of a more traditional revival, from the GITIS group— Lithuanians who had gone to study at the Russian Academy of Theatre Arts in Moscow.[2] At GITIS, they studied under many famous actors and theatre teachers, including Maria Knebel and the actor and teacher Vasili Orlov.[3] The director Henrikas Vancevičius returned from GITIS a fully formed theatre artist, as did the actors who would later form the core of the Kaunas Drama Theatre: Kęstutis Genys, Antanas Gabrėnas, Leonardas Zelčius, Laimonas Noreika, Birutė Raubaitė, Marytė Rasteikaitė, Genovaite Tolkutė, Regina Varnaitė, Antanina Mackevičiūtė, Danutė Juronytė, and others.[4] I got to know some of them quite well during my own studies in Moscow.

Director Vancevičius played a very important role in our theatre's development—he staged a lot of Lithuanian plays, which was very important at the

---

2   GITIS—Lunacharsky State Institute for Theatre Arts, one of the largest theatre schools in Europe and the world, with roots dating to 1878. Currently called the Russian Institute of Theatre Arts.

3   Maria Knebel (Rus. Мария Кнебель, 1898–1985)—actor, director, pedagogue.
Vasili Orlov (Rus. Василий Орлов, 1896–1974)— actor and pedagogue.

4   The Lithuanian class studied under Vasili Orlov and Maria Orlova at GITIS in 1948–1952. After completing their studies, they were hired by the Kaunas Drama Theatre. Vancevičius completed directing studies in 1953 and was head director of the Kaunas Drama Theatre 1953–1966.
Kęstutis Genys (1928–1996)—actor (worked at Kaunas State Drama Theatre 1952–1990), poet, director.
Antanas Gabrėnas (1922–1984)—theatre (worked at Kaunas State Drama Theatre 1952–1982) and film actor.
Leonardas Zelčius (1928–2015)—theatre (worked at Kaunas State Drama Theatre 1952–2010) and film actor.
Laimonas Noreika (1926–2007)—theatre (worked at Vilnius State Academic Drama Theatre 1963–1998) and film actor, poetry reciter, and social activist during the independence movement.
Birutė Raubaitė—theatre (at Kaunas State Drama Theatre from 1952) and film actor.
Marytė Rasteikaitė (1930–1988)—theatre actor (Vilnius State Academic Drama Thatre 1956–1988)
Genovaitė Tolkutė-Gabrėnienė (1923–2008)—theatre actor (Kaunas State Drama Theatre 1952–2003).
Regina Varnaitė-Eidukaitienė—theatre actor (Kaunas State Drama Theatre 1952–2010).
Antanina Mackevičiūtė-Berčienė (1926–2011)—theatre actor (Kaunas State Drama Theatre 1952–2002).
Danutė Juronytė-Zelčiuvienė (1933–2015)—theatre (Kaunas State Drama Theatre 1952–2010) and film actor.

time. Staging Lithuanian plays during the Soviet period was, in itself, taking a certain position which, both then and now, I interpret as an effort to preserve our culture—to speak to the audience in the familiar and understandable language of Lithuanian literature and theatre classics.

Vancevičius staged such works as Lithuanian playwright Juozas Grušas's *Herkus Mantas* (1957), Kazys Binkis's *Generalinė repeticija* (General rehearsal, 1957) and Kazys Inčiūra's *Žemaitė* (1959). These were very important productions at the time. They may not have been cutting edge plays, but during that period, which was one of sovietisation and intense ideological pressure, it was especially important for theatre to look back at the real foundations of Lithuanian culture.

I would like to separately mention Vancevičius's productions at the Lithuanian Academic Drama Theatre (now the Lithuanian National Drama Theatre) in particular Lithuanian poet Justinas Marcinkevičius's trilogy of poetic dramas: *Mindaugas* (1969), *Katedra* (Cathedral, 1971) and *Mažvydas* (1978). These were events of immeasurable importance. I still remember perfectly how the audience repeated the word "Lie-tu-va" (Lithuania) like a prayer—that word was so important during the Sąjūdis years.

Justinas Marcinkevičius's *Mindaugas* reminded me a lot of *Macbeth*.[5] Mindaugas committed numerous crimes and killed a great many people, but he did so to preserve himself and unite Lithuania—to establish a Lithuanian state. In that sense they differ, of course. When this poetic drama was staged in Soviet-occupied Lithuania, we tended to forgive Mindaugas's misdeeds because he was forming, creating our state.[6] But not much attention was given to the fact that, because of his brutality, betrayals, and polarization of the aristocracy, he did not actually succeed in pulling Lithuania together; these questions seemed to remain offstage. Watching the play, we only saw the famous and handsome actor Regimantas Adomaitis—our Mindaugas. We were dreaming of independence, so we were proud to have had our own king! But Mindaugas was terribly

5   *Mindaugas* (1200–1263)—Lithuanian Grand Duke who established the Lithuanian state and was Lithuania's first and only monarch (christened 1251, crowned 1253).

6   During the Soviet period, Lithuanian historians had few opportunities to research early Lithuanian history and the formation of the Lithuanian state, including Mindaugas and his policies. For that reason, Justinas Marcinkevičius's poetic drama about Mindaugas and theatrical productions based on it were important events in the spheres of literature, historiography, the politics of history, and the country's cultural memory.

brutal, which seems to be reinforced when he says, in Justinas Marcinkevičius's play: "Where there are two Lithuanians—there is sure to be a knife …"

But at the time—and perhaps still today—the audience cared most about the play's idealization of Lithuania's history, although, as I have just emphasized, Marcinkevičius also revealed the paradoxes in that history.

Like texts, performances speak to audiences differently, depending on those people's experiences and context. For example, Irena Bučienė's 1975 production of *Mindaugas* in Georgia was interpreted very differently—there, from what I have heard, people associated the main character with Stalin.[7] They had a completely different understanding of the play …

In my own memory, *Cathedral* remains a play that explored the question of internal resistance and the importance of remaining true to oneself—of upholding one's values and building a Cathedral, a temple within oneself, even under the conditions of the Church's dictatorship.[8] I can clearly remember Laimonas Noreika's performance as Archbishop Masalskis, and the character of Laurynas, who was played by Arnas Rosenas, an actor with an exceptional voice and diction. I can remember Vancevičius's *Mažvydas* less clearly. Vytautas Paukštė's performance of the character of Mažvydas, at the Klaipėda Drama Theatre, made a bigger impression on me.[9]

It is an undisputed fact that Marcinkevičius's poetic dramas were very important to Lithuanian society during the Soviet period. But historians and literary scholars are tormented by one question: why did the Soviet censors allow Marcinkevičius to write and to publish these plays, and how were theatre directors allowed to stage them? According to one theory, Mindau-

---

7   *Mindaugas*—dir. I. Bučienė, staged at the Ordzhonkidze State Drama Theatre in the Ossetian language, 1975.

8   Justinas Marcinkevičius's poetic drama *Katedra* [Cathedral] is set in Vilnius 1792–1794. It describes the young architect Laurynas Stuoka-Gucevičius's efforts to rebuild the city's Catholic cathedral, which had been destroyed in a storm, and the complicated relationship between the artist and his patron (Archbishop Ignotas Masalskis).
Laimonas Noreika (1926–2007)—theatre actor (Vilnius State Academic Drama Theatre 1963–1998). Arnas Rosenas (1933–2002)—theatre and film actor (Vilnius State Academic Drama Theatre 1956–1990).

9   The main character of Marcinkevičius's play *Mažvydas*—Martynas Mažvydas—was the author of the first Lithuanian book, *Katechizmas* [Catechism] (1547).
Mažvydas—dir. P. Gaidys, 1976. Indeed, Gaidys also directed a 1969 production of Mindaugas, in which the main role was also played by Vytautas Paukštė.

gas could have been allowed because some Party official at that time said "something like that is needed . . ." How would you explain this curiosity?

Unfortunately, I don't have an explanation. I can only say that Marcinkevičius was recognized by the Soviet authorities and had received all of the highest state awards. Perhaps, in the beginning, when he wrote his 1956 long poem *Dvidešimtas pavasaris* (Twentieth spring), he believed in Komsomol ideals; or perhaps he overcame his reservations or was forced to make compromises, and could therefore later allow himself more leeway.[10] But I would rather believe that Marcinkevičius was always utterly sincere.

You are, of course, familiar with Alexander Shtromas and Tomas Venclova's conversation about Marcinkevičius, which appeared on the Lithuanian television program "Krantai" on June 6, 1991. What do you think about the ideas expressed in that conversation?[11] Perhaps you yourself have spoken with Shtromas and Venclova about how Marcinkevičius's activities and personality should be judged?

Yes, I have spoken to them about this, and at length. And they have both written on the subject. It was a very painful question.

Indeed, when Justinas Marcinkevičius published the short story "Pušis, kuri juokiasi" (The laughing pine), there were rumours in Vilnius that it had been commissioned by the KGB and that it depicted Tomas Venclova, Alexander Shtromas, Juozas Tumelis, and their friends, who were, if I remember correctly, at that very time being interrogated over Alexander Ginzburg's underground dissident publication *Sintaksis*.[12] I cannot say how much truth there was

10   *Dvidešimtas pavasaris* [Twentieth spring]—Marcinkevičius's 1956 pro-Soviet, propagandist poem.

11   Reference to Alexander Shtromas's and Tomas Venclova's theory that Marcinkevičius's 1961 story "Pušis, kuri juokėsi" [The laughing pine, 1961] drew on records from KGB interrogation protocols.

12   *Sintaksis*—a journal conceived by Alexander Ginzburg and several other individuals. It was typewritten and contained literary works, in particular poetry, which had been rejected by Soviet censors. At the end of 1959, Ginzburg produced and circulated the first issue of *Sintaksis* among friends. The almanac became the cultural and social event of the year and up to 300 copies (including various secondary copies) were circulated. What was especially innovative was the fact that the name of the publication's editor was not concealed. Ginzburg managed to publish three issues of *Sintaksis* and to edit a fourth and fifth issue, but was arrested in 1960, while other individuals connected to the almanac suffered harassment by police and special forces.

in that rumour. Shtromas believed that, even though Vladas Grybas and Justinas Marcinkevičius were sincere communists in their youth, when they began their literary careers, they were always—in particular Marcinkevičius—sympathetic to the Lithuanian national cause.[13]

Unfortunately, that short story contained many passages of narration and dialogue that were strongly suggestive of Tomas Venclova and that poet's conversations with his friends. It is a great pity that Marcinkevičius himself did not leave us any more thorough explanations about this question, or, in any case, I never saw them.[14]

Why do you think Marcinkevičius's plays have not been staged very often since the restoration of Lithuania's independence? To what degree is this author's work no longer suitable for a theatre that is not so much interested in celebratory productions that reinforce grand narratives, as in seeking to create a new theatrical reality?

Apparently, it is not very suitable.

What did you think about Oskaras Koršunovas's 2012 production of Marcinkevičius's Cathedral?

I am a great admirer of Koršunovas, could even be called a "fan," in today's language. But although I consider him to be perhaps the most interesting director working in independent Lithuania, I'm afraid that his *Cathedral* left me indifferent. He recreated the Marcinkevičius poetic drama that I valued most of the three, but his production did not say anything new to me.

So let's go back to Vancevičius . . .

---

13 Vladas Grybas (1927–1954)—poet who consistently supported communist ideas in his work. Committed suicide.

14 Justinas Marcinkevičius chose silence—he did not respond to accusations from Tomas Venclova, Alexander Shtromas and others. This most popular of poets opened up in his autobiographical text "Taburetė virš galvos" [A stool over my head], fragments of which were published in the book *Pažadėtoji žemė* [Promised land] (Lietuvos rašytojų sąjungos leidykla, 2009). In this text, the poet denied having collaborated with the KGB and maintained the position that Tomas Venclova did not understand his creative intentions.

In my opinion, Henrikas Vancevičius staged great plays—classics by authors such as Anton Chekhov, Federico Garcia Lorca, Shakespeare, and Henrik Ibsen. His productions followed in the best traditions of Konstantin Stanislavsky and twentieth century Russian theatre, while at the same time referencing the artistic language of Russian socialist realism, as well as Lithuanian interwar theatre traditions and Borisas Dauguvietis's productions. But Lithuanian audiences wanted something new.[15]

Another kind of theatre—one that could respond to the need for "something new" that I have alluded to—was at that time being established in the northern Lithuanian city of Panevėžys. I am speaking about Juozas Miltinis's theatre.[16] Miltinis was unique in that he was the only director and actor who had been educated not only in Lithuania but in Western Europe. He was therefore someone with a different training, a different way of thinking. He knew the French existentialists and had thorough knowledge of drama of the first half of the twentieth century. He had excellent taste and knew how to distinguish between that which has value and that which does not.

If I am not mistaken, in 1940, during the first Soviet occupation, the Minister of Culture at that time, Antanas Venclova (Tomas Venclova's father), transferred Miltinis from Kaunas, where he had formed his own theatre troupe, to Panevėžys, and appointed him head of that city's drama theatre.[17] As far as I remember, all of the famous actors from the Kaunas troupe—Blėdis, Babkauskas, Banionis, Masiulis, Karka, Kosmauskas—moved to Panevėžys to continue working with Miltinis.[18]

---

15   Borisas Dauguvietis (1885–1949)—Lithuanian theatre director, actor, pedagogue.

16   Juozas Miltinis (1907–1994). Studied acting at the State Drama Theatre in Kaunas. In 1932, moved to Paris, where he attended exhibitions, museums, and lectures at the Sorbonne, studied French, and circulated among the elite of the art world. In 1933–1936 studied at Charles Dullin's theatre studio, connected to Théâtre de l'Atelier. Participated in that theatre's productions together with well-known French directors and actors Jean Vilar, Jean Louis Barrault, Roger Blin and Jean Dasté, and also appeared in French films. Following his studies in Paris, Miltinis became director of theatre studies at the Work Palace in Kaunas (1938–1940).

17   On November 18, 1940 Lithuanian SSR Commissar for the People's Education Antanas Venclova issued a decree allowing the establishment of a drama theatre in Panevėžys. Juozas Miltinis won the competition and on December 1, 1940 arrived in Panevėžys with a troupe of actors from the Kaunas Work Palace theatre studio.

18   Valcovas Blėdis (1920–1999)—theatre and film actor (Panevėžys Drama Theatre 1941–1991) and director (head director Panevėžys Drama Theatre 1956–1959).
Bronius Babkauskas (1921–1975)—theatre and film actor.
Donatas Banionis (1924–2014)—theatre and film actor (Panevėžys Drama Theatre 1941–1991).

This is how the foundations for the famous Miltinis theatre were laid. I have been in the old wooden building of the Panevėžys theatre, which looked more like an old cottage than a theatre. In this kind of environment, in a small provincial city, Miltinis succeeded in creating something that was original and unusual within the context of the entire Soviet Union.

In analysing the Miltinis phenomenon, it is important to stress that he was as cunning as Ben Johnson's Volpone, a role that he himself acted.

In 1954 or 1955, Miltinis was thrown out of the theatre for ideological reasons.[19] I can remember perfectly well how, even though I was not yet a theatre critic, I felt terrible for Miltinis when this happened. But even then, Miltinis did not leave the theatre. They would throw him out through one door and he would come back in through another. One person who helped him a great deal during that time was his close friend, the actor and director Vaclovas Blėdis. Miltinis knew how to adapt to situations so that he could achieve the goals he had set out for himself. One of these adaptation techniques was the following: by including some Soviet rubbish in his repertoire he would gain the right to stage the productions that were important to him. You see, during the Soviet period a repertoire had to contain a certain proportion of Soviet, Western, and Lithuanian plays. By making a good many compromises, Miltinis "earned" virtually all of the titles that a theatre director could hold during that period, as well as the privileges that went with that. In 1967 he was even able to build himself a new theatre.[20]

Miltinis was at his height during the 1960s and 1970s, which is when his most important productions were staged. Foremost among these was his *Macbeth* (1961), with the lead played by Stasys Petronaitis, an actor who never received the recognition he deserved, or who perhaps simply did not stay in the theatre long enough.[21] Petronaitis was an actor-celebrity whose Macbeth was

---

Known for roles in Lithuanian films and in films directed by famous Russian directors (Grigori Kozincev, Andrei Tarkovsky).

Algimantas Masiulis (1931–2008)—theatre and film actor (Panevėžys Drama Theatre 1948–1976).

Gediminas Karka (1922–1991)—theatre and film actor (Panevėžys Drama Theatre 1941–1991).

Steponas (Stepas) Kosmauskas (1918–1985)—theatre and film actor (Panevėžys Drama Theatre 1941–1985).

19   Juozas Miltinis was dismissed from the theatre by a 1954 order issued by Lithuanian SSR culture minister Aleksandras Gudaitis-Guzevičius.

20   Architect—Algimantas Mikėnas.

21   Stasys Petronaitis—actor (Panevėžys Drama Theatre 1951–1972).

unforgettable—I can still vividly remember specific scenes from that play. He succeeded in revealing his character's tragedy by developing his humanity. I must also mention such fantastic Miltinis productions as Borchert's *Outside the Door* (1966), Dürrenmatt's *Frank V* (1969, and revived in 1978) and Strindberg's *Dance of Death* (1973). I recall that his 1972 production of *Hedda Gabler* received mixed reviews; it did not make much of an impression on me.

Summing up, it must be said that Miltinis was an exceptional figure not only in the context of Lithuanian theatre, but of the theatre of the Soviet Union. One of the people who contributed to the creation of the myth about Miltinis and his theatre was the famous Russian theatre critic Natalia Krymova.[22] She was a great admirer of the director and steadily constructed a myth about Miltinis and his theatre, with the result that the entire Soviet theatre elite would gather in the small Lithuanian provincial town to see his plays.

Konstantin Stanislavsky has said that theatre begins in the cloakroom. But it Miltinis's case it was certainly not the women working in the cloakroom or the café that were responsible for the intense aura around the theatre, but its quite extravagant director. Following performances he would hold discussions and gatherings, and a good deal of champagne and wine was drunk . . . There was even a legend at the theatre that Miltinis bathed his dog in champagne.

At Miltinis's theatre, everything happened a bit differently, and that "a bit differently" can best be described as the existence of a "Western spirit" around the place. Festivals were held and famous people were constantly visiting Miltinis, which further reinforced the legend around him. Miltinis was a great authority during the Soviet period, but, as the writer Tomas Sakalauskas has said, the Panevėžys Theatre died together with him.

I would like to stay with the theme of Miltinis for a moment. Was there a difference in Miltinis's theatrical language when he was staging masterpieces as opposed to Soviet nonsense?

I'm afraid that I cannot answer that question, as I never saw any of those "Soviet nonsense" productions, or, if I did see any, I can't remember anything. One

---

22   Natalia Krymova (Rus. Наталья Крымова, 1930–2003)—theatre critic, art historian; wrote articles about Panevėžys Drama Theatre and Miltinis's productions for the Soviet press.

must remember that Miltinis's performances took place not in Vilnius, but in Panevėžys. So I simply did not waste my time to go see the plays with which he was "paying his dues" to the Soviet authorities. I can recall that he staged a weak play by Jokūbas Josadė, but, even though I had read the text, I did not travel to see the performance.[23]

If we are talking about the Miltinis myth, it must be noted that he was not, by any means, an angel. Although it was interesting to work with him, it was not always easy. I have heard a lot of people say that he could be abusive toward actors and theatre personnel. But when so much time has passed, I would prefer to remember his great achievements.

The cultural field is one of constant competition, and that is perfectly natural. I wonder if members of the Vilnius theatre community did not feel some envy for Miltinis. If so, how might such envy have manifested itself?

I never sensed any of that envy, so I cannot say anything about it. But I did have numerous opportunities to interact with him. Most of our conversations were about the French existentialists, the theatre, his experiences in France, and wine and champagne.

We can leave Miltinis at peace for now. If I am not mistaken, we should now turn our attention to another theatre director, Jonas Jurašas.

To my great pain and disappointment, Jonas Jurašas is not sufficiently valued today. And yet it is Jurašas who created the new Lithuanian theatre! In one of those paradoxes of fate, this director worked during an ill-fated period, so that almost nothing of his stunning early work in Kaunas has survived. At that time—he headed the Kaunas Drama Theatre from 1967 to 1972—there were no technological means for recording his productions, and very little was written or recorded in other ways. Of course, Jurašas's extremely dignified and principled stance complicated things—because of it, he was harassed in all sorts of ways, and was ultimately forced to leave Lithuania.

---

23 Jokūbas Josadė (1911–1995)—writer, playwright, literary critic. Miltinis staged his play *Tardytojas* [The prosecutor] in 1978.

In my opinion, the theatre that Jurašas created in Kaunas produced the best theatre in Lithuania at that time. But it survives only in the older generation's memories, as younger people never saw any of those performances.

As you can probably sense, I could speak about Jurašas a great deal. I can't quite remember how we met, but it may have been through the playwright Kazys Saja. Jonas was studying in Moscow, where he was supported and championed by Maria Knebel.[24] In Moscow, Jonas met his first wife, a very pleasant Russian director named Lidia Kutuzova, who returned to Lithuania with him, learned the language, and had a successful career as a director at the Kaunas Drama Theatre.[25] I first took notice of Jonas as a director when he staged Sławomir Mrożek's *Tango* and Leonid Zorin's *Warsaw Melody* at the Vilnius Academic Drama Theatre in 1967. There was something very interesting and real about those performances. Then, in 1967, Jurašas was appointed head director of the Kaunas Drama Theatre.[26]

As I have already mentioned, it is in Kaunas that a period of flourishing and modernisation in Lithuanian theatre began, and it is Jurašas who began to create our metaphorical theatre. I have sometimes been told that I am making too much of a legend out of Jonas, but I am convinced that I am not mystifying or exaggerating anything, and feel very strongly about the value of his productions dating from that period.

Three of Jurašas's productions—Kazys Saja's *Mamutų medžioklė* (The mammoth hunt, 1968), Juozas Glinskis's *Grasos namai* (House of threat, 1970) and Juozas Grušas's *Barbora Radvilaitė* (1972) represent the apex of his career and should be recognized as Lithuanian theatre classics. In them, Jonas encoded his protest against the lies in which we were drowning; he found a way to express his passionate search for TRUTH by developing a new theatrical language that was based not on words or the text of a play, but rather on the actors' physical actions. Jurašas created a unique Aesopic language and, as I have said, a metaphorical theatre. It was only after Jurašas's productions that those of later great Lithuanian directors such as Vaitkus, Nekrošius, Tuminas, and others were possible.

---

24 Jonas Jurašas graduated from Lunacharsky State Institute for Theatre Arts (GITIS) in 1964. Maria Knebel (Rus. Мария Кнебель, 1898–1985)—theatre critic, actor, art historian, pedagogue.

25 Lidia Kutuzova (Rus. Лидия Кутузова)—theatre director and pedagoge. Worked at Kaunas Drama Theatre (1967–1972).

26 Jurašas held this position until 1972.

I can remember taking my students to Kaunas to see Jurašas's *Mammoth Hunt*. In a discussion following the play, Jonas used an endless stream of synonyms to say that the goal of the theatre was to say, shout, speak, whisper, express...the TRUTH. That was his credo. And he paid dearly for it.

With his values, taste, and multiple talents—Jonas drew beautifully and was very musical—Jurašas was an exceptional person. But he may have sometimes lacked diplomacy. Not everyone tolerated his determined and uncompromising manner.

Life is not easy for people like Jurašas. I think he was also affected by heavy childhood traumas. During the first Soviet occupation his mother was a high school principal. At the very beginning of the war, early one morning the "white armbands" shot Jonas's parents right in front of their house. Jonas and his older sister saw the execution from a window of their apartment. Left an orphan at four and a half, Jonas was separated from his sister and raised by relatives. She died in 1944, while fleeing from Lithuania.

Such experiences either toughen or break a person. Jonas never speaks about his parents' murder. But once, when we were in Panevėžys, he took me to see his parents' home and the place where they were shot. This is only my theory, but I am convinced that this tragedy caused Jonas to develop into a very strong person, which is something that could be felt in each one of his productions.

I will never forget his *House of Threat*. It was a meeting of two very powerful personalities—the writer Juozas Glinskis and the director Jonas Jurašas—resulting a synergetic effect.[27] Although the play and the production are about the Lithuanian poet Antanas Strazdas (Strazdelis), who lived at the turn of the nineteenth century, one feels that it is a play about the present, about the fate of the poet—freedom's bard—during the period of the Soviet occupation. I will never forget the scene when the poet's inner censor (played by Česlovas Stonys) hides under Strazdelis's cassock.[28] Later, when Jurašas was thrown out of the

---

27 Juozas Glinskis—writer and playwright. The characters in his play *Grasos namai* [House of threat]—a poet-priest, an archivist, a bishop—are imprisoned in cells and isolated from the world; they continuously relive grotesque images from the past that rise up from their subconscious minds. Published by Vaga in book form (1971, 1983). Both script and book text were subjected to censorship; on orders from Lionginas Šepetys, Minister of Culture at that time, some scenes were deleted and the ending of the play was altered.

28 Strazdelis was played by actor Algirdas Voščikas.

theatre, Stonys and the actor Jonas Pakulis also left it out of solidarity and protest. That kind of thing is quite rare in our world . . .

There are rumors that . . .

. . . that I saw the only authentic performance of Jurašas's *Barbora Radvilaitė*? It's true. I have a very clear memory of that Jurašas production. I have had many intense theatre experiences—I have seen plays by Peter Brook; by the Russian directors Tovstonogov, Liubimov, Efros, Dodin; by Georgian directors Robert Sturua, Rezo Gabriadze, Mikhail Tumanishvili, and others.[29]

But Jurašas's *Barbora Radvilaitė* is certainly one of the plays that had the most profound emotional impact on me. The play itself, by Grušas, is beautiful but not exceptional. But what Jurašas did with it was simply miraculous! There were probably a number of factors that caused me to have the intense experience that I will try to describe, including the fact that one of the main themes in the play is love, and at that time I was madly in love myself!

When you recall Jurašas's Barbora Radvilaitė, *what is the first thing that comes to mind?*

First of all, the set design, by Janina Malinauskaitė, was very impressive. The columns of Cracow Castle were sewn from satin fabric.[30] They seemed almost to be moving, which created a feeling of instability. It seemed that the ground under Barbora's royal castle was unstable beneath her feet—after all, while living in Cracow she felt rejected and foreign.

The true, but at the same time fragile, love between the Lithuanian, Protestant Barbora and the Catholic king Žygimantas Augustas collided with the ruthlessness of power, and political and religious intrigues.[31] To this day, I can-

---

29   Robert Sturua (Geor. რობერტ სტურუა, Rus. Роберт Стуруя) – theatre director.
     Revaz (Rezo) Gabriadze (Geor. რევაზ გაბრიაძე, Rus. Реваз (Резо) Габриадзе)—artist, screenwriter, director, founder of Tbilisi Puppet Theatre (1981).
     Mikhail Tumanišvili (Geor. მიხეილ თუმანიშვილი, Rus. Михаил Туманишвили, 1935–2010)—director.

30   Set designer for the production—Janina Malinauskaitė.

31   Barbora Radvilaitė (1522–1551)—noblewoman of the Grand Duchy of Lithuania, Queen of Poland and Grand Duchess of Lithuania (from 1550).

not forget the love scenes between Barbora, played by Rūta Staliliūnaitė, and Žygimantas Augustas, played by Kęstutis Genys.[32] When the Polish king sneaks into Barbora's bedroom, their passion takes the form of a dance—without even touching, they experience the highest ecstasy of love. That scene made an even greater impression on me than any of today's naturalistic sex scenes.

At the end of the performance, Barbora, who has been poisoned by Queen Bona, is dying, but in Jurašas's production it is love that triumphs.[33] The director introduced a character that did not exist in Grušas's play—an artist who is shown painting Barbora's portrait through the entire performance.[34] After she dies, he frames his painting—Staliliūnaitė-Barbora—and carries it from the stage. At the same time, a glowing, golden painting of Our Lady of the Gates of Dawn seems to descend from Heaven, accompanied by a beautiful hymn sung by a soprano voice. Love has triumphed.

According to legend, the painting of Our Lady of the Gates of Dawn was indeed commissioned by Žygimantas Augustas and was a portrait of Barbora Radvilaitė.[35]

After the curtain fell, I could not leave the theatre—I simply could not get up from my seat. My eyes welled up with tears and I simply sat there, sobbing…

But, at the same time, the committee that was to decide whether the play was acceptable was already meeting. I pulled myself together and went to lis-

---

Žygimantas Augustas (1520–1572)—King of Poland (1548–1572) and Grand Duke of Lithuania (1544–1572).

Barbora Radvilaitė's life has been shrouded in endless myths and rumours. From the eighteenth century, the life of this unusual woman began to be depicted in a romantic light, with a primary focus on the theme of a grand and tragic love between two people were not fated to be together. To this day, Barbora Radvilaitė's personality and her relationship with Žygimantas Augustas fascinate historians, writers, and theatre and film directors.

32 Rūta Staliliūnaitė-Matulionienė (1938–2011)—film and theatre actor (Kaunas Drama Theatre 1963–1993).

33 Bona Sforza (1494–1557)—Queen of Poland and Grand Duchess of Lithuania (from 1518), mother of Žygimantas Augustas. Played by actress Aldona Jodkaitė.

34 The artist was played by actor Viktoras Šinkariukas.

35 The painting of the Blessed Virgin Mary, Mother of Mercy at the Gates of Dawn in Vilnius is shrouded in legends. According to one legend, it is a Byzantine icon that Grand Duke Algirdas brought back from the shores of the Black Sea in the fourteenth century; a second claims that the painting is newer and the work of a monk, and was painted in Kiev in the eighteenth century; according to the third, Barbora Radvilaitė's features are recognisable in the Blessed Mary's face. Extensive research has determined that there is no foundation to any of these legends and that the image of Mary was painted in the seventeenth century.

ten to the discussion, which, before my eyes, degenerated into a complete farce.[36] Jurašas was accused of "nationalism," "excessive spirituality" and similar things. I can't remember all of the terms and expressions used, and I have to say that each was more ridiculous than the last. But the subtext of these absurd accusations was menacing. Jurašas was being accused of trying to deceive the authorities—during the first preview performance of the play, which was attended by Sigizmundas Šimkus from the Central Committee of the Lithuanian Communist Party, the painting of Our Lady of the Gates of Dawn was not shown.[37] The set design crew had not yet finished making it. The second preview, which is the one that I saw, was supervised by a representative from the Ministry of Culture, a Mr. Jakučionis.[38] That time, the painting was lowered over the stage. As I have mentioned, the committee read "excessive spirituality" as well as nationalist and religious subtexts into the play. As you know, the production was banned. It was later restaged, but with substantial cuts by the censors.

After the discussion, Aušra Sluckaitė, whom I had invited to see the preview with me, Jonas Jurašas and I went to Grušas's home.[39] It was a very grim and sad night.

You are perfectly aware of how this story ended: Jurašas wrote a very principled letter of protest against the mutilation of his play and was thrown out of the theatre.[40] Left with no work or source of income, Jonas roamed around, helping artists like Vladas Vildžiūnas and Teodoras Valaitis in their studios.[41]

---

36 For more about this preview performance c.f.: Aušra Marija Sluckaitė-Jurašienė, *Egziliantės užrašai: esė, portretų eskizai, atsiminimai, impresijos* [Notes from exile: Essays, portrait sketches, memories, impressions] Kultūros barai, 2008, 144–151. Also: Goda Dapšytė, "Teatras ir cenzūra. Režisieriaus Jono Jurašo atvejis" [Theatre and censorship: The case of Jonas Jurašas], *Menotyra*, 2007, Vol.14, Nr. 4, 69–78.

37 Sigizmundas Šimkus (1931–2009)—Soviet Communist Party figure; at the time of the attacks on Jonas Jurašas, head of the Culture Department of the Central Committee of the Lithuanian Communist Party (1969–1983).

38 Meilutis Raimundas Jakučionis (1929–1992)—theatre critic; at the time of these event, head of the Arts Council, Ministry of Culture, Lithuanian SSSR.

39 Aušra Marija Sluckaitė—playwright, journalist, critic. During the Soviet period worked at Vaga Publishing House (1959–1970). Head of the Literature Department at the Lithuanian State Youth Theatre (1970–1974).

40 For Jonas Jurašas's August 16, 1972 letter to the Ministry of Culture of the Lithuanian SSR, Kaunas Drama Theatre, the Lithuanian Theatre Association and the editors of the weekly culture magazine *Literatūra ir menas* c.f.: *Jonas Jurašas*, Ed. Audronė Girdzijauskaitė, Vilnius: Gervelė, 1995, 276–278. Also c.f.: *Lietuvių teatro istorija: Trečioji knyga: 1970–1980* [The history of Lithuanian theatre: Third book: 1970–1980], Vilnius: Kultūros, filosofijos ir meno institutas, 2006, 218–219.

41 Teodoras Kazimieras Valaitis (1934–1974)—artist.

At that point, the end of socialism was not in sight. Jonas left Lithuania knowing that it may be the end of his career as a director, but, also, that it was his only
chance. I remember speaking with him about how each director has his hours
of greatness and that it is not easy to sustain such heights. Jonas had visited the
United States with Miltinis and, like I, he must have been entranced by the creative freedom that existed there. But we never spoke in more detail.

I am telling you a lot about Jurašas because he was such an important figure in my life at that time. He was not only a friend but an example of a strong
human being and artist. I value him a great deal and believe that he was responsible for establishing the modern Lithuanian theatre.

During the period of Jurašas's persecution, I stayed by his side and did everything I could to support him. I saw his romance with Aušra develop, attended their wedding, and saw them off when they emigrated.

Indeed, when Jurašas lost his job at the theatre, I tried to organize a meeting for him with Miltinis, who, by that point, was a highly recognized "people's
artist" and the head director at the Panevėžys Theatre. I thought that he might
be able to give Jonas a job in his theatre. I remembered how Stanislavsky gave
Meyerhold a job at the MHAT when the latter was thrown out of his own theatre, even though they held very different, even opposing theatrical principles.[42]

Jonas and Aušra drove to Panevėžys. Miltinis received us very nicely at the
theatre and said that Jurašas was the best director in Lithuania after he himself,
but that he would only enter the Panevėžys Theatre as a director after Miltinis's
own death. So, Miltinis refused to help Jurašas. This was a great shock to me.

When Jurašas returned to Lithuania after independence was restored, he
staged a series of productions at Kaunas Drama Theatre: Sluckaitė's *Smėlio klavyrai* (Sand claviers, 1990) and Ariel Dorfman's *Death and the Maiden* (1992); then
Verdi's *Aida* and Bronius Kutavičius's *Lokis* (2000) at Vilnius Opera Theatre; and
then, back at Kaunas Drama Theatre, Sluckaitė's *Barbora*, in 2014.[43]

---

42 MHAT—Московский художественный академическийтеатр—Moscow Art Theatre. Estab-
     lished in 1898 by Konstantin Stanislavsky and Vladimir Nemirovich-Danchenko.
     Vsevolod Meyerhold (Rus. Всеволод Мейерхольд, 1874–1940)—theatre director and pedagogue
     who developed his own acting system.

43 The libretto for *Lokis* was written by Aušra Marija Sluckaitė based on motifs in the Prosper Mérimée
     novella of the same title.
     Smėlio klavyrai [Sand claviers]—script by Aušra Marija Sluckaitė based on Johannes Bobrovski's 1966
     novel *Lithuanian Pianos* and his poetry.

Of course, Jonas continued to work as a high-level theatre director. He travelled and saw many things and staged a good number of plays abroad, but, in my view, he never again reached the heights he had achieved in Kaunas during the Soviet period. His later productions never received the same kind of acclaim, but times change . . . But nor am I really qualified to say much about it as there are many plays of Jonas's that I did not see. His American production of Russian playwright Nikolai Erdman's *The Suicide* was considered a masterpiece and travelled to Broadway, but Jonas did not know how to take advantage of that enormous recognition and financial success. He did not want to repeat himself, which is what American theatre practice and conventions expected of him to do. Personally, of Jonas's later plays, I found the Kaunas productions of *Smėlio klavyrai* (which created a very innovative and experimental space) and *Balta drobulė* to be the most interesting.[44]

Before we go on to another director, I would like to ask you a question with regards to Barbora Radvilaitė. As far as I know, you had another "encounter" with that character?

When I think of Barbora Radvilaitė I have to say that she always impressed me as a very intelligent, educated woman. Her tragic love story moved me deeply. She was a Protestant, and so different from other women of her times and context.

When, many years later, in 2006, I received the Barbora Radvilaitė medal for contributions to Lithuanian culture and education, I took it as a sign and a gift. I was the third woman to receive it, after Maya Plisetskaya and Gražina Ručytė-Landsbergienė.[45] It was a great honour. It was a very emotional experience when Barbora came back into my life in that way.

The figure of Jonas Vaitkus often flashes through our conversations. Since we have discussed Jurašas's work, it is time to move on to Vaitkus. What

---

Barbora—script by Aušra Marija Sluckaitė based on motifs in Juozas Grušas's play *Barbora Radvilaitė*.

44 *Balta Drobulė* [The white shroud]—Aušra Marija Sluckaitė's adaptation of Antanas Škėma's 1958 novel *Balta Drobulė* [Eng. trans. *White Shroud*, Karla Gruodis, Glasgow: Vagabond Voices, 2018].

45 Maya Plisetskaya (Rus. Майя Плисецкая, 1925–2015)—Russian ballet dancer, prima ballerina at the Bolshoi Theatre (1948–1990). Plisetskaya had Lithuanian citizenship and a home in this country, and was interested in Lithuania's cultural life.
Gražina Ručytė-Landsbergienė—pianist, social activist, wife of Vytautas Landsbergis.

did you find interesting about him—both in terms of his person and his productions?

Jonas Vaitkus became the head director of Kaunas Drama Theatre following Jurašas's departure. He was a student of the Leningrad, rather than Moscow, school of theatre.[46] He was absolutely in love with the theatre and lived for it, much like an ascetic.

Vaitkus is probably one of our most productive directors. At the time, you couldn't say that he was continuing the work that Jurašas had started, because it was not even possible to mention that "rebel's" and "outcast's" name. But now, weighing all of the pros and cons, I would hazard to say that Vaitkus could not have happened without Jurašas.

Vaitkus's theatre made an enormous impression upon me. I admired his energy, his original theatrical interpretations, and his search for new forms. As the literary critic Vytautas Kubilius once said, Vaitkus does not so much stage literature as interpret it.[47] Each of his productions was different, but each one was ethically and politically charged. In that sense, I believe that Vaitkus was continuing Jurašas's tradition.

I have very clear memories of Vaitkus's productions of Eugenijus Ignatavičius's *Svajonių piligrimas* (Pilgrim of dreams, 1975), Alfred Jarry's *King Ubu* (1977), Gorky's *The Last Ones* (1978), Ivan Radoyev's *Red and Brown* (1979), and Ibsen's *The Master Builder* (1980), in which Juozas Budraitis emerged as an excellent actor. There was also Juozas Glinskas's *Kingas* (1980), and Mikhail Shatrov's *Blue Horses on Red Grass* (1982). I found his production of the Estonian playwright Mati Unto's *The Most Important Rehearsal* very interesting and current, and my husband was preparing to stage it in Tallinn. But it was Vaitkus's productions of Camus' *Caligula* (1983), and his *Literatūros pamokos* (Literature lessons, based on Saint Exupery's *The Little Prince* and *Night Flight*, (1985) and *Golgota* (based on Aitmatov's novel 'The Scaffold', staged in 1987) that made the greatest impression on me. These latter plays spoke directly to the viewer and demolished stereotypical theatrical expression. Vaitkus creat-

---

46 Jonas Vaitkus studied at the Leningrad State Institute of Theatre, Music and Cinema, and was a director at Kaunas Drama Theatre (1975–1978) and head director (1980–1988).

47 Reference to a discussion about a Kaunas Drama Theatre tour in Vilnius. C.f.: "Po penkerių metų" [Five years later], *Literatūra ir menas*, September 5, 1981, 6–9.

Valentinas Masalskis in Caligula. *1983*

ed a theatre which one went to see not to relax, but to think. Caligula was brilliantly acted by Valentinas Masalskis, and Rūta Staliliūnaitė played Drusilla. I attended that performance with my students, who were assigned to write reviews afterwards. Audra Žukaitytė's review stood out from all that rest, and it was thanks to it that I "discovered" her. And with *Golgota*, I believe, we travelled to a theatre festival in Kaliningrad. The impression of that no man's land, of a destroyed city, stayed with me throughout the whole trip to Kaliningrad, and has to this day. Vaitkus's *Golgota* acquired even greater relevance when performed in that city.

Vaitkus was, and continues to be, a very tough character. I can remember how, on the way to Tallinn, my husband and I were stunned when, by the seaside near Riga, he for some mysterious reason forced himself to eat some very large ants. And I have another memory of Vaitkus getting very drunk at a reception in Tallinn. I reminded him that he had once said that he never drank in front of his actors, but he shot back, saying that he knew where he could drink. Indeed, the actors there were Estonian, not his Lithuanian troupe. It seems to me that Vaitkus was often inspired by anger, an intense argument or struggle. I once told him that he should stop fighting constantly and wasting his energy on unimportant things, but he replied that struggle lifts him up and inspires him.

And what about Vaitkus's 1990 production of Joshua Sobol's play **Ghetto?**
When I first mentioned it, you smiled and said that it was you who were
responsible for bringing it to Lithuania.

Yes, it was I who initiated the idea of staging that play in Vilnius. I even received
an award for an article I wrote in *Kultūros barai* about Sobol, who was still unknown to us at that time. I had been to the National Theatre in London, where
I had seen a performance of *Ghetto*.[48] It is a very interesting play. That time, I
had gone to the theatre wearing an amber broach. Jacob Gens' granddaughter,
who was also there to see the play, understood that I was from Lithuania, and
we became acquainted.[49] As it happened, she was quite outraged that the production depicted her grandfather as a drinker.

Joshua Sobol was a very interesting person. He had studied philosophy at
the Sorbonne, was a true humanist who suffered terribly over the Israeli-Pal-
estinian conflict, and was a famous director at the Gesher Theatre in Tel Aviv.
While writing his trilogy about the Nazi occupation of Vilnius during the Second World War, he consciously refused to visit the city for fear that reality
might constrain his imagination.[50]

To be honest, I am not even sure why Vaitkus staged that play. I think he
may not have appreciated it fully and, wanting to avoid the documentary and
the concrete, abstracted it too much.[51] From what I remember, he stressed that
it would not be about Jews and Lithuanians, or about the Holocaust in Lithuania, but would explore more universal themes. The critics and the public did
not receive the play very well, and it was soon dropped from the repertoire. Indeed, Sobol has written many interesting plays that, in my view, would have
suited Vaitkus better.

In Lithuanian theatre, the Jewish theme was probably best explored in
Rimas Tuminas's 1994 production of the writer Grigory Kanovich's
Nusišypsok mums, Viešpatie *(Smile upon us, o Lord).*

---

48 *Ghetto*—dir. Nicholas Hytner, Royal National Theatre 1989.
49 Reference to Jacob Gens (1903–1943)—Jewish-Lithuanian doctor, head of the Vilnius Ghetto Jewish
    police force.
50 Joshua Sobol's so-called "Vilnius trilogy" consists of the plays *Ghetto, Adam,* and *Underground.*
51 C.f.: Irena Veisaitė, "Getas be istorijos" [An ahistorical ghetto], *Kultūros barai*, 1991, Nr. 5, 30–35.

Smile Upon us, o Lord. *From left: Vytautas Grigolis, Audrius Žebrauskas,*
Sigitas Račkys, Vytautas Šapranauskas. 1994. Photo by Dimitrijus Matvejevas.

I agree with you completely—it is a masterpiece, one of Tuminas's best plays. It is
perfect in every way: Kanovich's script, the cast (Grigolis, Šapranauskas, Girdvainis,
Račkys, Žebrauskas), the score by Faustas Latėnas, Adomas Jacovskis's set design...[52]
It is a very concrete play, about a group of Jews from a small Lithuanian town travelling to Vilnius in an attempt to free a young Jewish townsman being held in a
tsarist prison after attempting to assassinate the Governor. At the same time it is a
very universal, metaphorical play about the eternal human quest for justice.

Now Tuminas has staged the play, apparently with great success, in Moscow, where he directs the Vakhtangov Theatre.[53]

Indeed, although there has been more than one attempt, a play has yet to
have been staged that would fully reveal the tragedy of the Lithuanian Jews.
Audrius Juzėnas attempted to touch on this theme in his 2005 film *Vilniaus*
getas (Ghetto). Most likely because of lack of funds, the film was directed more

---

52   The theatre adaptations of Grigory Kanovich's novels *Nusišypsok mums, Viešpatie* [Smile upon us,
      Lord] and *Ožiukas už porą skaičių* [A kid for two pennies] were written by Rimas Tuminas and Al-
      mantas Grikevičius.
      Vytautas Grigolis—Šmulė Senderis; Vytautas Šapranauskas—Chloinė Genechas; Gediminas Gird-
      vainis—Avneris Rozentalis; Sigitas Račkys—Efraimas Ben Jokūbas Dudakas; Andrius Žebrauskas—
      Palestinietis.
53   Rus. Улыбнись нам, Господи—Vakhtangov State Academic Theatre, premiere—2014.

like a play. The director may not have succeeded in every way, but it was the first serious and sincere attempt to deal with this theme, which is a very painful one for Lithuania. It is very moving and contains some excellent scenes and performances (in particular the characters of Kittel and Gens), and has a powerful score by Anatoly Shenderov.[54]

I set great store by the poet Daiva Čepauskaitė's play *Duobė* (The pit), which was staged, as *Diena ir naktis* (Day and night), at the Kaunas Chamber Theatre by the director Stanislovas Rubinovas, who has since passed away.[55] Although I had known Stanislovas for a long time, we became much closer during the last decade of his life. We would meet at the Baltic House festival in Saint Petersburg and would exchange impressions and talk about personal matters.[56] Stanislovas told me about how, at the beginning of the war, his father was shot in Paneriai; about how, for three years after that, he and his mother had hidden in the forests of the Vilnius region and Belarus, helped by local farmers; and about how, after the war, he hid that he was a Jew. His son, the actor Aleksandras Rubinovas, only learned that his father was Jewish at the age of 35.

I urged Stanislovas to open up, to write his autobiography. Before his death he published a wonderful book, *Miške ir scenoje* (In the woods and on the stage).[57] It is made up of two parts: the first describes his Holocaust experiences; the second tells of his encounters with members of the Lithuanian and Russian cultural communities. It is a powerful, shocking book. Stanislovas once said it was only in writing the book that he finally "left the forest." That is yet another example of how important it is that people remain true to themselves.

Stanislovas Rubinovas had established an acting studio at the Kaunas Chamber Theatre, and I believe that his last production was Daiva Čepauskaitė's *The Pit*, which I referred to earlier. The play was a sincere and an impressive attempt by the playwright and director to approach the theme of the Holocaust. Both the play and its staging moved me deeply.

---

54 Kittel—Sebastian Hülk; Gens—Heino Ferch.
55 Stanislovas Rubinovas (1930–2013)—actor, singer, director, founder of Kaunas Chamber Theatre (now Kaunas City Chamber Theatre).
56 The international theatre festival Балтийский дом [Baltic House] in Saint Petersburg has been held annually since 1991.
57 Stanislovas Rubinovas, *Miške ir scenoje: Režisieriaus, Kauno kamerinio teatro įkūrėjo ir meno vadovo atsiminimai* [In the woods and on the stage: Recollections of the director and the founder and artistic director of the Kaunas Chamber Theatre], Vilnius: Versus aureus, 2013.

What did you think of Yana Ross's production of **Our Class,** *which premiered at the Lithuanian National Drama Theatre in 2013?*

I did not find the director's choices with regards to how the action should be depicted as convincing. Tadeusz Słobodzianek's tragic play is structured around fourteen lessons.[58] The action begins in 1935, the year that the Polish president Piłsudski died, and continues to our times.[59] Exploring the destinies of students from one class, the playwright succeeds in revealing the Polish tragedy with great subtlety. It seemed to me that, instead of highlighting the classmates' distinct personalities and tragic fates, the director used too many "show" elements. The director herself has told me that she made a conscious choice not to represent the tragedy, as she wanted to focus more on the theme of friendship.

That begs the questions of why the director chose that particular play and what she was trying to say.

I honestly do not know what Yana Ross was trying to say by making those choices. In personal conversations she stressed, several times, that her production was not only about the Holocaust, but about the Second World War in general and its effects on Poland.

One way or another, I have to admit that it was daring of Yana to take on such a difficult play. Perhaps she consciously added the "show" elements to draw in the viewer? The director achieved her goal: her production of *Our Class* continues to be well attended, the playwright was happy with it, and it has been performed and well received in Warsaw.

The playwright, essayist, and translator Rolandas Rastauskas's initial idea of organizing a reading of the play seemed very sincere in comparison to what we saw on the stage of the National Drama Theatre.

---

58 Polish playwright, theatre critic and director Tadeusz Słobodzianek's play *Nasza klasa* [Our class, 2008] is one of the most conceptual and powerful texts about the Holocaust in Central Europe.

59 Józef Klemens Piłsudski (1867–1935)—military officer, politician, statesman, de factor leader of Poland 1926–1935.

Rolandas's idea—and his translation of the play into Lithuanian was excellent—was deeper and closer to my heart. But perhaps you and I should see the play again. I have heard that Ross has made considerable changes to it.

You have also seen Oskaras Koršunovas's 2015 interpretation of Słobodzianek's play at the Oslo National Theatre. When we spoke on the telephone after the premiere, you said that it was a strong, mature production, that you liked it a lot.

That was definitely one of the most powerful theatre experiences I have had in recent years. Koršunovas felt Słobodzianek's text deeply, and succeeded, through the characters, to depict the tragedy of Poland in the twentieth century. The director does not condemn anyone, but we suffer each character's terrible fate. He shows us how circumstances determine a person's actions: both the Poles and the Jews shed blood, and, in doing so, they destroy their own and their children's lives. That is why only Abraham, who emigrates to America before the war, remains untouched and continues his line.

Bloodshed always begets more bloodshed...

At the beginning of Koršunovas's production of *Our Class*, we see that Rysek is in love with his Jewish classmate Dora, but then, when the Nazis come, he participates in her gang rape. In his play, Słobodzianek is referring to the Jedwabne tragedy, which took place on July 10, 1941, when the Poles of that village drove their Jewish neighbours into a barn and burned them alive, Dora and her child among them. Rysek is an active participant in that massacre. With the arrival of the Soviets, he too dies and finds himself in the land of the dead, where Dora approaches and embraces him. It is a chilling scene that bears witness to the meaninglessness of earthly hatred. The first act ends with the fire—people are being burned alive, the village is burning, and through the flames we can see an old Jewish man, an eternal wanderer. This character (perhaps Menachem?) is a rough, rather primitive man and a communist sympathizer. He has taken brutal vengeance upon his classmates, ended up in Israel, and, following his son's death, committed suicide, and now he walks across the stage singing the Yiddish poet Mordechai Gebirtig's famous song "Unzer shtetl brent"—"Our Village is Burning"...[60] And it feels as

---

60   Menachem is played by actors Øystein Røger and Lasse Lindtner.

though the whole world is burning . . . Everyone in the audience, myself included, simply froze in their seats.

Oskaras chose the actors perfectly. In the play, the first victim of the Holocaust in Poland—the Jew Jacob Katz—is drawn to communism, dreams of being a teacher, and initially believes the Soviets' propaganda. Oskaras chose two wonderful actors for that role, so that we see a young man looking at the world through innocent, childish eyes.[61] After he dies, this character, like the rest of the dead classmates, remains on the stage, observing what becomes of the village. Among them is Zigmunt, who is played by a very intelligent-looking actor.[62] Zigmunt is probably the least attractive character because he becomes an informer—he adapts to each regime in turn, and is an active collaborator. The twentieth century destroys all of their lives. As I said, bloodshed always leads to more bloodshed . . .

I could speak about that production forever—about Gintaras Makarevičius's profoundly meaningful, metaphorical sets, in which we see both classroom benches and a judge's tribunal, and an authentic monument of the period; about the composer's subtly selected and composed score; and, of course, about the unforgettable acting!

After the curtain fell, the usually restrained Norwegians stood applauding for a long time. The play received the highest assessment of six stars. It is not at all surprising that the Norwegian critics consider Koršunovas's *Our Class* the best play of recent years.

We will come back to Koršunovas in a little while, but now I would like to return to those great directors who shaped Lithuanian theatre following Jurašas's departure. After reading your review of Eimuntas Nekrošius's 1980 production **Kvadratas** *(The square), it occurred to me that you may have been first to understand what he was really trying to say.[63]*

---

61 Katz is played by actors Emil Johnsen and John Emil Jørgensrud.

62 Zigmunt is played by actor Kai Remlov.

63 Eimuntas Nekrošius (1952–2018)—theatre director.
Irena Veisaitė, "Dar kartą apie „Kvadrato" stogą" [Once more about Kvadratas's roof], *Literatūra ir menas*, February 14, 1981, 12. This review was a polemical response to an article by critic and playwright Gražina Mareckaitė: "Ar reikia stogo Kvadratui? [Does Kvadratas need a roof?], *Literatūra ir menas*, January 31, 1981, 14.

I doubt that I was the first—I am certain that my colleagues understood everything too. But perhaps I was simply incapable of remaining silent when Nekrošius was criticized for having created what I believed was a brilliant and innovative production. Because it was a breakthrough in every possible way— in terms of both form and content. There was a lot of physical action, which was performed by excellent actors: Kostas Smoriginas (as Him), Dalia Overaitė (as She), and Remigijus Vilkaitis (as the Host). To this day, I could speak about that play scene by scene—that is how deep an impression it made on me. After all, the Square was a metaphorical representation of the Soviet Union as a prison. We were all living within that square!

While preparing for our conversation, I came across the review you mentioned and would like to quote a few sentences from it: "Eimuntas Nekrošius's play cannot be judged by the laws governing everyday life and reality, but only by the theatrical principles he establishes on the stage. Here everything has welled up to the point of an excruciating poetic explosion. And if the director and actors were to add a roof to the fragile structure they have erected—if they were to answer all the questions and provide psychological justification for every word—would not the entire production be diminished, reduced to yet another moving melodrama? And, most importantly, would not the audience be robbed of a space for experience and reflection?"

I hold the same view today. In short, Nekrošius was creating a new kind of theatre—one in which the word was no longer the main component of a production. Ramunė Marcinkevičiūtė wrote about that in more depth in her excellent, seminal book about the director, *Erdvė už žodžių* (A space beyond words).[64]

Nekrošius's rise was facilitated by the early support he received from another director, Dalia Tamulevičiūtė, who was probably the first to notice his talent. Dalia accepted him into the Vilnius Conservatory's acting department and later sent him to Moscow to study with the director and actor Andrey Goncharov.[65] Dalia herself was a theatre reformer. She headed the Youth Theatre, taught, and rose to fame with her lively and cheerful production of the chil-

---

64 Ramunė Marcinkevičiūtė, *Eimuntas Nekrošius: erdvė už žodžių* [Eimuntas Nekrošius: A space beyond words], Vilnius: Scena, Kultūros barai, 2002.

65 Dalia Tamulevičiūtė was head director at the State Youth Theatre of Lithuania 1974–1988. Nekrošius studied theatre at the Lunacharsky Theatre Arts Institute and graduated in 1978. Andrey Goncharov (Rus. Андрей Гончаров, 1918–2001)—theatre director, pedagogue.

*A scene from the play
Pirosmani, Pirosmani.
Vladas Bogdanas and
Irena Kriauzaitė.
1981.
Photo by Audrius
Zavadskis.*

dren's play *Bebenčiukas*, which was full of physical action and was performed by her "troupe of ten."[66] I am sure that Dalia knew perfectly well that Eimuntas would soon present her with stiff competition, but she did not hesitate to ask him to join her theatre, where, working with her troupe, he created the best productions of his early period: *Kvadratas*, Vadim Korostyliov's *Pirosmani, Pirosmani...* (1981), Chingiz Aitmatov's *The Day Lasts More Than A Hundred Years* (1983) and Chekhov's *Uncle Vanya* (1986).[67] I greatly admired Dalia's selfless and creative attitude and conduct.

Even Nekrošius's very first plays—Shelagh Delaney's *The Taste of Honey* (1977), Saulius Šaltenis's *Duokiškio baladės* (The ballads of Duokiškis, 1978), and Chekhov's *Ivanov*— were fascinating, especially the last two, in which the young director's talent for creating a unique theatrical atmosphere, with exactly the right music, was very evident.

I was simply stunned by Nekrošius's ability to create theatrical metaphors and by the originality of his interpretations. For example, in *Piros-*

---

66 Dalia Tamulevičiūtė's "group of ten" was made up of actors Kristina Kazlauskaitė, Irena Kriauzaitė, Algirdas Latėnas, Dalia Overaitė, Vidas Petkevičius, Violeta Podolskaitė, Kostas Smoriginas, Dalia Storyk, Arūnas Storpirštis, and Remigijus Vilkaitis.

67 Eimuntas Nekrošius worked at the State Youth Theatre 1979–1991.

mani, Pirosmani ... in which Vladas Bodganas played Pirosmani and Vidas Petkevičius played the Guard, everything—set design, music, acting—blended together into an integrated whole. Petkevičius played the Guard without speaking a word ... Irena Kriauzaitė gave one of the best performances of her career. When I think of that play it is not words but the unforgettable images from the production that come to mind.

I recall that *Pirosmani, Pirosmani...* was filmed, but when I saw the recording I could not recognize Nekrošius's production.[68] That was when I understood that it is not possible to mechanically transfer the action, spirit, and mood of a theatrical work to the screen.

I felt that Nekrošius's productions always conveyed his love of the Earth. His metaphors were concrete, often related to nature, water, or fire. Nekrošius himself has mentioned to me that his father was very unhappy by the career that his son chose, and would warn him that, working as a director, he would never build a house or put food on the table.

But I won't say any more about Nekrošius, because Ramunė Marcinkevičiūtė can do that much better. But I just have to add one more thing about this brilliant director—that I remember him as a very good, empathetic person.

When my husband, Grigori Kromanov, came to Lithuania and was looking for work here, he suddenly found that all doors were closed to him because there were rumours that I wanted to take him to Israel with me. That was complete nonsense. I knew that people were also saying that I was going to take Jurašas and Saja away as well...

That time, we had travelled to a theatre festival in Panevėžys, where Nekrošius was as well. Understanding the difficult situation in which my husband and I were in, Nekrošius promised to give him work.

Indeed, they understood one another very well. My husband was enormously impressed with Eimuntas Nekrošius and his productions, and wrote about them in the Estonian press.

You have already spoken today about Rimas Tuminas and his production of the play* Smile Upon Us, O Lord. *I would like to discuss another one of

---

68 *Pirosmani, Pirosmani...*—film recording of the play (dir. Juozas Sabolius, 1987)—access through Lietuvos radijo ir televizijos (Lithuanian Radio and Television) website (www.lrt.lt), "Mediateka."

his plays, Chekhov's The Cherry Orchard, *which Tuminas staged in 1990.*
That must have taken some courage?

Tuminas always remained close to Russian culture, and that did not require much courage. First of all, he often staged the classics. Tuminas has created some very meaningful productions, and with excellent actors, but I always found that they did not have the social impact—or perhaps it was simply different—of Nekrošius's or Vaitkus's works.

In a recent documentary film, Tuminas explains that his mother was Russian Orthodox and his father Lithuanian, and I think that these two elements coexisted very successfully within him.[69]

And one final detail: I wrote one of my first reviews about Tuminas's production *Viduržiemis* (Midwinter).[70]

Would you then say that Tuminas's consistent attention to the Russian classics can be explained by his maternal heritage?

Not necessarily. The Russian classics always were, and continue to be, important to us. Let us not forget that most of our earliest actors and directors were students of the Russian school of theatre. During the interwar years, Mikhail Chekhov lived in Lithuania for several years; he was a giant of the theatre and undoubtedly had an influence on the development of Lithuanian theatre.[71] I believe that Borisas Dauguvietis was also of Russian descent. The long Soviet period also inevitably brought us closer to Russian culture, although, as I have said, the Russian classics have always been important to us. We learned from both Stanislavsky and Meyerhold—two very different, distinct, and powerful influences on the development of theatre. Only Juozas Miltinis, about whom we spoke earlier, represented the French, rather than Russian, theatre tradition.

---

69 Reference to Ramunė Sakalauskaitė's documentary film *Pakeliui į prieplauką* [On the way to the pier], 2014.

70 *Viduržiemis* [Midwinter]—based on Jordan Radichkov's play *Viduržiemis*, Lithuanian State Academic Drama Theatre, 1978. C.f.: Irena Veisaitė, "Horizontalės ir vertikalės" [Horizontals and verticals], *Kultūros barai*, 1978, Nr. 6, 72–73.

71 Mikhail (Michael) Chekhov (1891–1955)—Russian director and actor who worked in Lithuania at the State Drama Theatre (1932–1933), directed the plays *Hamletas* [Hamlet] and *Revizorius* [The inspector] and taught acting technique.

I believe that our musical culture also received a boost from the possibility, during that era, to study in Moscow or Leningrad under the best professors
and true musical greats.

Since I have been speaking about Russian literature, I would like to stress
that it is important not to conflate Russian culture with Russian imperialist
policies. While we distance ourselves from the imperialist politics, we do not
abandon cultural ties.

Indeed, the Russian intelligentsia and Russian dissident communities have always supported us. In 1991, my friends from Moscow stood with us at the Supreme
Council building, holding Lithuanian flags and clearly expressing their support for
Lithuania's freedom.[72] Of course, it is sad that people with that kind of culture are
in the minority, and that this minority often remains powerless, that its voice is often too weak. Russian culture is global—it formed not only me, but you as well, if
you have read classics like Dostoevsky, Tolstoy, Chekhov, or have studied the poetry of Mandelstam, Tsvetaeva, Pasternak, Akhmatova, or Brodsky. So, interest in
true Russian culture has always been and continues to be relevant and alive here.
I am very disturbed by the growth of Russophobia in Lithuania today.

And one more important point: when I speak about Bolshevik Russia, I always
try to avoid using the word "Russian," preferring instead "Soviet," or, these days,
"Putinist." I have many friends among the Russian intelligentsia who are deeply
ashamed of what is happening in Russia today. Fear has been sown in Russian society, and the aggression directed at neighbouring countries reminds me of the Soviet period. In short, there are two Russias, and it is important to remember that.

The same applies to my views about Adolf Hitler's Germany. I avoid saying
"Germans" and instead use the term "Nazis." After all, the Nazis had nothing
in common with the true German culture of Lessing, Goethe, Schiller, or, later, Mann, Brecht, Grass, and many others.

*If we could return once more to Tuminas, I would like to ask you: which of
his productions have you personally found most interesting?*

Probably *The Cherry Orchard* [1990] and Mikhail Lermontov's *Masquerade*
[1997], as well as, of course, *Smile Upon Us, O Lord*, and his production of

---

72 Supreme Council building—currently the Lithuanian Parliament.

Chekhov's *Uncle Vanya* with the Vakhtangov Theatre. I also found his production of Pushkin's *Evgeny Onegin* [2013], in which both Onegin and Lensky are
played by actors of different ages, interesting.

*If we are speaking about your relationship with Lithuanian theatre, it
must be noted that you have not only attended a great variety of performances, participated in discussions about them and wrote reviews, but you
also helped to nurture two of the most distinct directors of the post-inde-
pendence period—Oskaras Koršunovas and Gintaras Varnas.*

That is a bit of an exaggeration. Yes, both Koršunovas and Varnas were my students.[73] As I mentioned earlier, Varnas was the strongest student I ever had—
he was very well read and had broad general knowledge. And Oskaras, as I also
said, was the opposite—as a student he was a *tabula rasa*; he read none of the
required texts and his head was probably full of Daniil Charms; he was working on his first production (based on Charms's *There To Be Here*, 1990), which
he began to develop while still studying at the Conservatory.[74]

Yes, I had contact with these two talented young people, but I doubt whether I had any significant impact on their development. They were both part of
a cohort under the very powerful director Jonas Vaitkus. That, in my opinion,
was the most significant factor.

I think that, before that, Oskaras was also influenced by his high school
teacher Violeta Tapinienė, who would mount theatrical productions with her
students.[75] I saw Oskaras play the lead in her production on Ray Bradbury's
Dandelion Wine. He was like an angel—such a beautiful, pure boy, and he carried the entire production. Now Oskaras is very well read, a highly original director, and the leading figure in our theatre. From his earliest productions of
Charms works, he has introduced utterly new and unseen things into Lithuanian theatre.[76]

---

73 Oskaras Koršunovas graduated from the Conservatory in 1994, Gintaras Varnas graduated in 1993.
74 Daniil Charms, a.k.a. Daniil Juvachov (Rus. Даниил Хармс, 1905–1942)—poet, writer and play-
     wright, classic writer of absurdist texts.
75 Violeta Tapinienė was a Lithuanian language and literature teacher at Vilnius High School Nr. 9 (cur-
     rently St. Chistopher's High School) who led the school's theatre club (1966–2002).
76 Oskaras Koršunovas's first production was *Ten būti čia* [There to be here]; other early plays include
     Senė [Old lady] and *Senė 2* [Old lady 2] (based on Charms and Vvedensky, 1992 and 1994), *Labas,*

From that point, Oskaras never stopped growing. One need only recall his productions of Mark Ravenhill's *Shopping and Fucking* (1999), Marius von Mayenburg's *Fireface* (2000), Sophocles' *Oedipus Rex* (2002), Shakespeare's *Romeo and Juliet* and *Miranda* (The Tempest, 2011), and, his recent so-called trilogy: *Hamlet* (2008), *The Lower Depths* (2010), and *The Seagull* (2014), which have travelled all of Europe and beyond . . . Each is full of discoveries—direct interaction with the audience, interactivity, and true authenticity.

I can remember all of these performances very well, but I hesitate to discuss them. In them, I think that Koršunovas is clearly discussing his own painful experiences and the times he lives in. I would recommend that you read the poet and critic Dovilės Zelčiūtė's book *Kelionė su Oskaru Koršunovu* (A journey with Oskaras Koršunovas), which at least begins to reveal this director's creative process.[77] If I were any younger, I would perhaps write a book about Koršunovas myself. Though we belong to different generations, I think I understand the world that he creates. I find him interesting and familiar. But I just don't have the energy . . .

If we are speaking about Varnas, during the early Independence period I was very impressed by his 2008 staging of two madrigal operas by Claudio Monteverdi: *The Fight Between Tancred and Clorinda* and *Dance of the Ungrateful Women*. These were excellent productions in which everything was in perfect harmony—the music, the actors' baroque voices, their physical movements, and set designer Julija Skuratova's wonderfully expressive dolls. I also liked his productions of several operas: Piotr Tchaikovsky's *The Queen of Spades* (2001), Giuseppe Verdi's *Rigoletto* (2003), and Onutė Narbutaitė's *Kornetas* (2014).

Varnas has perfect taste—he is an aesthete in the best sense of that word. I am also impressed by his social engagement, his courageous defence of birds, the environment, and, of course, the theatre.

Although they studied under the same director and graduated from the Lithuanian Conservatory in the same year, Oskaras Koršunovas and Gintaras Varnas are very different artists. And that is wonderful.

Sonia, Nauji metai [Hello Sonya new year] (based on Vvedensky, 1994). All were staged at what is currently called the Lithuanian National Drama Theatre.

77 Dovilė Zelčiūtė, *Kelionė su Oskaru Koršunovu: teatrinis koliažas: esė, repeticijų fragmentai, spektaklių, gastrolių įspūdžiai, interviu, recenzijos* [A journey with Oskaras Koršunovas: A theatrical collage of essays, rehearsal fragments, tour impressions, interviews and reviews], Vilnius: Alma Littera, 2014.

Does Eastern European theatre have its own specificities? How do you see the Lithuanian theatre scene in the context of Eastern European theatre?

Your question does not quite fit into the framework of our conversations—it requires a special study or at least a thorough article. So I will only express a few thoughts.

Eastern European theatre has its own specific characteristics because the conditions under which it developed were fundamentally different from those that existed in Western Europe. While Western Europe was celebrating a hard-won victory over Germany and Hitler, Eastern Europe was experiencing a new occupation. Eastern European theatre developed in the post-war period, when some parts of Eastern Europe were incorporated into the Soviet Union, while the so-called "people's democracies" of Central Europe also fell under the Soviet sphere of influence. Communist ideology and strict censorship reigned throughout the region. Eastern European theatre, like other art forms, was looking for paths of resistance. With the Church being persecuted, Eastern and Central European theatre was virtually the only public space where it was possible to express anything about human existential questions, morality, or true humanist values. Because the communists had answers to all of life's questions, Eastern and Central European theatre had to create and perfect an Aesopic, or metaphorical language if it was to circumvent the censors and express its ideas. Although each director naturally had his or her own style and means of expression, this was characteristic of all theatre in this part of Europe.

In their plays, the text sometimes had only a secondary role, allowing the visual plane to dominate. What was most important was interpretation of the work and the roles, and the search for ways to make classical theatrical plots contemporary. Here it suffices to remember productions by Brecht, Kantor, Grotowski, Jaan Tooming, Adolf Shapiro, and many other Eastern and Central European directors. In Lithuania, Aesopic and metaphorical theatrical language reached great heights in the plays of Jonas Jurašas, Jonas Vaitkus, and, in particular, Eimuntas Nekrošius.

When you were speaking about Soviet-era theatre, you presented the thesis that the theatre was a space in which existentially important questions could be raised. What, in your opinion, is the mission (if we can

*even speak of such a thing in the postmodern era) of contemporary Lith-
uanian theatre?*

That is a difficult question to answer. I think that theatre no longer has a special
mission and, today, is very diverse. Some theatres (e.g., Domino Theatre) offer
entertainment, while others try to reflect upon our times. The latter approach
is clearly evident in the repertoire that Audronis Liuga and Martynas Budraitis
have been developing for the Lithuanian National Drama Theatre.

Today, directors, actors and set designers from different generations work
in the theatre, so different schools of theatre inevitably collide. But I am not prepared, at this point, to classify or evaluate them.

※

People Developed
Close Relationships
Within "Islands"

Irena Veisaitė, her daughter Alina, and Alexander Shtromas. Tarusa, late 1960s.

Drawing on Aron Gurevich's ideas, you often repeat that it is a mistake to apply today's categories of good and evil, resistance, conformism, and so on to the Soviet period. On the other hand, there is an opposing view, which declares that there were only two alternatives—"one or the other"—during that period. With that in mind, I would like to ask you: what do you think would have been the right thing to do? Be a "boiler room intellectual," or enter into compromises with the Soviet authorities in order to be able to work in the theatre and speak to the audience in metaphorical language?

That is a very complicated question, and one that every person resolves in their own way. I have personally confronted that problem on different levels.

It seems to me that, during the Soviet period, there were three types of people in Lithuanian society: the dissidents, individuals who adjusted to the regime in different degrees, and open collaborators.

The first category—the dissident—includes individuals such as Antanas Terleckas, Viktoras Petkus, and Nijolė Sadūnaitė.[1] To some degree, they chose to be outsiders—they refused to recognize the Soviet regime and to work with it in any way, and did not participate in the social life of the era. I would call them "boiler room intellectuals." I remember meeting Jaan Kaplinski in Estonia.[2] A highly regarded Estonian poet and writer, intellectual, Orientalist, and

---

1   In 1978, Antanas Terleckas and a group of like-minded people established the Lithuanian Freedom League—a political organisation that fought for the restoration of Lithuania's independence. The dissidents Viktoras Petkus and Nijolė Sadūnaitė were members of the Lithuanian Helsinki Group, founded in 1976.

2   Jaan Kaplinski—one of the authors of the "Letter by 40 Estonian Intellectuals," published in 1980. The "Letter" criticised the Soviet policy of Estonia's russification.

author of pointed articles criticising the Soviet regime, he worked in the botanical gardens and completely detached himself from Soviet reality. That was a matter of principle for him.

Another example is someone very close to me, my brother from Mrs. Stefanija Ladigienė's family, Algis Ladiga. He was very bright and was drawn to art and philosophy. During the first independence period, he had begun studies in architecture at Kaunas University, but broke them off when the war began. Algis spent the Nazi occupation years at his parents' estate in Gulbinėnai, and, when the war ended, he entered Kaunas Seminary. He completed his studies but was never ordained, because he was deported to Siberia in 1948. He spent eight years there, and then returned to Lithuania and settled in the town of Anykščiai, where he and his wife Marytė raised two wonderful sons—Linas and Tomas.

Algis was very well read, a serious intellectual, and he refused to make compromises on any level. In order to avoid any contact with the Soviet reality that so repulsed him, he became a land reclamation engineer. He had to feed his family…

After his mother's death, Algis began to sculpt a monument from a large stone, in effect for both of his parents; General Kazys Ladiga, Mrs. Ladigienė's husband, was executed in 1941 in Sol-Iletsk.[3] No one knows where he was buried. Algis worked on the sculpture in his spare time, and a rumour began to spread through Anykščiai that he was creating a monument for the Lithuanian partisans. One night, the monument simply vanished; some soldiers apparently carted it off and exploded it. And the monument was so close to being completed… But then Algis, not deterred by threats from the KGB, found another stone and began to sculpt a new monument, which now stands in Saltoniškių Cemetery in Vilnius, where Mrs. Ladigienė is buried.

The people I have been speaking about were specific kinds of outsiders. They refused to enter even into the slightest compromises with the Soviet authorities. Of course, this group of brave and highly principled people made up a very small portion of the society of that time.

---

3   Kazys Ladiga was arrested by Soviet authorities in September 1940. At first he was imprisoned in Lithuania, but, with the start of the war between Germany and the USSR, was transferred to Russia and imprisoned in a special regime prison colony in the town of Sol-Iletsk in the Orenburg region. He was condemned to death in October 1941 and executed in December 1941.

Tomas Venclova, Alexander Shtromas, Juozas Tumelis, and Pranas Morkus had similar views to the first group, but they did not sever all ties with the public sphere.

The second group of people generally consisted of intellectuals who had adjusted to the conditions imposed upon them—but only externally, not within themselves. They avoided compromises but were not able to do so completely, because they had to survive. That is the group that I belonged to, and I did have to make some compromises. But of course, as the years went by and my values and attitude toward life took shape, I increasingly avoided them. As I read Solzhenitsyn and Shalamov and met some of the Russian dissidents, I increasingly felt the need to protest actively. But I must immediately acknowledge that I never became a true fighter. I remember how Andrei Sakharov, a person whom I respected immensely, came to Vilnius during Sergei Kovalyov's trial; I so badly wanted to go and congratulate Sakharov, to support him, but ... I did not do so.[4] Out of fear. On the other hand, Monsignor Kazimieras Vasiliauskas received Sakharov and spent time with him. I am still ashamed to remember that episode.[5]

Another person who was very dear to me and whom I could include among the outsiders was the rather eccentric and multi-talented Alfredas Andrijauskas. His was a tragicomical story. An organ player and composer, he was also studying German language and literature and had great difficulty making ends meet. Although I knew very little about his life, it seemed to me that he was very lonely. Professor Vitas Areška, who headed the Faculty of Philology at the Pedagogical Institute for about five years, and later became head of the Department of Lithuanian Literature at Vilnius University, sent Alfredas to me so that I would supervise his thesis about Schiller's aesthetics.[6] Alfredas was naïve

4   Sergei Kovalyov was arrested and accused of spreading anti-Soviet propaganda in December 1974; his trial was held in 1975 in Vilnius. Prominent dissidents, including the academic Andrei Sakharov, travelled to Vilnius to show their support for Kovalyov. The fact that Sakharov was in Vilnius during the trial, when the Nobel Peace Prize was being awarded to him in Oslo at the time, helped attract Western media attention to Kovalyov's trial.

5   Kazimieras Vasiliauskas (1922–2001)—Lithuanian Catholic priest and deportee. When Vilnius Cathedral was returned to Catholic believers in 1989, Vasiliauskas was named its pastor. Vasiliauskas maintained contact with members of the Lithuanian anti-Soviet resistence, including members of the Lithuanian Helsinki Group. Andrei Sakharov and other people close to Kovalyov stayed in Vasiliauskas's home while in Vilnius for the former's trial.

6   Vitas Areška was head of the Faculty of Philology at Vilnius State Pedagogical Institute (1968–1971) and (with pauses) head of the Department of Lithuanian Literature at Vilnius University (1971–1991).

and very sincere, a very pure-minded person and a serious Catholic—an ideal-
ist par excellence. He wanted to defend his thesis and he seemed to be ready to
make one or two small compromises, for example to cite Marx or Lenin somewhere in his dissertation—to "put up a lightening-rod," as we used to say—but
he simply could not do it. I remember saying to him more than once: "My dear
Andrijauskas, you must make up your mind—do you want to defend your thesis or write a book about Schiller. If you want to write a book, then it will eventually be published, as manuscripts don't burn. I will be happy to help you. But
if your goal is to defend your thesis, you simply must include some quotes from
the Marxist classics. Otherwise it will not get past the VAK."[7] I could see that
he was trying, but it was all for naught. He simply could not do it. Alfredas
never defended his dissertation, but his book about Friedrich Schiller was published after Lithuania regained independence.[8] In some ways, Alfredas can be
compared to Justinas Mikutis. Of course, he was not a philosopher of the same
calibre as Mikutis, but there are similarities of character and behaviour. Except
that Alfredas didn't drink at all.

Alfredas was deeply moved by the Jewish tragedy in Lithuania and even
wrote a poem on the topic. It was also he who brought me Matilda Olkinaitė's—
she was the daughter of the pharmacist in the town of Panemunėlis, and was
shot by the "white armbands"—notebook of poetry written in 1938–1940,
which Father Matulionis, the late parson of Panemunėlis, had preserved.[9] I have
it in my home and treasure it to this day. Now the director Saulius Beržinis is
making a film about Matilda. He once told me how, when he was in the Neth-
erlands, a Dutch colleague refused to greet and shake hands with him—he had
learned that Saulius was Lithuanian and, in this Dutch man's view, Lithuania
was a nation of Jew-killers. Saulius was very disturbed by this and began to learn
more about the Holocaust in Lithuania.

---

7   VAK (Rus. Высшая аттестационная комиссия)—Higher Attestation Commission—Soviet insti-
    tution that controlled academic dissertations and gave the final approval needed for the awarding of
    academic degrees.
8   Alfredas Andrijauskas, *Frydrichas Šileris ir lietuvių drama* [Friedrich Schiller and Lithuanian drama],
    Vilnius: Vaga, 1990; *Frydrichas Šileris* [Friedrich Schiller], Vilnius: Vyturys, 1997.
9   Matilda Olkinaitė's (1921–1941) diary and notebook of poems is almost all that is left of this talented
    young person's work, which Irena Veisaitė has steadily worked to present to Lithuanian readers. For
    more about Matilda Olkinaitė c.f.: Irena Veisaitė, "Poezija. Matilda Olkinaitė" [Matilda Olkinaitė's
    poetry], April 1, 1989, 8–9. Also see Veisaitė's text about Olkinaitė and some of the young author's po-
    ems in *Krantai*, 1997, Nr. 3, 104–107.

But to return to the theme we are exploring today, it must sadly be said that many members of the intelligentsia, and of other sectors of society, adapted to the regime, pursued their careers, and morally compromised themselves. They can be said to belong to the third type of people in Lithuania during the Soviet period, whom I would call pure conformists or even collaborators. Of course, most of them claimed that they were joining the Communist Party for patriotic reasons—in order to preserve Lithuanianness, to save Lithuania. The dominating opinion of the time was that the only way to achieve anything tangible was to be a Party member. And there is some truth to that.

But there were different types of conformists: those who believed in Bolshevism and its goals; those who were trying to succeed in their careers; and those who conformed purely out of fear. Sadly, this kind of thing is unavoidable under conditions of terror and dictatorship, because people want to live. Understanding that, I am disinclined to condemn all of them. But while I didn't like turncoats and don't to this day, I am against any universal "hunting down" of communists.

I would like to explore another theme—that of "islands of like-minded people." During the Soviet period, people were overwhelmed by fear and mistrust, and in that kind of atmosphere the need to find like-minded people with whom one could share thoughts about books, performances, and ideas became even more acute. What do you think—am I not over-idealising those times?

During the Soviet period, we did indeed feel a strong need for social interaction. People would form groups of close friends that were bound by mutual trust, respect, and a community of spirit. Within these so-called "islands" especially close relationships were established—we would have intimate conversations, discuss the books we had read, share our news and concerns, all of this accompanied by tea, sometimes a little vodka, or Armenian or Georgian cognac . . . The Moldovan cognac "White Stork" was also popular, as far as I can remember. This was the origin of the so-called kitchen culture, because we often sat in each other's kitchens. These groups of friends were quite closed, because we were never free of the feeling that we were being followed. For that reason, we often had to warn our assembled friends: "We can't speak openly today, because we'll have a guest whom we don't know very well!"

And now I can tell you about some specific "islands." There were certain homes that became magnets, and the first one that I would like to recall was the very special home of the Vildžiūnas family in the neighbourhood of Jeruzalė, on the outskirts of Vilnius. It all began with Stefanija Ladigienė's return from Siberia in 1957. After her daughter Marytė's marriage to Vladas Vildžiūnas, a very respectful and close relationship developed between Stefanija and her son-in-law.[10] She loved and deeply appreciated Vladas, and that very close relationship lasted until her death. As long as she was alive, Mrs. Ladigienė was, indeed, the soul of that home . . .

At Marytė's, Vladas's, and Stefanija's home we truly felt free. One could talk about anything. The most diverse people gathered there, including some representatives of the interwar intelligentsia: Juozas Keliuotis, Father Petras Rauda, the composer and choral director Konradas Kaveckas and his family, Teofilia Vaičiūnienė, and the actress Elena Žalinkevičaitė (Petrauskienė)—the mother of Aušra Petrauskaitė and an exceptionally attractive, creative, and good woman.[11] When the 1951 anti-Semitic "Doctors' Case" was taking place and rumours were circulating that all Jews would be deported to Siberia, she told me that, if any danger should arise, I was to run to her for shelter.[12] Those kinds of things are simply impossible to forget.

Vytautas Landsbergis and his family were also guests of the Vildžiunases.[13] Justinas Mikutis also found refuge there, as did other people who were persecuted by the authorities. Mrs. Ladigienė was also visited by my "Siberian sis-

---

10   Vladas Vildžiūnas (1932–2013)—sculptor who, in his home in the Jeruzalė neighbourhood of Vilnius created an oasis for free-thinking people, and also a sculpture garden which later became the Jeruzalė Art Centre.

11   Juozas Keliuotis (1902–1983)—editor, writer, translator.
     Petras Rauda (1894–1974)—Catholic priest.
     Konradas Kaveckas (1905–1996)—composer and choral director.
     Teofilia Vaičiūnienė (1899–1995)—actor.
     Elena Žalinkevičaitė-Petrauskienė (1900–1986)—actor, playwright, poet.
     Aušra Petrauskaitė-Šimoliūnienė—artist.

12   The Petrauskas family rescued Jews, including the violinist Danutė Ponceraitė, during the Second World War. Elena ŽalinkevičaitėPetrauskienė was honoured as one of the Righteous Among the Nations in 1999.

13   Vytautas Landsbergis—music and cultural historian, activist, politician. On March 11, 1990, Landsbergis was elected head of the Supreme Council of the Republic of Lithuania and was in charge of its first session on that same day, when the session voted to restore the independence of the Republic of Lithuania. According to the Temporary Constitution he was the state's highest official—its de facto leader.

ters"—that is what a group of young women she had cared for in Siberia called themselves: Stasė Niūniavaitė, Aldona Kalpokaitė, Marytė Biekšaitė, and Julija Šerkšnaitė. When Jonas Jurašas was thrown out of all the theatres and was being harassed by the authorities, he also found refuge in this special home. Others who visited included Teodoras Valaitis, Antanas Kmieliauskas, Vincas Kisarauskas, Vytautas Valius, and their families. One could also say that the entire "quiet modernists'" group—Stanislovas Kuzma, Ksenija Jaroševaitė, Vladas Urbonavičius, Mindaugas Navakas, and many others—found their "island" at the Vildžiūnas home.[14]

Strange as it may sound, some left-leaning people also came there. Mrs. Ladigienė always remained true to herself but she never turned anyone away, even if they had different views. Even the architect Danielius Todesas would visit—at the time of Mrs. Ladigienė's case was being examined, he was the Soviet security forces employee responsible for it.[15] I believe they met through Bela Zelieskaja, a German literature scholar who later represented Lithuanian literature at the Moscow Writer's Union.[16] Bela was a relative of Todesas' and a friend of Marija Ladigaitė-Vildžiūnienė. When he would come to visit, Todesas would kiss Mrs. Ladigienė's hand. He was a member of the intelligentsia, and, it seemed to me, in the end understood a great deal. Or perhaps he didn't. I never spoke to him about it. Much later, his son Daumantas Todesas told me that, when his father was close to death, he wrote Mrs. Ladigienė a letter of apology. So I suppose that my hunch was correct.

---

14   Irena Veisaitė refers to some of the most prominent artists of Soviet-era Lithuania: Teodoras Valaitis (1934–1974)—sculptor and painter; Antanas Kmieliauskas—sculptor; Vincas Kisarauskas (1934–1988)—painter, graphic artist, set designer; Vytautas Valius (1930–2004)—graphic artist, painter, book illustrator.
"Quiet Modernism"—a metaphor referring to a process (1962–1982) during which Lithuanian artists trasngressed the vague boundary between official and unofficial activities. For more detail c.f.: *Tylusis modernizmas Lietuvoje, 1962–1982* [Quiet modernism in Lithuanian 1962–1982], ed. Elona Lubytė, Vilnius: Tyto alba, 1997.
Representatives of the "quiet modernists" that Veisaitė refers to: Stanislovas Kuzma (1947–2012)—sculptor; Ksenija Jaroševaitė—sculptor; Vladas Urbonavičius—sculptor; Mindaugas Navakas—sculptor.

15   Danielius Todesas—member of the Lithuanian Communist Party active in the communist underground during the interwar years; from 1940, working for the Lithuanian SSR's NKVD and KGB, was active in the mass arrests, deportations, and repression of Lithuanian citizens. After leaving the special forces, worked as an architect.

16   Bela Zelieskaja, while working at the Writers' Union of the USSR, was responsible for ties with Lithuania.

Model for a sculpture of Barbora Radvilaitė in the Vildžiūnas garden. Vilnius, c. 1981.

Indeed, some people condemned Mrs. Ladigienė for welcoming people like that former KGB agent into her home. Perhaps in that sense she was similar to Monsignor Vasiliauskas? As I have said, one way or another, Mrs. Ladigienė remained true to herself.

I was a regular visitor to the Vildžiūnas home; my husband, our daughter Alina, and I even spent our summer holidays in Jeruzalė so that we could be closer to Mrs. Ladigienė. My cousin Alexander Shtromas, my lifelong friend Tadas Masiulis and his wife Janina, and many others were also her guests. What unforgettable evenings we spent there! And how entertaining it was when the actress Rūta Staliliūnaitė was there. Dressed as Barbora Radvilaitė in costumes from Jurašas's play, she would wander regally around the Jeruzalė sculpture garden, whose centrepiece was a copy of Vladas Vildžiūnas's sculpture of Barbora Radvilaitė. The original now graces Vokiečių Street, one of the central streets of Vilnius.

Vladas filmed many of those magical evenings . . .

Indeed, even after Mrs. Ladigienė's death, the Vildžiūnas home remained an "island"—a place where members of the Lithuanian intelligentsia, artists, and a large circle of friends would gather. Vladas and his wife Marija Ladigaitė continued Mrs. Ladigienė's "open house" traditions.

There were other "islands" in Vilnius during that post-war era. One of them was Aldona Liobytė's home in Žvėrynas.[17] Aldona was a true *vilnietė*, a writer and editor, and an attractive, good and openhearted woman with a terrific sense of humour. I would visit her home as well, but not as often as that of the Vildžiunas family. The Lithuanian intelligentsia would gather in Aldona's home—people like Antanas Vengris, Kazys Saja, Jonas Jurašas, Jokūbas Josadė and his wife, Dr. Sideraitė.[18] Aldona had very firm moral principles; she was not afraid of criticising people—even her closest friends—and saying what she thought straight to their faces. She was especially critical of divorce.

Aldona was very important to me and I still stay in touch with her daughter Gintarė.[19]

I absolutely must mention the home of Virgilijus Čepaitis and his wife Natalia Trauberg.[20] Their guests would include Joseph Brodsky and many other Russian dissidents.[21] Frequent visitors included Ramūnas Katilius and his wife Elė, Ramūnas's brother Adas, Venclova, Morkus, Shtromas, Tumelis, and others—all of them very interesting, creative people.[22] Indeed, even if the latter group never ended up in the Soviet lagers, they should, in a certain sense, be included among Vilnius dissident types. These people have all played a very important role in my life.

Indeed, it was in Natalia's home that I was introduced to British author G.K. Chesterton; she considered him very important and translated him into Russian. This writer was an important discovery for me.

---

17 Aldona Liobytė-Paškevičienė (1915–1985)—children's author, translator, journalist. For more c.f.: *Šmaikščioji rezistentė Aldona Liobytė: publicistika, laiškai, atsiminimai* [Aldona Liobytė, the playful resistant: Articles, letters, recollections], ed. Rūta Saukienė, Vilnius: Lietuvos rašytojų sąjungos leidykla, 1995. Also c.f.: *Korespondencijos fragmentai. Aldona Liobytė (1915–1985)* [Aldona Liobytė (1915–1985): Correspondence fragments], ed. Giedrė Jankevičiūtė and Gintarė Paškevičiūtė-Breivienė, Vilnius: Lietuvos rašytojų sąjungos leidykla, 2015.

18 Aldona Liobytė's home attracted the Vilnius cultural elite, including: Antanas Vengris (1912–2014)—theatre and literary scholar, translator; Jokūbas Josadė (1911–1995)—writer and playwright. Šeinė Sideraitė (1921–2005)—medical doctor (endochrinologist), wife of Jokūbas Josadė.

19 Gintarė Paškevičiūtė—surgeon.

20 Virgilijus Čepaitis—literary figure, translator, politician. Natalia Trauberg (1928–2009)—translator, essayist.

21 Joseph Brodsky (1940–1996)—poet and essayist. Nobel Literature Prize laureate (1987), considered one of the most important inheritors of the "silver age" of Russian poetry.

22 Ramūnas and Elė Katilius were close friends of Joseph Brodsky in 1966–1970. The Ramūnas and Elė Katilius Archive, a collection of Brodsky's works, photographs and documents, was given to Stanford University. For more detail c.f.: *Josifo Brodskio ryšiai su Lietuva: draugų atsiminimai* [Joseph Brodsky's Lithuanian connection: Friends' recollections], ed. Ramūnas Katilius, Vilnius: R. Paknio leidykla, 2013.

Kazys Saja and Grigori Kromanov during a rehearsal for Saja's play Šventežeris. Tallinn, 1971.

I was very close friends with the writer Kazys Saja . His home was not one of these kinds of "islands" but I felt very comfortable there, and we had many interesting conversations. Dear Kazys would read his new dramas, comedies and novellas aloud and then we would discuss them. He was someone who was constantly searching—a restless soul—and he always remained true to himself.

Naturally, I was not acquainted with all the Vilnius "islands." I am sure that there were more in both Vilnius and other Lithuanian cities. It is perhaps enough to mention Father Stanislovas's home in Paberžė, which attracted people from across the Soviet Union.[23]

Earlier, you mentioned Justinas Mikutis. What do you remember about him?

I remember him in many different ways. I remember him expounding his philosophical views and his theories about Russia's feminine nature (he divided the world into "feminine" and "non-feminine"), and how he would predict the world's future. I cannot recreate everything. We started our conversations too

---

23   Algirdas Mykolas Dobrovolskis (Tėvas [Father] Stanislovas, 1918–2005)—a priest, monk, and preacher who sheltered addicts and other socially disenfranchised people.

late in my life. It is terrible how the memory begins to fade . . . Sadly, I also remember him as sickly, unwashed, and drunk to the point of almost falling down
. . . To be very honest, I still feel guilty when I think about Justinas—I am haunt-
ed by the thought that I should have paid him more attention, that I should have
helped him in some way . . . There was no alcohol in my grandparents' and parents' culture, so to this day I shrink when I see someone drunk. The Vildžiūnases
took much better care of dear Justinas, who was one of their frequent visitors.

*Besides Mikutis, did you meet anyone of that visionary calibre in Vilnius
during that period?*

Not like Mikutis.

*Would it be correct to say that alcohol was sometimes the only thing that
could bring people solace during those horrific times?*

The inner feeling that one is not free is not a justification for drinking. I don't
believe that it forces people to drink. The habit of turning to drink is probably
most of all determined by the household culture in which a person grows up.
My second husband was Estonian—more precisely, in terms of ethnicity, he was
half Russian and half Estonian, and he belonged to both the Estonian and Russian cultural worlds. He was never a drinker and claimed that his weak health
had saved him from that. But everyone around him drank . . . Unfortunately, I
often found myself among drunk artists. Most of the time I would cringe and
withdraw from the group; I could never understand and was never interested in
those kinds of interactions between drunk or half-drunk people.

*Were books a more reliable way to escape, into one's thoughts, from Sovi-
et reality?*

I would not say that books were only a means of escape. Perhaps even the opposite. After all, we were not only reading fairy tales or detective stories, but works
that helped us to better understand humanity, its history and existential problems, and the tragedy of our situation. So they also helped us to successfully "rid
ourselves" of Soviet ideology.

Did not another realm of art and imagination—film—also occasionally offer refuge?

My husband was a film and theatre director and was often invited to screenings in both Vilnius and Tallinn, and I joined him whenever I could. So, even during the period we are speaking about, I saw Italian neo-realist films and the works of French directors like François Truffaut, Alain Resnais, Godard, and many others.

Lithuanian film was also very important to me. Indeed, strange as it may sound, I probably see its value now more than I did then.

Could that be because you can now compare Lithuanian film of that era to today's?

No, not because of that. I simply realise that they were very good films for their times. In viewing them today, I also have the opportunity to see some of my favorite actors—the ones who have kept me company all through my life—in their youth. I have great sentiments for them. I am thinking of works such as Vytautas Žalakevičius's *Niekas nenorėjo mirti* (Nobody wanted to die, 1965), Algimantas Grikevičius's *Jausmai* (Feelings, 1968) and *Ave, vita!* (1969), the films of Arūnas Žebriūnas—I see my past, the years of my youth in those films... [24]

That I feel a great affection for Lithuanian film is also the result of the fact that I lived, and continue to live, within a Lithuanian arts context. Later, I also became close to the Estonian arts scene, when I became involved in my husband's work—one year I even took an unpaid leave from my teaching and worked as assistant director on his film *Dead Mountaineer's Hotel*. [25]

Let us return to the question of the "islands"... They were not only created within private homes or apartments—the Neringa café in Vilnius also became an important refuge during the Soviet era.[26] Today we know that

---

24 Irena Veisaitė mentions great Lithuanian Soviet-era films by major directors Vytautas Žalakevičius (1930–1996), Almantas Grikevičius (1935–2011), and Arūnas Žebriūnas (1930–2013).

25 *Dead Mountaineer's Hotel* (Est. "Hukkunud Alpinisti" hotel)—a 1979 feature film in the fantasy genre, directed by Grigori Kromanov at Tallinnfilm Studios, based on the novel of the same title by Arkady and Boris Strugatsky.

26 Reference to the famous Neringa Café at 23 Gedimino Prospect in Vilnius, for which the architects Algimantas and Vytautas Nasvytis created a unique interior that caused controversy not only

the Neringa was also very convenient for the KGB as all of the freethinkers gathered in one place, they drank, they talked ...

The opening of the Neringa was very important to people in Vilnius. I was ecstatic when I saw that café and its architecture and interior, which included motifs from Lithuanian mythology rather than Soviet ideological symbols. Those curved lines that recall the waves of the sea, the little pond in the middle—it was all very beautiful.

Nor did the KGB's listening devices—a well-known secret—interfere with our enjoyment of the Neringa. At the time, I was very upset with the criticism that the Nasvytis architects and Lithuania received from Moscow.

But in terms of the life of the Neringa, I have to admit that I was not a regular visitor there. I didn't have time, as I had to prepare lectures, meet with students, and go to the theatre, and besides, I never adapted to our alcoholic culture. I certainly went there to hear the Ganelin–Chekasin–Tarasov Trio, and more than a few times.[27] They were a unique phenomenon not only in Lithuania, but within the whole Soviet Union. Although I was not a jazz expert, I sensed the smell of freedom in that music and eventually came to love it.

Since we have touched on the Neringa, I would like to ask you a broader question, about disappearing Vilnius. The city has changed a great deal since 1990, and continues to change rapidly. What do you think about this new city? Is there anything that you miss from that bygone era, which is increasingly receding from the city's streets?

Though I was born in Kaunas, I am now a true *vilnietė*. I fell in love with this city, I feel and am drawn to its history, its mystical spirit. I find Vilnius incredibly beautiful at all times of the year, in every kind of lighting. I am very pained

---

in Lithunia, but throughout the Soviet Union. From its opening, Neringa Café was a favorite gathering place for intellectuals and bohemians including Vladimir Vysotsky, Bulat Okudzhava, and Robert Rozhdetsvensky. For more c.f.: *Neringos kavinė: sugrįžimas į legendą* [The Neringa Café : Return to the legend], ed. Neringa Jonušaitė, Vilnius: Mažoji leidykla, 2014.

27   Ganelin Trio—formed in 1971, actively created and performed within and outside the USSR and became the first jazz band from the USSR to gain recognition in Western Europe without imitating famous US jazz musicians.

by the changes that are altering the city's unique atmosphere—the taller buildings going up, the plastic window displays.

I'm sorry that there are no more cinemas in the centre and I miss the old
ones—the Helios, Maskva, and Lietuva movie theatres.[28] I'm sorry that the park
opposite the Evangelical Reformed Church is so neglected and lifeless. I often
walked there with my daughter. Sometimes it pains me to walk through the little streets of the former ghetto, where so many Jews once lived. I remember all
of those murdered people, those destroyed lives . . .

The smells and signs of Vilnius that are most dear to me have almost all
disappeared. I'm glad that I live in a building whose inner courtyard has walls
that are still full of Second World War cartridges.[29] After all, I myself am a relic
of that war. Freshly painted Vilnius is not my Vilnius, which is more likely the
grey, dusty, still wounded post-war city, partly in ruins. At the same time, I am
happy to see our capital being revived and modernised, the Old Town being reconstructed. I love Vilnius in all of its states. I understand, after all, that there
is nothing permanent except change, and that one must accept that.

✳

---

28 For more about the Soviet-era cinemas that have disappeared from Vilnius life, c.f.: Sonata Žalne-
    ravičiūtė, *Vilniaus iliuzionai: miesto kino teatrų istorijos* [Vilnius Illusionists: History of a city's cine-
    mas], Vilnius: Vaga, 2015.
29 From 1965 Irena Veisaitė has lived in an apartment on Basanavičiaus Street.

Why Was
Faust Redeemed,
Even After Making
a Pact with the Devil?

Irena Veisaitė and Nora Pärt. Vilnius, 1970s.

I would like to talk about books. How do you find and choose them? How often do people recommend books to you, and are you inclined to trust those recommendations? Do you read book surveys and reviews?

That depends on who is recommending the book. Of course, reading itself and the love of books begins with one's parents' home and their library. Later, when one becomes a conscious member of society, public discourse comes into play. But classical literature—for both children and adults—has remained a point of reference throughout my life.

During the Soviet period, I often read *samizdat* publications and books that I would receive for several days—or, more precisely, several nights. They would come to me from the hands of trusted people, which was the best kind of recommendation. When I worked at the Pedagogical Institute I also read a great deal of literary and professional literature.

If I look back upon my own reading habits, I have to admit that I am one of those people who cannot read several books at once. If I start a book, I always try to read it to the end, and I also used to take copious notes—I had the thickest notebooks full of all sorts of quotes. When reading a book that I owned, I always underlined thoughts that I liked, so most of my books are heavily marked up.

Through that marking up, I met someone who became very important in my life—a like-minded person and friend. The playwright, writer, and journalist Nikolai Davidovich Otten once came to the Russian Drama Theatre.[1]

---

1   Regarding Otten and his family, c.f.: Note Nr.28, p. 116

Nikolai Otten. Tarusa, c. 1966.

He needed a copy of Georg Büchner's play *Danton's Death* (Ger. *Dantons Tod*, 1835). Someone from the Russian Drama Theatre asked if I had a copy. I lent them the book, apologizing that it was marked up. Having seen my notes, Otten became interested in me—he said that I had underlined everything that he would have. That was how we met, and we became very close friends. As I mentioned earlier, it was through the Otten family that I met many of the Russian dissidents.

Reading habits vary depending on the period in one's life, and one reads academic and literary texts differently. A novel must be read from beginning to end—one has to enter it deeply and grasp it. With academic literature it is completely different—you can't, after all, read all of the professional literature related to your dissertation topic!

While writing my doctoral dissertation, and later my most important articles, I used the following method: I would carefully read the most fundamental, seminal work on a topic from beginning to end, while only scanning other books to see if they contained anything that I did not yet know. That helps to speed one's reading up and makes it possible to cover more ground and access more information. At Moscow University, Professor Roman Samarin, of whom I was not very fond, used to say that a philologist must read 200 pages per day. That thought used to help me to justify my scanning of academic literature.

So, one cannot read everything over the course of one's life, but one must try to read as much as possible.

The Soviet period presented every reading person with a challenge—one had to truly "hunt" for books. Tell me about how you succeeded in meeting that challenge? How did you create and supplement your library?

Mostly, I would buy books in bookstores or antique shops. I also tried to subscribe to serial publications of classical literature and works by different authors and on different themes, both in the originals and in translation. It was not so easy to acquire those subscriptions—it usually involved spending a day in a long line outside of the bookstore that processed subscriptions.

Having mentioned serial publications, I must acknowledge that Russian classical literature publishing culture was at a very high level, and the texts included excellent comments.

You have said that in each of our personal reading histories our parents' library is an important point of departure. Could you elaborate upon this some more?

What I remember of my parents' library is many encyclopaedia titles in Lithuanian, German, Russian and French, and a great variety of authors' names. When I began my studies in the Faculty of Philology, I discovered that my classmates did not know anything about many books that, in a certain sense, were not news to me. Certainly, I had read very few books from that library—I had simply been too young for them—but I have clear memories of what they looked like, of the authors' names on the spines. For example, my mother was interested in psychoanalysis, so the names of Freud, Adler, and Jung were familiar to me from childhood. I am convinced that it was my parents' library that taught me my great respect for books and my understanding of how varied literature is—how vast and multilingual. Besides, in my parents' home, I had my own library, which contained all sorts of fairy tales as well as books that we had to read in primary school.

I began to read very early, at the age of four or five. I recall that, at the time, special German literature for girls was very popular, that there were even special series, such as *Nesthäkchen und ihre Puppen*.[2] But they could not have had much long-lasting value, as I cannot remember their contents. I can only remember that those books existed and that I read them with pleasure.

If you were to look at my library today , it would reveal the different periods of my life and my varied interests. I know perfectly well that I will never again read some of the books it contains, but I still cannot give them away as I simply can't imagine my life without them. To this day, books are probably my greatest treasure.

Today's youth probably find that difficult to imagine. Besides, books are no longer people's main source of knowledge, as they have been replaced by the "all-powerful" Internet.

And now let us move from libraries to the specific books that had the greatest influence on you. Let us begin from those you read in childhood.

The Jonas Biliūnas stories "Brisiaus galas" (Brisius' end) and "Kliudžiau" (I hit the mark) had a great impact on me.[3] These works instilled in me the feeling of compassion for the weak. I will never forget the scene in which the dog Brisius continues to gaze trustingly at his owner, who is about to shoot him. Reading these works filled me with disgust for betrayal and helped me to grasp the importance of loyalty. I also have a clear memory of the same author's story "Laimės žiburys" (The light of good fortune)—the idea of pursuing good, something more beautiful and ideal, stayed with me. I have no doubt that fairy tales shaped me as well. My dissertation supervisor, Professor Tronskaya, used to say that it is essential that children be read fairy tales: they shape a child's values, understanding of life and sense of justice. After all, in fairy tales good always triumphs!

Naturally, I only understood the value and meaning of fairy tales much later, but I certainly sensed their influence from a young age—I was always opposing any kind of injustice and discrimination. I also loved Mayne Reid and Karl May; it was not their novels' motifs of adventure and heroism that played an

---

2   Series by German writer Else Ury, published 1913–1925.
3   Jonas Biliūnas (1879–1907)—Lithuanian classic writer of novellas; developed psychological prose in Lithuanian literature.

Irena Veisaitė at her home. Vilnius, 2016.

important role in my life, but the importance and meaning of truth and justice that remained with me from fairy tales. In this context I should probably mention that the novel that has had the greatest impact on me is Harriet Beecher Stowe's *Uncle Tom's Cabin*, which instilled in me a lifelong opposition to racism and any kind of humiliation of others and a yearning for equality which have lasted to this day.

I could also add Frances Hodgson Burnett's *Little Lord Fauntleroy* to the list of my favorite childhood books.

Sadly, I cannot boast of having a very good sense of humour, though I value it in others and suffer from this personal shortfall. I am grateful to the books of Samuil Marshak, Kornei Chukovsky, and Erich Kästner, and especially Wilhelm Busch's little book *Max Und Moritz*, while Mark Twain's *Tom Sawyer* and *The Adventures of Huckleberry Finn* introduced me to true humour.[4] Later, as an adult, I read the popular books *Winnie the Pooh*, by A.A. Milne, J.M. Barrie's *Peter Pan*, as well as Lewis Carroll's *Alice*.

Russian literature has probably influenced me a great deal. I read Fyodor Dostoevsky's *Crime and Punishment* before entering the ghetto. I was especially moved by the character of Sonia—her inner beauty, virtue, and self-sacrifice.

4   Wilhelm Busch's rhymed story *Max Und Moritz: Eine Bubengeschichte in sieben Streichen* [Max and Moritz: A story of seven boyish pranks], first published in 1865, quickly became popular in Germany and beyond its borders.

I also loved to read Charles Dickens, and for some reason especially enjoyed *David Copperfield*. Ivan Turgenev's story "Mumu" also made a great impression on me. Perhaps as great as Biliūnas.

The authors and books that I have just mentioned shaped me during my childhood and early adolescence. Then there was a long break—for three years books barely existed in my life, so I longed for them and greedily read anything that came into my hands. After the war, when I entered Salomėja Nėris High School, and especially when Vanda Zaborskaitė became my teacher, I entered a very intense period of reading and discovering the classics. It is difficult to single anything out.

It goes without saying that the German classics were very important to me. I can remember reading Friedrich Schiller's *Ballads* while still at the underground school in the ghetto. The *Ballads* devote a lot of attention to loyalty, friendship, heroism, self-sacrifice and humanism. There I was, thinking about what a horrific world we live in—one in which the Nazis are killing us—only to discover that the German classics wrote about such high ideals . . . It was probably then that I gradually began to understand that one should not identify Nazi ideology with the German nation and culture. But we have already talked about that.

Later I became acquainted with Gotthold Ephraim Lessing and his drama in verse, *Nathan the Wise*, which is permeated with the spirit of tolerance, human brotherhood and love. That was a very important book for me. I was constantly talking about it with my students, even though it was not part of the official curriculum. I am very happy that there is finally an excellent Lithuanian translation of it, by Lithuanian poet Antanas A. Jonynas. It is my view that Lessing surpasses even Goethe—not in terms of talent, but in his profound humanity and humanism. I hope that *Nathan* will one day be staged in Lithuania.[5] The ideas in that play have not become out-dated, though they might require a contemporary dramatic interpretation.

As you know, my initial university studies were in Lithuanian literature, so Lithuanian prose and poetry are also important to me. I attentively read Vaižgantas, Nėris, Maironis, Žemaitė, Putinas, Sruoga, Mačernis, Boruta, and

---

5   Irena Veisaitė's former student Gintaras Varnas staged Lessing's play *Nathan the Wise* at Kaunas State Drama Theatre, in part as a result of her intense mediation. The premiere took place in December 2017.

many others.[6] They were all very important to me. When I left to study in Moscow, the infinite strata of Russian and Western literature were revealed to me. To this day my favorite literary hero is Don Quixote.

I also read philosophical texts and was profoundly influenced by Solovyov and the French existentialists, especially Camus.[7] Antanas Maceina also had an impact on me, though I was later disappointed when I learned that he had contributed to the development of the nationalist ideology of the "Tautininkai."[8] And, of course, there were many others, but it is impossible to list them all here . . . Probably the last important revelation that I experienced in terms of philosophy was the work of the sociologist Zygmunt Bauman.

I have just mentioned many authors, but I could also speak about books that were key sources of revelation to me, and there have been many of those: the works of Kafka, Hemingway's *For Whom the Bells Toll*; the works of Solzhenitsyn, Shalamov, Tsvetaeva, Akhmatova, Mandelstam, and Brodsky's early texts . . . Tomas Venclova—as both a poet and essayist—is always important to me, and I greatly admired his civic stance. I should also add Rabelais, Corneille, Racine, Molière, Voltaire, Diderot, Rousseau, Balzac, and Stendhal; and, from the twentieth century, Brecht and the Swiss writers Frisch and Dürrenmatt . . . The writers, poets and philosophers whose works speak important truths to me are endless; I really cannot list all of them . . .

When you mentioned Don Quixote, you partially answered another question I wanted to ask. I would like to know with which literary hero you most deeply identified, or the reverse—is there a character with whom you see yourself in contrast, so that distancing yourself from him helps you to define yourself?

6　Veisaitė refers to classic authors of Lithuanian literature:
　　Juozas Tumas-Vaižgantas (1869–1933)—Catholic priest, writer, one of the most prominent figures of the first half of the twentieth century, active in the Lithuanian national rebirth movement and advocate of modern culture.
　　Julija Beniuševičiūtė-Žymantienė "Žemaitė" (1845–1921)—prose writer, playwright, journalist, activist.
　　Vytautas Mačernis (1921–1944)—poet, famous for intellectual work marked by internal, existentialist searching.
　　Kazys Boruta (1905–1965)—writer and translator.

7　During the Soviet period, the French existentialists (including Camus) were tolerated, and their texts were translated and published. On the other hand, Vladimir Solovyov (Rus. Владимир Соловьев, 1853–1900)—writer, religious author, mystic—was on the censors' "black lists."

8　Antanas Maceina (1908–1987)—Lithuanian Christian philosopher, poet, author of works of religious and cultural philosophy.

I feel a close kinship with Don Quixote, though I am probably more "sober" than him. But I have read so many books that it is very difficult to say with which characters I could identify myself... To some degree, I can identify with Goethe's Faust—his searching, his desire to improve the world and himself... When our teacher Vanda Zaborskaitė asked to write about "the questions that concern me the most today" I wrote: "There is no question that does not concern me. I am interested in all the inner and outer phenomena of the world. I am like a little Faust or Andrei Bolkonsky—I am looking for the meaning of life, a goal, the truth. I am tormented by the lack of a strong foundation beneath me. Abstract, detached answers and questions do not interest me."[9]

To this day, I am fascinated by the relationship between Mephistopheles and Faust. Although Faust, in his quest for perfection and his desire to change the world, fails on every level, at the end of the work it becomes clear that he who seeks truth, and does not give up, will be redeemed. It doesn't matter if one never finds it—the most important thing is to seek it. A lot of time passed before I understood *Faust* in this way. I understood that although we are incapable of saving the world, we can try to save our souls.

Earlier, you mentioned that you were always especially drawn to twentieth-century literature, and in saying so you began to answer another one of my questions. On the other hand, I would like to be certain that I understood you correctly, so I will ask once more: which epoch and literary genre were most important in your own individual development?

That is a very interesting question, because it also touches on one's relationship with postmodern literature. At first, I was very impressed by the idea of de-ideologisation, which was so necessary after the Soviet period. I could probably say that I understand contemporary or postmodern literature, music, and painting on an expressive level, but that, at the same time, I have a strong sense that they are rather marked by destruction and the primacy of form. To me, form in itself—without any idea or internal values—is not interesting. For it to be "my kind" of art, it has to have meaning.

---

9   C.f. full text on page 303.

As I just mentioned, I see destruction in postmodernism, and I fail to find anything positive or holy (in a non-parochial sense) within it; but that may be a matter of my own limitations ... Indeed, when postmodern art is being discussed, the same questions is always asked: "*How* was that done?" And to me, as I have said, this is not the most important aspect. I care more about *what* is being said.

I look to art to find something positive, perhaps even hopeful. I am not only interested in the horizontal plane of the narrative, but the vertical one. Of course, in saying that I have to ask myself: "Do I think this way simply because I have grown old?" And I also need art to affect me directly—I need it to make me think, to move me, so that I would not need any of those lengthy explanations that are so often necessary these days ... about "what the artist wanted to say" or "how they want to be understood." I am convinced that good art affects people directly, so that one feels lifted above the ground, above the everyday.

I remember that, when I was studying in Moscow, I would experience that feeling of elevation when listening to Richter's concerts (he had just returned from Siberia); during Jurašas or Nekrošius performances; reading the poetry of Pushkin, Rilke, Mandelstam, Tsvetaeva, Putinas, or Mačernis; or viewing exhibitions of works by Čiurlionis, Van Gogh, or Modigliani.[10]

But it would be impossible to convey all of those experiences here ...

What are literary classics to you? Is their role to quiet "the noise of the present" or, as the Italian writer Italo Calvino put it, to help us hear this "noise" and find something meaningful in it?

It would be difficult for me to answer that question. It seems to me that classical art allows us to feel a sense of harmony, perhaps even come close to grasping perfection, the ideal. That kind of art affects both the conscious and subconscious minds, that higher order that exists within each of us. A believer would probably say that classical art brings them closer to God, to man's essential calling ... I once saw a film called *Water*, which vividly showed how water molecules

---

10 Mikalojus Konstantinas Čiurlionis (1875–1911)—Lithuanian composer and artist, especially known for his visual art, who sought to achieve a synthesis of several art forms. In Čiurlionis's paintings, biblical, Christian motifs interweave with a pantheistic worldview. During the Soviet period, this artist's paintings were especially important to Lithuanian society because they contained elements from folk art.

change in reaction to different kinds of sounds.[11] Classical music harmonizes their structures, while dissonant music creates chaos within them.

Which Lithuanian books, or books by Lithuanian authors, have most moved you personally—were important "events" to you—during the Soviet period and then after Lithuania regained independence?

Hmm . . . I would have to think about that for a long time.

During the Soviet period, it was probably Icchokas Meras's novels: *Lygiosios trunka akimirka* (Stalemate), *Ant ko laikosi pasaulis* (What the world depends on), *Geltonas lopas* (The yellow patch), and *Striptizas* (Striptease).[12] Meras's thinking and style were highly original, somehow Biblical, and not at all related to Socialist Realist literature. I was very excited by Romualdas Granauskas's *Gyvenimas po klevu* (Life under the maple tree); Marcelijus Martinaitis's *Kukučio baladės* (The ballads of Kukutis); the poetry of Sigitas Geda; Grigory Kanovich's novels about the lives and fates of Lithuania's Jews—*Свечи на ветру* (Candles in the wind, 1979), *Слёзы и молитвы дураков* (The fool's tears and prayers, 1983), as well as his later books, all of them beautifully translated into Lithuanian by Feliksas Vaitiekūnas; the plays of Kazys Saja; and almost everything written by Tomas Venclova, many of whose texts I have first read in manuscript form.[13]

---

11 Water: *The Great Mystery* [Rus. Вода]—dir. Julia Perkul, Anastasia Popova.

12 Icchokas Meras (1934–2014)—writer and screenwriter. As a child, Meras lost his parents in the Holocaust; miraculously, he survived and was rescued and raised by a family of Lithuanian farmers. His childhood experiences are reflected in the book of short stories *Geltonas lopas* [The yellow patch, 1960].
  Lygiosios trunka akimirką [Stalemate; Eng. Trans. *Stalemate: A Novel*, Lyle Stuart, 1980]—the first Soviet-era Lithuanian novel to have discussed the painful question of the Holocaust, and it did so very subtly.
  Icchokas Meras's novel *Striptizas, arba Paryžius–Roma–Paryžius* [Striptease, or Paris–Rome–Paris] was published in 1971 in the journal *Pergalė* (Nr. 11–12) because it was clear that, because of problems with Soviet censorship, it would not be possible to publish it as a separate book. *Striptizas* was published in the US in 1976: *Striptease, or Paris–Rome–Paris,* Southfield, MI: Ateitis. For more about Meras, c.f.: *Besikartojančios erdvės: pokalbiai su Icchoku Meru ir kūrybos interpretacijos* [Repeating spaces: Conversations with Icchokas Meras and interpretations of his work], ed. Loreta Mačianskaitė and Skaistė Vilimaitė, Vilnius: Baltos Lankos, 2009.

13 Here, Irena Veisaitė mentions Soviet-era Lithuanian literary works that were innovative in both form and content: Romualdas Granauskas's short novel *Gyvenimas po klevu* [Life under the maple tree, 1988] offered a critical interpretation of the disappearance of traditional Lithuanian rural life and the erosion of traditional agrarian culture and society during the Soviet period; poet Marcelijus Marti-

In the period following the restoration of Lithuania's independence, I have been interested in the same authors—Martinaitis, Venclova, Kanovich, Granauskas. And authors of the younger generation: the works of Valdas Kukulas, Sigitas Parulskis, Marius Ivaškevičius, Kristina Sabaliauskaitė . . .[14] And recently I have noticed a certain shift in myself. I am increasingly interested not so much in novels as in memoir-type literature—in narratives about individual destinies, experiences, and reflections on the road already travelled.

You have mentioned that you were close friends with some Lithuanian authors. It would be very good if you could elaborate on this somewhat. Who were the writers that played some kind of a role in your own life?

In answering this question I will begin from far away. I could say that I would be very sad to die because I am madly in love with human creativity—I have tremendous admiration for the creative process and the fruits and discoveries it produces. Even this conversation is a form of creativity, as we are both trying to grasp, to create something. And life itself, to me, is a type of creativity, something we have already talked about. It is probably because I so worship creativity—even in everyday life, even in the kitchen—that I have always been, and continue to be, attracted to creative people.

I knew most of the Lithuanian writers of my generation. When I began my undergraduate studies in Lithuanian Literature, our group included Anta-

---

naitis's *Kukučio baladės* [The ballads of Kukutis, 1977] used the mask of the old-fashioned, naïve oddball character Kukutis to explore the dramatic encounter between tradition and modernity, and the absurdity of Soviet ideology; Sigitas Geda's poetry injected new life into a Lithuanian poetry constrained by Socialist Realism, modernising Lithuanian lyric by offering innovative interpretations of ancient cultural sources.

Grigory Kanovich—one of contemporary Lithuania's best-known and most productive Jewish authors (who has lived in Israel since 1993). Kanovich has written a total of 11 novels, which together form a saga of Lithuanian Jewish life from the eighteenth century to this day. His writing has been translated into 13 languages. Kanovich writes in Russian, so his books appear first in that language. Feliksas Vaitiekūnas has translated the majority of Kanovich's works into Lithuanian.

14 Valdas Kukulas (1959–2011)—poet, essayist, literary critic.

Sigitas Parulskis—poet, playwright, essayist, one of the most important figures in contemporary Lithuanian literature and the most-translated contemporary Lithuanian author.

Marius Ivaškevičius—writer, playwright, director. Ivaškevičius distinguishes himself in contemporary Lithuanian literature for his recreations and renewals of national myths

Kristina Sabaliauskaitė—art historian and author of a unique four-volume cycle of historical novels titled *Silva Rerum* (2008–2016).

nas Jonynas, Jonas Lapašinskas, Mykolas Sluckis, Jonas Macevičius, Mulikas Rozinas.[15] I also knew the students above me, who later became literary scholars and researchers, including Ale Naginskaitė, Irena Kostkevičiūtė, Aurelija Rabačiauskaitė, and Ona Pajedaitė.[16] I spoke earlier about Vanda Zaborskaitė, with whom I maintained a close relationship, though always one between student and teacher. Without question, I had the closest relationships with the authors Icchokas Meras, Grigory Kanovich, Juozas Grušas, and Kazys Saja.

Among Russian writers, I was close to Otten and his friends; Nina Demurova, who produced a brilliant Russian translation of Lewis Carroll's *Alice*; the playwright Alexandr Volodin; the poet Nikolai Panchenko; the Shklovsky family; Galich.I knew many interesting, highly educated and intelligent people, not all of them necessarily associated with literature or theatre.[17] Through my husband, I probably knew all of the important Estonian writers and artists of that era.

※

15   Antanas Jonynas (1923–1976)—writer.
      Jonas Lapašinskas (1923–1997)—poet, journalist, editor.
      Mykolas Sluckis (1928–2013)—writer.
      Jonas Macevičius (1922–1999)—philosopher, Soviet party figure.
      Mulikas Rozinas—artist.
16   Irena Kostkevičiūtė (1927–2007)—scholar of Lithuanian literature and art.
      Aurelija Rabačiauskaitė—Lithuanian literature scholar.
17   Nina Demurova (Rus. Нина Демурова)—literary scholar, translator.
      Alexandr Volodin (1919–2001)—Soviet and Russian playwright, screenwriter and poet.

I Felt a Powerful
Connection with
My Spiritual Brothers

Tomas Venclova and Irena Veisaitė. Vilnius, c. 1976.

*C*ould you tell me about how you met Kazys Saja and Juozas Grušas, *who both eventually became very close friends of yours?*

As I have already mentioned, I have always been drawn to creative people. I felt a powerful connection with my spiritual brothers. From the time when I began my studies in Vilnius, I had many friends in the arts. Somewhat later, I came to know Kazys Saja closely. He had a restless soul and was always searching for truth and for answers to existential questions. He was a critical thinker who, during the Soviet period, had the courage to say things that others tried to suppress.

I think it would be correct to say that he contributed to the development of Aesopic language in Lithuanian literature and theatre. We were very close and our families spent a lot of time together. I have many fond memories of that period. One of the most vivid is of our trip to Tallinn in 1971 to see Grigori Kromanov's production of Saja's play *Šventežeris* at Kingissepp Drama Theatre.

Another time, Kazys staged a sensational event, pretending that he had unearthed some historic treasures at his cottage near the Merkinė River. Alina and I and my grandsons even drove there to see it. It made a powerful and convincing impression on everyone. It was only much later that Kazys admitted to me that the treasure was not real and that he had come up with the idea of the adventure to entertain my grandsons. I don't even know if they ever learned the truth.

Kazys was a very lively and inventive person. We are close to this day, even though we barely ever see each other—we were separated by a stupid conflict in which Saja had a terrible disagreement with my cousin Aliukas over Vytautas

Landsbergis. They both respected Landsbergis and held him in high esteem, but my cousin had some critical opinions about the man; these angered and insulted Kazys, who literally ran out of my apartment. I tried to catch up with him, to calm him down and prevent him from leaving. Our relationship somehow broke down after that conflict, because, as I learned somewhat later, Kazys had formed the impression that I, too, had taken a stand in the argument and had supported Alexander Shtromas, which was certainly not the case. I still do not understand what the essence of that dispute was. After some time, the tension subsided, and Kazys wrote some beautiful remembrances following Shtromas's death.[1] After all, they had been close, like-minded friends; I think that Aliukas was an important influence on Kazys Saja, and he even wrote the first review of a Klaipėda Drama Theatre production of Saja's play *Septynios ožkenos* (Seven goats), and introduced him to *samizdat* literature.[2] Aliukas was not a conflictual person. He loved Kazys and was very sad following their conflict. He never said, and certainly never wrote, an unkind word about Kazys.

Kaziukas always called me his sister.[3] I don't even understand why our close friendship broke off in that way—perhaps we no longer have time or space for each other in our lives, maybe the need is no longer there, I simply don't know … One way or another, he remains a very dear and special person to me. I consider him my brother and have only positive, bright memories of him. I already mentioned that Grigori Kromanov staged a production of Saja's play *Šventežeris* in Tallinn. Kazys Saja took me with him as a theatre critic, and that is how I met my second husband. I may speak more about that later …

And now tell me about how you met and became friends with Juozas Grušas.

I can't remember when and where, during the Soviet period, I met Juozas Grušas, but it was probably through the theatre. But whenever it was, a state of complete trust was immediately established between myself and Grušas, and also with his wonderful wife, Pulcherija. That did not happen very often dur-

---

1   C.f.: *XX a. žmogus: Aleksandro Štromo portretai* [A twentieth century person: Portraits of Alexander Shtromas] ed. Leonidas Donskis, Vilnius: Versus aureus, 2008, 92–94.

2   Kazys Saja, *Komedijos* [Comedies], Vilnius: Valstybinė grožinės literatūros leidykla, 1957.

3   Kaziukas—diminutive of the name Kazys.

Irena Veisaitė and Juozas Grušas in the playwright's garden. Kaunas, c. 1985.

ing Soviet times. I greatly admired Grušas's nobility, his deep and sincere humanity. We were connected by our love of Don Quixote—perhaps that endless quest for the meaning of life. I can remember sitting with him in what used to be called Konradas Café in Kaunas, which was renamed Tulpė (Tulip) during the Soviet period, and how we talked for three hours.[4] He told me about his love for the writer Salomėja Nėris, his relationships with friends and neighbours, about what had shaped his worldview. I always thought that I should have recorded those conversations, but I knew that, had I pulled out a tape recorder, the intimacy of our conversation would have vanished in an instant. After all, during the Soviet period, tape recorders were associated with the KGB and informers. That close connection and our conversations were too precious to me, but I sensed that it was all historical material . . .

Grušas was terrified of old age but he lived to see it. During the last years of his life, he no longer avoided being open about his thoughts, but I still never got around to writing anything down, and I regret that to this day. I could so easily have returned home and at least noted down some of the key details of our conversations! My only consolation is that I brought many of my students

---

4   A favorite café and gathering place of artists, writers, actors, and architects during both the interwar period and the Soviet years (when it was re-named Tulpė).

to him. Under my supervision, two of my best students—Audra Žukaitytė and Reda Noreikaitė-Pabarčienė—wrote their final undergraduate papers on Juozas Grušas. They had gained the writer's complete trust, spent a great deal of time with him, and, I think, collected quite a lot of information. I had faith that other students also preserved Grušas in their memories and their hearts. Sadly, it seems that everyone's memory fades; details are lost and all that is left is a general impression. All that remains from our meetings is quite a lot of photographs.

But several events remain lodged in my memory. Having the best of intentions and out of love and admiration for Grušas, my friend Otten wanted to translate Grušas's play *Meilė, džiazas ir velnias* (Love, jazz and the devil) into Russian, so that more people would know about it and that it would be staged more frequently throughout the Soviet Union.[5] As he translated, Otten tried to "correct" the play a bit so that it would get past the censors. He was doing this only out of very good will, but it was nevertheless painful to Grušas. I'm only relieved that, despite it all, we remained friends.

Could you tell me about Grušas's relationships with other writers, such as Salomėja Nėris, whom you have already mentioned today?

As far as I can remember, Grušas was hopelessly in love with her, but, when she finally began to be more interested, he was already dating his future wife, Pulcherija. He would talk about Salomėja's affair with Juozas Eretas, about her complicated relationship to her husband, but I can't remember the details of our conversations.[6] Sadly, nor could Audra or Reda help me. We all remember that Grušas valued Salomėja highly as a poet, always stressed her exceptional sensitivity, never accused her of betrayal, and never even touched on that subject. [7]

---

5   In the play *Meilė, džiazas ir velnias* [Love, jazz, and the devil, 1966], Grušas explores the challenges faced by humanist values during the twentieth century, raising questions about freedom and responsibility, and exploring the causes of war. The main characters of the tragicomedy are three young wanderers who are having trouble finding their life paths.

6   Juozas Eretas (Ger. Jozeph Ehret, 1896–1984)—Lithuanian-Swiss literary historian.

7   In the post-Soviet period, Salomėja Nėris's biography has been the object of intense debate about questions of collaboration and resistance. Observing these discussions, Irena Veisaitė has consistently stressed the importance of understanding the poet's fate and the capacity for forgiveness.

"Off camera," you have mentioned to me that you also interacted with Grušas under rather uncomfortable circumstances, when he was under intense attack. Could you speak in more detail about that period in the writer's life?

Yes, and I remember that episode well. Grušas's play *Meilė, džiazas ir velnias*, which was staged at the Panevėžys Drama Theatre by Blėdis, under the title *Pražūtingas apsvaigimas* (A deathly intoxication), was supposed to be discussed at what was then called the Lithuanian Theatre Association.[8] The meeting was supposed to be chaired by a colleague of mine, who inexplicably asked me to take his place. I agreed. Everyone who had gathered was very worried; the atmosphere was very heavy as there was a sense that the Central Committee had a negative opinion of the play. Even its title had been changed, which suggested a critical attitude to the youth of those times. When the time came to present the assembly with the complaint that had been written by some of my colleagues from the Pedagogical Institute (I do not want to mention any names), I read it out with the same exalted Levitan's voice that I sometimes used with my students, in that way distancing myself from the text and ironising its contents. Everyone understood.

After this discussion, Juozas Grušas was not condemned. At the time I considered it a personal victory.

But I still do not understand why Grušas was not condemned. Was it because, despite the complaint that had been submitted, the participants of the Theatre Association meeting did not undertake to "critique" Grušas using all of the "canons" of Communist criticism and self-criticism?

I am afraid that I can no longer remember all of the details. But I am certain that the majority of those assembled were on Grušas's side, and perhaps my reading of the complaint helped them to grasp its absurdity. At the time, at least, it seemed to me that I had contributed with the ironic tone I applied to the complaint. Besides, this was after Stalin's death.

---

8   Lithuanian Theatre Association—now called the Lithuanian Theatre Union.

Besides Jonas Jurašas and Juozas Grušas, did any more of your acquain-
tances or friends find themselves in those kinds of situations, in which
there was an attempt to criticize or even condemn them?

All sorts of things happened, but I never participated in "criticism and self-criticism sessions." Nor did I ever sign a letter of condemnation. Indeed, keen col-
lectors of signatures for such petitions knew there was no point in coming to
me—that I would never sign.

Of my friends, Tomas Venclova was very negatively viewed in official cir-
cles. From the beginning, Tomas was distinct in his principled stance; he was
very consistent and always held firmly to his positions. I could sign my name below almost every one of his ideas as they correspond to my own—only Tomas
expresses them much better. He expresses himself very precisely and backs up
his points with irrefutable arguments. We are also connected by long-standing
personal friendship. To this day I follow everything that Tomas does and writes.

Here, in this room in which we are speaking, I celebrated New Year's Eve in
1975 together a group of close friends, Tomas among them. It was a very mem-
orable New Year's Eve. During our party we elected Sakharov as the hero of the
year. Tomas's romance with his future wife Natasha Oguy was at its height.[9]
Sadly, their relationship did not last, but they have a wonderful daughter, Maria, who now lives in the United States.[10]

Many of my memories are in some way connected to Tomas Venclova. One
of them is quite painful to me. I can't remember exactly, but I think it was the
early 1980s. I was in London visiting my daughter and other people dear to me,
and I met with Tomas and Aliukas. We were walking through London and they
were both explaining to me, as though in one voice, that it was not possible to
become a full-fledged human being and scholar in the Soviet Union, that that
was possible only in the West. I can't remember all of the details, but eventually I broke down in tears. It was very painful to me. I was convinced that, even
in the Soviet Union one could be a decent person and a true scholar, despite the
unfavorable conditions. Tomas later admitted that he had been wrong and that

---

9   Natasha Oguy-Ramer (Rus. Наташа Огай-Рамер)—director at the Lithuanian Drama Theatre (direct-
     ed plays at Šiauliai Drama Theatre, Vilnius Youth Theatre, and the Lithuanian Russian Drama Theatre).
10   When Tomas Venclova emigrated in 1977, his wife, Natasha Oguy, and daughter Maria remained in
     Lithuania. They left for the West five years later.

the opinion he had expressed at the time was typical of the hangups of people beginning their lives in the West.

I was very happy when Tomas came to Weimar in 2012, when I was awarded the Goethe Medal.[11] After Lithuania regained independence, Tomas travelled here regularly. We always meet when he comes to Vilnius, usually at the home of our close mutual friends Ramūnas (a former classmate of Tomas') and Elė Katilius. The evenings we spent together there were very special, unforgettable times. These were meetings of friends and like-minded people, and Tomas was always the centre of attention. Elė would prepare some simple, but very delicious, dishes. I still remember the taste of her boiled potatoes, which were somehow especially delicious. We drank wine, talked about the past, discussed the situation in Lithuania and in the world, and remembered friends. Tomas Venclova is a fantastic storyteller. Perhaps I should mention at least a few of the names of those who participated in those get-togethers: Adas Katilius, Pranas Morkus, Zenonas Butkevičius, Donata Mitaitė, and Nina Mackevič.[12] During Tomas's visits to Vilnius, even more like-minded people would gather at the Venclova Museum and Home, whose director, Birutė Vagrienė, would organize everything. Birutė has contributed a great deal to the dissemination of his work; she is constantly organizing events with him—readings of Tomas's poetry and various discussions about themes in his work.

Am I correct in imagining the situation—that, during the Soviet period, Tomas Venclova was anathema to members of the nationally oriented intelligentsia, who saw him as too cosmopolitan?

Yes, I can confirm that, only I would replace "nationally" with "nationalistically." In my view, Tomas's cosmopolitanism was very positive and it distinguished him from more nationalistically oriented members of the intelligentsia.

---

11 Irena Veisaitė was awarded the Federal Republic of Germany's Goethe Medal in August, 2012 for promoting the German language and culture and encouraging cultural exchange.

12 Pranas Morkus—screenwriter, journalist, essayist.
Zenonas Butkevičius (1936–2012)—journalist, early promoter of ecological journalism in Lithuania.
Donata Mitaitė—literary scholar, editor of Tomas Venclova's creative biography, *Tomas Venclova: Biografijos ir kūrybos ženklai* [Tomas Venclova: Biographical and creative signs], (Vilnius: Lithuanian Literature and Folklore Institute, 2002).
Nina Mackevič—Lithuanian journalist.

It was as though Tomas was ahead of his times. I know that he was and is a true Lithuanian patriot, but he also respects and understands the "other." Those who today shout "Lithuania for Lithuanians"—who oppose themselves and their nation to others—promote hatred and ultimately degrade themselves. I cannot, I'm afraid, consider them true patriots worthy of respect.

During the twentieth century, the concept of patriotism was sullied by both the Soviets and the Nazis, and therefore now has a negative connotation. In the post-war years, many, such as Frisch and Dürrenmatt, did not even use that word. The concept of "patriotism" eventually shed its shameful baggage from the past, but it should still be used carefully, with absolutely no hatred of others or un-founded self-aggrandizement. During my lectures, I frequently reminded my students that we love our homeland because this is where we were born, because it was given to us, but that it is no way superior to any other. The same applies to language. We all love our language because it is our own and we love it like we love our mother—not because she is the best and most beautiful woman in the world, but simply because she is our mother. It is horrible to see and hear contemporary election campaign messages in which the concept of patriotism sounds like it stepped right out of a Soviet slogan. I want Lithuania to be a free country, but I am a patriot in Venclova's mould. In this respect, I identify completely with him and with his statement that, if forced to choose between truth and the nation, he will always choose truth. Besides, a true patriot also sees their nation's weaknesses and errors, and tries to correct them, even at the risk of being accused of slander.

In speaking about your relationship with Tomas Venclova, you have more than once described the two of you as "twins in terms of values." I would imagine that it must have been very difficult for you to lose your "twin brother" when Tomas decided to leave the Soviet Union for the West.

Yes, without a doubt it was very difficult. It was a great loss, but I also understood perfectly well that there was no other option, because Tomas simply could not fit into the cage of Soviet life. He needed to see the world. As a member of the Helsinki Group, he felt the constant threat of arrest—we all felt it, so I completely agreed with his decision.

Although Tomas's departure was a great loss for all of Lithuania, the most important thing was to save him. Indeed, he did a great deal for Lithuania during the Soviet occupation, both while in Lithuania and after he left, and following the restoration of independence. I always felt, and continue to feel him near by.

After Tomas's emigration, were you able stay in touch with him? I am asking what may sound like a banal question, because, as a historian, I know perfectly well that any correspondence with a "black sheep" like Tomas could have caused you numerous complications.

After Tomas emigrated, I ceased having any direct contact with him. We did not correspond, but we met several times abroad during the Gorbachev years. I received regular news of him from Aliukas and the media.

Tomas Venclova celebrated his 80th birthday in 2017. In thinking about that, I remembered the late literary scholar and editor Bronius Savuky-nas's point that major birthdays are dangerous because they can reveal that some of the work or other phenomena attributed to the person being celebrated already belong in a museum and are no longer of contemporary relevance. I would be interested to know what you think: of all of the ideas that Tomas has formulated and spent a lifetime defending, which remain most relevant to twenty-first century Lithuanian society? Which of his texts should we be looking at and reading most closely today?

I would go so far as saying that all of Tomas's writing is relevant to us. I can't even think of anything that I would leave out or could say has become out-dated. Tomas always was and continues to be a very important thinker for me. In a certain sense he is Lithuania's conscience. But sadly, there is a segment of Lithuanian society that still does not understand or appreciate him, and accuses him of either cosmopolitanism or of betraying his homeland. Some were angered by his article "I am Suffocating," which was seen as an insult to Lithuania. That was untrue and a misinterpretation of his views. Even though he has lived in different countries around the world and has a perfect command of Russian, Polish, and now English, Tomas was and remains a true Lithuanian patriot. But at the same time, he is a citizen of the world. I greatly admire his courage, his ability to powerfully, and without compromise, express his ideas and defend his values. You ask which of his statements and arguments are most important today. It is all important—his poetry; his respect for other cultures; his position that, whenever there is a conflict between ethnic interests and truth, he will always choose the side of truth. His battle against manifestations of nationalism in our own and other cultures is especially important. I would gladly put together a glossary of his main ideas, so that we could all draw wisdom from it. But of course, only those who do nothing are free of errors.

Without Tomas, I would probably not have become such a Lithuanian patriot myself, though other role models shaped me as well. I find that a person's view of Tomas is the perfect litmus test for revealing their values. I am happy that, despite all the attacks, Tomas is valued in Lithuania—his 80th birthday was celebrated as an important cultural event. That gives me great cause for optimism. Indeed, Tomas has been recognised in other countries as well: he has received the highest state honour awarded to a foreigner by the Polish government, and the Borderland Foundation has proclaimed him an honorary "Borderlander" . . .

Let us speak in more depth about Tomas's text "I am Suffocating."[13] *It was first given as a paper at the 2010 Santara-Šviesa conference and then appeared on online media platforms, and it was quite a bombshell.*[14]

Tomas's article did, indeed, cause a lot of anger in Lithuania.

I should at once say that I did not see it as a bombshell. It was a very courageous article that was ahead of its times. The words "I am suffocating" were said by Socrates in Aristophanes' play *The Clouds*. As it is well known, Socrates was condemned to death for his views, which were in conflict with those of

---

13   Tomas Venclova's public lecture "Aš dūstu" ["I am suffocating"], given at the June 26, 2010 Santara-Šviesa conference in Alanta, Lithuania, caused an especially dramatic and emotional polarisation of opinion in Lithuanian public discourse. In the lecture, Venclova expressed heavy condemnation of Lithuanian intellectuals who, in his view, were "fetishizing independence" and promoting a system of ideas and values that is satisfied with a primitive nationalist paradigm; this, Venclova argued, prevents Lithuania's incorporation into the global cultural polilogue and hinders its sociopolitical development.

14   Santara-Šviesa, "Santaros-Šviesos federacija" [Concord-light federation]—Lithuanian émigré organisation founded in 1957 by liberal intellectuals. Unlike other Lithuanian émigré organisations, Santara-Šviesa maintained contact with occupied Lithuania. Since the restoration of Lithuania's independence, the organisation's annual conference has been held in Lithuania.

Athenian society of the time; Aristophanes himself was probably on Strepsiades' side.

History has shown that Socrates was right. When I read *The Clouds* (quite a long time ago, I have to admit), I sympathized with Socrates; Strepsiades seemed to me to be ossified in his thinking and his defense of conservative elements in his society.

Socrates' words "I am suffocating" were said in the context of his conflict with his own society. Venclova uses Aristophanes as a kind of metaphor that he applies to our times, echoing Socrates' views in his own opposition to deep-rooted stereotypes.

The article was, indeed, very critical. Venclova expresses many bitter truths about us. One could take issue with the views of Russia expressed in the article, but it is important to remember that Tomas wrote the article in 2010 and that much has changed since then.

Now that we have discussed Tomas Venclova, let us come back to two people you know well and are close to in many ways—Icchokas Meras and Grigory Kanovich. How and when did you get to know these two individuals, and what sort of relationships did you have with them?

I can't at all remember how I first met Icchokas Meras.[15] Our paths probably crossed as a result of our common views. I was also very interested in his writing, which, in the context of Lithuanian literature of the time, was unique and innovative. We were also connected by our common experiences—he, too, was rescued from the Holocaust as a child. It may sound strange, but we were also connected by our shared love for Lithuania; we never blamed the entire Lithuanian nation for the murders of the Jews.

We had complete trust in one another and talked a great deal. Meras would bring me his latest manuscripts and would ask for my impressions and feedback.

The decision to leave for Israel was a difficult and painful one for him.[16] I, too, was saddened when he decided to emigrate. It was the early 1970s. His novel *Striptease* had been published recently and had received a great deal of

---

15   C.f. note 27, p. 85.
16   Icchokas Meras and his family emigrated to Israel in 1972.

criticism. Meras then admitted to me that he could feel the "internal censor" taking hold of him, which means death to any artist. Then I asked him whether he was not worried that, by emigrating, he would lose his connection to the language, his creative wellspring, and his readers. We talked for a long time, but Meras had already decided to leave. And he did. In the West, he hoped to find a publisher and the freedom to create.

Sadly, as he wrote to my cousin Margarita in 1972, he quickly realized that it is impossible to make a living from writing in the West. He "consoled himself" with the fact that he had an engineering degree as a fallback and so would not die of starvation.

My prediction, unfortunately, was to some degree fulfilled—even though he wrote *Sara* (1982) and several short stories after he left, it was not the same Meras.

On the other hand, he never really left Lithuania—he wrote only in Lithuanian, represented Lithuania in Israel, and longed for his native Kelmė and Vilnius. He visited Lithuania in 1996, but later became seriously ill and was no longer able to return.

I was very moved by a poem by Meras's cousin, which was shown to me by the writer Vanda Juknaitė, a close friend of Icchokas and his family. I will cite only the last four lines:

> *Does the sun still melt into the Baltic?*
> *Does Ona still reach for the sky?*
> *Tell Lithuania—we long for it.*
> *Tell Lithuania—we will not return.*[17]

I cried when I read those pain-drenched lines . . .

Our conversation about relationships with creative people forces me to return to a question that we already discussed when we were comparing the different feelings of freedom in Soviet-era Vilnius, Moscow, and Leningrad. But this time, I will formulate it completely differently. You have

---

17　Ar dar skęsta saulė Baltijoj? / Ar dar stiebias į dangų Ona? / Pasakykite Lietuva—pasiilgome, / Pasakykite Lietuvai —negrįšime. (Lith.)

mentioned that, to a certain degree, life was freer and better in Lithuania than anywhere else in the Soviet Union at that time, including for Jewish artists. Could you elaborate on that?

What I had in mind was that, immediately after the war, various Stalinist processes—the "Doctors' Plot," the anti-Semitic "Campaign against Cosmopolitanism" and so on—passed through Lithuania more gently. I think that that was largely to Sniečkus's credit.[18] Sniečkus was not an anti-Semite and generally avoided extremes whenever he could.[19] Indeed, Russian intellectuals such as Brodsky viewed Lithuania as a Western nation. We were independent during the interwar period, while Russia, Ukraine, and other republics had been under the yoke of the Soviet Union, of the dictatorship of the Communist Party.

But Lithuania as "the West of the Soviet Union"—was that not a myth? True, we had the Old Town of Vilnius, the coast, and one or two other sites that may have given the impression of a "Western spirit" to a tourist from one of the "brotherly republics." On the other hand, we have spoken a lot about what you saw and read, whom you interacted with in Moscow—how that was on a completely different level.

Yes, I did see, read, and hear many things there. But unfortunately, the Russian intelligentsia was an absolute minority within the Soviet Union. I am very grateful that I had the opportunity to meet and interact with them.

By no means do I want to create the impression that there was more freedom in Lithuania during that time. There was censorship in Lithuania and

---

18 Regarding "Doctors' Plot" and "Campaign against Cosmopolitanism"—c.f note 10, p. 109.

19 Indeed, this anti-Semitic campaign was not as intensive in Lithuania compared to other Soviet republics. On the other hand, Jews in Soviet Lithuania were pushed out of the Party and accused of "conspiracies"; they were mistrusted, their cultural activity and religious practice were limited, and some attacks against Jews who had survived the Holocaust took place in smaller towns, as a result of which there were even debates about concentrating all remaining Jews in Lithuania's largest cities. The Vilnius State Gaon Jewish Museum, founded in 1913 and the only such museum to have existed in the Soviet Union, was closed in 1949. The "gentler" anti-Semitic processes that took place in Soviet Lithuania were less the result of Antanas Sniečkus's or the Lithuanian Communist Party's policies as of an objective fact—that a very small percentage of Lithuanian Jews survived the Holocaust. C.f: Vladas Sirutavičius, Darius Staliūnas, Jurgita Šiaučiūnaitė-Verbickienė, *Lietuvos žydai: istorinė studija* [Lithuania's Jews: An historical study], Vilnius: Baltos Lankos, 2012, 485–507.

there was no way for us to get around it; but sometimes it was more tolerant, in comparison with censorship in Soviet Russia, in its evaluations of cultural phenomena. Besides, as I have already mentioned, we had had two decades of independence before the war, so we had other traditions. And our artists learned the "white poodle rule" very well and applied it expertly.[20]

Indeed, the Estonians were sometimes even more successful than we were in finding some crack through which freedom of thought could find expression. They published Kafka, and their writers—Jaan Kross, Jaan Kaplinksi, Mati Unta, Vaino Vahing, and others—allowed themselves more free rein.[21] While we did not. I don't quite understand why it was like that. Perhaps the Estonian language was less understandable to potential censors, or perhaps it was because we had more communists. But I do know that anyone who says that there was no art or culture in Lithuania during the Soviet period is absolutely wrong. Much was destroyed, but much was also achieved in literature and especially theatre, and in documentary and feature film, music, the visual arts, and photography. After all, it was during the Soviet period that such world-class photographers as Antanas Sutkus, Algimantas Kunčius, Vitas Luckus, and others emerged.

Let us return to someone else you know well—Grigory Kanovich.[22]

Grigory Kanovich is a completely different kind of person than Icchokas Meras. I saw him undergo a complete transformation. At first he was a Soviet screenwriter.[23] I have not read all of his screenplays, but he must have written some good ones, as he was never short of talent, irony, and wit. I know that my hus-

---

20 According to the "white poodle rule," an artist or writer would deliberately include a fragment of "fodder" to feed the Soviet censors, in the hope that the censors would demand that that specific element be changed and that other elements, that were more important to the artist and society, would be allowed to remain.

21 Franz Kafka's *Stories* were published in Soviet Estonia in 1962 and *The Trial* in 1972 (while only in 1981 in Lithuania). Other "oddities" of Soviet Estonian cultural life included the publication of texts by T.S. Eliot, Federico García Lorca, James Joyce, Dylan Thomas, Elias Canetti, and Fernando Pessoa.
Jaan Kross (1920–2007)—writer, most translated Estonian author.
Mati Unt (1944–2005)—writer and theatre director.
Vaino Vahing (1940–2008)—writer and playwright.

22 C.f. note 27, p. 86.

23 Grigory Kanovich worked at the Lithuanian Film Studio 1962–1972.

band wanted to make a film based on Kanovich's screenplay *Svetimas* (The foreigner). It is the story of a German army deserter who finds himself with a Lithuanian peasant family: he gets used to the Lithuanian family and falls in love with a Lithuanian girl, but, when a dangerous situation arises, the family hands him over to the Soviet security forces, because he is a foreigner. The censors immediately forbade Kanovich to present a positive image of a German, so he changed the character into an Austrian.

That theme was very interesting to my husband, who was half Russian, half Estonian and therefore knew what it is like to feel like a foreigner. In Russia he was an Estonian, but in Estonia he was often seen as a Russian. Unfortunately, Moscow forbade my husband from making a film based on Kanovich's screenplay; it was given to another, perhaps less independent, Estonian director.[24]

With time, Kanovich and his writing evolved, and he developed a more authentic voice. His true talent was revealed when he began to explore the Jewish theme and created his series of novels about Lithuania's Jews. I believe that Kanovich immortalised himself as the writer of the Lithuanian Jewish epic. I am happy that there is no hatred in his writing. Kanovich's writing uses a Biblical style and contains plenty of Jewish humour. His narratives are at once local and universal.

I greatly admire Kanovich and his wonderful wife Olga.[25] They are both very sensitive people. Grigory's searching and constant creative growth reflect his inner freedom, his liberation from all fear and violence. But I was probably never as close to him as I was to Icchokas Meras. And although our close connection has broken down, probably because we no longer have the energy to overcome physical distance, I follow his writing and feel that, if he isn't angry with me for some reason, we could at any point resume our friendship.

Sadly, the Kanovich family emigrated in 1993. The writer and his wife settled in Israel, and it seems that they are doing very well there. I am so happy that Grisha has not lost touch with Lithuania—that he keeps up with what is going on here. Differently from Icchokas Meras's case, his creative output did not wane with the move to Israel: he has written two more novels and some interesting critical articles. Kanovich's case is very special and unique: he is a Lithu-

---

24   Reference to Olav Neuland's film *Tuulte pessa* (1979), based on Kanovich's screenplay *Svetimas* [The foreigner].

25   Olga Kanovich—her husband Grigory's first reader and editor of all of his texts.

anian writer living in Israel, who writes about Lithuania's Jews in Russian and is then translated into Lithuanian, Hebrew, and other languages. Kanovich's writing has garnered universal recognition. [26]

Listening to you, I realised that you have not yet mentioned another Lithuanian literary figure with whom you were connected by close friendship. I am thinking about Jurga Ivanauskaitė.[27]

Yes, that is true. My late friendship with Jurga was one of the most profound, painful, and yet deeply enriching—on a spiritual level—experiences I have ever had. I had known Jurga for a long time, but we had never been close. I had been more intimate with her mother, the art historian Ingrida Korsakaitė. From a certain distance, I deeply sympathised with Jurga for the especially complicated relationship she had with her father, the artist Igoris Ivanovas, who essentially abandoned her.

From what I remember, Jurga and I met at the 2002 Frankfurt Book Fair, where she was the centre of attention following the publication of the German translation of her novel *Ragana ir lietus* (The witch and the rain).[28] We met again in early 2003, in Kaunas, when we were both nominated for the Person of Tolerance Award. So we met as "competitors." That time it was I who was given the award, though I had been sure that it would go to her. She had done so much to support the Tibetan cause that I could not compare myself to her. That day, I strongly sensed Jurga's exceptional purity of spirit. She was most sincerely happy for me. I have a lovely photograph of the two of us from that day.

---

26 Theatre critic Rūta Oginskaitė created a portrait of Grigory and Olga Kanovich in her book of conversations *Gib a kuk. Žvilgtelėk. Pokalbiai Olgos ir Grigorijaus Kanovičių namuose* [Gib a kuk. Conversations with Olga and Grigory Kanovich in their home], Vilnius: Tyto Alba, 2017.

27 Jurga Ivanauskaitė (1961–2007)—Lithuanian writer and activist; one of the most popular writers of that period.

28 Lithuania was guest of honour at the 2002 Frankfurt Book Fair. During the fair, Jurga Ivanauskaitė and her work received a great deal of attention, and the first print run of the translation of *Ragana ir lietus* (*Die Regenhexe*, trans. Markus Roduner, Munich: dtv, 2002)(8000 copies) sold out during the few days of the fair.
Ragana ir lietus interweaves three story lines—a contemporary woman's love for a Catholic priest and the stories of a medieval witch and Mary Magdalene. First published in 1993, the novel was the most scandalous of this author's works, inspired anger among some segments of society, and was one of the first bestsellers of the independence period.

In 2005 we both found ourselves at the Gottenburg Book Fair, and I was deeply impressed by Jurga and came to love her.[29] She was the "star" of that fair. We spoke a great deal and felt a keen spiritual connection. Jurga was already suffering from pain in her leg. I felt terribly sorry for her, and when I later learned the cause of that pain—a very aggressive, life-threatening form of cancer—I was devastated. I wanted to help her, to try to save her, to be closer to her. That was when our true friendship and correspondence began. I began to read her books more closely and was stunned by her premonitions of death; I was moved by her expressions of loneliness, her longing for her real father and for true love, and much more . . . I was especially intrigued by her paintings, and deeply admired her physical and inner beauty. She was searching for both love and God, and I found that tremendously moving. Jurga simply became the dominating presence in my life.

After the Gottenburg fair, Jurga had planned to travel to Jerusalem, but when she learned that she was very ill, she was forced to give up her trip to the "Eternal City." Instead of going to Jerusalem, she found herself on an operating table in Sweden. Let me read to you what I wrote about this wonderful woman following her death, for the commemorative book *Jurga*: "There, in Sweden, she waged an inconceivably difficult battle with an incurable illness. Through her mother Ingrida, I sent Jurga a small, gold-colored stone from Jerusalem, as a talisman. To the end of her life, Jurga kept that little stone close by her as a sign of hope. In a postcard to me she wrote: 'Dear Irena, every morning and every evening I pray to Faith, Hope, Love, and, most importantly, to Life, with your little gold-colored stone from Jerusalem in my hand . . .'"[30]

Many years have gone by, but I still cannot come to terms with Jurga's death. I deeply wished for her memory to be preserved, that her unique apartment (in an Art Nouveau building on Šaltinių Street), full of her drawings, paintings, photographs and books, be preserved. For more than five years I was a member of the Jurga Ivanauskaitė Heritage Committee together with the artist Ramunė Valiuvienė, the journalist Ramunė Sakalauskaitė, the cultural historian Vytautas Rubavičius, the television host Edita Mildažytė, the director of Jurga's publisher, Tyto Alba, Lolita Varanavičienė, the orientalist Vytis

---

29   The Swedish translation of Jurga Ivanauskaitė's *Ragana ir lietus* (*Häxan och regnet*, trans. Jonas Öhman, Stockholm: Tranan, 2005) was presented at the 2005 Gothenburg Book Fair.

30   *Jurga: Atsiminimai, pokalbiai, laiškai* [Jurga: Memories, conversations, letters], ed. Dovilė Zelčiūtė, Vilnius: Tyto alba, 2008.

Vidūnas, and, most importantly, her mother, Ingrida Korsakaitė, and her sister, Radvilė Racenaitė.

Thanks to the intense efforts of the Heritage Committee, in particular Ramunė Sakalauskaitė and Lolita Varanavičienė, it was possible to publish Jurga's final books and a book of recollections, to erect a monument to her cat in Aguonų Square, to organise exhibitions of her works, to found a literary prize in her name, and more.[31] Thanks to her family's efforts, her unique, museum-worthy apartment has been preserved.

I believe that Jurga will never be forgotten.

I would like to believe that too. But constant effort is needed if we are to prevent important things from slipping into the twilight of forgetting. I, too, see our conversations as a form of resistance against forgetting. So we should remember one more individual who had a remarkable fate, and with whom you were connected by many years of friendship—Ugnė Karvelis.

I first saw Ugnė Karvelis in 1979, during the "East-West" festival in Die, to which I had travelled together with about 80 people from Lithuania: writers, literary scholars, actors, agronomists, farmers, and others.[32] A very elegant woman came from Paris to visit us. As soon as I saw Ugnė Karvelis, it was clear that she was an exceptional person. She was already a recognised diplomat, cultural activist, translator, and the Republic of Lithuania's special and commissioned ambassador to UNESCO.[33] That time I did not even dare to approach her; she was the focus of the Die participants' attention and, unfortunately, did not stay for very long. Quite some years later, I believe in 1998 (but am not sure of the exact date), we met in Vilnius and our friendship began. We were both surprised to discover that we had the same views of many things and had shared values, except that Ugnė was more experienced and connected to European culture. She loved Lithuania but at the same time she was a citizen of the world; she had little patience for provincial thinking or any kind of nationalism. Her friend, the

---

31   Sculptor of the monument—Ksenija Jaroševaitė.
32   Fr. Festival Est–Ouest—annual festival of East European culture, held in Die, France.
33   Ugnė Karvelis (1935–2002)—temporary chargé d'affaires of the Republic of Lithuania (1993–1995), Lithuanian ambassador to UNESCO (1995–2002), from 2000 appointed a member of the Intangible and Oral Cultural Heritage Commission.

artist Antanas Mončys said that she was always seeking the impossible, breaking down stereotypes, that she operated very independently, sometimes like a playful colt. But at the same time, in the artist's words, "she was a queen"—both in her life and when dying from an incurable disease.[34] We developed projects together. I wanted the Open Lithuania Foundation to organise an event with Ugnė on the theme "Returning Without Returning," but we kept postponing it because she was always so busy, and then because of her illness. She called me as soon as she learned that she had cancer. Ugnė remained composed and immediately began to wonder who could replace her, though it seemed to me that she was irreplaceable. Individuals of Ugnė's calibre are born only rarely. Eventually, I drew her attention to Ina Marčiulionytė, whom she knew, respected and trusted, and Ugnė finally named Ina as her successor. She worked until she took her last breath. I deeply admired Ugnė and learned a great deal from her. I simply cannot convey how important and impressive a person she was.[35]

I was very close to Ugnė during her illness, if not physically, then spiritually. She told me a great deal about her life, about the love of her life—the writer Julio Cortázar—and about her son, Christophe Thierry Pierre.[36] She often remembered her childhood and her birthplace, the town of Noreikiškės in Kaunas Region. Up to her last breath, she was full of plans and ideas. Already very weak, she longed for Latin America and ignored her doctors' orders by traveling to Brazil. That was her last journey. She told me that she would leave this life when she became a complete invalid. That day came. In early morning on March 4, 2002.

Ugnė was not religious and did not want any kind of church ceremony. Before passing away, she invited her closest friends, including the writer Valdas Papievis, the violinist Martynas Švėgžda von Bekker, and others.

The table was laid as it always was. Martynas played and Ugnė wrote her

---

34 Antanas Mončys (1921–1993)—Lithuanian sculptor, lived in Paris from 1950.

35 During Karvelis's tenure at UNESCO, the Neringa Peninsula, the Old Town of Vilnius, and Lithuanian iron cross art were included in UNESCO's world heritage list. Karvelis initiated many projects that were very important to Lithuania, including the establishment of a UNESCO Cultural Management and Cultural Policy department at Vilnius Art Academy, the M. K. Čiurlionis exhibition in Paris (2000), and the international conference "Dialogue Between Civilisations" (Vilnius, 2001).

36 Ugnė Karvelis worked at Éditions Gallimard 1959–1983, where for a long time she was in charge of its department of Latin American, Spanish, Portuguese and East European Literature. This work led her to meet Julio Cortázar, who became her partner.

farewell letter, which was addressed to me as well. I have it here and would like to quote from it: "To all of you sitting on the other side of the oxygen tank, I send very many good wishes and happy thoughts. Every day this hemisphere wanes, it wanes and runs out." These words were not written in her hand, but after them, with trembling fingers, she wrote the names of the nine people, including Asta, Ina, Valdas and myself, to whom it was addressed. And below that, in her barely legible hand, she wrote: "I think of you all devotedly and hope that we will meet again. I embrace you, Ugnė."

When Ugnė became too tired they helped her into bed and she left us.

Following Ugnė's last wishes, her son, alone, scattered her ashes into the Baltic Sea.

We usually meet to talk in the mornings. In the past, our conversations were often interrupted by one phone call—your friend Dalia Sruogaitė would call you, or you yourself would remember, "We haven't spoken yet today," and would dial her number.[37]

Yes, even though a year has passed since Dalia's death, I still miss those phone calls and almost daily letters.

We shared experiences, political and cultural news, and our aches and pains for close to fifteen years—from the time that Dalia and her daughter came to Lithuania. Sadly, Dalia, who was a very active and creative person and a dedicated member of Santara Šviesa, returned to her homeland a bit too late, when her physical strength was already waning, and there remained very little time to adapt and be active in her new surroundings. Dalia was disappointed by many things in her homeland, in particular our political life. She felt lonely, as though her friends had abandoned her; in around 2012, she wrote that she was entering a depression and was missing America, where most of her friends and associates remained. She found some comfort in her cats, Opus and Lapu, she liked to feed the birds, enjoyed the flowers on her balcony, and read a lot. While weakening physically, she retained her perfect memory and sharp mind to her final days.

---

37 Dalia Sruogaitė-Bylaitienė (1925–2015)—theatre critic, social figure.

Indeed, during those years Dalia managed to accomplish a great deal: she published an excellent memoir, which she had long debated writing.[38] Dalia gave me the manuscript to read and I succeeded in convincing her that it was a truly talented and interesting text. By the time it had to be proofread, she had some difficulty, but still managed to finish it. Dalia was very concerned about her father, Balys Sruoga's, legacy.[39] She never called him "Father"—only "Balys." They were friends. It especially angered her when Balys and the others who had been arrested with him were referred to as "Stutthof prisoners." They were hostages, Dalia argued, and insisted that they be referred to as such. Dalia was actively involved in the Sruoga Museum in Kaunas and the opening of the Sruoga room in the Mykolaitis-Putinas Memorial Apartment-Museum in Vilnius. She also worked on the extensive archive that she had brought with her from America and later donated to the museums.

Her closest friends in Lithuania were the writer Vanda Juknaitė, Mrs. Ladigienė's daughter Jonė Ardžiūnienė, Romas and Emilija Sakadolskis, the literary scholar Dalia Kuizinienė, and the editor Donata Linčiuvienė.[40] To the very end, she was cared for by her beloved daughter, Aušrinė Byla. More than once, Dalia wrote to me that she did not want to burden her daughter. She would often say that old age was the most terrible nonsense and that she hoped to end her days with as much dignity as possible.

She also often said that meeting me had been a real blessing to her. I was delighted to hear that, of course, and have to say that I too considered our late, but still lengthy, friendship to be a great, invaluable gift of fate.

During one of our meetings you mentioned that we should also speak about several other writers you knew—those from outside the Lithuanian cultural sphere.

My life has been enriched by friendships with many wonderful writers. I have talked about these contacts many times in the past, but in speaking with you

---

38 Dalia Sruogaitė, *Atminties archeologija* [The archeology of memory], Vilnius: Lithuanian Literature and Folklore Institute, 2012.

39 C.f. note 29, p. 142.

40 Romualdas (Romas) Sakadolskis (1947–2016)—American-Lithuanian journalist. Emilija Pakštaitė-Sakadolskienė—musicologist, pedagogue.

and trying to answer your very interesting, and never banal, questions, I now see that it is impossible to convey the whole of a life, even one's own.

Today, I will try to tell you about some of the writers I have been close to. For example, the Russian poet Nikolai Panchenko.[41] I felt a very strong spiritual connection with him and we stayed in touch right up to the end of his life. I deeply admired his inner freedom, nobility, and capacity for empathy. During the Second World War, Nikolai served in the Soviet army and, just imagine, already in 1944 wrote "Ballad for a Broken Heart," in which he states that in shooting at others, even at enemies, you also kill yourself.[42]

And I must say a few words about my friend Aleksandr Volodin.[43] He was an extremely modest and sensitive person. Aleksandr once told me that, while still a student, he knew he wanted to be a writer, and was always looking for interesting material. So he tried to get to know famous, interesting people, to go everywhere, but nothing came of it. Then it occurred to him that if he found other people's stories interesting, perhaps others might find him interesting as well. When he began to write about and through himself he finally became Volodin. I will never forget Aleksandr's story about how, exhausted from all the attention, he disconnected his phone and lived like that for two months. But eventually he so longed to hear another human voice that he answered a random phone call and was thrilled to spend the longest time chatting with someone he did not even know. Then he once again disconnected his phone. If I'm not mistaken, he even wrote a short story about the experience.

I usually met people like Nikolai or Aleksandr through my cousin Alexander Shtromas or my friends the Ottens.

It was Aliukas who introduced me to Aleksandr Galich, who was a very well known and recognized Soviet Russian screenwriter, though later he became even better known as a songwriter and singer.[44] As a bard, he succeeded in revealing the absurdity and criminality of everyday reality in the Soviet system with great depth, emotion, a fantastic sense of humour and irony. He would sing in private homes—at friends' homes that were gathering places for dissidents, members of the Moscow intelligentsia, and like-minded people.

---

41   Nikolai Panchenko (Rus. Николай Панченко, 1925–2005)—poet and editor.

42   Rus. "Баллада о расстрелянном сердце."

43   Aleksandr Volodin (Rus. Александр Моисеевич Володин, 1919–2001) —playwright, screenwriter, and poet.

44   C.f. note 28, p. 118.

Irena Veisaitė's second husband, Grigori Kromanov. Russian Drama Theatre, Tallinn, 1982.

My husband organised a Galich concert in Estonia, which was a very daring thing to do—Galich was not very well liked by the Soviet authorities, to put it mildly. I had many conversations with Galich, mostly at the kinds of above-mentioned gatherings of the Moscow intelligentsia. He created a very special atmosphere with his songs—one felt spiritually exalted, a type of refreshment of the soul that it may only be possible to experience while living in a totalitarian regime.

Having mentioned my husband Grigori, I must say that I met some very interesting people, who fundamentally enriched my life, thanks to him.

Did you perhaps have the opportunity to get to know another famous bard—Bulat Okudzhava?

I knew of Bulat Okudzhava and heard him sing, but never knew him personally nor even met him. His songs appeared earlier than Galich's and were a kind of liberation from Soviet marches and the pomp of Socialist Realism.[45] Okudzhava sang not about the homeland or the Party but about simple, human matters. To this day, I like him very much and often listen to his songs. They introduced an intimacy, they spoke to you and about you.

Just being and remaining human was in itself a heroic endeavour during the Soviet period.

---

45 Bulat Okudzhava—(Rus. Булат Окуджава, 1924–1997)—poet, singer, writer and screenwriter.

I would guess that, of the three we have mentioned, another bard, Vlad-
imir Vysotsky, would have been the least close to your heart in his themes
and expression?[46],

I would not say that Vysotsky was the least close to my heart. His hoarse voice
and temperamental performance style were very appealing to me. I also knew
and very much admired him as an actor.

I will never forget his performance as Hamlet in a 1971 production directed by Yuri Liubimov at the Taganka Theatre. Vysotsky gave a tragic, brilliant
performance—from the very first scene, in which he came onto the prosceni-
um with a guitar and stood by the grave pit reading Boris Pasternak's poem
"Hamlet" [1946]:

> *The din dies down. I enter from the wings.*
> *Leaning inside the doorway to the stage,*
> *I try and catch an echo in the distance,*
> *A sense of what shall happen in my age.[47]*

From the very beginning, it was clear that, in rotten Denmark, Hamlet was
doomed to die. And the audience members all understood clearly that the play
was not referring to Denmark but the Soviet Union.

Vladimir Vysotsky's Hamlet and Liubimov's production as a whole were
very relevant to us at the time. It was a play about *us*.

I also saw Vysotsky perform in a production of Bertold Brecht's play *The
Good Person of Szechwan* [1964].[48] It is a brilliant play, one of Brecht's best, about
how it is almost impossible to live in an exploitative society and remain a good,
moral person. Although the play was purportedly speaking about capitalist society, it was clear to everyone what Liubimov was trying to say. As in *Hamlet*,
Vysotsky also appeared with a guitar on stage and sang.

I especially admired Vysotsky's protest, courage, how he spoke the truth,

---

46 Vladimir Vysotsky (Rus. Владимир Высоцкий, 1938–1980)—poet, singer, film and theatre actor.
    One of the most popular bards in the Soviet Union.
47 Гул затих. Я вышел на подмостки. / Прислонясь к дверному косяку, / Я ловлю в далеком
    отголоске, / Что случится на моем веку. (Rus.) [Eng. trans. A.Z Foreman].
48 Vysotsky only played the role of Yang Sun from 1969.

and also, if you will, his manliness. Those qualities were very rare at the time and so all the more valuable. I believe that Vysotsky had a very sensitive soul, and it is sad that he abused alcohol and so destroyed himself. But I'm afraid that I did not know him personally.

We started talking about bards and it seems we strayed from the theme of your friendships with writers . . .

I have a very close friendship with the highly sensitive and subtle German writer Ulla Lachauer. I believe that we met in Nida, at Thomas Mann's summerhouse, through Ruth Kibelka-Leiserowitz, who is currently the chair of the Thomas Mann Cultural Centre's curatorial committee. We had many common interests. Ulla suffered deeply over the crimes of the Nazis and was interested in the tragedy and fate of the Jews as well as in Russian history, Prussia, the fate of Germans in Lithuania and Siberia, and of Germans in Kazakhstan. She has written many books and is a well-known documentary filmmaker. She is a true voice of the German conscience. She sought resolution to the problems of her era through the destinies of specific people. When we met, she had just finished writing her documentary story "Paradise Street," about Lena Grigoleit, an East Prussian farmer of German descent.[49] Lena had married a Lithuanian and stayed in Lithuania, was deported to Siberia and later returned to Soviet Lithuania, where she gave birth to and raised two daughters, to whom Ulla introduced me. Ulla lived for quite some time in Lena's farmstead where they worked together and had many conversations. That was Ulla's creative method—deeply authentic, convincing, moving. "Paradise Street" tells us about the intersection of two, even three cultures during the twentieth century—Lithuanian, German, and Russian. The story raises questions of identity and is impressive for its representation of Lena's incredibly strong, principled, and unshakeable personality.

My friendship with Ulla is very dear to me and we still correspond. Distance and time, and perhaps age also, have their effect. The connection is there but it weakens and gradually becomes part of the past, only to once again be renewed.

---

49 *Paradiesstraße. Lebenserinnerungen der ostpreußischen Bäuerin Lena Grigoleit* [Paradise street: Memories of a farmer, Lena Grigoleit] Rowohlt: Reinbek bei Hamburg, 1996.

Since you mentioned that you met Ulla at the Thomas Mann Festival,
perhaps this is an opportunity to ask you to speak about how that unique
event, and the Thomas Mann Cultural Centre, came to be.

Thomas Mann and the Thomas Mann Centre are very important and dear to me.

I heard this writer's name mentioned often, and with the deepest respect, in my parents' house, and that kind of thing stays in the memory. The German versions of his books stood in my parents' library, though of course I did not read them at that time.

After the war, as a student of German literature, I learned of the lives and work of Thomas Mann, his children, and his brother Heinrich Mann in more detail. Mann's first, almost biographical novel, *Buddenbrooks*, for which he won the Nobel Prize in 1929, was especially interesting to me. It was from the funds that Mann received for the prize that he built himself a fisherman's-style summerhouse in Nida.

I was also very interested in the shifts in Mann's views: his stance, writing, and activities under the Nazi dictatorship; after emigration; and when he decided to never again return to his homeland after the war.

After Lithuania's independence was restored and when it was discovered that Thomas Mann's summerhouse was still standing (if a little worn down) on the shores of the Curonian Lagoon, the idea of establishing a Thomas Mann cultural centre naturally began to circulate. Among the most active people in this discussion were the historian Alvydas Nikžentaitis; then Vice Minister of Culture Vytautas Balčiūnas; the musicologist Onutė Narbutienė; and Vitalija Jonušienė, a teacher living in Nida. Ruth Kibelka-Leiserowitz, then a young historian of East Prussian descent who knew Lithuanian and other Eastern European languages, was very active in developing the centre's program and became its first director.

We received considerable support from Dietmar Albrecht, a historian at the Baltic Academy in Lübeck. We collaborated actively with East Prussia historian Professor Robert Traba and with well-known German historian Joachim Tauber, who even learned Lithuanian.

There were no doubts in my own mind that the centre would attract interest and activity. But there were many who thought differently and worried about "rich Germans" returning and buying up land and buildings in the Klaipėda area and "taking over" the region, in particular Nida and Klaipėda.

Finally, in 1995, renovations of Thomas Mann's summerhouse were completed and the Thomas Mann Cultural Centre was opened. All events there are held in two languages—Lithuanian and German. The annual Thomas Mann Festival attracts more and more guests to Nida each year. Our hopes were clearly fulfilled.

You attend the Thomas Mann Festival, which takes place in mid-July, every year. Have you established this tradition because the festival happens in a beautiful setting and at a nice time of the year? Or should we say, rather, that it not only offers the possibility of combining rest with intellectual activity, but is also unique in the context of other related events?

I can answer this question without hesitation: I attend the Thomas Mann Festival every year because it is a unique event and we created it ourselves after a long search for the appropriate format. The beautiful landscape of Nida and the pleasant time of the year—the third week of July—are just nice additions. The current festival combines several programs: music, talks, art exhibitions, and film screenings. All of these programs are in one way or another related to Thomas Mann's biography and writing, his family history, his worldview and values, as well as the period in which he lived. It is a small, "chamber" festival (and thank God for that, because Nida and the unique Neringa landscape are not suited to mass events and would quickly be damaged by them)—an elite event that attracts regular visitors from Lithuania, Germany, and other countries. Each year it attracts more and more young people. If I am not mistaken, the twenty-third Thomas Mann Festival took place in 2019.

※

I Regret Nothing, But I Continue to Pay Dearly for My Decisions

Irena Veisaitė and her daughter Alina. Vilnius, c. 1958.

Today I would like to shift to more personal themes . . . How and when did you meet your first husband? How long did your first marriage last?

I met my first husband at the Moscow University library, when I was in my fourth year. At the time, I was writing an essay about Heinrich Heine. Since my youth I have had the habit of taking a nap in the afternoon, and I used to do that in the library. I would lay my head on my books and doze for about twenty minutes. One of those times, I woke to find the following note: *Ваш Гейне скучает по Вас*!—"Your Heine longs for you!" Surprised, I looked around me and saw Yasha, my future husband.[1]

He was from Moscow and was studying economics. He was one year ahead of me and was a veteran of the Second World War: he had been conscripted as soon as he finished school, in 1939, and had served for six years, almost his entire youth . . . We became friends quite quickly and found we had much to talk about. I was deeply moved by his tales of life on the front. Imagine, of all of his classmates, he was the only one to survive the war! In his old age he finally wrote a memoir about his experiences during the Second World War.[2]

Yasha turned out to be a very attentive, caring person, I would even say something of a father figure. We were married in 1952. He knew that I wanted to return to Lithuania so he found a job in Vilnius, and a year later I finished my studies and also returned home. Our daughter Alina was born in 1955.

---

1   Jakov (Yasha) Boom.
2   Jakov Boom left his memoir, dedicated to his grandchildren, in manuscript form, in three notebooks that are in Alina Boom's personal archive.

Jakov Boom, Alina Boom, and Irena Veisaitė, c. 1960.

What were the most important experiences that stayed with you from your first marriage?

We lived together very nicely for twenty years. And although we divorced, we remained friends until his death in 2012. I believe that, for a marriage to be successful, the couple must have common tastes, interests and values, and that both partners must respect, not stifle one another—so that each may flourish rather than feel that his or her freedom is limited. In a marriage it is also important to maintain a dynamic relationship and not to give into routine and domesticity.

I am grateful to my first husband for a great deal, and I respect him. He always supported me and never shirked the domestic duties that can take up so much time, especially for a woman. I believe that it was diverging interests that caused a distance to grow between us. Yasha never learned Lithuanian and could not actively participate in my intellectual and cultural life. As a result, a certain kind of emptiness began to grow between us . . .

Your first marriage, the birth of your daughter, your dissertation . . . You have suggested that starting a family presented you with a considerable challenge, which was perhaps resolved by your decision to pursue doctoral studies in Leningrad. How did you—a person of books and ideas—man-

age to reconcile family, intellectual pursuits, and intense involvement in cultural life?

These things are not so difficult to reconcile, especially if one has the support of the people around one. People are multifaceted, after all.

Tell me about your decision to stay in Lithuania when your daughter was planning to emigrate.

Oh, that was one of the most painful decisions I made in my life . . .

My daughter emigrated from the Soviet Union in 1974. While in school, she had not joined the Communist Youth League, though I had encouraged her to do so. "It's your ticket to university," I told her at the time. But Alina did not want to make compromises, to go against her conscience, to lie or swear that she would "loyally serve the ideals of the Communist Party." To this day I deeply respect her for that.

Alina was a student at Salomėja Nėris High School, was at the top of her class and had straight "fives." She was a candidate for a gold medal, but did not receive one. In her final year, she suddenly received grades of "four" for the subjects of history and the constitution. My daughter is not excessively ambitious, and I would even say that she could use more of that, but that time it seemed to me that she was quite hurt by this blatant injustice.

Alina had planned to go to university after high school, but she eventually decided to leave Soviet Lithuania . . . At the time, I was already divorced from her father, who also wanted to emigrate.

In speaking with Alina about her future I made an enormous mistake—one which cost me a great deal. But looking at it from today's perspective, one could say that everything turned out well in the end.

What mistake did you make?

I asked Alina if she would leave Lithuania even if I decided to stay. She answered that she would. I have to admit that I had not expected her to say that. For various reasons I did not want to leave Lithuania. Of course, I would not have sacrificed Alina's future for my own interests, but when I heard her answer—that she would leave without me—it occurred to me that perhaps it was not neces-sary for me to leave.

I made a second, equally big mistake during that conversation with my daughter. When I learned about her decision, I said: "If you have decided to leave, you should not begin your university studies, because you would be taking a place away from someone else." Alina listened to me and did not apply. But it is entirely possible that, during that first year of her studies, she might have de-cided to stay after all. And when she gave up the opportunity to study, she had nothing to do. What could she do? . . . She began to audit some lectures at the Pedagogical Institute, but that was not the same as full-time studies.

We went through a very difficult period . . . Eventually, I made the decision to leave with Alina and began to organise the paperwork. Not surprisingly, I soon encountered various problems. As soon as the rumour that I was planning to emigrate began to circulate, all of my articles in a planned textbook on for-eign literature were thrown out. I avoided seeing certain people in case they were labelled anti-Soviet. For that reason I did not contact Sniečkus, who undoubt-edly could have helped me to resolve certain artificially created challenges. But Sniečkus himself wrote me a letter in which he said: "If you truly wish to go and live near your father, I will let you leave and, as long as I am alive, you will always be able to return to Lithuania. You are not Alexander Shtromas (at the time they were not communicating at all). But if you want to go to Israel, our rela-tions will cease, because that state is our enemy."[3] I am quoting from memory . . .

I prepared the extensive documentation necessary for emigration and Alina, her father, and I went to the OVIR office at the end of Gediminas Pros-pect. OVIR stood for *Отдел виз и регистрации*, or "Visa and Registration Department."

On the way to the OVIR office I began to feel ill—I began to shake and my head was spinning . . . It was clear that I was making a decision that went against my will. Yasha was a very noble person. Seeing how I was suffering, he said that he did not want me to pay such a high price by emigrating. So that time, we did not take over our documents, and Alina and her father submitted theirs later. They left Lithuania in May 1974. I remained. .

---

3   The mass emigration of Jews from the USSR occurred most intensively in 1969–1973. Soviet laws only permitted such emigration based on the principle of family reunification.

So it was a very difficult decision?

On the one hand, it was a difficult decision, but on the other hand there was simply no other way that I could have behaved. To this day, I feel some kind of magical force connecting me to this land. It is the only place where I feel at home, though I will not hide that there is much that I do not like, and that it is sometimes very painful. But this place is mine. This is where my life is, where my friends and graves are. Besides, I twice witnessed situations in which someone I knew lost a great deal by leaving the country. I believe that Icchokas Meras made such a decision and perhaps Jonas Jurašas as well. We have already spoken about this, but this theme is so important to me that I am returning to it again. As I have already described, both Meras's and Jurašas's professional lives broke off just when they were at the height of their creativity. On the other hand, a person has to leave if they feel they can't breathe. Meras was suffocating from an increasingly oppressive "internal censor," while Jurašas was no longer able to work in the theatre. I had never felt that same kind of oppression. On the contrary, I felt that my word could only mean something if spoken in my native land. It seemed that it was only by staying in Lithuania that I could be useful and find meaning in my existence. I have been, and continue to be, pained by the antagonism between the Lithuanians and the Jews, because I myself am an "authentic" Litvak, i.e., a Lithuanian Jew, or, if you will, a Lithuanian of Jewish ethnicity. Both of those cultures are alive in me. I am speaking first of all about mentality. If I could, with love, help to overcome this antagonism and contribute to the country's Europeanization, then that was probably the most important reason why it was worth staying in my own land.

There were also some very personal reasons that prevented me from emigrating.

I have no regrets, but the cost of my decisions was, and continues to be very high . . . Now that old age has finally caught up with me, I am living far away from my beloved, only daughter, from my beloved grandsons . . .

Perhaps, then, we should move on to how you met your second husband and the "Estonian" period in your life?

Estonia was an enormous turning point in my life—in both practical and spiritual terms. As I explained earlier, I first went there quite accidentally, to the pre-

miere of Grigori Kromanov's production of Kazys Saja's play *Šventežeris*. I liked
the production very much; it seemed to me that the Estonian director grasped
and conveyed the essence of the play perfectly, much as I understood it. After
the performance, we were invited to meet with him at a nightclub. While in
Tallinn I had already arranged to visit the Kamusher family (during the Stalinist era they had lived in Vilnius to avoid deportation, and after their return to
Tallinn, we had maintained close and friendly relations). Grigori accompanied
me to their home and said that he would be expecting me at the nightclub at
10:30 pm. I danced through the night with Kazys and Grigori alternately. At the
end of the night, Grigori would not let me go and we danced the last dance. It
was very hard to say goodbye . . . That heaviness was still with me in the morning, when I got on the plane, and by the transfer in Riga I understood that I
was in love. We began to correspond. I wrote a short review of his production
of Kazys's play and eventually we met in Moscow, where we both understood
that something momentous had happened between us.[4] But it seemed that it
would be impossible for either of us to change anything in our lives: we were
both around forty, had families and jobs, and were intensely involved in our cultural worlds. He did not speak Lithuanian and I knew no Estonian. After a year,
we attempted to separate, but to no avail. That was when I understood that no
obstacles or barriers can stand in the way of true love. Eventually, we decided to
live together. My first husband, whom I respected and admired, left for Great
Britain together with our daughter. Grigori left his family.

It was all very difficult—but at the same time it was probably the happiest
period of my life . . .

We travelled constantly, one or the other of us going from Tallinn to Vilnius or from Vilnius to Tallinn. We were together—we worked together, dreamt
together, and felt as though we were on a higher spiritual plane. I became friends
with Grigori's former wife and their children and he came to love my daughter Alina. At first it was very difficult, because I did not understand a word of
Estonian, and the Estonians did not like to speak Russian; Grisha did not understand Lithuanian, so in Lithuania I was his simultaneous translator. New
worlds opened up to each of us. The Estonians accepted me very warmly and

---

4   Irena Veisaitė, "Rūstus optimizmas" [Measured optimism], *Literatūra ir menas*, May 29, 1971, 11. C.f.:
     "Voices from the Past" section, p. 306.

I never felt any hostility. Quite to the contrary. I became acquainted with Estonian culture—reading Tammsaare's five-volume work helped me to understand the Estonians' character and history, their relationships to the land, to nature, to people.[5]

I can so well remember how, driving from Tallinn to Vilnius, or the reverse, we would often stop in the town of Velžys for a short visit and chat with my friends Stasė and Benediktas Valeckas. Mrs. Stasė would not let us leave without a cornucopia of treasures from her orchard and garden. When we spent holidays in Lahe, in the former summer residence for Lithuanian theatre workers, we always tried to visit our close friend, the famous Estonian composer Arvo Pärt's mother, who lived in the town of Rakvere. As we left, she, just like Mrs. Stasė, would present us with a gift from her garden: a little bouquet of parsley, dill, or something like that. It was always a very small, more symbolic amount, but it was exactly the same feeling that Mrs. Stasė conveyed—it contained just as much warmth. Estonians have a different relationship to the land—our land is more generous, while the Estonians' is less fertile. That was when I understood that Estonians are beautiful, generous people; because of their living conditions, they simply express it differently from Lithuanians. I somehow managed to overcome the barrier of the Estonians' characteristic reserve, though sometimes it took a stiff drink. Gradually, the Estonian mentality became understandable and familiar to me.

I also found 1970s Estonian theatre, directors, and actors fascinating.[6] I was fortunate to meet most of the key figures of Estonian theatre of the period. I also became familiar with Estonian cinema, as my husband was considered one of the best Estonian film directors; his films were well known and successful even beyond Estonia's borders. To this day, his film *The Last Relic* is a cult classic; in 1971 it was sold to over sixty countries.[7] I participated in some of his final film projects, and was even assistant director on one of them, *Dead*

---

5   Anton Hansen Tammsaare's novel *Tõde ja õigus* [Truth and justice, Est. 1926–1933; Lith. 2009], which presents a broad picture of Estonian country and city life at the turn of the twentieth century, is often referred to as Estonia's epic.

6   For more about Estonia during that period, c.f.: Irena Veisaitė, "Ieškojimų kelyje" [The path pf discovery] *Literatūra ir menas*, April 4, 1977, 9; April 16, 1977, 10; April 23, 1977, 11.

7   *The Last Relic* (Est. *Viimne reliikvia*, Tallinnfilm, 1975)—historical adventure film based on a novel by Estonian writer Eduard Bornhöhe, set during the sixteenth century Livonian War. In 1971 the film was seen by 44.9 million viewers in the Soviet Union.

Mountaineer's Hotel.[8] For one year I worked in Estonia, on unpaid leave from the Pedagogical Institute.

One of the greatest gifts that fate gave us was our close friendship with the composer Arvo Pärt and his wife Nora. For a year we lived with them in their apartment in Tallinn. During that period I became acquainted with Estonia's leading cultural figures; I became friends with my colleagues, the film critics Lea Tormis, Ivika Sillart, Lilian Vellerand, Kajlu Haanu; and became very close with Grisha's colleagues from Tallinnfilm, in particular Raimond Feld, who produced all of his films.

I'm very happy that I managed to learn some Estonian; I certainly never mastered that difficult language, but could at least understand what was being spoken about.

I would like to clarify one detail: you were working at the Pedagogical Institute and your husband was staging plays in Estonia, so did you only meet on weekends?

It wasn't quite like that. For one year, as I mentioned, I worked in Estonia. The Estonians even offered me a longer-term position, but I could not give up my work at the Pedagogical Institute. But we had a "Zhiguli" car, with which I drove to Tallinn, sometimes even twice a week. And when Grisha did not have to be in Estonia to work—if, for example, he was writing a script or screenplay— he would come to Vilnius to be with me. But, sadly, he was often ill; he had serious heart problems and medicine was not as advanced as it is now, so he spent quite a lot of time in hospitals in both Vilnius and Tallinn.

Grisha wanted to, and tried to, live and work in Lithuania. We truly made every effort so that he might establish himself here, make films and direct movies. He even began rehearsals at the Russian Drama Theatre with the famous, very nuanced actress Valentina Motovilova as the lead in William Luce's *The Belle of Amherst*, a play about the famous American poet Emily Dickinson.[9] He was also thinking about mounting a production of Goethe's *Iphigenia*, and had other ideas, but soon the rumours began to fly that he was only there so that I

---

8   See note 25, p. 196.
9   Orig. *The Belle of Amherst*, 1976.

Irena Veisaitė and Grigori Kromanov. Nida, c. 1972.

could take him with me to the West. Indeed, there were similar rumours around my friendships with Jurašas and Saja. It is therefore not surprising that, in the end, my husband did not find work in Lithuania. In Estonia, on the other hand, he was revered; that was where he had invested all of his efforts. And I was afraid that if I gave up my position in Lithuania, it may be difficult to find another one. As it was, the authorities at the Institute did not like me very much; I did not have a very good reputation with the nomenklatura types.

That question of where to live was probably the only one that we never resolved. We were both too entrenched in and connected to our own country's cultures. For myself, I would probably have made the move to Estonia. I had learned the language, so I would have found something to do. The Estonians offered me all sorts of work, probably hoping to keep Kromanov there, but I knew perfectly well that my husband's health was very poor, that he would not be able to work much. So what would we have lived on while I learned Estonian and tried to establish myself in a foreign country?

Despite all of the difficulties and problems, our life was very interesting. We created together. Of course, Grisha was the main creator, but many of his ideas were born during our conversations. I helped him to rewrite scenarios, to select actors. I had qualities that he lacked, and he had qualities that I needed, so we complemented one another beautifully. We were both truly happy . . .

That constant travelling to see one another—it sounds like a Soviet version of the American lifestyle . . .

I have to admit that those trips were also quite tiring. When we drove together, the time naturally went by faster. I would drive and he would read me books or interesting articles. We would stop to rest in beautiful places where we could soak up nature. But I often had to drive by myself. In 1982, Grigori had a serious heart attack. I was told that he was in a very serious condition. I rushed to get to Estonia, and while on the bus I did not even know if I would find him alive . . . But I did!

I brought him to cardiologists here as well. Before that 1982 heart attack he had been offered the option of surgery, but by then it was too risky. An actor he knew had recently died on the operating table, so we were not, in the end, ready to take the risk. And after the heart attack he was no longer offered that option. So there was no solution . . . But still we tried, we did what we could. Grisha badly wanted to make a film based on Jaan Kross's *The Tsar's Madman* and had written a scenario, but Moscow did not let him pursue the idea; he did not have a good name with the authorities there and was considered ideologically unreliable.[10]

In 1984 Grigori was invited to teach at the Tallin Conservatory. He was an excellent, respected, and well-loved teacher, but it is difficult work that takes strong nerves. I knew that he should not take on such responsibilities, but was not able to persuade him to give it up. After the final exams, we once again went to Lahe for a holiday, to the same Theatre Union resort. On the third day of our holiday, as I was picking berries and he, mushrooms, a dark cloud crept over the sky and it began to rain. Suddenly I heard him shout in a strange voice: "Irenushka!"

Grisha had a heart attack and took his last breath in the forest . . .

The period after his death was unbearable. I did not want to live any more, and probably only survived because I was working on a book about him, so that, in a sense, we were still living together.[11] I wanted to write about his life and the work he had been unable to finish. He had suffered so many prohibi-

---

10 Jaan Kross, *Keisri hull*, Tallinn: Eesti Raamat, 1978; *The Czar's Madman*, transl. George Kurman, London: The Harvill Press, 1992.

11 C.f. note 4, p. 11.

tions and there were so many unrealised ideas—I wanted them to be heard, to be known. I worked on the book for about seven years. I spent every spare minute I had in Estonia gathering material; at the same time, a large portion of the future book was being translated into Estonian, and friends helped me to properly understand the Estonian texts. It was complicated work, but finally, in 1995, the book was published—in independent Estonia. Arvo Pärt contributed funds toward its publication, and it was designed by a very sensitive designer named Jüri Kaarma. I was so happy that the book was very well received in Estonia and sold out quickly.

You mentioned that the censors were always very critical of your husband's work. Which of his works was the most heavily "pruned"?

Probably the two-part film *Diamonds for the Dictatorship of the Proletariat.*[12] That was a very special and interesting film based on Yulian Semyonov's novel of the same name. The main character was the popular Soviet spy Isaev, who also appeared in the television series *Seventeen Moments of Spring.*[13] But Grisha did not want to create just another detective story; he succeeded in depicting the tragedy of the Russian intelligentsia following the October Revolution. You can imagine what Moscow thought of that . . . Yermash, the head of the Soviet cinematography committee, shouted: "Where did Kromanov put the million?"[14] Naturally, after such a "warm" reception of the film in Moscow, Tallinnfilm received the order to make heavy cuts.

Which of your husband's films was the most dear and interesting to you?

As I mentioned earlier, to this day *The Last Relic* is considered a cult film in Estonia, but both Grisha and I probably most cared for those *Diamonds,* with their complicated fate. The very title of the film is deceptive: it is not about the

---

12 *Diamonds for the Dictatorship of the Proletariat* [Est. *Briljandid proletariaadi diktatuurile,* Rus. *Бриллианты для диктатуры пролетариата*] Tallinnfilm, 1975.

13 The fictional Soviet spy Maxim Isaev was created by writer Yulian Semionov as a counterpart to Ian Fleming's James Bond character.

14 Philip Yermash (Rus. Филипп Ермаш, 1923–2002)—chairman of the USSR State Cinema Committee (1972–1986). Filmmakers called this period the Yermash era or stagnation era, while the chairman himself is remembered as a staunch defender of official dogma.

wealth needed by the dictatorship of the proletariat, but about a fateful internal conflict experienced by the nation and the tragic demise of the Russia's true
diamonds, its intelligentsia. The film starred wonderful Russian, Estonian, and
Lithuanian actors, and the score was composed by Arvo Pärt. It is a great pity
that that film was so heavily damaged by the censors. At one and the same the
time, Grisha was in hospital and his film was being massacred . . . He felt as
though it was not film tape, but his heart, that was being cut up. Although my
husband was not allowed to execute his idea fully, I value what remained of it.

**Could we try to compare Estonian and Lithuanian culture of that era? Do
you see any differences?**

Yes, there were some differences. The Estonians often seemed more daring to me.
That may have been because their language was less comprehensible to me, as I
found it much more difficult than Lithuanian. Their journalism and media were
different too. It would be enough to compare their cultural weekly *Sirp ja vasar*
(Hammer and sickle) and our *Literatūra ir menas* (Literature and art).[15] As I have
already said, the Estonians published many more of the great world classics during the Soviet period. Another aspect was that the Estonians were much more interested in and valued the Russian dissidents, and they had their own, such as the
philosopher, poet, and cultural critic Jaan Kaplinski. Their theatre was also very
strong, but on that front we were in no way inferior, and perhaps even the opposite. It is interesting that today, Russian citizens seeking asylum from Putin's dictatorship more often request it from Estonia than from Lithuania.

I think that, compared to the Estonians, we were more conservative.
Throughout the Soviet period, Estonians could watch Finnish television; they
could travel to Finland and Finns themselves were quite free to visit Estonia,
so they had good opportunities to interact with a non-Soviet country. Lithuanians, on the other hand, had far fewer opportunities to do so—after all, Poland
was part of the Soviet bloc. Grisha liked to say that "Lithuanians are romantics,
dreamers; Estonians are much more rational." I am not sure if the Estonians
are doing better or worse than us today, but I think that they have handled the
Communist past much better than we, and that is very significant.

---

15 *Sirp ja vasar* [Est. *Hammer and sickle*]—Soviet-era Estonian cultural weekly.

During the Soviet period, I was always very impressed that important leadership positions, such as appointments to head Estonian ministries of the time, were held by quite young people. I would ask them, "Why are you working for the government?" They would answer very simply that they saw it as a way of expanding their horizons and gaining useful knowledge, contacts, and skills; their plan would be to stay in such a position for no more than five years, so as not to become infected by Soviet bureaucracy, and then afterwards apply their experience to pursuing their own goals. Perhaps that was one of the reasons why the Estonians were able to more radically deal with their Soviet nomenklatura following the restoration of independence.

And now I have one more Estonian question. The character of Arvo Pärt has frequently visited our conversations. You have a portrait of the composer, a few of his paintings, and even some pieces of his furniture in your apartment. Your life trajectories are also connected by one of this Estonian composer's most famous works, **Für Alina.** *Could you tell me about the events surrounding its composition?*

I met Arvo and his wife Nora in 1975, during the filming of *Diamonds*, for which he wrote the score. We had an instant connection. Arvo and Nora had decided to join their lives not long before Grisha and I. Arvo had separated from his first wife and spent three or four years living in the country and eating only raw food he had grown himself, because he suffered from kidney stones. He had had one kidney removed and the second one had to be saved—it was a matter of life or death. During that period, he did not compose anything, found his faith in God, and became a deeply devout Orthodox Christian.

Then he met Nora, who was preparing to emigrate to Israel with her parents; they fell in love and he could not let her leave. She stayed. Arvo and Nora were married and had two wonderful boys—Immanuel and Michael. The family lived in an apartment inherited from Nora's parents, on Mustamäe Street in Tallinn. It was there that Arvo discovered his *tintinnabuli* style, which garnered him worldwide fame.[16]

---

16   *Tintinnabuli*—(Lat. tintinnabulum—"bell")—a compositional style that Arvo Pärt first applied in the work *Für Alina* (1976), and then in *Spiegel im Spiegel* (1978). Pärt's tintinnabuli works are notable for their clear asceticism and minimalist composition.

During the same period, Grisha and I did not have a roof over our heads, and the Pärts offered us one room in their three-room flat. We lived together for about one year, perhaps a bit more, until Grisha was able to buy a cooperative housing apartment with the honorarium he received from *Diamonds*. I remember that period of living together with Arvo and Nora as one of the most uplifting and interesting of my entire life. Arvo and Nora had an enormous impact on me. Nora, who was quite a bit younger than me, was very wise and good, while Arvo simply seemed like a holy man to me.

Both they and we were madly in love. Nora's health was fragile and Arvo took care of her beautifully. I remember once returning home to find him washing diapers. I said, "Arvochka, let me do that, and you can write your music." To which he replied: "As long as my conscience is not clear and I have not done my duty, I cannot write music. After all, it is not I that write it—I simply pass on the sounds that come to me from the heavens. For them to come, I must first of all ensure that my conscience is pure; I must be clean." I cannot exactly convey those several sentences, but that is an exact rendering of his meaning.

I remember how a character named Misha used to visit Arvo and Nora. They had met him while visiting a monastery. Misha had diabetes and did not adhere to any dietary or hygienic rules, but had the gift of clairvoyance. I would call him a true *juródivyj*.[17]

Once he warned Arvo and Nora that the KGB was going through their apartment while they were at the monastery. They raced back home to find a broken mirror and other signs that a search had taken place. Misha also urged Arvo and Nora to emigrate, though that was truly a difficult decision to make.

When Misha came to visit them, Nora would first of all lead him to the washroom for a bath, dress him in clean clothes, and feed him. She was tiny, and Misha was tall, fat and heavy. It reminded me of Justinėlis and how I had failed to help him.

After they became Orthodox Christians, Arvo and Nora maintained regular contact with monasteries in Estonia and, later, England. I once accompanied them on a visit to an Orthodox monastery in Essex.[18] It felt like being on a utopian island. Each of the monks spoke at least four to six languages and most

---

17   Rus. *юрóдивый*—from *юродъ*—idiot, oddball, madman; Orthodox concept referring to wandering monks and/or very religious types seen by society as "holy madmen" or "blessed madmen."

18   Reference to the Patriarchal Stavropegic Monastery of St. John the Baptist in Essex, UK.

had university degrees. I was there simply as a guest and one day went to attend morning prayers. The monks and nuns were singing hymns, and suddenly I hear them singing in Lithuanian! It was their way of honouring my country and me. I was moved to tears.

Nor will I ever forget the culinary and eating culture at the monastery. First of all, they grew all of their food themselves. It was simple, but healthy and very tasty. During the meal, one of the monks would read from the Bible, which created a very special, spiritual atmosphere.

When Arvo was composing in the *tintinnabuli* style, he often also drew, but then threw those drawings into a wastebasket. As you have probably understood, by that point I already worshipped Arvo and his music, which gave one a strong sense of Heaven, eternity, unearthly purity, love, and beauty. I treasured anything that was connected to him and Nora. While helping them to tidy the flat, I would take those drawings from the wastebasket. They did not object. Now that makes me feel very wealthy—I have his self-portrait and a glowing cross, both drawn on pieces of staff paper. These drawings hang on the wall in my room.

When he discovered the *tintinnabuli* style and began to write sacred music, Arvo stopped writing music for films. At the time, a famous Viennese music publisher offered to buy everything that he would write while still alive. I would think that must have helped Arvo and Nora to think about emigration more concretely, as the atmosphere in Soviet Estonia was becoming more and more oppressive.

I have a vivid memory of another episode connected to this unusually pure and true man. During an annual meeting of the Estonian Composers' Union, Arvo made an open statement criticising the cultural policies of the day. Although I was in the room and observed people's reactions—he received unanimous support and seemingly endless applause—I did not understand everything. It was clear afterwards, however, that he would never again receive a state commission; his music was banned and he had no means of supporting his family. That was when Arvo and Nora decided to emigrate. When the Communist authorities heard about this they "became concerned" about the couple's fate. I can recall how they were visited at home by one of the Central Committee secretaries, who wanted to understand the reasons for their decision to emigrate and offered to help. Arvo swiped his hand across his neck and said, "I'm fed up." I should admit that Arvo recalls this incident differently. According to him, the

Central Committee secretary advised them to emigrate to Israel, where Nora's parents were already living.

Arvo and his family departed for Vienna in 1981. They travelled by train through Vilnius, where we said our farewells, but our relationship did not end there. I lived, and continue to live with Arvo's music. I listen to it all the time, especially when I feel despair about the imperfection of the world and humanity ... My apartment is full of objects and furniture given to me by Arvo and Nora when they left. In 1984, when my husband died, he wrote a wonderful psalm for him, *Ein Wallfahrstlied*.

I would visit them in Berlin, and would stay in their flat when visiting Tallinn. They are both incredibly dear to me, as are their children. Unfortunately, I do not know their grandchildren.

And now to get back to your question about Arvo's work *Für Alina*, which was written in the *tintinnabuli* style. It is named after my daughter, whom he had not yet met. She had already immigrated to England, and Arvo could see and feel how much I missed her. When asked during an interview with Estonian television who that Alina was, he stood up and stepped backwards, and, saying "*kaugel, kaugel*," left the room. In Estonian that meant "far away, far away."

In around 1976 or 1977, Grisha and I had the great fortune of attending a single, unforgettable concert that took place, by some miracle, at the Tallinn Philharmonic. Gidon Kremer and Tatyana Grindenko performed violin duets of Alfred Schnittke's *Concerto Grosso* and Arvo Pärt's *Tabula Rasa*.[19] Daring to take responsibility for the performance of these works, our famous Lithuanian maestro Saulius Sondeckis was conducting. As far as I can remember, Tatyana Grindenko (and perhaps Gidon Kremer as well) was at one point banned from performing in the Baltic States, so everyone was taking some kind of risk.

No words can convey the experience of that evening—it was the kind of pinnacle that one reaches only once in a lifetime. Everything came together—brilliant, yet-unheard compositions, perfect execution, and internal protest against an oppressive regime.

In 2003, one of the most amazing people I have met in my life—the actor, visionary, and intensely creative Krzysztof Czyżewski, who founded and runs

---

19   Alfred Schnittke (1934–1998) dedicated his work *Concerto Grosso No. 1* to its first performers: Gidon Kremer, Tatjana Gridenko, and Saulius Sondeckis.

the Center of Borderland Cultures in Sejny—decided to award Arvo the honorary title of "Borderland Person."[20] It was necessary to reach Arvo and find out if he would accept the honour, so Krzysztof and I travelled to see Arvo and Nora in Berlin. Arvo never liked public forms of recognition, but he could not always avoid them. Eventually, we managed to convince him that this was not some kind of bureaucratic, state award but a way of honouring him as a composer and a person, and he agreed. That week in Sejny, which is recorded in a film, was very special.

You once said that Krzysztof Czyżewski has created a utopia in Krasnogruda. What did you mean by that?

In calling Krasnogruda a utopia I had in mind that it is a place that is in utter contrast to our contemporary world and the hatred, mistrust, conflict, and lack of respect that mark so much of it . . .

Set against a beautiful natural background, near a lake and the Polish and Lithuanian towns of Sejny and Žagarė, in the Miłosz family manor in the village of Krasnogruda, this international centre for dialogue keeps Czesław Miłosz's ideals of creativity and tolerance alive. It attracts and connects not only people living in this borderland region, but from Lithuania and around the world. It contains a substantial library related to borderland peoples. It is a place where respect for the person flourishes, artistic workshops are held, performances are staged, a klezmer band plays, animated films are created, and the songs of many different nations can be heard. One feels as though one has entered the kind of paradise about which, these days, it is only possible to dream.

When and how did you get to know Krzysztof? Is it only your common ideas that connect you, or do you have some other mutual interests?

Our friendship probably began in 1990–1991, shortly after Lithuania declared independence and the Open Lithuania Fund (OLF) was formed. Lithuanian-

20 Pol. Fundacja Pogranicze—foundation and centre established in 1990 with the goal of supporting the cultural identities of borderland inhabitants, and to promote understanding and cooperation between different national, religious, and cultural communities. Located in the village of Krasnogruda in the district of Sejny in north-eastern Poland, close to the border with Lithuania.

Polish relations were very important to the new Lithuanian state, especially given the painful and controversial history of these nations' connections and separations. The OLF was therefore looking for ways to connect with our Polish neighbours. As far as I can remember, Krzysztof invited us to visit the Borderland Foundation, which was created at the same time, and we immediately found much in common. You were correct in saying that we found a connection through our common values; that connection eventually grew into a close friendship and, I would even say, love. I saw Krzysztof not only as an artist—a very creative, talented person—but also as a truly exceptional individual. I was entranced by him and his wife Małgorzata, a woman of great sensitivity, and also their daughter Weronika—a young historian with a rare talent for acting. After fifty years of Soviet rule, it simply felt like a miracle to meet people like Krzysztof and Małgorzata.

Together with their colleagues—the like-minded actors and musicians Wojciech and Bożena Szroeder—Krzysztof and Małgorzata had recently arrived in Sejny, a small borderland town that changed hands eleven times during the First World War. A good number of Poles had been killed there by Lithuanians, and Lithuanians by Poles. Eventually, Sejny came to belong to Poland. Scores were still being settled in this small town, with each side calculating how much it had suffered. Krzysztof was looking for a new modus vivendi—a way of reconciling the Lithuanian and Polish communities. As OLF representatives, we were invited to one of the first celebrations organised by all of the town's residents. Everything took place in the Sejny White Synagogue, which had been given to the Borderland Foundation. I immediately sensed the pain Krzysztof felt about the Jewish tragedy, and his respect for Jewish culture. Seeking to revive the musical traditions of the Jews who had lived there, he and his friend Wojciech had formed a klezmer ensemble, for which they eventually became quite famous.

The windows of the synagogue were lined with life-sized photographs of the Jewish residents of Sejny who had been killed. By the entrance to the synagogue lay ruined Jewish gravestones and a menorah stood in the middle of them. All of it moved me very deeply because I had long since understood that one can only be freed from the painful and tragic burdens of the past by acknowledging them. And also, of course, through empathy.

Krzysztof himself, a former actor and dissident, was the soul of the whole event—he spoke and danced with everyone. I remember how he twirled—per-

haps even a hundred times. I had never seen anything like it and could not believe that a person could dance that way. His wife Małgorzata sang Jewish songs.
The Lithuanian community had prepared delicious food.

There were rumours circulating around Sejny that Krzysztof himself was a
Jew or a gypsy, because his hair was black. He had arrived in Sejny in a wagon
loaded up with all of the family's belongings. But Krzysztof's entire group—his
wife Małgorzata and the actors Wojciech and Bożena—have nothing to do with
either Jews or gypsies. They are true ethnic Poles, and Wojciech and Bożena are
Kashubians.[21] I had certainly never met any group of people like them, but I was
immediately fond of them and wanted to get to know them better.

We did many things together and I later recommended that Krzysztof be appointed to the Open Society Institute's board in Budapest, and we made a good
many trips to places in Central Asia, the Caucasus, the Balkans and elsewhere.

Krzysztof is a great friend of Lithuania's. Like his teacher Jerzy Giedroyc,
he is very concerned with the relationships between close neighbours. I am happy that Lithuania recognised Krzysztof's work by awarding him a state medal.

*In Krzysztof Czyżewski's Borderland Center of Arts, Cultures and Na-
tions, the word "borderland" is very important. What does this concept
mean to you personally? Do you—like Krzysztof—see yourself as a "borderland person"?*

Yes, in a sense I do. A "borderland person" is someone who lives at the intersection of several cultures. As a child, I spoke three languages, and when I began to attend Sholem Aleichem High School, I learned Yiddish. But I have already spoken about that.

As I have already said, Sejny is a borderland town; its long-time residents have
included Poles, Lithuanians, Ukrainians, Jews, Roma, Belarusians, and other nationalities. Like Sejny, Lithuania is a multi-cultural, and, in a sense, a borderland
country. I would say that borderland people are not only those who live in borderland regions but also those who respect different cultures and do not feel hatred for the Other. A borderland person usually speaks several languages and per-

---

21 Kashubians—a western Slavic nation living in the territory of the Republic of Poland, primarily to the
    southeast of Gdansk and Gdynia, in Eastern Pomerania.

haps feels more wealthy than someone who only identifies with one culture. Every two years, the Borderland Foundation elects someone as honorary "Borderlander." This distinction has gone to people like Tomas Venclova and the composer Arvo Pärt. I sometimes think that perhaps the whole world is a borderland . . .

I would hazard to say that Krasnogruda is also important to you because of its connection to Czesław Miłosz, as it was one of the "bases" of the Miłosz clan. How did you discover Miłosz's texts? Which ideas, of Miłosz's enormous intellectual legacy (the fate of Central Europe, Vilnius as an idea and an object of nostalgia, the tragedy of the captive mind, his identity as "the last citizen of the Grand Duchy of Lithuania, Lithuanian-Polish relations, etc.) are most important to you personally?

You are correct in saying that Miłosz's legacy and his connection to Krasnogruda are very important to me.

I believe that I only became better acquainted with Czesław Miłosz's work after the restoration of Lithuania's independence. Before that, I had thought about him more as a relative of Oscar Milosz. Czesław Miłosz taught me a great deal and most of his concepts are perfectly aligned with my own beliefs and values. He explained to me what happened with Central Europe, he showed me the tragedy of the captive mind that allows totalitarian regimes to take hold.

Miłosz's humanism and tolerance always impressed me greatly. I should say that I became more aware of him thanks to Alexander Shtromas and Tomas Venclova. I met Miłosz in person when he visited Vilnius in 1995, which was especially interesting: I sensed his respect for others, for Lithuania. But when we were walking together along Didžioji Street, on the way to the Gates of Dawn, near the Astoria Hotel, he told me that he would never again return to Vilnius, because he was tired of being endlessly asked whether he was a Pole or a Lithuanian. He said that he is both a Pole and a Lithuanian, and, most importantly, that he was the last citizen of the Grand Duchy of Lithuania. Unfortunately, I did not have the opportunity to understand what he meant in more detail as I could only read translations. To this day I regret not having learned Polish.

※

It is Probably Only Possible to Feel a Part of History Once in One's Lifetime . . .

Irena Veisaitė in the courtyard of Vilnius University, 1990. Photo by Antanas Sutkus.

*H*ow *do you remember the late Soviet period?*

The Brezhnev era was a time of hopeless stagnation.[1] No one, with the exception of my cousin Alexander Shtromas, who argued that the USSR would not last for long, would have believed that it would all end soon. Most people thought that the system would go on functioning forever. On the other hand, having limited hopes for the future and having lost faith in the ideals of Communism, people simply went on with their lives. What most oppressed people of that era was the hopeless permanence of it; in contrast, people today are overwhelmed by the fear of never-ending change. As I like to say, these days, there is nothing permanent—except change.

For me, personally, it was a time during which I sorely missed my daughter Alina, who had emigrated to Great Britain with her father in 1974. But it was also a time of good fortune, love, interesting contacts, friendships, and creative work. And there was another aspect to that period; the late Soviet period was a time of great flourishing for Lithuanian theatre.

Scholars of the late Soviet period cannot agree: some argue that, for audience members, the theatre of metaphor was a space of spiritual protest, while others claim that the metaphors that spoke to them from the screen or stage were so polysemous that they could at once mean anything and nothing.

---

1   Leonid Brezhnev (1906–1982, Rus. Леонид Брежнев)—Communist Party and political figure, General Secretary of the Communist Party of the Soviet Union and de facto leader of the USSR (1964–1982).

A lot depended on the audience that was viewing a specific play or film. But I would certainly not agree with the sceptics. The theatre of that period had an enormous impact, it was a great force. I have clear memories of so many productions: by Liubimov, Efros, and Dodin in Moscow; by Lininsh and Shapiro in Latvia; by Tooming, Komissarov and Kromanov in Estonia; and by Jurašas, Nekrošius, Vaitkus, Tuminas, Gaidys, and Varnas in Lithuania. All of these productions communicated clear, powerful values. You cannot imagine the long lines stretching from the ticket booths, the theatres packed to the rafters. These were performances that urged people to think independently within a system that imposed uniformity. At the time, it was a form of protest against Soviet stereotypes and lies. And I would go even farther: the theatre was the only place where human existential questions were explored. It was a sacred, spiritual place.

Of course, you could not openly or freely discuss the ideas that a performance stimulated—you could lose your job or harm the director or theatre. But nevertheless, that spirit of opposition to the absurdity of the Soviet regime grew, and the need for deeper and more complex understanding of human existential questions intensified. That was also evident in literature, especially in Russia. Unfortunately, when Lithuania declared independence, it became clear that not many works had been written "into the drawer." But there was plenty of veiled opposition, especially in the theatre...

Why did Lithuanians not write "into the drawer"?

That is a complicated question. Could it have been because there were plenty of opportunities to express oneself both in public and private in Lithuania? After all, things were always a little bit freer in Lithuania, especially after Stalin's death.

There was also plenty of fear. I know perfectly well that, during the formation of the Sąjūdis independence movement, strong opposition could be felt from the Lithuanian Communist Party; it was only after Alexander Yakovlev, the "architect of *perestroika*," came to Vilnius and said those fateful words, that Sąjūdis truly gained momentum.[2] Perhaps we did not have enough courage? Or we had suffered too much? Or did not trust our own strength?

---

2   Reference to Alexander Yakovlev's (Rus. Александр Яковлев, 1923–2005)—Soviet and Russian Communist Party figure and one of the ideologues behind Gorbachev's initiated *perestroika* reform policies—and his August 11–13, 1988 visit to Vilnius.

But when the Sąjūdis movement began, all the dams burst . . . It was an exceptional period—a rising up of the entire nation—during which there was certainly no shortage of courage or determination. It is probably only possible to feel a part of history once in one's lifetime . . .

To continue the theme of texts hiding in drawers . . . During that period of epochal change, did you read any text that had been written "into the drawer," or that was published once conditions allowed, and which you would now say was fundamental, that caused a breakthrough in your own worldview?

In that context, I would first of all mention Russian *samizdat* literature: Sakharov, Solzhenitsyn, Shalamov, and the writing and activities of the Russian dissidents in general. The Lithuanian equivalents were Tomas Venclova, Antanas Terleckas, my cousin Alexander Shtromas, and the "Helsinki Group."[3] Once, from my friend Tadas Masiulis, I learnt about the unique attitude and work of the artist and builder Eduardas Jonušas in Nida.[4] It turned out that Jonušas's wife, Vitalija Jonušienė, who was the soul of the Thomas Mann Museum and Cultural Centre, was Tadas's cousin; she later became a close colleague of mine. As I mentioned before, at the time I did not know anything about the Chronicle of the Catholic Church in Lithuania.

In answer to your question, it would probably be more accurate to say that the breakthrough happened gradually. My understanding of literature and cultural phenomena in general was greatly influenced by the Leningrad School, Zhirmunsky, and Mariya Lazarevna Tronskaya, who introduced me to the Leningrad cultural elite; later, the books of Bakhtin, Gurevich, and Lotman were

---

3   Antanas Terleckas—economist, dissident, social and political activist.
    Helsinki Group—on August 1, 1975, the Final Act of the Conference on Security and Cooperation in Europe was signed in Helsinki (known as the Helsinki Accords). In it, 35 states, including the Soviet Union, committed to respect human rights. The reality, however, was different, and the Soviet Union continued to violate human rights. The Soviet dissident movement, led by academic Andrei Sacharov, developed the idea of researching violations of the Helsinki Final Act and informing the global community about them. The Lithuanian Helsinki Group was formed on November 25, 1976. It was modeled after the Moscow Helsinki Group but was an independent organization.
4   Eduardas Jonušas (1932–2014)—an exceptional individual within the Soviet-era Lithuanian art world: painter and philosopher; recorded, restored, and protected ancient Neringa Region socio-cultural artefacts.

very important to me; and my friendships and exchanges with Venclova, my cousin Shtromas, Vytautas Kubilius, Ramūnas Katilius, Monsignor Vasiliauskas, and the Estonian intellectual elite had an important impact. It would be impossible to list all of the small and big things—texts, contacts, discussions— that shaped my thinking and worldview.

Besides, do not forget that I was born in the interwar period, in still independent Lithuania, so I had a different point of reference . . .

How did you and other people in your circle see Mikhail Gorbachev's rise to power and that general secretary's announcement of a new age of glasnost *and* perestroika?[5] *Was there any fear that this was just one more deception?*

We began to have hope. We all felt that the times were changing, and that brought a great sense of relief.

Nikita Khrushchev implemented a policy of "thaw," but this could not in any way be compared to *perestroika* and *glasnost*.[6] Although we placed great hopes in Gorbachev, he still represented the USSR. I can remember how disappointed I became in this man when he would not let Sakharov speak during a congress of Supreme Council deputies. That is when I began to have doubts about him. Those doubts only grew after the bloody events that took place in Tbilisi, Riga, and especially Vilnius.

I believe that Gorbachev had no intention of dismantling the Soviet Union and so was very surprised when things began to move in that direction. And yet he did a great deal . . . truly a great deal. Although I am angry with this politician for the above-mentioned events in Lithuania and Georgia, and many others, I am nevertheless grateful to him for many things. I am convinced that without Gorbachev we would have been trapped in Brezhnev's system for much longer.

When did you sense that the processes in part inspired by Gorbachev were very serious, that there was no turning back?

---

5   "Restructuring" and "openness." [Rus.]
6   "thaw"—Rus. оттепель.

As I mentioned, our liberation from the fear of terror did not happen suddenly. It was a gradual process, because each one of us had been touched by various forms of terror, so the fear was very deeply rooted. I remember how, even after Lithuania's declaration of independence, my friends noticed that whenever political topics were touched I always lowered my voice—even in England. On the other hand, the realisation that the times were changing came to me very suddenly. *Perestroika* and *glasnost* gave me a certain feeling of freedom, even though there were no guarantees and the idea of independence did not seem acceptable, or, to be more accurate, realistic.

I cannot boast that I was a big Sąjūdis activist, but I contributed to the Sąjūdis group at what was then called Vilnius Pedagogical Institute, and participated in the first Sąjūdis Congress, in 1988. It was very impressive. I was so happy to see that, on the stage of the Sports Palace, people were beginning to speak openly about the oppression and terror we had experienced under the Communist regime. It was a period of euphoria. At the same time, I have to admit that, while listening to the Sąjūdis Congress, I did occasionally ask myself: "What am I doing here if no one is talking about what Lithuania's Jews have suffered, about the heavy toll that the Holocaust had on my family—about my brutally murdered mother, uncle, grandfather . . ." At the time, I quickly brushed those thoughts aside, telling myself they were too egoistical. I was happy that the prisoners of the Gulag were finally speaking out. With all my heart I was happy—with them and for them. I too wanted to walk onto that stage and to loudly proclaim the names of people who had saved Jews, as I considered them saints and true heroes of the resistance, but I did not dare. But the next day I took a short article containing my thoughts to the newspaper *Gimtasis kraštas* (Native land) and it was printed.[7]

I can still recall how my friends and I felt as we left the Sports Palace after the congress . . . It was an hour of joy and triumph. It seemed that we had been surrounded by many like-minded people and that a new, honourable, and just democratic Lithuania was about to be born.

Some years later, I helped keep watch over the Seimas, took food to the people guarding it, and spoke with my students about the epochal changes that were taking place. I did also feel some fear that the Soviets would seek revenge—that

---

7   Irena Veisaitė, "Nepasakytas žodis" [Left unsaid], *Gimtasis kraštas*, November 10-16, 1988 11 10–16, 6. C.f.: "Voices from the Past" section, p. 310.

blood could be spilled—but I tried not to show it. During the conflict between Brazauskas and Landsbergis I was firmly on Landsbergis's side, though I sometimes thought to myself, "*Тише едешь — дальше будешь*."[8] Soviet coercion and the fear of it were clearly deeply engrained in me. For that reason, I have the utmost respect for Landsbergis and deeply admire him for having taken such a brave position. I can remember how, in 1991, the entire young generation of the Ladiga and Vildžiūnas families went to help guard the Parliament. The Ladigas's grandson, Andrius Eiva, who was a US army officer, had also come and contributed greatly to the defence of the Parliament.[9] All of the younger members of the Ladiga and Vildžiūnas clan had inherited their parents' courage and principled stance. They had a particular kind of toughness and determination. At the time, I said to Marytė Vildžiūnienė: "Don't let all the children go to the Seimas at once. Keep at least one at home—if none of them come back the whole Vildžiūnas family will perish." She just laughed at me and ignored my advice. As I said, that boundless courage and determination were family traits, for which I feel the greatest respect.

On January 12, 1991, my cousin Margarita was visiting me from London. My cousin Alexander Shtromas and his wife Violeta, and Jonas Jurašas were also in Vilnius. That evening, Margarita and I once more took some food down to the people guarding the Lithuanian radio and television headquarters on Konarskio Street. But I did not feel comfortable going to the Parliament with her. We returned home, went to sleep and then, at around one in the morning, we began to hear gunfire. I wanted to run outside to see what was happening, but I felt responsible for my cousin, so I stayed with her, though I am sorry and feel some regret about that. But that is how it was. With great emotion, we watched the last frames of the television broadcast as the building was seized.[10]

How quickly were changes reflected in life at the Pedagogical Institute?

---

8   Algirdas Mykolas Brazauskas (1932–2010)—Communist Party and political figure. First Secretary of the Central Committee of the Lithuanian Communist Party and de facto leader of the Soviet Republic of Lithuania (1988–1990). First president of the newly restored Lithuanian state (1993–1998). Irena Veisaitė is referring to Brazauskas and Landsbergis's Sąjūdis-era disagreement about the movement's goals and whether it should seek the restoration of independence, a position that Landsbergis firmly defended. *Тише едешь—дальше будешь*—"The slower you drive, the faster you will arrive." [Rus.]

9   Andrew Eiva—US military officer of Lithuanian descent. In January 1990, helped those defending the Lithuanian Parliament organize the defense of the building and of the deputies working within it.

10 C.f. note 13, p. 46.

It is possible to change a government and flags overnight, but it takes more time to change people's thinking. The administration of the Vilnius Pedagogical Institute changed and the new rector was the universally respected Antanas Pakerys. Most of us began to shed the fear of saying what we thought. Communist Party members handed in their party membership cards. But how much did these changes reflect fundamental changes in the life of the Institute? Sadly, I cannot answer that question in more detail. I have to admit that I had some concerns that communist ideology would be replaced by nationalist ideology.

During the reestablishment of the Lithuanian state, when did you feel that the transitional period was over and that something permanent had taken shape?

Quite quickly. I felt responsible for my country—I felt that I must help it get on its feet. Although we still did not know what tomorrow would bring, we tried to have faith and behave as though we would be free forever.

We understood that we had to act. In 1990, as a newly independent Lithuania was being created, efforts began to create the Open Lithuania Foundation. It was a way of expressing our personal positions—that we supported democracy and Lithuania's efforts to become free. To this day, I keep repeating that we must feel like masters of our own country—not life serfs. We must be responsible for what happens in our homeland and be active citizens within it. And that meant actively countering outdated stereotypes.

It is paradoxical—state-level anti-Semitism was really strong in the USSR, but, on the level of everyday life, I felt it more keenly in Lithuania during the Soviet period. I often felt like a second-class citizen. With the restoration of Lithuania's independence, that feeling disappeared; I felt that I truly was a Lithuanian citizen, as Lithuanian as I was Jewish.

So, Lithuania's independence also meant liberation from Soviet anti-Semitism. Landsbergis's first decrees were also related to the Holocaust: a Day of Mourning was announced and other important steps were taken. At the state level, therefore, the tragedy of the Jews was sufficiently grasped and remembered.

Already in 1988, professor Česlovas Kudaba was initiating the formation of cultural foundations.[11] I contributed to the creation of the Jewish Cultural

---

11   Česlovas Kudaba (1934–1993)—geographer, social and political activist.

Foundation's statute and bylaws and participated in its founding meeting. But I decided to leave that organization because, during discussions about the bylaws, the decision was made not to include a point recognizing that there were Jews who collaborated with Soviet repressive structures, and to leave a point about how some Lithuanians contributed to implementation of the Holocaust in this country. I was very upset and was convinced that this was a wrongful decision. I gave a harsh speech, which was filmed by Laima Pangonytė, and left the room.[12] A young friend of mine, American-Lithuanian journalist Ina Navazelskis, left with me, and Audrius Butkevičius spent a long time helping us to calm down.[13]

Today I am a member of the Jewish community, and, when invited, am happy to participate in its events. I respect the Jewish community and admire much of their work, but I am not an activist. There is not enough time for everything. I have never renounced my background—my wonderful parents, grandparents, and nation—but I feel strongly that I am a Litvak, that is, both a Jew and a Lithuanian. Now I would also add that I am a European.

I am often critical of European Union policies and feel the divide between Western and Eastern Europe, but I am firmly convinced that our collective future depends on whether the dream of a unified Europe survives.

Although my professional work and interests have been very broad, the Open Lithuania Foundation became my most important life's work. The focus of that work was to open Lithuania to Europe, and Europe to Lithuania.

How did the work of the Open Lithuania Foundation begin?

At the very beginning, the creation of the Foundation was entrusted to Kazimiera Prunskienė.[14] But when George Soros' envoy Anthony Richter came to Lithuania, he saw that Prunskienė did not have time to delve into the foundation's principles and goals. Most importantly, she became Prime Minister, and,

---

12 Laima Pangonytė—documentary filmmaker, video documenter of the Sąjūdis movement and the changes it inspired.
13 Ina Navazelskis—US journalist of Lithuanian descent, project coordinator at the Holocaust Memorial Museum in Washington, DC.
    Audrius Butkevičius—doctor and politician, active member of Sąjūdis, first Minister of Defense of the newly independent Republic of Lithuania.
14 Kazimiera Prunskienė—economist, politician, first Prime Minister of the newly independent Republic of Lithuania (March 17, 1990–January 10, 1991).

Irena Veisaitė and George Soros, c. 1995.

according to the general regulations of the Soros Foundation, political activity was incompatible with the work of the Foundation.

It turned out that the people chosen to meet with Soros in Dubrovnik in the spring of 1990 were Professor Česlovas Kudaba, who had participated in the OLF Board (at that time headed by Prunskienė) from the beginning, and myself. Professor Kudaba spoke neither English nor German, so all communication had to go through me. Incidentally, at the time Soros had tremendous faith in Gorbachev and even criticised the Lithuanians for wanting "a great deal right away." He told us that we were like small children who want all the toys right away, and that we were disrupting Gorbachev's plans. During those meetings in Dubrovnik, Soros was therefore unsure about whether it was the right time for establishing an Open Society Foundation in Lithuania. We were greatly helped in our attempts to convince him otherwise by the Hungarian philologist and Baltic Studies scholar Endre Bojtár, who was a great friend of Lithuania's.[15] Ultimately the decision was made to create the Dubrovnik Committee and monitor the situation.[16]

---

15   Endre Bojtár (1940–2018)—Baltic Studies scholar, literary historian, translator, and steady promoter of Lithuanian culture in Hungary.
16   While reviewing the manuscript, Irena Veisaitė added the following: "From the very beginning, the Dubrovnik Committee consisted of Professor Česlovas Kudaba, Vytautas Kubilius, Ramūnas Katilius, Ina Marčiulionytė, Natalija Kasatkina, and myself."

The Dubrovnik Committee completed all of the required tasks and in this way Soros's trust was gained. On October 5, 1990, after less than half a year of work on the part of the Dubrovnik Committee, the Open Lithuania Foundation was established. It was registered on December 19. Kazimiera Prunskienė was very helpful in organising all of these matters.

What ideas did you explore during the first meetings of like-minded people who had formed the Dubrovnik Committee?

What was most important to us was to demonstrate that we could work in a conscientious way, execute projects, and find sponsors in Lithuania. Rimvydas Valatka, who at the time was editor of the weekly *Atgimimas* (Rebirth) still likes to say, with his characteristic sense of humour, that he is probably the only person in the world to have financed Soros himself. He and Liuba Chiornaya, who was editor of the Russian weekly *Soglasije* (Unity) gave us 15,000 rubles as Lithuania's contribution to the establishment of the OLF. I am grateful to them for that to this day.

How was the general strategy for the Foundation's work developed? Who played the most important roles in that process?

On the level of ideas, the main role was played by the OLF Board of Directors, which consisted of truly enlightened people.[17] The first Executive Directors of the Foundation were journalist Algis Lipštas, financial expert Audra Misiūnienė, and international business expert Vytautas Gruodis.[18] The latter two had come from the free world: Audra from the United States and Vytautas from Canada. They had matured and worked in countries untouched by to-

---

17 During the review of the text, Irena Veisaitė made the following addition: "The first OLF Board of Directors consisted of the Dubrovnik Committee (with the exception of Ina Marčiulionytė, whom we asked to join the foundation's administration) as well as Kęstutis Nastopka, Vytautas Karpus, and, later—Stasys Stačiokas, Giedrius Uždavinys, Darius Kuolys, Egidijus Aleksandravičius, Arūnas Sverdiolas, Teodoras Medaiskis and others. The administrative office was made up of Algis Lipštas, Ina Marčiulionytė, Diana Vilytė, and Rimas Banys."

18 Algis Lipštas—journalist. OLF Executive Director (1990–1991).
Audra Misiūnienė (Misiunas)—businesswoman. OLF Executive Director (1992–1993).
Vytautas Gruodis (1930–2019)—businessman, OLF Executive Director (1993–1997).

talitarianism, so their contribution was enormous: they spoke English perfectly and had substantial work experience. We always received practical help from New York, in particular from Anthony Richter, who supported us through all the stages of the Foundation's establishment, and whom we called the "OLF's godfather."

Where were the Foundation's offices? How did you manage practical matters?

Prior to its formal establishment, the Foundation did not have its own offices. The first meetings took place at my home, Professor Kudaba's department office at Vilnius University's Faculty of Natural Sciences, and I can remember that we also met at Ina Marčiulionytė's apartment. We chose our staff very carefully. We were especially afraid of corruption and dishonesty, as we were dealing with very large sums of money. Thank God that we managed to avoid such problems. That is largely to the credit of our financial director, Diana Vilytė, who later became the OLF executive director.[19]

I remember how the Dubrovnik Committee implemented one of its first international projects—we sent a group of farmers to the United States to gain experience. Imagine someone like that receiving a paid trip to the United States in 1990! People could not believe that they didn't need to give anyone a bribe! To thank the foundation, they presented a carp from one of their own farms, but even that was accepted very reluctantly. Diana has told me about how careful they were with Soros's money—they would not even buy coffee with it. Later, when Audronė Misiūnienė became director, she reorganised the internal structure and explained that it was all right to use OLF funds to purchase coffee and water that were drunk at work. During the entire time that the OLF existed, there was not a single financial transgression. Even when the newspaper *Respublika* was waging a huge campaign of slander against us, the revenue agency did not even come to inspect us![20]

---

19 Diana Vilytė—OLF Director of Finance (1991–1995) and Executive Director (1997–2007).

20 From 2004, the Respublika publishing group waged a campaign of attacks against the OLF and George Soros that frequently descended into slander. Through articles in the daily newspapers *Respublika* [Republic] and *Vakaro žinios* [Evening news], the publishers steadily promoted the opinion that Soros and the foundations he supported were involved in criminal activities, that the OLF was recklessly interfering in Lithuanian government matters, destroying the state, and seeking to demoralise Lithuanians and erode their national identity.

One of our principles was that it is we who serve society, not the reverse. We instructed employees on how to answer the telephone, how to interact with applicants. We did everything we could to avoid becoming bureaucratic. We wanted our visitors to immediately sense that they had not come to a government institution. The Foundation gradually became a magnet: people such as the philosopher Arvydas Šliogeris, members of our board and expert committees, and other interesting and enlightened characters would simply drop by to talk, to discuss things.

I'm sure that many people in the humanities in Lithuania would agree that the "Open Lithuania Book" series shaped intellectual fashions to some degree. Please describe how that series came about, how decisions were made about which books to publish, how you selected staff and worked with publishing houses.

I would probably replace the word "fashions" with "directions." The publishing program was definitely one of our most successful, and perhaps one of the most significant of our programs. One journalist even referred to it as "a cultural revolution in Lithuania." We understood perfectly well that we had been isolated for many years, that we were very far behind and out of touch with European and world intellectual developments, that we did not know the main humanities and academic works of the second half of the twentieth century. It was therefore decided that such a publishing program must be developed. The historian Darius Čuplinskas and the journalist and translator Karla Gruodis had come to Lithuania from Canada in fall 1989. We had immediately found much common ground. They were very well read young people with broad interests, so I invited them to work with the OLF.

Darius Čuplinskas, whom the philosopher Arūnas Sverdiolas referred to as a "miraculous person" who had arrived in Lithuania, became the director of the publishing program and the creation of that program is entirely to his credit. He developed an all-encompassing program. We needed to dismantle the publishing monopoly held by the Mintis, Vaga, and Šviesa publishing houses, train publishers to work under market conditions, and nurture translators. The humanitarian sciences had been utterly starved for literature during the Soviet period. We understood that we needed to catch up with the world in a very deliberate and rapid fashion, so we worked very carefully and responsibly. In choosing books for the program we drew on the recommendations of academics and teachers; final selections were made by a special OLF committee headed by Arūnas Sverdiolas. From the many recommendations we tried hard to select the foundational texts that were needed to compensate for our long period of postwar isolation.

The texts were often translated by qualified specialists from academic and research institutions, some of which had been closed after the restoration of independence. This provided some of these individuals with an occupation and source of income, and therefore a reason for not emigrating.

In seeking to dismantle the state publishing monopolies, we tried to support private publishers, such as Baltos lankos and Alma Littera, by giving them work, and in this way I know that we helped them to become established.

A special program for training publishers was also created: we invited an expert from Great Britain to lead seminars for local Lithuanian publishers, thus training them in matters of market dynamics, marketing, and so on.

It is wonderful that this broad-ranging educational and academic publishing program had an effect. As I have mentioned, that is all largely to Darius Čuplinskas's credit.

When Darius left Lithuania to work in Budapest in 1995, his responsibilities were smoothly and creatively taken over by his assistant, Giedrė Kadžiulytė, who later founded and now runs the small, but top-level, publishing house Apostrofa.

Did you yourself actively participate in shaping the "Open Lithuania Book" (OLB) series? Did you make any specific recommendations or participate in the selection committee's discussions about which books were needed?

Yes, I did participate. Of course, today it is difficult to remember any concrete suggestions. It was very important to me that we publish key philosophical and historical works. At that time in Lithuania, not even Alexis de Tocqueville had been published; there were no books about the Holocaust or twentieth century history.[21] The list of books we published was very long. The head of our selec-

---

21 Alexis de Tocqueville's seminal work *Democracy in America* was published in Lithuanian as *Apie demokratija Amerikoje* (Vilnius: Amžius, 1996).

tion committee, Arūnas Sverdiolas, was responsible for compiling it; scholars and experts such as Kęstutis Nastopka and Stasys Stačiokas, and, from abroad, Alexander Shtromas and others, actively contributed to the process.

Were there any unsuccessful projects within the publishing program?

I do not think that any of our books failed to interest, or be understood by anyone at all. There was only one misunderstanding, around Nijolė Gaškaitė's *Pasipriešinimo istorija: 1944–1953* (A history of resistance: 1944– 1953). But we were able to reach a compromise: a forward written by Egidijus Aleksandravičius, including several clarifications, was glued into the already published book.[22]

Which books from the "OLB" series were most important and dear to you personally?

All of the books that were published in the series were important to me. But perhaps the most important to me personally were those that analysed twentieth century history—that tried to understand what happened to us, to Europe, before, during and after the Second World War. I cared especially about the texts of Czesław Miłosz, Vytautas Kavolis, Emmanuel Levin and Hannah Arendt, and I found the books by Norman Davies, Ernest Gellner's studies of nationalism, and many others to be fascinating.[23] I must not forget to mention the new

---

22   In the above-mentioned introduction, Egidijus Aleksandravičius raises and explores to what degree specific topics and analyses in Nijolė Gaškaitė's book conform to established, universal criterial for interpreting history and memory.

23   The following books by authors mentioned here by Veisaitė were published as part of the Open Lithuania Book series: Czesław Miłosz, *Tėvynės ieškojimas* [In search of a homeland], Vilnius: Baltos Lankos, 1995; *Ulro žemė: esė* [The land of Ulro: Essays], Vilnius: Baltos Lankos, 1996; *Lenkų literatūros istorija* [Literary history of Poland], Vilnius: Baltos Lankos, 1996; Vytautas Kavolis, *Civilizacijų analizė* [The analysis of civilisations], Vilnius: Baltos Lankos, 1998; About Kavolis: *Vytautas Kavolis: asmuo ir idėjos* [Vytautas Kavolis: The person and his ideas], Vilnius: Baltos Lankos, 2000; *Emmanuel Levinas, Etika ir begalybė: pokalbiai su Philippe'u Nemo* [Ethics and infinity: Conversations with Philippe Nemo], Vilnius: Baltos Lankos, 1994; *Apie dievą, ateinantį į mąstymą* [About God coming to thinking], Vilnius: Aidai, 2001; Hannah Arendt, *Tarp praeities ir ateities: aštuoni politinės filosofijos etiudai* [Between past and future: Eight political philosophy etudes], Vilnius: Aidai, 1995; *Totalitarizmo ištakos* [The Origins of Totalitarianism], Vilnius: Tyto alba, 2001. Norman Davies, *Dievo žaislas: Lenkijos istorija* [God's Playground: A History of Poland], Vilnius: Lietuvos rašytojų sąjungos leidykla, 1998, Vol. I and II; *Europa: istorija* [Europe: A history], Vilnius: Vaga, 2002; Ernest Gellner, *Postmod-*

kinds of textbooks for school children that were published through the program "Education for Lithuania's Future."

Then it is an excellent time to speak more about that particular program.

I have to admit that I was like a cat stalking a mouse as I waited for the historian Darius Kuolys to resign from his government position, because we could not invite people involved in politics to work directly with the OLF.[24] As soon as Darius resigned as Minister of Culture and Education—I believe the very same day—I called him and asked to become involved with the Foundation and to join the board. Darius more or less created our education program; he was the board member responsible for it, while Ina Marčiulionytė was the program director. When she left, Eglė Pranckūnienė took over her position.

"Education for Lithuania's Future" was developed as a five-year program and had many offshoots. One of these was the publication of textbooks, and we were the first to publish European-style textbooks in Lithuania. Through the program we organised professional teacher development courses, were intensely involved in the modernisation of libraries, and founded didactical, career, and debating centres that are functioning to this day. I believe that the program had a powerful impact on the entire Lithuanian education system.

Since we have been talking about publishing and education, I must ask you about another individual who had a tremendous impact on Lithuania during that period. The émigré sociologist Vytautas Kavolis's visits to Lithuania were very important to the development of Lithuanian liberalism (as an intellectual attitude, not a political strategy)—in particular his attitude as a social and cultural critic and, later, his teaching at Vytautas Magnus University in Kaunas. When and how did you meet Kavolis?

Vytautas Kavolis was a classmate of my cousin Aliukas in Kaunas, at Ateitininkų High School, where they were both students during the interwar period.

---

ernizmas, protas ir religija [Postmodernism, Reason and Religion], Vilnius: Pradai, 1993; *Tautos ir nacionalizmas* [Nations and Nationalism], Vilnius: Pradai, 1996.

24 Darius Kuolys—first Minister of Culture of the newly restored Republic of Lithuania (March 17, 1990–December 1, 1992).

I likely first heard Kavolis's name from Aliukas after the war, during the Soviet occupation.

Later, the émigré cultural journal *Metmenys* (Outline), which Kavolis edited and which was very close to our own views, reached us through various channels, and we read it with great interest. It provided both knowledge and the hope that Lithuania would one day be free and democratic.

When Aliukas went to America, he immediately connected with Vytautas and the Santara-Šviesa group, and became an active member of that circle. It meant a great deal to me that its members were open to and interested in what we were doing in Lithuania, despite the fact that we were living in an occupied country that was called Soviet Lithuania.

I can't remember when Kavolis first came to Lithuania, but I immediately got to know him and his wonderful wife Rita, a woman of rare goodness. She would travel to Lithuania with suitcases full of "deficit" items and medications, which she handed out to everyone as presents. That was when I began to acquaint myself with Kavolis's writings, his articles and books. After the restoration of Lithuania's independence, Kavolis's influence and input seemed especially important to me because we had to decide which direction Lithuania was going to go in—what kind of state it would be. Because the Open Lithuania Fund had a higher education program, our board decided that we must try to bring Kavolis to Lithuania. It was a very expensive idea. We would have to "buy out" Kavolis from Dickenson College for half a year, and that, as far as I remember, cost at least $300,000.

Having come to an agreement with Vytautas Magnus University (the historian Egidijus Aleksandravičius; the director of the Greimas Centre for the Study of Semiotics, Saulius Žukas; and the semiotics professor Kęstutis Nastopka played pivotal roles in this), we submitted an application to the Open Society Institute for funding. Kavolis's name was not that well known and there were some doubts about his qualifications, so we did not receive the funding immediately. Then I, as chair of the OLF board at that time, collected everything I could about Kavolis's publications and achievements and travelled to Budapest. Oxford University professor Bill Newton Smith was head of the Institute's academic program at that time. I cannot remember all of the details of our conversation, but I managed to convince him that Professor Kavolis had exceptional academic qualities, had written many works of sociology, and was especially needed in Lithuania at this time. In the end, we succeeded in "buying" Vytautas Kavolis for half a year. He and his wife came to Lithuania, and he lectured in Vilnius and Kaunas. It is hard to say, but I think this was one of the OLF's most successful projects. Professor Kavolis's lectures and interaction with students were indispensable and he developed a large following. Quite a few of his books were published through the OLF, and a Santara-Šviesa community became established in Lithuania, its work continuing to this day and increasingly popular with young people.

Tragically, during his second or third visit, Kavolis suffered a sudden and fatal heart attack. This was a great loss and blow to our culture, but by that point, thankfully, his work had already had a great impact on the humanities in Lithuania.

Kavolis left many students and followers. One of them was Leonidas Donskis, another scholar who left us much too young and who considered Kavolis to be his teacher.[25]

Which of this intellectual's ideas seemed to you most important for post-Soviet Lithuanian society's being and existence?

Personally, what I considered most important were professor Kavolis's liberal views, his critique of nationalism, his humanism, and his very open, deep and analytical way of looking at the world and different cultures, and his ability to see Lithuanian culture's role and value within this diversity. "Santara Šviesa"— Vytautas Kavolis was that organisation's conceptual leader—is a truly unique phenomenon that had no analogues in Lithuanian émigré history. After all, people living in the emigration tended to be more insular; as I have already mentioned, "Santara" had a completely different view of Lithuanianness, the occupied homeland, and the world.

Looking at the history of the OLF from today's perspective, what were some of its other key achievements?

A whole book could be written about that. The art historian Agnė Narušytė is trying to summarize the work of the OLF and I hope that her book will be

---

25   Leonidas Donskis (1962–2016)—philosopher, political theorist, historian of ideas, and one of Lithuania's most prominent public intellectuals. A close and long-time friend of Irena Veisaitė's.

published soon. There is already an Internet catalogue of the books that we published and financed. Rima Kuprytė, long-time director of the international Public Library Innovation Program, is working with other OLF employees on the project "A Virtual Exhibition of OLF Initiated, Supported and Published Books," which will illustrate the scale of the OLF publishing programme.

It seems to me that all of our programs were meaningful.

I think that our early childhood education programs, which we implemented together with the Danes and Americans, were very important; as were the debating, civil society, and law programs, which were numerous; the economics program; the Junior Achievement program; and the library support program, through which it was possible to implement important changes in the area of library modernisation. Personally, I cared a great deal about the culture program. Its scope was so wide that it is impossible to mention everything here. Perhaps it is worth at least mentioning the models for modern cinema, music, theatre and children's theatre festivals that we developed. The centres that we established also played an important role. Among these were the Journalism Centre; the Kaunas centre, which implemented several of the Foundation's programs; the Study Information Centre; and the Children's Support Centre.

And what would you consider to be the Foundation's failures?

I'm not sure how I can answer that question. The greatest and most fundamental failure is probably that we did not succeed in preserving the Foundation—that we did not find other sources of financing, so that it would not be solely dependent on Mr. Soros's money, which is something that Poland's Stefan Batory Foundation managed to do. On the other hand, as Diana Vilytė argues, even our failures were meaningful as experiments.

It would probably be correct to say that our Stateless Culture Centre was a failure. Its goal was to study and support the ethnic cultures in Lithuania that do not have their own state status: Karaim, Roma, Tatar, Old Believer, and Yiddish (from the time when Jewish Yiddish culture thrived in the territory of Lithuania and before the foundation of the state of Israel). The Centre began to function; its first director was the cultural historian Dovid Katz, a man of great erudition and tremendous energy. Unfortunately, certain circumstances led Professor Katz to resign as director and create a separate Yiddish Institute, which functions to this day. We attempted to keep the Centre alive and it continued to function for a while, but it did not play a significant role in the long run.

I hope that we will be able to re-establish the OLF—not as it was, perhaps not as multifaceted, but such that it would still be needed in Lithuania. After all, we are still on the path to creating a truly democratic state and society.[26]

In 1990–1993, you were vice chair and in 1993–2000 you were chair of the OLF board. Up until 1997, you taught at Vilnius Pedagogical University. How did you manage with such a workload? The responsibilities of heading the OLF board would probably have been enough work for several people. Were there perhaps some "effective time management" or "work optimization" rules that helped you to stay on track?

It was, indeed, impossible to fulfil all of these responsibilities. I sensed that I did not have enough time to get ready for my lectures, and I would never have dared to stand before my students unprepared. I simply had too much respect for their time, and, of course, for my own reputation. In 1997, after working at the Pedagogical Institute for 43 years, I gave up my teaching position. I also thought that it was time to make room for someone younger. I left my courses with my tremendously talented and hardworking student and graduate student Reda Pabarčienė, who is now a professor. And I have no regrets.

As chair of the OLF board, how often did you have to travel to meetings, training sessions or consultations for leaders of Soros-financed foundations?

That happened quite often. For five years I was also a member of Soros's main international board of directors in Budapest and a board member of the central

---

26   The Open Lithuania Foundation was re-established in 2017. In the twenty-first century, the foundation sees its mission as fostering the development of a mature, responsible, active, tolerant civil society, and the further development of the state through democratic institutions and human rights. At this time, the Foundation is implementing three programs: "A Strong Society," "Public Policy Analysis," and "Rethinking Europe."

Culture, Higher Education and East-East programs. At that time, I travelled a great deal with Mr. Soros and the entire international board to the Caucasus region, Central Asia, Russia, and throughout Eastern and Central Europe. And there were a great many meetings and all kinds of gatherings both abroad and in Lithuania. Only after my term as chair of the board ended did I realise what a burden and responsibility had been lifted from my shoulders. But I never thought about that while I was working.

What kind of a person is Mr. Soros? Did your opinions about fundamental matters differ often?

Our opinions rarely differed because, at the time, he maintained the position that we knew better what our countries needed than he did. I deeply respect him for that attitude and for all of his work. I learned a great deal from him.

I felt that I had Mr. Soros's complete trust. He is a highly intelligent person with a very intense, original, and paradoxical way of thinking. Mr. Soros always finds an unexpected solution—he never takes the well-trodden path. When we talked, it always felt like we were playing ping-pong. It was extremely tense . . . He knew how to get more out of you than you yourself are capable of. I remember how once, during a gathering of board chairs, he scheduled a 45-minute conversation with me. That day I had begun to have very severe back pain. I went to a pharmacy and bought a tablet that contained a lot of caffeine. That made me feel worse, my blood pressure went up, and I felt absolutely awful. But the thought of missing my meeting with Soros never entered my mind. So, my colleagues walked with me to the restaurant where we were going to have lunch. When I saw Soros I completely forgot how ill I felt. We had an intense and fascinating conversation that lasted not the scheduled 45 minutes, but, as I later noticed, an hour and a half, and then said our goodbyes. My colleagues helped me back to the hotel, and, although I felt half dead, I was very happy to have withstood the strain.

I was especially impressed by Soros's creativity, his capacity for critical thinking, and also his ability to acknowledge his mistakes. It was incredibly interesting to work with him. I am very proud of the dedication he wrote when he gave me the book *George Soros im Gespräch mit Krisztina Koenen* (George Soros in conversation with Krisztina Koenen, Frankfurt: Eichborn, 1994): "To Irena Veisaitė, my fellow-traveller in spreading the ideology of no ideology. With affection, George Soros."[27] That dedication is a good riposte to those who accused us of spreading the ideology of cosmopolitanism, which some people considered dangerous to Lithuania.

I would like to repeat a question that Kęstutis Nastopka formulated very precisely during a panel discussion about the OLF's work, held at the 2014 Santara-Šviesa conference: In the work of the Foundation, how did the patron's broad international goals coexist with Lithuania's interests?

I have already spoken about that to some degree. Soros's views were incongruous with those of conservatively oriented people such as some nationalistically inclined "patriots." Sometimes he wanted to create programs for which we were not yet ready. For example, we had problems regarding the treatment of drug addicts with methadone and with attitudes regarding homosexuality . . . But when it came to criticism of the scale levelled by *Respublika* in 2004 and later, we simply did not respond.

I have no doubt that you often found yourself in arguments with people who attacked the OLF for spreading the "ideology of cosmopolitanism." How did you defend yourself from such "arrows"?

I have to be honest and say that it was mostly the Education program that experienced that kind of disapproval. But it had very qualified staff and was headed by Darius Kuolys, so they managed to defend themselves very well.

To me, personally, it was very important that all of our programs maintain a balance between global and national interests, that democratic thinking and values develop as organically as possible, and that respect always be shown to those who think differently.

What do you think—to what degree did the OLF succeed in "dislodging" an image that is deeply engrained in Lithuanian mentality, and that I myself have formulated as "living in a besieged fortress"?

---

27 *George Soros im Gespräch mit Krisztina Koenen* [George Soros in conversation with Krisztina Koenen], Krisztina Koenen (Frankfurt: Eichborn, 1994)

I think that it succeeded to some degree—not everywhere and not always. We wanted to open ourselves up to Europe and open Europe up to ourselves. In Lithuania today there are certainly many things that have English names, fancy restaurants and shopping centres, and we follow European fashions. But these are all only external signs. Not enough time has passed for deeper changes, for a spiritual rebirth to take place. But I am an optimist and believe that a new and younger generation is growing that is free of the stereotypes that oppressed us. On the other hand, our future is hard to predict. Throughout much of Europe there is a danger of flooding from a new wave of radicalism.

In 2004, the newspaper **Respublika** *began a steady and brutal campaign of attacks against the OLF, specific members of its staff, and Mr. Soros. While observing that process at the time I formulated three questions, which I would like to pose to you now. First of all, why does a large portion of our society still need that kind of "media" and those kinds of "themes"? Secondly, does* **Respublika's** *campaign of lies and hatred not demonstrate that the idea of an open society was not realized? And thirdly, why did Lithuania's public intellectuals turn out to be cowards when they failed to defend either the OLF or the people associated with it, who were being smeared with mud?*

I will try to answer your questions in order.

Regarding the first question: that kind of media reflects the moods of people belonging to a certain segment of society. Take a look at the kinds of things said in online comments and it will all be clear. Intelligent comments are very much in the minority. Read Akunin's philosophical novel *Aristonomia*, which is set in 1915–1922 Russia.[28] It is an excellent analysis of the revolutionary period, during which the intelligentsia were a helpless minority that was powerless in controlling the brutal terror of the Bolshevik revolution. We, too, still need a lot more time.

Now regarding your second question. You are right—we did not succeed in achieving the idea of an open society. But the concept of one has entered our discourse, and that, in itself, is a great victory.

---

28   Борис Акунин, Аристономия, Москва: Захаров, 2012.

And as for the last one . . . Only isolated individuals, such as Father Arūnas Peškaitis, stood up in our defence. But on the other hand, who was actually supporting *Respublika* and *Vakaro žinios*? Maybe it was just those same online commentators? There is another factor—our decades-long fear of speaking openly and going against so-called public opinion. I can testify to the fact that all sorts of people would come up to me and tell me, in private, that they were grateful to the OLF. Naturally, that silence was painful to us, even extremely so.

Everything takes time. Whether we will have enough remains to be seen.

Our conversations are taking place during a time when you are working with a group of like-minded people who are trying to revive the OLF. Why did you decide to do that? What are the main challenges that the OLF and the people working there hope to meet?

We decided to renew our activities because, as you have said yourself, the idea of an open society is not yet fully realised in Lithuania. There are many new problems—not only in Lithuania, but around the entire world.

We must combine our efforts to try to solve them. Mr. Soros wants to encourage mutual understanding among the nations of Europe. That is also very important to us. As the saying goes, "Drop by drop, the stone will be hewn."

✳

More and More Questions, But Fewer and Fewer Answers

Irena Veisaitė at her home. Vilnius, 2016. Photo by Artūras Morozovas.

Our "marathon" of conversations is almost over, so I am very curious to ask what you are thinking and how you feel about the process we have gone through. In what ways did we succeed and fail?

It is impossible to accurately repeat that which one has lived through or experienced, and memory is often deceiving. On the other hand, I want to believe that our conversations, which will soon appear as a book, will help to reveal how we think and what we feel today. I have often noticed that people speaking to me want first of all to learn certain facts, while what is most meaningful to me is to try to understand *how* we look at those facts and events and *why* it is worth remembering them again. I have faith that your—our—book will contribute to that kind of understanding.

I also believe that conversations can be a good way of promoting the kind of reflection and self-awareness that you refer to. On the other hand, a sceptic could say: "Irena's and Aurimas's efforts are doomed to failure. All that history can teach us is that nobody every learns anything from it."

But if we should succeed in bringing one person closer to the truth and encouraging them to reject stereotypes, that in itself would be meaningful. I do not mean to suggest that, in speaking about the past and the present, we have the capacity to save people and lead them onto the path of truth. But if our conversations should encourage people to learn more about, and more deeply understand, the past—to forgive and to have more empathy for each other—then it is worth remembering for that. As I said when we were discussing *Faust*—we cannot save the world, but we can each try to save our own souls . . .

We recorded our conversations with various breaks and over almost three years. At any point did you have any shadow of doubt about that we are doing here?

I never doubted you, but I doubt myself constantly. I have said that I find it difficult to reveal myself. I understand perfectly well that I cannot relate everything and that I will fail to mention many events and people that played important roles in my life, so I wish to apologise for that in advance. But at the same time, I would like to believe that our conversations will not have been pointless—that they may help someone grasp what happened to and is happening to us.

I have constant doubts about whether anyone will be interested in reading what we have talked about, but, despite these uncertainties, I am happy to be able to speak with you about the things that brought meaning to my life.

On the other hand, over the course of those three years, during which we have met so many times to talk, the world has changed a great deal. There are more and more signs that are cause for alarm. I am always reacting to the present, but that present is constantly shifting. What one says today may be out of date tomorrow.

And there is one more thing. During our conversations, you were always asking me about one thing and another and I have tried to answer your questions, but I have no idea about your own relationship to what we have managed to accomplish. So I would like to interview you.

I am used to being the one asking and listening. On the other hand, our interviews, which, in the long run, turned into conversations between two like-minded people, no longer adhere to a strict division of roles between listener and narrator. For that reason, I am happy to answer your question. I would like to begin from the more general: I treasure every moment of every meeting or conversation during which people tell me their life stories. These conversations help me to imagine, understand, and feel the historical episodes that are the constant focus of my research and analysis. And listening to testimonials about things experienced during the twenti-

eth century helps me to better understand and feel the unsettled nature of the twenty-first century.

And there is one more thing. I often speak to people who have lived long, interesting, and meaningful lives and are inevitably nearing the end of their own paths. Being with people like that simply forces one to look at one's own life, the rapid passage of time and the horizon of the future, and to continually ask the following questions: "How much time do I have left and how should I spend it? What is the meaning of my existence here and now? How can my thinking about the past help me to live in the present?"

What you are saying is interesting, but I would also like to understand what my own narrative has opened up to you, what it has helped you to understand and to feel. Or perhaps this is not the time to ask such question? Perhaps some distance is needed for consideration of that question to be possible? Please try to think about that a little now and open yourself up to me a little.

During our conversations, you have said a few things that I think about constantly and will likely continue to think about more in the future. Your decision to forgive those Holocaust participants who sincerely repent for their dark deeds, and your forceful stance that these people's crimes against humanity should not lead us to condemn the entire German or Lithuanian nation—this is, existentially, very important to me. I keep wondering: how is it possible to do that when you have experienced such awful things, when you lost your entire world?

I have to be honest—that question truly surprised me . . . And what alternative is there?

It is clear that we are alike in some ways, that we are connected on certain levels of ideas and existential attitudes, but, at the same time, as your reaction indicates, our experiences are very different. And, naturally, I don't know of any alternative.

There is one more thing that I think about when remembering our conversations and which is related to the lifestyle each of us has chosen: we both live in the world of books. Your pedagogical experience of working with classrooms full of young people, of using the interpretation of classical texts to talk to them about ideas and values that were generally belittled and negated, is very important to me.

If I had to name which subjects and themes in our conversations were especially interesting and important to me as a scholar, I would have to mention many things that are related to twentieth-century mentality, everyday life, and cultural history. But here I will limit myself to one example: in our last conversation, we devoted a lot of our attention to discussing the work around the creation of the independent Lithuanian state. That is especially important to me because I am convinced that we do not think deeply enough about that, and therefore still do not know how to talk about our new epoch of freedom.

Thank your for sharing your thoughts. It was very important for me to understand something about how you think and what you feel. And as far as the capacity to forgive is concerned, I believe that you understand perfectly well that there simply is no other path. Seeking revenge is senseless and revenge only leads to more bloodshed. As my friend the sculptor Elena Gaputytė, may she rest in peace, said: the human path is the *path of forgiveness and that is the only path to life.*[1]

And as far as the miracle of the restoration of our independence and the disappointment we have sometimes felt since then are concerned, we will be thinking about that for a long time . . . But whatever anyone may think, it was a miracle.

And now I would like to return to my usual and more familiar role and ask this: our conversations were not a "sprint" but rather a "marathon." If you had to prepare for another marathon like this, what would you do, now that you have had this experience?

A great deal would depend on the person with whom I would have the conversations. But one thing is certain—it would be very important for me to keep

---

[1]   Elena Gaputytė (1927–1991)—artist whose central themes include the tragic fate of Eastern Europe in the twentieth century and the importance of compassion for all those who suffer.

our attention focused on the dimension of the present, and, also, to leave space for doubts and questions. With the passage of time, some people claim to have learned or understood everything, or almost everything. But I have to say that with every year that passes I realise that I have more and more questions—and fewer and fewer answers . . .

✻

Voices from the Past

The texts in this section return the reader to questions that we discussed in various conversations, and offer several additional points of access to Irena Veisaitė's biography.

In seeking to respect the genre, structure, and scope of this book, I was determined to include, in this chapter that draws a curtain over my conversations with Irena Veisaitė, several documents that give voice to the past and the people who lived in it.

The first document, from 1947, contains Irena Veisaitė's answers to a questionnaire that her high school teacher, Vanda Zaborskaitė, asked her students to complete. In it, Veisaitė expresses several key ideas that would serve as existential guidelines when she had to make crucial decisions at different points in her life.

A theatre review dating from the Soviet period makes it at least somewhat easier to grasp the scope of my heroine and co-author's interests; her review of the play *Šventežeris* also marks the beginning of a new period in Irena Veisaitė's biography. Several other texts and statements—"Left Unsaid," "The Holocaust in My Life," and "Does Litvak Culture Have any Future on Lithuanian Soil?"—offer the reader further opportunities to experience how Veisaitė has created her own relationship to the Holocaust, her murdered Litvak tribe, and memories of these things in contemporary Lithuania.

Excerpts from letters by Veisaitė to her future husband, Grigori Kromanov, not only speak about the growth of feelings but also the birth of intellectual connections, and thus help us to, at least in part, answer the question: how did like-minded artists and academics in Soviet-era "islands" think, and what sorts of questions did they grapple with?

The past speaks to us in various ways—one only needs to be open to hearing these narratives. Knowing this, I hope that the texts in this section of the book will offer the reader additional opportunities to ask questions and think, and in that way create their own dialogue with the past—a dialogue which allows us to see both ourselves and the Other in history.

Aurimas Švedas

WHAT QUESTIONS MATTER MOST TO ME NOW?

High School Questionnaire

1. What questions matter the most to me now?

There is no question that does not matter to me. I am interested in all external and internal phenomena. I am like a little Faust or Andrei Bolkonsky—I am searching for the meaning of life, for a goal, for the truth. I am troubled by the lack of a firm foundation. Abstract, detached answers and questions do not satisfy me.

But these fragmentary thoughts also lack concreteness. Apparently, they are typical of youth. Right now, I am standing on the threshold of my life, and the future is one big question mark. What will I be? Will I succeed in justifying my life?

This year I will graduate from high school. I must choose a profession. I am drawn to a profession that has no future and which, under current circumstances, it would not be interesting to study. So I must choose something else. I am thinking about medicine, music theory and criticism, or literature. As is the case for all of my friends, this is the question that matters most to me today.

I devote much attention, time, and thought to my own development. I want to grow, to improve myself, to correct my errors. I used to think that my feelings were special in some way. Only recently did I notice that I am no different from anyone else and that I do not have even the tiniest grain of originality. This thought was very upsetting. I no longer knew how to escape from a vicious circle. How can I find myself?

I am also concerned with the question of Woman, and have no idea how to resolve it. Is there a realistic, practical solution? What is a woman's first calling? How does one create a happy family? Life offers us many examples of the opposite. The first requirement of a happy family is self-sacrifice and negation of one's own interests (at least 90 per cent of them). And that is incredibly difficult. Family and love should only be a support—not the goal in itself. I am a true egotist and therefore often ask myself: "Where will I find happiness and satisfaction?" And I definitely want to find happiness. Already now, I would like to find a future direction, some elementary principles, at least a grain of truth. And that is incredibly difficult, when such a great *battle of truths* is taking place in the world.

I could definitely not confirm that the things that I have written here are the questions that are most important to me. It reflects only a small fraction of them, since each thing one notices in life raises many new questions, most of which remain unanswered. But all thoughts, desires, and questions can be summarised in a few words: "What makes a full-fledged human being? How does one become that?"

In the end, at this point I am trying (as much as I can) to follow some advice I have received: "Don't think about yourself too much. Let some time pass for all the questions that have arisen to settle; they will sort themselves out naturally."

2. What do I expect from my homeroom teacher?

My friends and I recently debated the question of friendship and we came to the conclusion that one should not place any great demands on a friend. But a teacher is not a friend. A teacher is the person from whom we hope to receive the theoretical and practical knowledge we will need in our lives. So demands, or perhaps more accurately desires or hopes, naturally arise. And although it may not sound nice, we have been told, "Use your teacher in every way you can." I am trying to follow this piece of advice. I am trying to grasp and absorb my teacher's every word.

I would like that, at least in terms of authority, for my teacher to be like a mother. Of course, most girls from the country do not have anything in common with their parents. But my own mother was like a friend and a teacher to me. I had tremendous respect and admiration for her. Sadly, I lost her at a very young age. And with her I lost someone whom I respected deeply and could trust implicitly. Every person and book has a different opinion. How is one to find a middle ground? That is a very difficult task.

But now there is my Homeroom Teacher, whom I respect and love deeply. Almost every word she says is the truth to me. So it is very important to me that our Teacher never ceases to be an authority figure to me. I very much hope, if it is possible, that our Teacher would not refrain from sharing with her students her opinions on every possible question. I would like our homeroom classes to be more frequent and more in-depth, and that we be able to reach a conclusion about every subject. I want to use my Homeroom Teacher in every way I possibly can! Please do not understand that the wrong way. All other requirements are being fulfilled 100 per cent.

3. What do I think about our class?

A homeroom class is the first and last intimate collective that a person experiences in life. I would like to experience it deeply and fully. We spend a large portion of each day among our classroom friends. We are connected by common interests and goals.

At the beginning of the year, students gathered from all corners of Lithuania. The old students made up only half of the class. It is hard for everyone to get along instantly, to avoid petty misunderstandings. But nevertheless, the life of our class is developing nicely and is moving forward. What is especially beautiful is the love all of the girls have for our Teacher, through whom we are all connected.

Review: "Measured Optimism"
Impressions from the premiere of Kazys Saja's *Šventežeris* in Tallinn

The premiere of Kazys Saja's *Šventežeris* recently took place in Tallinn's Kingi-sepp Theatre.

In Estonia there has long been interest in Lithuanian dramaturgy and theatre. Kazys Binkis's play *Atžalynas* (The undergrowth, 1938) was staged at the Tallinn Workers' Theatre in 1941. The plays of Juozas Grušas, Augustinas Gricius, Viktoras Miliūnas, Kazys Saja, Raimundas Samulevičius, and Regina Mikalauskaitė have been translated into Estonian and quite a few of them have been staged. Juozas Grušas's *Meilė, džiazas ir velnias* (Love, jazz and the devil) is currently playing at the Viljandi Theatre in Ugala, and Raimundas Samulevičius's *Tiltas į tolimąją naktį* (Bridge to a distant night) is playing in Pernu.

Kazys Saja has been known to Estonian audiences since 1956, when his play *Lažybos* (The gamble) was staged at Pernu Theatre, and Tartu Student Theatre performed *Nerimas* (Anxiety). But *Šventežeris* has been honoured in a very special way: it is the first Lithuanian play to be staged at the main theatre of the Estonian capital in the post-war years.

It is difficult, without understanding Estonian, to form a broader opinion of this production by Grigori Kromanov, who appears to me to be a very subtle artist. Nevertheless, it is impossible not to notice that the Tallinn team took a different route than the one taken by the Kaunas theatre, and in doing so they found a very unique theatrical solution for *Šventežeris*. In highlighting the dramatic, and, in some places, tragic subtext of Saja's play, the director suppresses the comic plane. Underplaying the author's characteristic witty retorts and amusing situations, Kromanov has created a production that is about varied individuals' complex fates and interpersonal relations within the context of contemporary civilization and progress. Here Šventežeris represents the generosity of the land that provides refuge to all of us. But different kinds of people live in that land—often failing to understand each other, looking for only their own truths, and defending their own interests, they abuse both the land and each other... But that is only one aspect of a very rich and multifaceted production. The stream of associations is endless... Both director and actors succeed in not only communicating Saja's text but in drawing out the many thoughts and feelings hiding within it.

The internal rhythm of the play hooks the audience in the first act. Here the director is most concerned with two characters—Izolda and Ramunė—through whose portraits the main problems of the play go on to be developed.

Acclaimed Estonian SSR actress Ita Ever's portrayal of Izolda is one of the play's greatest successes. Using external means of characterisation with taste and moderation, the actress reveals her heroine's complex world. In appearance, Izolda—Ever—is somewhat vulgar, a little woman who likes to talk loud and dirty; but her uncoordinated movements and certain other details quickly reveal the unhappy creature's internal fragility, her human helplessness. This is especially made evident in the daring resolution of the scene depicting Izolda's epilepsy attack. Ever subtly demonstrates that behind Izolda's somewhat vulgar and eccentric character hides a woman's beautiful and childishly pure, if somewhat primitive, soul. The viewer marvels at how the actress precisely hits the intonations of a small, hurt child when she asks Dr. Butrimas to help her, and how she becomes petulantly angry when she does not receive any help. Finally, in the third act, Ever shows us an Izolda who is now completely broken by life (if she does not always understand that herself)—who will never recover and can only seek shelter with one or another, or, in the author's words, will sway like a reed in whichever direction the wind blows.

The role of Ramunė is played by Liina Saari, a nineteen-year-old toy store clerk and amateur actress. This is Saari's first substantial role and one cannot fail to enjoy her directness, sincerity, and intuition. Ramunė—Saari—is utterly convincing: when, in the first act, the sixteen-year-old girl observes, with both curiosity and revulsion, Izolda standing in the bushes with Dunzila; when she is horrified by how the geologists mock Izolda's epilepsy; when she attacks Liukpetris—Hans Kaldoja—seeking to pour out all of her anger and pain; and finally, when Ramunė, right then senses Liukpetris's humanity and nestles close to him, whimpering and crying like an abused little dog. In the second and third acts, the director is not generous with Ramunė. Although her misfortune becomes more of an object of the other characters' experiences, interests and debates, she still succeeds in attracting the viewers' attention. Her parting from her mother sounds like a farewell to a cosy childhood and the warmth of the home. The actress Saari does not know if they will return to Šventežeris... This question mark at the end of the play becomes especially meaningful and impressive, and forces the viewer to think.

It is perhaps more difficult, without knowing the Estonian language, to understand Dr. Butrimas (Eduard Ralja), whom the author gives many opportunities to contemplate and debate. It seems that this man of determined voice and movement speaks convincingly about man and nature, but he much too easily leaves Šventežeris and Mrs. Daugvilienė.

In *Šventežeris*, director Kromanov accords especially great significance to Mrs. Daugvilienė, who is played by USSR People's Artist Aino Talvi. At the beginning of the play, she perhaps seems too reserved and static, but her deep and passionate personality breaks through in the second act, and by the end of the play we see that her reserve was very meaningful. It is difficult to convey the power that this woman, who has not been pampered by life, reveals when she suddenly begins to shout: "Drown him, little lake, drown him!" At that moment, it seems that Daugvilienė—Talvi—is not thinking of revenge toward the drowning Dunzila, or the geologists, but is cursing all that befouls nature and man. In my own understanding, the direction of the play allows Daugvilienė to rise above all of the other characters; when, having lost everything, she firmly states "Tomorrow we will drain the well," what had seemed to be a bleak, even tragic play becomes an optimistic one—a play that asserts the human determination to persevere, survive, preserve . . . As long as people such as Daugvilienė protect Šventežeris, we can still hope that its water will remain clear . . .

Watching this premiere, I was also struck by the remaining actors' impressive dramatic culture, their refusal to cater to the audience's tastes or to use cheap effects, and their success in establishing a consistent poetic atmosphere and psychologically convincing characters. I was also struck by the great demands that the director and actors placed on themselves. For example, Dunzila (richly portrayed by the actor R. Gutman) lifted weights and "warmed up" before coming on stage in order to appear before the audience in the required mood and appearance.

The set designer, Lembit Roosa, supports the director's efforts, but, in my view, he could have been more inventive. The decorations add neither Lithuanian nor Estonian color and only convey the general impression of a dying country village: three dried-up trees rise against a black background and there is nothing to suggest the greenness of the fields, the variety of the meadows, or the blueness of the lake. Even the landscape, by Lithuanian photographer Antanas Sutkus, that is projected onto the back of the stage, as though through dark clouds, is in black and white and therefore does not help to add any local color to the set. The photographs that are inventively projected on a screen during the hypnosis scene are a strong solution on Kromanov's part, as they seem deeply significant (and this is the scene that brought the author so much grief from Lithuanian critics!). When Izolda, ordered by Dr. Butrimas, weaves a wreath of flowers, a meadow of daisies appears on the screen; the hypnotized geologists seem to see running, bare-legged girls and young men enjoying ice cream on the screen, a clear indication of their inner, spiritual poverty. One would like to once more thank our creative Estonian colleagues and hope that relations with Grigori Kromanov become even closer in the future—in collaborations with Kazys Saja and perhaps also other Lithuanian playwrights.

※

Texts and Statements

"Left Unsaid"

The first and founding meeting of our Sąjūdis independence movement has taken place. These have been very significant days for Lithuania. Every hour and every word spoken here were more precious than gold. I did not make a statement myself, but, like many others listening in the hall or watching on television, I have a great many and varied thoughts that I have kept to myself during these horrifying decades of silence. However, when I heard about a letter to Sąjūdis written by a fellow Jew, my childhood friend Dmitrijus Kopelmanas, I felt that I could no longer remain silent. I decided to appeal to the editors of *Gimtasis kraštas* (Homeland) and ask that they publish my long unsaid words.

Dear readers, to live in freedom is the inalienable right of every person and nation. It is their right, good fortune, and responsibility. As it was said here so beautifully: without it, "a humanoid cannot become a human, or a community—a nation."

But freedom does not depend only upon external factors or political systems (though one should not diminish their importance). It lies in a person's spirit, in their heart. World leaders have often become slaves to their own wealth or their governments, while many a shackled prisoner has felt free. Our recent history offers many examples of this.

During the years of Hitler's occupation, when the Jews lost not only freedom but the right to live, many Lithuanians stood up to save their countrymen. But there were also many other fates. My mother, Sofija Veisienė-Štromaitė, was killed at the Ninth Fort.[1] My beloved uncle, the great Lithuanian patriot Jurgis Štromas, was brutally killed during the first days of the war at the Lietūkis Garage. All of that was the product of a state under great stress; it is tragic and irreversible. Left an orphan, I found myself in the Kaunas ghetto. I did not seek delivery, but it came to me. The family of the Kudirkos Naumiestis organist, Bagdonavičius, for whom virtue was always the highest goal of existence, undertook to help me. Onutė Bagdonavičiūtė-Strimaitienė and her husband, the Lithuanian army officer Juozas Strimaitis (USA), procured an official document for me, and I became Irena Treigytė, daughter of the Principal of Marijampolė High School. They took me from Kaunas to Vilnius and always watched over me. I lived in the home of the surgeon Pranas Bagdonavičius (USA), then the late Marija Meškauskienė. My second mother was to be Stefanija Paliulytė-Ladigienė. She was a widow who had six children and was always short of food, but I stayed with her family even after the war, until her arrest in March 1946. I was supported by the pastor of St. Ignatius Church, Father Skurskis, the late nurse Marcelė Kubiliūtė, and the director of the Subačiaus Street orphanage, Dr. Rudaitis. There is much to say and write about all of that. Unfortunately, it was not possible to publicise my story, and those of many others, in the late, honourable Sofija Binkienė's (a woman who rescued Jews herself) book *Ir be ginklo kariai* (There are also unarmed soldiers); as Dimitrijus Kopelmanas rightly pointed out, among the rescuers there were many priests and devout lay people—in other words, "enemies of the people." It was not possible to praise them in such times. But today, during this time of spiritual cleansing and elation, I feel a responsibility to remember these people who are so dear to me, as they no doubt are to many others. May they be remembered always. Yes, thousands of unarmed souls can be killed by just a few men with machine guns. And those men risk nothing—except their souls. On the other hand, it can sometimes take the sacrifice and tremendous spiritual strength of many to save but one.

---

1   Ninth Fort—red brick building that belonged to the Kaunas Fortress defence systems. In 1924 the Ninth Fort was established as a hard labor facility of the Kaunas Prison; in 1940–1941 it functioned as an NKVD prison; during the Nazi occupation (October 1941 to August 1944) it was a prison and site of mass killings. In addition to Kaunas residents, citizens of various countries (Austria, Poland, France, Germany, the USSR) were imprisoned and executed there. According to preliminary data, approximately 50,000 were killed at the Ninth Fort during the Second World War.

Every nation has its saints and its executioners. To hate a nation or to condemn a nation is only possible if one is blind. It is always a specific person who is guilty. But it is especially painful to see one's own countrymen become executioners.

And today our enemy is not some nation, but a great variety of fanatics, stagnationists, Stalinists—no matter of what nationality. And how important it is for the citizens of our republic—Lithuanians, Russians, Poles, Jews, Belarusians, Ukrainians, and others—to understand this, so that blood may never again be shed on Lithuanian land on any of their behalf.

Let us free ourselves from hatred, let us hear each other, and let us join together for the general good of our beloved country. We were born and raised in it. There is no other country in the world that we can call our homeland.

"The Holocaust in My Life"

Some time ago, the esteemed pastor of the Bernardine Church, Brother Arūnas, asked me: "Tell me, Irena, what does the Holocaust mean to you?" That is a very personal question and I will attempt to answer it in as personal a way as I can. I have now been thinking about it for several months. I know that immediately after the war I instinctively avoided those memories. They were simply unbearable. After all, I had lost my mother, who was only 35 years old, my grandparents, my parents' entire generation, and countless friends and acquaintances. Their deaths were inexplicable and therefore unjustifiable. What had been the source of all of that sudden brutality? I did not understand why I too had been marked, humiliated, and hunted. I did not understand why, in the post-war years, this terrible crime—not just against the Jews but against all of humanity—was fundamentally either hushed up or distorted. At the time, the only thing that saved me from feeling total despair was the human kindness and self-sacrifice that I encountered during those inhumane times. What especially stuck in my mind were the principles my mother bade me to live by—that I must always live in truth and never seek revenge. I was only able to understand and appreciate them much later. I will never forget my rescuers, the Bagdonavičius and Strimaitis families; my second mother, Stefanija Paliulytė-Ladigienė; or Dr. Rudaitis, Miss Marcelė Kubiliūtė, and many others. In saving me, they risked their own and their children's lives. I could write a poem about each of them, and today, in the Bernardine Church, I once more bow my head in their memories. These people not only saved my life but, what is just as important, helped me to avoid hatred, showed me how not to give in to anger, and allowed me to trust.

But of course, no matter what I did to run from the terrifying memories of the Nazi occupation, I did not succeed in doing so. The best way that I can convey that is through certain details: I could never go into saunas, as they made me think of the gas chambers; I was always eternally grateful that I could feed my only daughter, Alina; I could never, and still cannot, throw out even the smallest slice of bread, and when I see a piece of discarded food on the street I always think that it could have saved some Holocaust or Gulag prisoner's life ... I have to say that the Holocaust and the Gulag are somehow intertwined in my subconscious. My second mother spent time in the Gulag. To this day, I cannot speak calmly about my mother's brutal death or the suffering Mrs. Ladigienė endured in Siberia.

Now that I have reached a venerable age, I understand that the Holocaust always was and continues to be a part of me and that, to a large extent, it determined the course of my life and the formation of my values. I must tell you, openly, that with every year the memories become more distinct, that they come to the surface of my consciousness more and more frequently. To this day, I fail to understand how it could all have happened in Europe, in the civilised world, in my native Lithuania.

In attempting to answer esteemed Brother Arūnas's question about what the Holocaust means in my life, I would say that, more than 60 years after those awful events, I am still trying to understand what lessons I have gleaned from them.

I know that I will never forget the dead, that I will always preserve their memories, but also that I will never seek to impose my pain on others. Each individual, whatever their nationality or faith, must establish their own relationship to the Holocaust.

I believe that the experience of the Holocaust taught me:

- · to always empathise with and understand others, and to never try to compare levels of suffering—for each person, their own suffering is the greatest;

- to not see myself as a victim;
- to never mark someone with the Star of David or any other nationalist, religious, or ethnic symbol that could have a humiliating effect;
- to never do to others what was done to me;
- to never blame a nation for crimes committed by individuals or even governments.

I realised that, if I wanted to go on living, I had to learn to love and to forgive, *even if that is sometimes very difficult* . . . I cannot say everything here. I would like to end with the words that the late artist and sculptor Elena Gaputytė, who lived in exile, said in her foreword to the Lithuanian and English language editions of Dalia Grinkevičiūtė's book *Lietuviai prie Laptevių jūros* (Lithuanians by the Laptev sea). That album contained photographs of Elena's installations, which used many small white stones, candles, and lanterns. She saw them, in her words, as "symbols of peace, eternal hope and eternal life. [...] Those burning candles remind us that the human path is the path to forgiveness, and that that is the only path to life . . ."

I do not know, dear Brother Arūnas, whether I answered your question, or even my own . . .

"Does Litvak Culture Have a Future on Lithuanian Soil?"

I am speaking from a personal perspective. I am not an historian, but I am a Litvak. The Holocaust brought the end of the Litvak tribe on Lithuanian soil: during the years of Hitler's occupation (1941–1944), it was physically annihilated in the traditional territory of the Litvaks, i.e., in contemporary Lithuania, Belarus, and Courland (Latvia). After the Holocaust, only approximately one in ten of the Jews that had lived in Lithuania remained.

The second Soviet occupation (1944–1990) did not affect the remaining living Litvaks physically, but, for 50 years, the Soviet regime destroyed their spiritual and cultural heritage: buildings and synagogues were demolished and cemeteries were destroyed; all the Jewish schools and museums were closed; the surviving Yiddish and Hebrew books were not burned, but were sent to recycling, and all Jewish media was banned . . . The long history of the Jews in Lithuania, including the Holocaust, was either hushed up or falsified to meet the political and ideological needs of the times.

With the declaration of the restoration of Lithuania's independence in 1990 and as the foundations for a new democratic state began to be laid, it became necessary to examine the recent past. It turned out that one of the most difficult problems would turn out to be the assessment of the Holocaust and the Jewish-Lithuanian relations connected to it. Barely beginning to create itself, the young state had to confront an especially painful truth—that some Lithuanians had participated in the mass killings of the Jews. This was a difficult task for the following reasons:

The Holocaust, in Professor Egidijus Aleksandravičius's view, was not embedded in the Lithuanian nation's collective memory; it was overwhelmed by the Gulag, from which the Lithuanian nation suffered especially harshly. In truth, so did Jews, but that detail was left unnoticed.

Deeply-rooted anti-Semitic stereotypes existed, in particular the views that the Jews were all communists and were responsible for the Soviet occupation of Lithuania and that the participation of certain Lithuanians in the killing of Jews was revenge for the betrayal of the homeland.

With independence restored and Lithuanian statehood being rebuilt, and with the country seeking to take its rightful place among the nations of Europe, it was difficult to speak about the catastrophe of Lithuania's Jews. As Professor Alfonsas Eidintas has put it, it did not correspond with our tradition of mythologizing and heroicising history, something which is, indeed, typical of many nations.

Events had to be reconstructed, facts and figures checked, analysed and assessed. Much has been done in this regard and this work continues intensively, especially among our middle generation of historians; the reality of the irreversible catastrophe of the Jews is increasingly, and always more courageously, recognised, bringing the realisation (as Vytautas Landsbergis has said) that what happened in Lithuania—even during the years of the Nazi occupation—is a problem that the Lithuanians must face.

With increasing examination of the history and consequences of the Holocaust, these questions were raised more and more frequently: What, in the end, have we lost? Who were those Litvaks and what was their role in Lithuanian history? What is their cultural legacy, and what does it mean to us today?

I can offer a short retrospective. According the *Encyclopaedia Judaica*, the Litvaks (as the Lithuanian Jews were called in Yiddish), settled in Lithuania's historical territory—i.e., the Grand Duchy of Lithuania, whose territory extended well beyond the borders of the Republic of Lithuania and, in the sixteenth century, included contemporary Belarus, Courland (Latvia) and Northern Poland. Litvak culture took shape during the seventeenth and eighteenth centuries. Litvaks are connected by Yiddish language and literature, and Misnagdic (Ashkenazy) religious views; they were famous for their religious schools, their yeshivas, and rabbis, and also, from the nineteenth century, their secular culture and arts.

I cannot, in this short address, offer an in-depth discussion of that culture's religious and secular manifestations. (A more detailed account of Litvak history is available in Jonas Morkus's book *The Jerusalem of Lithuania*, which was specially published for the Frankfurt Book Fair.) I would only like to point out that Lithuania is universally recognised as the cradle of Litvak religious and secular culture, and that Lithuania's capital, Vilnius, is known as the Jerusalem of Lithuania. This has been beautifully expressed by the famous classic Jewish poet Moyshe Kulbak, who was tragically executed by the Soviets in 1937. In 1926, he created one of the most beautiful poems about Vilnius—a city in which the Jews had put down deep roots and which was embedded in the metaphysical depths of their spirit:

> *You are a talisman planted in Lithuania,*
> *Woven in lichen and mosses grey;*
> *Each of your walls like parchment,*
> *Every wall—a holy script,*
> *Mysteriously placed and revealed in the night,*
> *When a water carrier stands frozen on the old synagogue*
> *His beard pointed up as he counts the stars.*[2]

But let us return to the question raised at the beginning: is a continuation of that unique Litvak heritage possible in twenty-first century Lithuania, and, if so, under what conditions?

---

[2]   Tu esi Lietuvon įstatytas talismanas, / Apipintas kerpėm ir samanom pilkom; / Kiekviena siena—pergamentas, / Kiekvienas akmuo—šventas raštas, / Išdėlioti mįslingai ir praskleisti nakčia, / Kai ant senos sinagogos sustirįs vandens nešėjas / Stovi ir barzdą užvertįs skaičiuoja žvaigždes. [Lithuanian translation]

It is a fact that there are hardly any Litvaks left in Lithuania. Of the roughly 4,000 remaining Jews living there, perhaps one quarter are Litvaks, and these
are very elderly people. Yes, the Litvaks' material and spiritual heritage has survived: the empty synagogues and community buildings, homes, and town layouts are still there; some of the spiritual heritage—books and other printed media, artisanal objects, and so on—has survived. Is it important to preserve and
make use of all of this in today's Lithuania, which is being shaped by globalisation and the process of re-entering Europe?

I will attempt to answer this question from two angles—from the positions
of both Lithuania's ethnic Jews and ethnic Lithuanians.

The position of Lithuania's ethnic Jews was perhaps best expressed in a
statement by Dr. Simonas Alperavičius, head of the Lithuanian Jewish Community: "We are recognised as one of the most active Jewish communities in
Eastern Europe—please do not bury us before our time." Indeed, even several Jewish communities have formed in Lithuania, and they are active not only
on a social level but in the cultural and educational spheres as well. The Jewish
newspaper *Lietuvos Jeruzalė* (Lithuania's Jerusalem) is published in four languages. In Vilnius there is a Jewish high school named after Sholem Aleichem,
a day care, clubs, the Vilna Gaon State Jewish Museum and Centre for Tolerance, and the Stateless Culture Centre and Yiddish Institute connected to Vilnius University, where, since four years ago, Yiddish courses have been attracting students from around the world. The National Martynas Mažvydas Library
has a Judaica department in which the miraculously surviving Litvak spiritual
and cultural heritage—books and print media—is preserved, systematised, and
studied. For that we must be grateful to the Book Palace's former director Antanas Ulpius, who, in 1949, ignored orders from the Soviet authorities to send
the contents of the Jewish Museum to recycling; he hid them in St. George's
Church, which was at his disposal and had been turned into the Book Palace's
warehouse. For almost fourteen years now, the National Library's Judaica department has been run by Fira Bramson-Alperienė, whom many in Germany
know. Vilnius Municipality and the director of the Tolerance Centre, Emanuelis Zingeris, have plans to reconstruct fragments of old Jewish neighbourhoods
in the city; a state resolution has already been adopted to that effect.

Litvak cultural traditions are also maintained by many prominent artists—the composer Anatoly Shenderov; the artists Adomas Jacovskis, Ada

Skliutauskaitė, and Solomonas Teitelbaumas; the writers Grigory Kanovich and Icchokas Meras (who both, indeed, now live in Israel), and others.

In 2001, following an initiative of the Lithuanian Jewish Community, a worldwide congress of Litvak communities was held in Vilnius. It attracted a great deal of attention and, it would seem, demonstrated that the Litvaks have survived.

But it is my view that we should not have too many illusions. As I have already mentioned, there remain very few Litvaks in Lithuania and most of them are of a venerable age. Young Litvaks are more oriented to Israel or other Western countries, and are not very interested in the preservation of Litvak traditions and their continuation in Lithuania.

As far as Litvak religious heritage is concerned, it seems that, if these traditions have not completely broken off, they have at least been substantially altered. Only Chabad Lubavitch, which represents the Eastern Litvak Hasidic tradition, which the Vilnius Gaon opposed so strongly during the eighteenth century, is still active in Vilnius today . . .

Looking at the picture soberly and assessing what is happening now, one would have to say that Litvak culture has no real future in Lithuania. It impossible to revive a culture if none of the people who live it remain; or, if they do, now live in a different world—in both geographic and spiritual terms. The majority of them, particularly the younger ones, no longer know the Yiddish language.

Today, the fate of Litvak culture in Lithuania depends largely on how ethnic Lithuanians see it. And how is that? First of all, inconsistently.

Indeed, quite a lot is being done at the official, state level: there are efforts to preserve Litvak heritage, state Jewish organisations are supported, and there is cooperation with and respect for what remains of the Jewish community. I have already mentioned various examples of this.

At the academic level, the ice has definitely been broken. Litvak heritage is increasingly seen as an integral part of Lithuania's cultural heritage. A good number of books and articles have been published on the subject of Jewish history, and documentary and educational films have been created. Lithuanians have begun to take an active interest in the Yiddish and Hebrew languages. But this is all still just a beginning. It must be recognised that, at the academic level, it is Holocaust studies that still dominate.

Sadly, the significance of Litvak cultural heritage has taken root in Lithuanian thinking as a whole more slowly. It is not that easy to overcome the syndrome of "otherness" that is so deeply ingrained in the nation's memory and consciousness. But here, too, one can see the beginnings of change. It would be enough to mention the activities of the NGO "Atminties namai" (House of memory). For three years now, it has held an essay contest on the theme "My grandparents' and great-grandparents' Jewish neighbours." Hundreds of school children from all over Lithuania have participated and have independently learned about Litvak history, and a collection of their essays has been published. Schools and museums have also become more active in this regard. In Kėdainiai, in a space within the former synagogue, a multicultural centre has been established that will place particular emphasis on the history of the region's Jews.

My time has come to an end, but I have still not provided you with an answer. That is because I do not have one.

In my purely personal view, the disappearance of Litvak culture in the territory of Lithuania is a fact, and the living continuation of that culture here, as anywhere else, is unrealistic, despite the fact that there are descendants of Litvaks living all over the world. But these people are no longer connected to their roots—they live in different cultural and historical contexts. The majority of them do not know the beautiful Litvak Yiddish language.

But it is also realistic and, I my view, necessary, to *preserve*, *study*, and *integrate* this unique Litvak culture into Lithuania's cultural context. And perhaps not only Lithuania's. I am deeply convinced that Litvak heritage does not only belong to ethnic Litvaks. It should be broadly studied, just like Ancient Greek or Roman culture. In today's globalised world, we should not feel or be isolated. It is my dream that Vilnius become an international centre of Litvak studies, just as it was up to the Second World War. I believe that would contribute to our global world's humanisation and, within the Lithuanian cultural context, to our country's spiritual enrichment.

NOTE: This text was a speech that I gave at the Frankfurt Book Fair, during a discussion titled "Litvak Heritage: Cultural Memory and the Present." The discussion was moderated by Professor Egidijus Aleksandravičius. The other participants included Professor Stefan Schreiner (Germany), the writer Krzysztof Czyżewski (Poland), and then Deputy Minister of Foreign Affairs Justas Paleckis (Lithuania).

Professor Stefan Schreiner provided a brief introduction to Litvak history. I found his point about the eighteenth-century Litvaks' experience in combining modern European education with ancient Jewish traditions to be especially relevant. That is a question that I believe is relevant today, in the context of globalisation.

The writer Krzysztof Czyżewski argued that it is only possible to study and integrate Jewish culture after thoroughly resolving one's relationship to the Holocaust. And that requires dialogue. He described how he himself felt relief after the general, national discussion about the tragic events at Jedwabne, where Poles participated in the slaughter of their neighbours. Only now, said Czyżewski, when the truth has finally been exposed, can he freely look his partners in dialogue—Jews—in the eyes.

Deputy Foreign Minister Justas Paleckis described how, after the restoration of independence, Lithuania has made efforts to deal with the effects of the Jewish catastrophe.

There were several questions from the audience. One of them—whether there is the same broad scale of discussions about the Holocaust in Lithuania as in Poland—was addressed to me. Because my answer to this question was presented in the Lithuanian media in a distorted way, I will attempt to reconstruct my answer from memory and in more detail.

I said that the historical situation in Lithuania was different and that discussions are taking place and spreading, but that they are not yet on the same scale as in Poland. Speaking about the urgent need for dialogue, I stressed that *dazu gehören zwei*—that "two sides are necessary"—in other words, that mutual understanding is needed. As a Litvak with deep roots in Lithuania myself and having lost my 35-year-old mother, my beloved uncle, my dear aunts and grandparents, my youngest cousin, and many other family members, I feel that I do have the right to express some criticism of my tribesmen.

It often seems to me that there are some Jews who are so focused on their own suffering and trials, which is understandable, that they are not sufficiently sensitive to the tragedy that their partners in dialogue, the Lithuanians, experienced. As is well known, the Molotov-Ribbentrop Pact made victims of both the ethnic Lithuanians and the Jews. I do not want to, here, compare the Holocaust with the Gulag, because it is impossible, and even immoral, to compare degrees of suffering, but the dialogue that is happening today, more than fifty years after the catastrophe, is with people who did not participate in the Holocaust and cannot be held responsible for it. That ought to change the tone of the dialogue. If historical truth and mutual understanding are to occur, it is necessary to not only accuse but to take some more interest in, to try to empathise with and more deeply understand the situation of one's partners in dialogue—both during the Second World War and today—and to better acknowledge their efforts at looking the tragic truth of history in the eyes. That is not an easy task. But it is my profound conviction that only that kind of position can encourage dialogue, speed it up, and take it to another level. *Dazu gehören zwei.*

※

LETTERS

Excerpts from Irena Veisaitė's letters to her future husband, Grigori Kromanov

April 25, 1971.

Dear Grigori!

Your premiere is coming up soon ... Once more, I wish you the greatest success. I hold you in my thoughts ...

I can now fulfil my promise and tell you about meeting Vilar. I saw him twice: in a small group of theatre people and at a concert. And both times I was greatly struck by his aristocratic appearance, intelligent face, and highly cultured manner of speaking—any one of our actors would be envious.

During the conversation, Vilar was asked three questions. Although he answered them in depth, it seemed that he was not so much responding to concrete questions as expressing his credo.

One of the most pressing questions for him is that of the relationship between politicians and artists, in the broadest sense. Vilar believes that in every era this relationship has been marked by irresolvable differences and conflicts. With great frustration, he described how, several years ago, the French government prohibited the staging of a play about General Franco in the National Theatre, simply because the French Foreign Minister, Michel Debré, was planning to travel to Spain to sign a trade treaty. And all of this happened under de Gaulle, who had so fought fascism!

The government's interference in the repertoire has a great effect on budgets. Vilar at length described the kinds of financial difficulties that a theatre director can face. He is also clearly burdened by this question. In speaking about a director's work, Vilar stressed that it is most important to avoid the use of the word "craft." An architect can build identical, high quality buildings in Paris,

Irena Veisaitė and Grigori Kromanov in Alma-Ata (today Almaty, Kazakhstan), 1978

Vilnius, or Kaunas, but a theatre director cannot stage identical productions. His work is irregular, and if a wife, lover, or wives—joked Vilar—begin to complain, they need to be told that happiness is not just making children. Then women retort that they do not want to be the victims of male egotism, which leads to revolution, though not of the political sort, said Vilar, ending his joke.

In speaking about his work with actors, Vilar stressed two aspects: 1) that an actor must know themselves, their body and soul, from head to toe, and that yoga exercises are very useful for this; and 2) that an actor must try to avoid egocentrism and individualism. One must have an open window, and for an actor that is the audience sitting in the theatre.

It is vital to promote equality in a theatre collective; that, in Vilar's view, is the basis of socialist art. It is therefore necessary to fight against the "star" system. The director must respect all his actors equally and work with each one, regardless of whether they have a small or big role. As examples, he gave Stanislavsky and Nemirovich-Danchenko who, in Vilar's opinion, never bowed to authorities. And where, asked Vilar, can you find someone in France or Russia who would dare to confront a famous director or actor—you won't!

When the conversation turned to the crisis in Western theatre, Vilar tried to explain that its source is the general crisis within society, which can be seen in the student protests of 1968. The theatre must find new paths, new ways of establishing contact with the public.

In speaking about the Avignon festivals, Vilar emphasized that they do not have financial goals but are all about art, creativity, and experimentation. The public does not always like that, but Vilar would not want the festivals to become a Museum of Theatre. As he concluded, Vilar very expressively and with great conviction said: "I have not told you anything new, but I have been completely open and sincere with you—perhaps that is my only worthwhile characteristic."

You see, Grigori, I have written you a whole report. I can feel you cursing my handwriting, but I have tried to write as clearly as possible.

Vilar's performance was very austere and without any external effects. The program included: anecdotes by Chamfort, Balzac's "Portrait of a Woman," some La Fontaine fables, excerpts from the correspondence between Voltaire and Catherine II, as well as texts by Maupassant, Hugo, and Renard. Vilar knows how to create a very intimate kind of atmosphere. It seems as though he is talking to himself; as he tells stories, he improvises and reflects, never losing sight of the essence, the main idea. He uses almost no external acting techniques and yet everything is executed with great care. He usually reads in a seated position. My only critique would be that he always had the text in front of him and consulted it continuously. I think he may be forced to do so because of his failing memory. His daughter, Dominique Vilar, is blessed with an exceptional sense of style. I especially liked her performance of a La Fontaine fable. She read it like a Comédie Française actress—with simplicity, logic, and grace. But enough about all that—your premiere is underway and I am already writing my review.

Dear Grigori, I await news but am certain of your success. I would only add that your interpretation of Šventežeris was very close to my heart and understandable to me, and yet it was also a great discovery . . .

My most heartfelt congratulations to your dear colleagues, especially Lilian and Kalju. I have such wonderful memories of Tallinn and am still revelling in the spirit of our encounter . . .

All the best, dear Grigori!

Yours,

Irena

May 7, 1971

Dear Grigori!
I just received your letter. I am so happy. I did not think anything about you, Grisha, I am simply thinking about you and am a little sad, as I would so like to see you ... The poster from "Pühajärve" hangs on my door—it makes Tallinn feel at least a little bit closer ...

    I can read your handwriting perfectly well. The quote from Blo— which, by the way, I did not know—is painfully understandable to me. It is a perfect expression of what moves me in *Hamlet*, *Don Quixote*, *The Idiot*, your *Šventežeris* (which I cannot forget), and in my own life. I have to admit that I never thought that it would be possible to find the things that you revealed in Kazys's play. I liked the play, but reading it was not a true poetic experience, while seeing your play was. I am generally moved by your ability to reconcile lifelike realism and simplicity with the highest level of poetry. I love Bergman and you somehow remind me of him. In my mind, the solution with Daugvilienė's painting is related to the end of Bergman's *Winter Light*, when Pastor Tomas stands at the altar and prays, even though the church is empty: "Holy holy holy Lord, God of power and might ..." That is just how Daugvilienė cleans the well ... I also found your Dr. Butrimas very interesting. Here is a man in an "extreme situation" which has revealed the emptiness of his words, his powerlessness. I could not, of course, catch all of the nuances of his portrait, but it all nevertheless moved me deeply, convinced me. I cannot, in truth, analyse your play objectively—I grasp it as "from one heart to another," to some degree ignoring the voice of reason.

    I submitted my review four days ago to our cultural weekly *Literatūra ir menas* (Literature and art). If all goes well, it will be published on May 5. If it does appear, I will send you a copy of the issue; if not, simply the manuscript. I only ask you, Grisha, be lenient and forgive me if I wrote anything incorrectly, if I misunderstood anything. It was very difficult for me: first of all, because they only gave me three or four pages (I wrote almost seven); secondly, because I did not attend the premiere. I only saw the play once, without an audience, and, although Milda and Kazys explained everything to me, it is difficult to see a play through the eyes of friends, even very close ones; and thirdly, because I do not understand Estonian and do not know your theatre. I am still not sure how I found the brazenness and courage to take up my pen.

Milda and Kazys returned very satisfied. Kazys said that, next to Jurašas's *Mamutų medžioklė* (Mammoth hunt), your production was the best premiere of one of his plays. He was very positive about your film and television productions. Unfortunately, I have seen neither one nor the other, but I very much hope that that can be remedied. Do you have copies of your work, or is that too naïve a question? Grigori, Kazys and I had an argument: in the first act, was it possible to briefly see the contours of a vague metal construction, perhaps a tower of some sort? If it turns out that I am right, I will win a bottle of champagne, so please help us settle our argument.

The Kaunas Drama Theatre is currently on tour in Vilnius. I was happy to see Jurašas's production of Glinskis's play for the third time. Aitmatov's *Motinos laukas* (A mother's field) was a disappointment. Jurašas tried to accomplish something, he looked for visual or rhythmic solutions for the play, but alas—it was dull, uninteresting, banal. It was especially difficult for the wonderful actress Staliliūnaitė, who played the mother—her physical and psychological makeup did not suit that role. And overall, I did not understand why Jurašas put so much effort and intelligence into a play that is so hopeless in the context of our theatre.

There is a lot of discussion here about Miltinis's *Volpone*—or, to be more precise, about the fact that he has once more returned to this production. Miltinis has returned on the scene after a break of several decades. He is working with two groups, actors and students, and, in my opinion the latter one is more interesting. I plan to see the play in the near future, in either Vilnius or Panevėžys. We are currently having such an intoxicating spring—horizons are beckoning, and I so feel like getting away somewhere that I can barely stay in my own skin.

Grisha, I can understand perfectly well how you feel empty and a little bit sad after such intense work. But it is always like that—it is unavoidable and will pass as soon as you begin something new. I would like to know what destiny will bring you next. I am certain that it will be something real, even though we are not always free to do what we want.

It is time to stop. You will soon be leaving for Moscow. I wish you a safe journey, that you are able to rest both your body and soul there, and to find new strength. And if you can allow illusions to warm you at all, try to believe in them ... You see, I believe in illusions, Grisha—I live from them. My favorite hero is Don Quixote. He lived as long as he had illusions, and when he lost them, he died. But it is sometimes frightening—one can be afraid to believe in them, especially when it feels so good . . . Then one must rely on one's self-defence mechanisms, one laughs at oneself . . . But one still believes.

Once more, safe travels—

Yours, Irena

May 14, 1971

Good morning, Grigori!

On my way to work, I will post a letter to you and I hope that you find it on your return to Tallinn.

I received the photographs, thank you. The editors chose two: Izolda with a bared Dundzila in Act 1, and Daugvilienė with Aura. My review will not be published on the 15th, because a review of *Motinos laukas* still has to come out. It is planned for the following issue. The article has been edited and is ready for publication, but it increasingly seems unresolved to me; I still want to make changes, additions. But there is nothing to be done; our print media could certainly be more efficient.

On the 17th we will celebrate the hundredth performance of *Šventežeris* in Kaunas. To be honest, I do not really want to see it. Yesterday, after *Juodoji komedija* (Black comedy), I was speaking with Jurašas and telling him about your production. There are many good ideas in *Juodoji komedija*, but they are not fully realised. Our actors are sorely in need of the Meyerhold School. Tell me, Grisha, what do you think about Liubimov and the Taganka Theatre?

I must stop now. There is work to do. In case you need it, here is my telephone number, as I did not give it to you when we met: 9-82-86.

I hope that your trip to Moscow was successful. I would be most grateful if you should drop me a few lines—

Yours,

Irena

May 27, 1971

Dear Grisha!

When I saw, in the city, a poster for an Estonian film festival, a spark of hope flashed in my soul...Just maybe, suddenly...I kept thinking that a taxi would pull up and there you would be...

I received your letter. Even from a distance, I can feel the tension you are experiencing. I am very curious about how your meeting in Moscow, with the Germans, went and whether you came to an agreement with them, whether you will have the opportunity to demand improvements to the script, the freedom to choose actors, and so on. DEFA, of course, is not the nicest film studio in the world, but, in this case, I think it is definitely worth trying. Of course, I do not know what alternative you have or what you are giving up with the film about Eduard Sõrmus, but that violinist's fate was truly interesting and tragic. You have thought long about him and your concept has developed over the years, which is so important, so I believe that DEFA will be a bit better than usual when dealing with you. I only hope that you will be able to preserve the film from the cheap lies and pseudo-meaningful demagoguery that DDR Germans are so inclined to.

Grisha, you write that art is a wonderful thing. And lately I am thinking a great deal about what art is in general. And it increasingly seems to me that it is not, or not only, what is written in aesthetics textbooks. It is impossible to define art precisely—there is much of the irrational, the personal, and the very intimate in it.

What you describe having experienced at the Van Gogh exhibition is exactly what I felt a few years ago looking at Matisse's paintings. I had never liked him; he seemed cold and decorative to me, and I found his colors jarring to the eye. But when I saw everything together, I suddenly felt that unforgettable internal quiver that only true art can cause. I suddenly realized that Matisse's markedly bright colors are a desperate attempt on the artist's part to see the beauty of the world—of a world in which harmony has been disrupted, in which the natural connection to nature and the artist's own sense of harmony have been lost. The rhythms, the screaming colors and the tendency toward primitivism all bear witness to that. And Kandinsky's colors?! All of Russia is contained in them; his abstract paintings say more than all of Levitan's landscapes.

I am very sorry that I did not see the Van Gogh exhibition. He has been my favorite artist since childhood. I wanted to go to Moscow specially to see the show, but then Milda put a damper on my enthusiasm when she said that the exhibition did not make a very big impression on her. What a pity...

Grisha, the *Šventežeris* review will appear this Saturday. I will send it to you, though I am a bit ashamed and would now change many things in it. The editors shortened certain parts, in particular the descriptions of specific scenes and your general comments about the play. I had V. Tobro's review translated. I liked it and agree with almost everything, and it was a relief to see that my own impressions were not entirely incorrect.

I found the 100th performance in Kaunas impossible to watch, though the audience received it warmly. The scenes you created were too vivid in my mind ... And afterwards a small group of us celebrated that round date and sent you a telegram at four in the morning...

Kazys returned only yesterday from Palanga, where he reworked his play *Dilgelių šilkas* (Nettle silk). He said he would soon bring me the revised version. And today Milda and Kazys are coming over with a bottle of champagne, as they lost our bet.

May 28, 1971

I did not have time to finish my letter yesterday. I want to convey Milda and Kazys's warmest greetings. Kazys brought me the new version of his play; I will read it today if our department meeting does not go on too long. On the 31st Kazys is travelling to the Armenian Writers' Conference. And the question of the champagne bottle remains unresolved. But now I have the chance to win two bottles! Kazys claims that the tower you refer to is that of a church rather than some metal, industrial construction. Grisha, my dear, please confirm that the metal tower does indeed appear—or something to that effect. And we will not drink the champagne without you. It will be waiting patiently...

Kazys, too, is very happy with Cde. Tobro's review, which I translated for him in detail, along with Cde. Haan's points. Kazys agrees with the comments about the end of the second act.

The Panevėžys Theatre has arrived in Vilnius for a series of performances. I am worried that I will once more be convinced that the legend and myth around that theatre are exaggerated. God willing, I will be proven wrong.

Grisha, you ask if the theatre community is not eager to send me to Tallinn. Alas! Do you remember how I told you about a dream that I had before leaving Tallinn? It was like a prophesy: I am lying prostate, chained to the floor of the Grotowski Theatre in Wrocław; I hear voices around me, someone is calling me, I want to stand up but the smallest movement causes intense pain, the chains are sinking deeper into my body, and above me flies the founder of the "Theatre of Cruelty," Antonin Artaud, cackling bitterly. You have certainly heard about him and know that he was more hideous than Voltaire. That dream haunts me to this day . . .

I teach until the 11th, with short breaks of two or three days. After the 11th I am more or less free. Kazys invites us to go kayaking on the lakes some time after June 17th. From July 1st Milda and Kazys and I have rented a small house on the Baltic coast, 5km from Palanga. It is a wonderful place. Pure silence—we are the only residents of the forest, the beach, and the sea. Hardly any holidayers ever pass through there, we see only local fishermen. We plan to live there until the end of August. In June I also expect to visit both Leningrad and Moscow. But there is another option—I might spend July and August in England. As you can see, it is all still unclear.

Grisha, if you will already be in Germany from the 10th to the 15th, it is unlikely that I will manage to say "see you soon" to you. So I would like to now wish you true, great creative joy, success and inspiration—to wish it so strongly that my wish must surely be fulfilled, no matter who might try to obstruct you . . . (It seems to me that you have accepted this offer.)

Well, I think I have written all that I had to and it is time to stop. And my conscience is clear since you have said that you can easily decipher my handwriting . . . It is so pleasant and warming for me to feel that I am speaking to you. It somehow seems to me that you understand everything: all that is written and all that is left unsaid . . .

Yours,

Irena

June 14, 1971

Good morning, Grisha!

How insufferably slowly the mail travels: your letter took seven days to travel from Tallinn to Vilnius! It is an entire eternity, and yet I thank the postal system for delivering it to me. It seems that I can once again hear your voice. Your every word, thought, feeling and even passing comment is familiar, understandable and dear (very dear) to me. People have become so alienated and have such difficulty understanding each other that I feel as though I have experienced a miracle . . . And that almost makes me more sad.

In recent days four foreign films have been shown here, mostly belonging to the "New Wave." They include: Lindsay Anderson's *If* and DDR director Peter Fleischmann's *Hunting Scenes from Bavaria*. In both films people hate one another; they have turned into beasts, especially in the German film—into thick-headed beasts.

From an artistic standpoint, the films are impeccable and very convincing, but they left me with an almost physical disgust and I kept wanting to scream, "It is all a lie!" And I so wanted to talk with you . . . Of course, Gorky was probably mistaken when he said "Mankind—how proud that sounds." But indeed, Grisha, certainly man is not a beast—is there not something good and pure in him? Can he not appreciate the heady smell of lilacs, enjoy the sun despite the soot and the smoke, defend his autonomy even when that is not really possible, and say, with Daugvilienė, "Tomorrow we will clean the well." Grisha, did you read Admonis's article, "The Myth of Thomas Mann's Creativity," in Issue Nr. 4 of *Novy mir*? If I may, I will copy out an excerpt that seems meaningful to me, even without the connection to the object of Lemm and Admonis's dispute. Admonis says:

"There have always, under all conditions, been people who were spiritually unbreakable, even if they often died before they had a chance to express the true power of their souls . . .

The twentieth century has powerfully demonstrated that the human spirit cannot be destroyed, and it has revealed the power of the human spirit. Even if we think about all of that "static" and conformist thinking, there is room within it—even if we consider only the Western world and leave the portraits of true revolutionaries and true revolutionary practice to the side—for people of remarkable individuality, inner freedom, for true nonconformists . . .

In the twentieth century, there are those who obey the demands of their souls and their consciences, who refuse to live a statistical, elementary, determined life. And even if these people make up the minority (and, during certain periods, a very small minority), they can never be ignored when speaking about the real-life context of the twentieth century...

It is precisely in the context of harsh and tragic reality that a person must constantly confront the question of their existence—the questions that force them to define their relationship to that horrific reality and their behavior in its context, by practically, but also generally, making internal decisions. It is catastrophic, rather than auspicious epochs that lead people to have the greatest need for deep examination of the broadest questions of their being and, within the options available to them, to choose their own path—even if this choice cannot actually be expressed."

I am probably wrong. There is probably a need for both Schedrins and Gogols, but sometimes one also wants to see an Alexander Chatzky. Admonis's article gave me some comfort, but I still cannot get the ugly mugs in that German film out of my head.

[...]

Grisha, I am with you on the side of Heaven.

Yours,

Irena

Post Scriptum

My conversations with Irena Veisaitė did not end with the publication of this book in Lithuanian in December 2016. Having become close friends, we continue to meet and discuss things that are important to us personally: we talk about films and performances we have seen and books we have read, and we analyse current events in Lithuanian, European, and global social and cultural life.

I would therefore like to share several excerpts from conversations that took place between Irena and myself in Vilnius and Nida during 2017–2018. These fragments of dialogue reflect questions that are very important to both of us: the dialectics of memory and forgetting, the process of learning to forgive, and Lithuanian society's efforts to speak about the most painful pages of twentieth century history.

Aurimas Švedas

"On Memory and Remembering"

Your conversation with Lithuanian cultural journalist Jolanta Kry-
ževičienė and University of Konstanz professor and memory researcher
Aleida Assmann was especially important to me personally.[3] During the
conversation, Assmann proposed the following thesis: "As we go back into
the past, we must, as Hannah Arendt said, understand that those things
should not have been allowed to happen. In other words, by applying our
own moral norms to the past, we say that this should not have been al-
lowed to happen. In doing so, we can be said to be acquiring a new mem-
ory. It is not that we simply forget, because it would be shameful to for-
get, but we find a new way of remembering, and in this way demonstrate
that we no longer think that way." To me, these words correspond to what
we have been trying to achieve through our conversations about pain-
ful history and history's scars. Would you agree with my interpretation?

Yes, that is still something to aspire to. It is difficult for us to speak openly about
what happened in Lithuania during the Nazi occupation, about the Lithuanian
administration of that time's involvement in the Holocaust, and so on. We have
still not yet absorbed the fact that what happened during the Nazi occupation,
and also during the Soviet occupation, was not only the Jews', but all of Lithuania's tragedy—Lithuania lost its citizens of Jewish descent, and some Lithuanians, no matter how few, contributed to the virtual annihilation of their countrymen. Until we understand and recognize that, we will not be able to heal our
wounds, and it would be so good to be able to do that. Perhaps that is why I devote so much attention to that question and so gladly welcome every step toward
the recognition of this tragedy. I agree with my cousin Aliukas's point, though
I can't remember where he said it. As a Jew he does not care about how the Holocaust is viewed in Lithuania; but because he also considers himself a Lithuanian, it is a question that concerns him gravely. We see things exactly the same
way—that it will not be possible to get rid of that "hunched back," that feeling
of guilt, until the tragedy has been acknowledged. Lithuanian collective mem-

---

3   Irena Veisaitė and Jolanta Kryževičienė's conversation with Aleida Assmann was aired on the Lithua-
     nian Radion program "Kultūros savaitė" [The week in culture] in August 2013.

ory still holds a fairly positive image of the German occupation, especially in comparison with the Soviet occupation. But it's a good idea to read about Hitler's once top secret "Ost" program, according to which German victory would have led to the deportation to Siberia of at least two thirds of Lithuania's residents because they did not meet racial purity requirements.

During all of our conversations, it is as though we are struggling with forgetting, which is constantly trying to swallow our memories of experiences, people we have met, books we have read. In that sense, forgetting is your and my enemy. But scholars who research the phenomenon of memory have pointed out that forgetting is not always a bad thing—that sometimes we need to forget so that we can continue to live. There is even, for example, something called "prescriptive forgetting," whose theorists argue that this kind of forgetting is sometimes needed (if agreed to by consensus) in societies that are restoring democracy after a long period of living under an authoritarian or totalitarian regime. What is your opinion about that—can forgetting do more than destroy? Can it offer possibilities for creating something new?

As far as I understand it, forgetting is unavoidable. It is necessary, but must first of all take place through knowledge and forgiveness. There have been many studies about that. Humanity's past is so difficult. There has been so much war, brutality, and killing. Neither faith, nor the Enlightenment, nor our so-called humanist, civilized age with its defense of human rights, have helped. Mass killing of innocent people happened intensely during the twentieth century and continues today. How can one live with such a heavy burden?

Forgetting is a natural process; it happens even without our will. But how do we deal with it without losing our conscience and humanity? I do not have a precise answer to that. I only know that it is only though comprehending and assessing the past that we can create our future.

Another feeling that has been present during our conversations and the whole process of writing this book is what you describe as "existing in a waiting room." You have often mentioned this state and reminded yourself and me that we must keep working because we do not know how much time we have. On the other hand, you have offered interesting descriptions of what it is to exist in a "waiting area" or a "waiting room." Could you perhaps return to these experiences of yours and tell me more about them?

That is a problem related to aging. I try to find something positive in every situation or period. Old age is not an easy stage of life. I would make the following comparison. A newborn child discovers something new every day; it develops and matures in terms of body and soul. A baby's abilities can't even be compared with those of a five-year-old child who can already speak, answer questions, and who grasps their environment and themselves better every day. When you are eighty or eighty-five years old, come what may, you lose something every day—the ability to move, to remember, to act—and that is natural. One must accept that as a given and as an inevitability because, thank God, we are mortal. I often remember Part III of *Gulliver's Travels*, when the hero finds himself on an island inhabited by immortals. It would be difficult to find people unhappier than these. As long as someone has not lost their mental capacities, they can observe that process of aging and loss, and can begin to see many things in a new light. They can appreciate and rejoice in what they have—not only understanding it, but also experiencing that it is temporary. The most important thing is to not complain. I have long felt my life's clock ticking, and that is also an interesting thing to observe. I feel grateful for everything that has been given to me, grateful to all the people who have accompanied me on my life's journey and have given me so much, and I am grateful to my family and my close friends. I wish each of them harmony, love, and a creative life. I have finally and clearly understood what it means to forgive, that it is no longer my time for teaching children or youth, and that I must now learn from them. As I have said earlier, there is nothing permanent in life except change. One should be learning until one takes one's last breath . . .

Old age gives us the opportunity to do so.

"An Important Meeting"

After our book came out in 2016, one of the most emotional experiences you have had—as far as I can tell—is related to your meeting with Reglindis Rauca. Tell me about it.

Meeting Reglindis Rauca was one of the most intense experiences I have had in recent years. Imagine that one day I look at my email and find a letter signed by Reglindis Rauca. The last name Rauca is connected to my most horrific experiences in the Kaunas Ghetto. Helmut Rauca directed the "Great Action" of October 28, 1941 and sent 10,000 Jews, from what I remember 4,000 of them children, to their deaths. I have already told you about my confrontation with Rauca and do not want to repeat myself. If I could once more describe his role and actions—as a Nazi party member executing Hitler's orders—then his behaviour with the German composer Edwin Geist (who was living in Lithuania at that time) and his wife Lyda paints a picture of a man of profound amorality.

Edwin Geist was born in 1902; his father, a German of Jewish descent, was killed in World War I. Geist was raised by his German mother and her sister. He studied music and became a composer, and, by the end of the 1920s, was known as a very promising young artist.

When Hitler came to power, Geist, as a half-Jew, found that he was prohibited from composing. At that time, a Lithuanian composer named Vladas Jakubėnas was studying in Berlin, and the two men became friends. It seems that, in 1938, Jakubėnas invited Geist to come to Lithuania, where Geist fell in love with and married a young Jewish woman named Lyda Bagrianskytė and settled with her in Kaunas. When the Soviets occupied Lithuania, Geist was not able to return to Germany. He was not even allowed to travel to attend his mother's funeral. Then, when the Nazis took Lithuania, Geist and his wife were sent to the Kaunas Ghetto. Unable to fully grasp what was happening and living in his own musical world, but deprived of a piano, Geist simply withered. His wife Lyda urged him to leave the ghetto. In 1942, Helmut Rauca agreed to let Geist leave the ghetto with the condition that he break off all communication with his Jewish wife. But Edwin devoted all of his time and energy to looking for ways to save her. All of that is described in his diary, which is dedicated to Lyda. Eventually, he succeeded in convincing Geist that Lyda was half Jewish, and Rauca let her leave the ghetto on the condition that they both undergo sterilisation and never have children. Ecstatic that he could once again be with his wife, Edwin lost his grip on reality. They both dreamed of having a son and had even picked out a name—Peterchen. Dr. Mažylis refused to sterilize Lyda, and so Rauca's order was not executed. Rauca arrested Edwin, incarcerated him in the Ninth Fort and shot him ten days later. Having learned of her husband's death, Lyda ended her own life.

Geist's story shows how Rauca played with Edwin like a cat with a mouse, demonstrating his sadistic tendencies. And there I was one day, discovering an email from someone with the same last name ... After the initial shock and having learned that Reglindis Rauca was in Lithuania, I looked her up on the Internet. I discovered that Reglindis is an actor and writer, that she never met her grandfather, and that her parents had hidden Helmut Rauca's role in the Nazi regime from her. In 1982 Helmut Rauca was extradited from Canada to West Germany, where he was to finally stand trial. Because Reglindis was then living in East Germany, the truth about her grandfather was only revealed to her in 2003, when she read an article about him on the Internet. It completely changed her life. Reglindis came to Lithuania wanting to meet eye to eye with descendants of her grandfather's victims and to somehow apologize to them. I understood that she was a person who was suffering, that she was deeply disturbed by her grandfather's story, and I realized that I wanted to help her.

I remembered a film that I had once seen on BBC television, called *Children of the Third Reich*. It made a great impression on me. It was about the famous Nazi Martin Borman's grandson, who became a Catholic and organized a trip of children of famous Nazis to Israel, where they met with the children of Auschwitz survivors. I believe that the trip took six days. The film showed different scenes from those meetings. At first the tension was immense. On the third day, I believe, the son of Auschwitz director Hans Frank read his father's deathbed letter, which was full of beautiful lines about how he loved his homeland and his family and had always served them. There was not a word about what he had done as a director of Auschwitz concentration camp. The Jews in the group sat frozen as they listened to the letter being read. Their eyes were filled with horror. But when Frank finished the letter and raized his eyes, they were full of tears, and he said: "But none of that was true." Then they all embraced. They had realized that both sides suffered and parted having understood each other.

It seemed to me that I now found myself in a similar situation. I invited Reglindis to dinner. I set the table and waited for her to arrive. The doorbell rings. I am trembling from head to toe. I open the door and see a middle-aged woman with a pretty face standing before me. And then a miracle happened. We embraced. We loved each other from the moment we met. That was the beginning of our friendship.

I look forward to seeing her again, when she comes at Easter.

"The Debate about *Our People*"

In our conversations we are repeatedly trying to answer the question: how is one to live today, while at the same time remembering, thinking, and speaking about the most complex aspects of twentieth-century Eastern and Central European history, and in such a way that memory does not become a source of conflict between Lithuanians, Jews, Russians, Germans, and Poles. It seems that we have come to the conclusion that painful and hurtful memories can only be soothed by continually remembering and talking about them, and constantly asking several questions: "Why did that happen? What does the painful past mean to us now, and how are we to live with it as we attempt to build a common future? What should we do, and how, with our lives so that the violence and destruction of the twentieth century do not repeat themselves in the near future?"

It is clear that there are no perfect answers to these questions. But, at the same time, it is also clear that one of the safeguards that can protect us from the return of catastrophic floods of nationalism, chauvinism, and totalitarianism is constant self-reflection and the effort to understand one another. The themes of understanding and empathy are especially important to you.

During our meetings we have often talked about various hopeful signs in our society indicating that people of different ethnicities, faiths, and beliefs in Lithuanian society are learning to talk about our common, and of-

ten sad and ugly, history and painful memories—that we are learning to be empathetic and to apologize to each other. You saw Rūta Vanagaitė's book Mūsiškiai *(Our people) and the discussion it generated in our society as one such hopeful sign of change.*[4] *I did not want to talk either about Rūta Vanagaitė or her book because, as a historian, I see the limitations of the book and, in some cases, the author's uncritical, dilettantish relationship to sources and historiography, her rushed generalisations, and her tendency to simplify, and in that way emotionally manipulate, the reader. On the other hand, I have restrained myself from criticising the book because Rūta Vanagaitė succeeded in achieving that which Lithuanian historians studying the Holocaust and its memory have failed to do for more than a quarter of a century—*Mūsiškiai *became a bestseller that has made a fundamental contribution to discussions about the Holocaust within Lithuanian society. And that last fact is especially important to me.*

Why have I decided to talk about Rūta Vanagaitė and Mūsiškiai *today? The answer is simple. As you well know, in an October 2017 exchange with a journalist during a presentation of another one of her books, Rūta Vanagaitė stated that the Lithuanian military officer and partisan leader Adolfas Ramanauskas-Vanagas was a KGB agent, and that she was therefore very critical of Lithuanian historians' and Lithuanian society's tendency to speak about that individual as a hero. As you know, this statement of Vanagaitė's was a bombshell, and the interviews she gave thereafter so further charged the atmosphere that, for a while, it was almost impossible to read online Lithuanian news media. Although Vanagaitė eventually admitted that she had made a mistake and apologized, her publisher, Alma Littera, announced that it was taking all of her books out of circulation. A painful war of memories erupted in our public discourse. Once again, various emotional statements—often lacking self-reflection, empathy or the appropriate insight into complex issues—were made about the*

---

4   Rūta Vanagaitė—theatre critic, founder and director of LIFE International Theatre Festival (1991–1998), author, producer, politician. In 2016, Vanagaitė published the book *Mūsiškiai: Kelionė su priešu* [Our people: Journey with the enemy, Vilnius: Alma Littera], co-authored with famous Nazi-hunter Efraim Zuroff (director of the Simon Wiesenthal Centre office in Jerusalem), about the search for historical truth about the Holocaust in Lithuania. *Mūsiškiai* was an instant best-seller and is broadly recognised as having contributed significantly to Lithuanian's reckoning with the darkest chapter in their country's history.

first and second Soviet occupations, the Second World War, the Holocaust and the tragedies that befell the Jews and Lithuanians during that time, and the Lithuanian partisan resistance. In other words, it took only a few thoughtless sentences said by one person to make it seem that all of the signs of hope that you and I had been seeing in Lithuanian society had never actually been there at all.

In the context of this war of memories, our efforts to speak calmly and without anger, but with empathy for the pain of the Other, about painful histories and traumatic memories seem to be a Sisyphean task.

I would answer that I both agree and disagree with you. I agree that we are engaged in a Sisyphean task because, at this moment, it seems that the boulder is rolling back down at an ever-increasing speed. I agree that Rūta Vanagaitė's statement, for which she later apologized, was a mistake, an especially serious one because she claimed something based solely on NKVD documents. These mistakes caused confusion and outrage. All of that is understandable. But it seems to me that we still have too narrow an understanding of freedom of speech. And Alma Littera's decision to take all of her books out of circulation was just as big an error. Thank God that there were no book burning bonfires and that, after warnings from Tomas Venclova and other intellectuals, the publisher came to the solution that they returned all of the books (most of which, indeed, had nothing to do with the Holocaust or the partisans) to Rūta Vanagaitė.

Another question altogether is how to see Rūta Vanagaitė's 2016 book *Mūsiškiai*, which was a major event. Most Lithuanians only finally understood what happened in Lithuania under the Nazi occupation after reading Vanagaitė's book. I am not an historian, and, while reading *Mūsiškiai*, I did not notice any significant errors. In discussing the Holocaust, Vanagaitė drew on archival documents and historical research. I would like to ask you what you mean by an "uncritical relationship"? It is my view that *Mūsiškiai* is a well-written book that was in part inspired by her own family history and the determination to confront the question of the Holocaust. After all, an entire tribe of people, who had lived in Lithuania for more than six hundred years, was annihilated. Men and women, children, and old people were piled in the pits.

I was immediately intrigued by the book's title, *Mūsiškiai*—"Our people." And if you turn open the cover, on the first page, under the title *Mūsiškiai*, you will see photographs of two young men. One of them is Isakas Anolikas, a talented athlete of Jewish descent who defended Lithuania's honour at the Paris and Amsterdam Olympics, and who was executed at the Ninth Fort. The other is a young Lithuanian man named Balys Norvaiša, who, from 1941 to 1943, headed a special battalion that conducted operations in which Jews were exterminated in various parts of Lithuania. These two young men—who also look quite similar—are "our own people." In the second half of the book, Vanagaitė describes her journey with "enemy number one" Efraim Zuroff, who, during the past few decades, has done more to increase anti-Semitism than to reduce it. This was a strategy on Vanagaitė's part; it enabled her to achieve her goal and to say things that many people in Lithuania still don't want to hear.

These are very subtle matters. I prefer to speak about the Holocaust differently than Rūta Vanagaitė. But I cannot deny that, while she inspired outrage, she also succeeded in deeply affecting people. That is why I see the book in a positive light.

As I have said, Holocaust history and memory are very subtle and sensitive questions that will long be difficult for our society. To me, an openly negative reaction to this book was not acceptable—that kind of reaction does not increase mutual understanding but stokes conflict. There are no Jews left in Lithuania, but anti-Semitism still exists. What can we do about that? I don't know.

As I have said before, the Germans' success in coming to terms with their difficult and painful past should be a model for us. It is only by truly acknowledging what happened that we will find the path to mutual understanding. I believe that, step by step, we are approaching it.

※

KEY BIOGRAPHICAL EVENTS

1928 Irena Veisaitė is born on January 9 in Kaunas, to Izidorius Veisas and Sofija Štromaitė-Veisienė.

1934–1941 Attends Sholem Aleichem Jewish High School in Kaunas.

1938 Parents divorce and father leaves Lithuania.

1941 The Nazi occupation of Lithuania begins. Irena's mother is executed and Irena finds herself in the Kaunas Ghetto.

1943 In November, Juozas and Ona Strimaitis procure documents for Irena and help her escape from Kaunas Ghetto and travel to Vilnius. In Vilnius, Irena is sheltered by Pranas Bagdonavičius, Marija Meškauskienė, and Stefanija Paliulytė-Ladigienė, who becomes her second mother.

1944–1947 Studies at Salomėja Nėris High School in Vilnius; graduates with a gold medal.

1947–1948 Studies Lithuanian Language and Literature at Vilnius University.

1948–1953 Persecuted by the Soviet security forces, Irena leaves for Moscow, where she enters the Department of German Studies at Lomonosov University. During some of this period Irena receives the Lermontov Stipend. She graduates in 1953.

1952 Marries Moscow economist Jakov (Yasha) Boom.

1953 Returns to Vilnius. From 1953 to 1997 Irena teaches at Vilnius Pedagogical Institute (from 1992 renamed Vilnius Pedagogical University). From 1965 she is an assistant professor, and, from 1999, a professor emeritus. She teaches foreign and German literature and founds a theatre club.

1955 Daughter Alina Bumaitė (Boom, later Boom-Slavinsky) is born.

1958–1960 Studies in the doctoral programme at Leningrad University.

1963 Defends doctoral thesis "The Late Poetry of Heinrich Heine: *Romanzero*" at Leningrad University.

1973 Irena's father, Izidorius Veisas, dies in Los Angeles.

1974 Divorces from first husband Jacov Boom who, in the same year, emigrates, with their daughter Alina, from the Soviet Union and settles in London, England.

1978 Marries Estonian film and theatre director Grigori Kromanov (1926–1984).

1979 Works as assistant director at Tallinnfilm studios, in Estonia, on the feature film *Dead Mountaineer's Hotel*.

1984 Death of Irena's husband, Grigori Kromanov.

1986 Birth of Irena's twin grandsons, Michael and Daniel Slavinsky, in London.

1990 Co-founder and Vice-Chair of the Board, Open Lithuania Foundation (OLF). From 1993 to 2000 Irena is Chair of the OLF Board, and in 2001–2002 she is a Board member.

1993 Studies at Oxford University.

1995 Receives Officer's Cross (4th Degree) of the Order of the Grand Duke Gediminas.

1995–2014 Irena is one of the founders of the Thomas Mann Cultural Centre. From 2003 to 2005, she is curatorial head, and from 2014 she is an honorary member of the curatorial board.

1995–2000 Member of the International Central Board of the Open Society Institute in Budapest.

1995–2001 Board Member, United World Colleges. Longtime board member of the Lithuanian Youth Psychological Helpline.

1998–2003 Founder and Chair of the Board, Lithuanian Ethnic Communities Study Centre.

1998–2005 Chair of the Board, Baltic Cultural Foundation.

2000–2005 Member, Lithuanian National UNESCO Commission.

2001–2014 Director, Lithuanian National Committee, United World College.

2003 Nominated and chosen as Person of Tolerance of the year by the Sugihara Foundation.

2003–2007 Member, Arts Council of the Lithuanian Ministry of Culture

2004–2014 Ombudsperson, Open Society Institute.

2006 Recipient, Barbora Radvilaitė medal.

2008 Recipient, Lithuanian Ministry of Education and Science honorary award for service in promoting Lithuanian education and science.

2008–2014 Member, National Culture and Arts Awards Commission, Lithuanian Ministry of Culture.

2008–2009 Member, Vilnius Capital of Culture board.

2009–2012 Chair of Board, George Soros Temporary Relief Fund for Lithuania.

2012 Recipient of the Goethe Medal for civic courage and lifelong efforts in promoting Lithuanian-German cultural exchange, Weimar.

Recipient, Lithuanian Ministry of Culture honorary award "Carry your light and believe" for strengthening dialogue, promoting national and religious harmony, national growth, and humanitarian values.

2015 Recipient, Lithuanian State Culture and Arts Award.

2019 Named an honorary Borderlander by the Borderland Foundation in Sejny, Poland, for her work countering stereotypes and building bridges between nations and religions.

Irena Veisaitė's parents,
travelling abroad, c. 1935.

Irena Veisaitė's friends and protectors Moishe Brauns and his wife Betty, c. 1947.

Irena Veisaitė with friend and fellow student Elena Markovich. Moscow, c. 1951.

Irena Veisaitė, Ona (Anuška) Štromaitė and Aleksandras Shtromas. Valakampiai, early 1960s.

At the Vildžiūnas home. From left, seated: Violeta Shtromas, sculptor Vladas Vildžiūnas and Marija Ladigaitė-Vildžiūnienė, and their daughter Liudvika Pociūnienė. Standing: Irena Ladigaitė-Eivienė and Irena Veisaitė. Vilnius, c. 1990.

Irena Veisaitė and her niece Jenny Kagan. Vilnius, 1993.

Irena Veisaitė and Nobel laureate, Polish poet and essayist Czesław Miłosz. Vilnius, 1995.

*Irena Veisaitė with her grandsons and representatives of the House of Memory
(a Holocaust and Jewish studies center in Lithuania founded by Linas Vildžiūnas)
at the Beth Shalom Holocaust Memorial Center. First from left is the center's founder
and director, Stephen Smith. Nottinghamshire, UK, 1998.*

Krzysztof Czyzewski and Irena Veisaitė. Nida, Lithuania, c. 2000.

Irena Veisaitė and Audra Žukaitytė. Trakai, Lithuania, 2001.

Irena Veisaitė, Estonian composer Arvo Pärt, and his wife Nora. Berlin, 2002.

Irena Veisaitė speaking in Berlin, at the Brandenburg Gates, on the occasion of Lithuania joining the European Union. 1 May, 2004.

Irena Veisaitė with her daughter Alina. New York, 2007.

Irena Veisaitė and Yves Plasseraud, author of the first book about her. Vilnius, c. 2005.

Meeting Queen Elizabeth II at the Palace of the President of Lithuania.
From right: Irena Veisaitė, President of Lithuania Valdas Adamkus, Queen Elizabeth,
Prince Philip, and Mrs. Alma Adamkienė. Vilnius, 2006.

Lithuanian philosopher and essayist Leonidas Donskis and renowned sociologist Zygmunt Bauman. Leeds, UK, 2009.

Irena Veisaitė with her daughter Alina, and her grandsons Michael and Daniel Slavinsky. London, c. 2010.

Irena Veisaitė and her close Moscow university friend Nina Demurova, translator of Alice in Wonderland into Russian and author of books about Lewis Carroll, c. 2010.

The last photograph of Irena Veisaitė, Margaret Kagan, and Valdemar Ginsburg together. Huddersfield, UK, 2012.

Rasa Rimickaitė (Lithuanian cultural attaché in Poland) and Irena Veisaitė, c. 2015.

Darius Čuplinskas, then director of the Open Lithuania Fund's publishing program, and UK cultural consultant Bill McAlister.

Irena Veisaitė and Reglindis Rauca on the balcony of Veisaitė's apartment. Vilnius, 2019.

Vytautas Toleikis and Violeta Toleikienė. Sejny, Poland, 2019.

Irena Veisaitė and her former student Marius Mikalajūnas selecting photographs for this book. Vilnius, 2016.

INDEX

CPSIA information can be obtained
at www.ICGtesting.com
Printed in the USA
FSHW020034151220
76899FS

9 789633 863596